T0270077

SUCCESSION

SEASON ONE

SUCCESSION

SEASON ONE

The Complete Scripts

faber

First published in 2023
by Faber & Faber Limited
The Bindery, 51 Hatton Garden
London ECIN 8HN

Typeset by Brighton Gray
Printed and bound at CPI Books Ltd, Croydon CRO 44Y

All rights reserved
Official HBO Licensed Product © 2023 Home Box Office, Inc. All Rights Reserved.
HBO and related trademarks are the property of Home Box Office, Inc.

Introduction © Jesse Armstrong, 2023
All rights reserved

The right of Jesse Armstrong, Jon Brown, Jonathan Glatzer, Anna Jordan,
Lucy Prebble, Georgia Pritchett, Tony Roche and Susan Soon He Stanton
to be identified as the authors of this work in accordance with
Section 77 of the Copyright, Designs and Patents Act 1988

This book is sold subject to the condition that it shall not,
by way of trade or otherwise, be lent, resold, hired out
or otherwise circulated without the publisher's prior consent
in any form of binding or cover other than that in which
it is published and without a similar condition including
this condition being imposed on the subsequent purchaser

A CIP record for this book
is available from the British Library

978-0-571-37974-3

Printed and bound in the UK on FSC® certified paper in line with our continuing
commitment to ethical business practices, sustainability and the environment.
For further information see faber.co.uk/environmental-policy

4 6 8 10 9 7 5

Contents

SUCCESSION
SEASON ONE

Introduction

My first vivid memory of the project which would develop into *Succession* was trying to get out of it. It was about 2008 and I was on location for the filming of *Peep Show*, the UK sitcom my long-time writing partner Sam Bain and I wrote together. Between that show and my work on *The Thick of It* and *In the Loop*, and a bunch of other things, I was feeling overcommitted. That particular day we were pretending a very normal field in Hertfordshire was a safari park. I sloped off from set and, hiding from imaginary lions, tried to elegantly step away from the project.

I failed. And in the following months as I wrote, slowly, I became certain the script was a dud. It was stodgy and odd. The original idea, a faux-documentary laying out Rupert Murdoch's business secrets, with them delivered straight to camera, evolved as I worked into a sort of TV play, set at the media owner's eightieth birthday party. Channel 4 were supportive, but it was an odd form, this docudrama/TV-play, and difficult to make happen. Around 2011, after a readthrough in central London where John Hurt played Rupert, the project essentially died.

My US agent was the first person I recall suggesting a totally different approach. A fictional family, a multi-series US show. For five years or so I dismissed the idea, certain that a portrayal of a fictional family would never have the power of a real one.

Four works changed my mind: HBO's excellent Durst documentary, *The Jinx*; Sumner Redstone's grimly business-focused autobiography, *A Passion to Win*; James B. Stewart's propulsive *Disney War*; and Tom Bower's fascinating Maxwell biography. These turned the idea of doing a media-family drama without a singular real-life model from a terrible betrayal of reality into a tantalizing chance to harvest all the best stories. Here was an opportunity to explore all the most fascinating family dynamics within a propitiously balanced fictional hybrid media conglomerate. I took a long, deep dive into rich-family and media-business research.

When Sam and I decided to bring things to a close on *Peep Show*, I flew out to pitch this media show around LA. I had a clear idea of where I wanted to develop the show, but my agent persuaded me appetites would be whetted if we had a number of potential homes. So, I spent three days doing a round of pitch meetings where I talked about this, as-yet-unwritten, idea in half-ironized terms as '*Festen*-meets-*Dallas*'. No stars, Dogme 95 camerawork. Scared of driving on the five-lane highways, I bumped around town in the back of a Honda Civic while a nice young man from my US agent's mailroom ferried me between rooms stocked with identical tiny bottles of water and executives of vastly varying degrees of interest.

Eventually I got to HBO, the place I most wanted the show to land, home to *The Sopranos* and *Six Feet Under*. I knew they might be receptive. Frank Rich – once known as the 'Butcher of Broadway' for his theatre criticism, but now an in-house consigliere – had championed my work there to the boss Richard Plepler and I'd previously developed a show with them. So, out the back of a French-style bistro on a three-cappuccino high, I pitched it to their head of drama and comedy, Casey Bloys. Sometimes a pitch stretches thin and threadbare, the fabric renting as you go, the other party peeping grimly through the holes. Other times, the air thickens, and you can feel the atmosphere in the room turn oxygen-rich as the enthusiasm you are trying to project transforms into an enthusiasm you are actually feeling.

By the time I left LA, HBO had made an offer and Adam McKay, fresh from *The Big Short*, had said he would be interested in directing. I'd written another *Succession* forerunner, a script about the US political strategist Lee Atwater, for Adam and his producing partner Kevin Messick. It had been one of the few LA experiences I'd had where the excitement expressed at the start of the project sustained through the writing and attempts to get it made.

This was 2016 and, once back in the UK, I wrote the pilot through the spring and summer in a one-room flat I rented on Brixton Hill, walking across Brockwell Park each morning, listening to podcasts and reading news about the Brexit referendum. Scotland had recently voted by a narrow majority to stay inside the United Kingdom and the abiding sense right before the Brexit vote was, yeah, change looms, it glistens, menacingly, promisingly, but it doesn't happen. Not really. Really, everything stays the same.

But then it did happen. And across the Atlantic, the Trump campaign was igniting – even if initially his candidacy felt like a slightly amusing, slightly too-vivid flash in the pan. Into early autumn, in fact, all serious people were still explaining to one another that Trump couldn't happen. Although I suppose, looking back, there was a notable lack of detail in terms of the mechanism by which he would be stopped.

I think a lot of the better films and TV shows I've been involved with have at their heart a quite simple impulse around which the more subtle layers are spun. *In the Loop*'s spark was anger at the Iraq War. Chris Morris's *Four Lions* I think was driven by his gut feeling that something was very wrong with the way we understood jihadi terrorism in the UK. *Peep Show* was about oddball male friendship, perhaps even 'masculinity'.

I guess the simple things at the heart of *Succession* ended up being Brexit and Trump. The way the UK press had primed the EU debate for decades. The way the US media's conservative outriders prepared the way for Trump, hovered at the brink of support and then dived in. The British press of Rothermere and the Barclay Brothers, Maxwell and Murdoch, and the US news environment of Fox and Breitbart.

The Sun doesn't run the UK, nor does Fox entirely set the media agenda in the US, but it was hard not to feel, at the time the show was coming together, the particular impact of one man, of one family, on the lives of so many. Right populism was on the march all across the globe. But in the fine margins of the Brexit vote and Trump's eventual electoral college victory, one couldn't help but think about the influence of the years of anti-EU stories and comment in the UK press, the years of Fox dancing with its audience, sometimes leading, sometimes following, as the wine got stronger, the music madder. It was politically alarming and creatively appealing: to imagine the mixture of business imperatives and political instinct that exist within a media operation; to consider what happens when something as important as the flow of information in a democracy hits the reductive brutality of the profit calculation inside such a company. How those elements might rebound emotionally and psychologically inside a family as it considered the question of corporate succession.

For Logan Roy, Murdoch, Redstone and Maxwell were my holy trinity of models. But Conrad Black, Brian Roberts of Comcast, Robert Mercer of Breitbart, Julian Sinclair Smith of Sinclair, Tiny Rowland, Rothermere, Beaverbrook, Hearst all fed in.

The three central models were wildly different, of course: the self-made refugee Maxwell and the already-rich Murdoch, a scion of Australian journalistic royalty, both so different from the tough Boston lawyer Redstone who started with a couple of his father's drive-in cinemas. But they were connected by a strong interest in a few things: a refusal to think about mortality (Redstone and Murdoch both used to make the same joke about their succession plan – not dying); desire for control; manic deal-making energy; love of gossip and power-connection; a certain ruthlessness about hirings and firings. And most of all, an instinct for forward motion, with a notable lack of introspection. Perhaps the best part of Redstone's autobiography for a casual reader is the opening, where he recounts clinging by one hand to a hotel balcony through a fire. Despite suffering third-degree burns over half his body, years of rehabilitation, excruciatingly painful skin grafts, he says this event, after which he made all his biggest business plays, had no impact whatsoever on the trajectory of his life.

Whether due to all this grist, or the aligning of the political planets (in)auspiciously, the pilot came unnervingly easily. Getting names in a script to feel real can be hard for me – they're a tell-tale sign of whether I'm living inside it. Kendall, Shiv, Roman, Connor. They all felt right straight off the bat. Their inspirations, I suppose, were the children of these magnates: three of the Maxwell kids, the ones closest to the business (the boys, Ian and Kevin) and to their father (Ghislaine). Brent and Shari Redstone, with whom Sumner played a tough and complicated game of bait-and-switch over CBS-Paramount succession. And the Murdoch children, Prudence, Lachlan, James, Elisabeth, Chloe and Grace.

But getting those names for the Roy children made them feel like their own individuals to me. It allowed me to pour in just what I wanted from the real world, fill each with all the faults they might have inherited, while giving me room to add some extra, just for them.

Greg and Tom came fast too. Tom from two roots. One was thinking about the sort of lunks I've occasionally seen powerful women choose as partners. Plausible manly men with big watches and a soothing affable manner. That mixed with the deadly courtier, a more eighteenth-century figure, minutely attuned to shifts in power and influence, an invisible deadly gas that occurs in certain confined places and rises to kill anyone unwise enough not to take precautions. A hanger-on sustained by some Fitzgeraldian illusions about the world, a sense that perhaps the rich really are different from us and a romantic ambition to make it in New York City.

Greg, I guess, was a distant relative of the sort of political advisor I had myself briefly been. Gormless, clueless, out of place and gauche. But not without an eye for a deal. And, I hope, a little more wheedling and insinuating than I ever was.

The charge between these two semi-outsiders struck me from the start as toxic and comic.

Tom, the interloper, is like an organism that has found a precarious but rewarding perch above some deep oceanic vent and adapted itself to conditions perfectly. He is not pleased at all to see a similar creature scuttling along hoping to share the same cramped evolutionary niche. That first half-bullying, half-provocative exchange they share in the outfield at a softball game in the pilot landed them right in the middle of a stew they've been cooking in ever since.

The scenes flowed. I had eaten a very large amount of research, but once I was writing I put it all aside and followed my nose and wrote pretty much exactly what I wanted. It felt funny but odd and broken-ended, fragmentary, abrupt, oblique and slightly brutal. When I emailed it off, I had the familiar feeling that Adam, Frank and HBO might email back to say not only was it not good, it wasn't even actually, technically, a script.

But their response was frighteningly positive. Almost as though the script was finished, after what was, I thought, a quick first draft. I think every other episode of *Succession* has gone to at least thirty drafts – usually fifty. The pilot barely hit fifteen.

We had our readthrough in New York on US election day 2016. Before we started, I made the sort of joke lots of people made that day, assuming the polls were right and Hillary Clinton was going to squeeze it. That night we gathered in Adam McKay's apartment to watch the results roll in. Much later, I walked a long walk back from Soho up to where I was staying near the United Nations looking at the electoral college numbers projected onto the Empire State Building.

We started filming the next day.

I still wonder whether *Succession* would have landed in the same way without the mad bum-rush of news and sensation Trump's chaotic presidency provided. Trump wasn't the firebombing of German civilians, and nor is *Succession Slaughterhouse-Five*, but I do sometimes think about Vonnegut saying no one in the world profited from the firebombing of Dresden, except himself.

Jesse Armstrong
March 2023

Note on the Text

This book contains the scripts as they stood when we started to film each episode.

Some screenwriters object to the suggestion that their scripts are mere recipes or blueprints towards the creation of the final film or TV show – I suppose because it undermines the sense that a script is a complete and achieved document in itself.

I think both things are true. It *is* only a recipe – a set of instructions for action and suggested dialogue. But this doesn't mean that it shouldn't have coherence and integrity in its own right; that you shouldn't be able to stand behind every word and choice and say: this is how I think it goes.

But the scripts are not the shows. They are simply important – very important – documents towards the creation of the shows, which are then made with a cast and crew and post-production staff of many and great talents.

If you read these scripts, you'll soon see that these important documents depart fairly often from the action and words as they finally appeared on screen. So, when they vary, what the hell happened?

Well, one of a number of things. In rough order of probable likelihood:

The edit: We shot the scene or line or beat but in the edit we decided to lose it – that happens a lot. I like to write long and I encourage my fellow writers to write long. I rewrite long. Mostly around seventy-plus pages per script, when sixty would be a more normal target. Some hours of TV have scripts squeezed down to around fifty. I think that the economies of scale on a TV shoot mean that filming a few extra pages per episode – provided they are largely dialogue, not car crashes – returns exponential rewards. It leaves you free to make choices in the edit, giving you the ability to refocus story: make it clearer if necessary, or more subtly expressed if possible.

That extra length also allows you to *not* make choices. So you don't have to make cuts when you're tired and snow-blind from forty drafts and redrafts and have forgotten why the line was ever good or the joke funny. That's the stage when, on another show, the producer or network or director might plead for you to cut some pages to come in on time or budget, and you end up making those choices you so regret later. To get the accursed page length down you can find yourself excluding those moments which have come to seem small or weird or nothingy – moments, perhaps, that people loved when they first read, but are now taken for granted and feel easy to cut. If you get to retain them at script, sometimes they do indeed get cut in the edit. But sometimes they become the heart of a scene or just a jewel of a moment, the detail which enchants a viewer.

It was an 'alt': For each day's filming, a day or two ahead, I select a few lines – sometimes none, sometimes ten to fifteen – where we might find a spot for something funnier or better or truer. Usually funnier. These go out to a group of three to five fellow writers who offer up 'alts'. I might whittle down ten to twenty options to five to ten that we then have in our pockets to consider on the day. Oftentimes, what is already in the script works and these alts never get fed in. But sometimes, after we have shot the scripted lines, we'll feed in a suggestion which feels apposite. Or sometimes just offer a bunch of alternative lines to the actor, have a quick chat about preferences, and let them try a few options out. (Kieran Culkin, in particular, was always able to load up a page of alts in a glance, then spray them out like a weapons system in subsequent takes.)

Late change: Close to shooting, too close to be recorded in the script, we made a dialogue or staging change. Often this was to fit the staging afforded by the particular location or some extra opportunity or problem that needed to be worked around or addressed or embraced. Then we either scribbled a change in biro or issued it ad hoc.

Fog of war: There are also lots of little changes of word order or individual words. I don't mind this – I don't stand at the monitor with my script in hand – I just watch the performances – and only look over the shoulder of script supervisors Lisa Molinaro or Holly Unterberger if something strikes my ear wrong. Most times, if the actor chooses to gently paraphrase, I take that as an implied note – that the line didn't quite have the cadence of natural speech for them. There's also a quid pro quo in operation here. I write and rewrite till late on, till we're actually shooting the episode. If you're going to tweak and change so tight against shooting you have to be understanding about how much text people can learn at short notice. Some sentences and constructions I can be prickly about getting precisely, but they are relatively rare.

Improvisation: We've always used a loose shooting style. Adam McKay encouraged it on the pilot. And I'd learnt it from Armando Iannucci on *The Thick of It*. Mark Mylod, our lead director, is very comfortable with this approach, coming as he does from the world of British comedy. So usually, after we have the scripted version on film, we'll do a 'freebie' take where improvisation is particularly encouraged. To my mind, more important than the occasional improvised lines we capture is that this improvisational method infuses all the takes, on-script and off, with a spirit of freedom and collaboration.

ADR: Some pieces of dialogue we change after the show is done – with Additional Dialogue Recording (ADR) to add plot clarification, or alter a plot detail or fill a gap or add a joke.

The remembrance of things past: We do a readthrough of the script a week or two before the first day of shooting. After which, there are always changes – sometimes just reorderings and sharpenings, sometimes a wholesale restructuring. The readthroughs mean that the actors have a knowledge of the development of the script, and memories of previous drafts. Sometimes on the day of shooting, an actor will stitch in a bit of an older script. So, on a loose take, or even before, a shard of something cut comes back: perhaps a link between two thoughts or speeches which we had come to think was extraneous – or a phrase that explained something to the actor, a joke or image or way of looking at something. It's a reassuring safety net to know that words you'd come to think unnecessary, ornament you'd stripped away as superfluous, can get pulled from the fire.

Jesse Armstrong
March 2023

SUCCESSION
SEASON ONE

SUCCESSION

SEASON ONE

Executive Producers	Jesse Armstrong
	Adam McKay
	Frank Rich
	Will Ferrell
	Kevin Messick
	Jane Tranter
	Mark Mylod
	Ilene S. Landress (pilot)
Writers	Jesse Armstrong
	Tony Roche
	Jonathan Glatzer
	Anna Jordan
	Georgia Pritchett
	Susan Soon He Stanton
	Lucy Prebble
	Jon Brown
Directors	Adam McKay
	Mark Mylod
	Adam Arkin
	Andrij Parekh
	Miguel Arteta
	S. J. Clarkson
Produced by	Jonathan Filley
	Regina Heyman (pilot)
Producer	Dara Schnapper
Associate Producers	Callie Hersheway
	Maeve Cullinane
	Maria Cerretani
Assistant to Mr Armstrong	Nathan Elston
Writers' Assistants	Bethan Gorman
	Ed Cripps
First Assistant Directors	Amy Lauritsen
	Christo Morse
Directors of Photography	Andrij Parekh
	Patrick Capone
	Christopher Norr

Editors	Ken Eluto, ACE
	Jane Rizzo
	Anne McCabe, ACE
	Mark Yoshikawa, ACE (pilot)
Composer	Nicholas Britell
Production Designers	Stephen H. Carter
	Kevin Thompson (pilot)
Costume Designers	Michelle Matland
	Catherine George (pilot)
Casting Directors	Francine Maisler, CSA
	Douglas Aibel, CSA
	Henry Russell Bergstein, CSA
Script Supervisors	Lisa Molinaro
	Holly Unterberger
	Jessica Lichtner (pilot)
Gaffers	John Oates
	Lee Walters
Key Grip	Christopher Skutch
Property Masters	Ron Stone
	Diana Burton (pilot)
Set Decorators	George DeTitta Jr.
	Susan Bode (pilot)
	Sophie Newman
Supervising Sound Editor	Nicholas Renbeck
Re-Recording Mixers	Andy Kris
	Larry Zipf
Music Editor	John Finklea
Production Sound Mixers	William Sarokin
	Ed Novick (pilot)
Hair Dept Heads	Michelle Johnson
	Jerry DeCarlo (pilot)
Make-Up Dept Head	Patricia Regan
Location Managers	Matthew Kania
	Dan Whitty
	Michael Kriaris (pilot)
	Patty Carey (pilot)

Episode One
CELEBRATION

Written by Jesse Armstrong
Directed by Adam McKay

Original air date 3 June 2018

Cast

LOGAN ROY	Brian Cox
KENDALL ROY	Jeremy Strong
MARCIA ROY	Hiam Abbass
GREG HIRSCH	Nicholas Braun
SHIV ROY	Sarah Snook
ROMAN ROY	Kieran Culkin
CONNOR ROY	Alan Ruck
TOM WAMBSGANS	Matthew Macfadyen
FRANK VERNON	Peter Friedman
LAWRENCE YEE	Rob Yang
COLIN STILES	Scott Nicholson
ALESSANDRO DANIEL	Parker Sawyers
RAVA	Natalie Gold
GRACE	Molly Griggs
TRAINER	Julia Murney
SARAH	Katie Lee Hill
MARIANNE	Mary Birdsong
PABLO	David Anzuelo
KID AT THEME PARK	Christopher Convery
THEME-PARK ATTENDANT	Raymond J. Lee
BUSINESS ALCHEMIST	Drew Gehling
PHOTOGRAPHER I	Ron Simons
LEFTIE (HELICOPTER PILOT)	Frank Lazzarini
ISLA	Noelle Hogan
SOPHIE ROY	Swayam Bhatia
IVERSON ROY	Quentin Morales
TOLLY	Jared Martinez
LOGAN'S PILOT	Julian Wheeler
KID 2 AT THEME PARK	Edan Alexander
PHOTOGRAPHER 2	Joseph J. Parks
KENDALL'S LAWYER	Phil Smrek
DOCTOR	Tim Miller
MALE NEWS ANCHOR	Logan Crawford
FEMALE NEWS ANCHOR	Cat Andersen
AIRPLANE PASSENGER	Sandra Colchado
FLIGHT ATTENDANT	Kim Rideout

INT. ROOM – NIGHT

Black. The unsteady POV of someone groping through a darkened room, hands out ahead—

Bang! A wall.

The figure we're following wasn't expecting that. Hands flat against the wall – hand over hand. Looking for an opening.

> LOGAN

Where am I?

Where are we? A prison cell? A maze?

Where the fuck am I?

Okay. Here's the opening our figure was seeking—

> MARCIA
> (off)

Logan? It's okay, Logan.

Our guy is in somewhere now, into the room he was seeking. Okay. Everything is okay. He knows what he's doing now—

> LOGAN
> (to himself)

Ugh. Okay. Okay.

The shuffle of bedclothes as Marcia climbs out of bed.

Then we hear the sound of . . . what? Water dripping? On to something soft—

And then boom—

You'll find a few footnotes scattered throughout. I've tried to limit these to spots where the reason for a change between script and screen might not be self-explanatory. Where these occur, I've sometimes also included a little flavour of the research that informed the show. Any errors, failure of memory or omissions are entirely mine. *J.A.*

Lights on! And all is bright and stark and sudden. And what do we have?

An eighty-year-old man, Logan Roy, in his shorts and T-shirt pissing towards a laundry basket in a walk-in wardrobe lined with freshly arrived suits and shirts.

Dark urine stutters across the deep white pile of the thick carpet, dampening it down like hot piss on wet snow.

Logan is momentarily terrified. But then a younger woman, early fifties, is in the doorway – her hands across her nakedness – pulling something on—

> MARCIA

It's okay.

> LOGAN

Where am I?

> MARCIA

It's okay. We're in the new place. It's okay, Logan.

NEW YORK. 4:12 A.M.

He computes this information as we cut from Logan's rebooting face to—

INT. CORPORATE BRIEFING ROOM – DAY

Logan Roy's face again. But confident. On a screen: a corporate headshot.

> CORPORATE
> (*voice-over*)

Waystar Royco is a family. A family that spans four continents, fifty countries, three divisions: Entertainment, News and Resorts. Working together. To provide a net that can hold the world, or catapult it forward. To the next adventure!

TORONTO. 7:15 A.M.

Greg (early twenties) in the front row, is nodding, pretending to be engaged. But he's zoning out and when he blinks—

INT. CAR – DAY

We cut through images of the recent past from Greg's POV—

He's smoking a hit of weed in a little pot pipe.

EXT. PARKING LOT – DAY

He slams shut the door of his small car in a big empty parking lot. Fumbles his keys. Sweating. Anxious.

INT. CORPORATE BRIEFING ROOM – DAY

He's back in the room. On the corporate message, a selection of Waystar holdings appear on screen:

The logo of a movie studio: Waystar Studios—

A selection of provincial Canadian and US local newspapers—

A US TV network: ATN and some cable channels, all their logos on screen at once in boxes: News, Cooking, Music, Spanish Language, Comedy Reruns, Sports (Ultimate Frisbee)—

A USA Today-style national US paper: The Correspondent—

Some mastheads of big-city and UK papers: Chicago Daily—

And finally the theme-park franchise: 'Waystar Studios Adventure'. With parks in California, outside London, and pinging on the onscreen map, Toronto.

On screen appears Kendall Roy.

He's chyroned: 'Kendall Roy, Divisional President'.

> KENDALL
> Joining Waystar Royco you're joining one of the most dynamic news and entertainment companies in the world. Feel it!

After the 'Feel it!' graphic there's a ™.

The trainer pauses the DVD on the graphic.

> TRAINER
> How we feeling. Ready to go?

11

Nods from the assembled trainees. But the trainer spots Greg is zoning out. Focusses in on him—

Okay? You in the room?

GREG

Uh-huh. Yep.

TRAINER

And who are you playing today?

GREG
(*by rote*)
I'm not playing anyone. I *am* Doderick.

TRAINER

And Doderick is?

GREG

Doderick is mild-mannered to a fault. Puppyish in my enthusiasms. Playful, eager and lacking in guile. I am the best friend to all I meet.

The trainer nods. Correct. Good kid. Looks to the manager at the back of the room.

TRAINER

Okay. Let's go, folks!

Greg takes a last look at Kendall paused on screen as we—

INT. LIMO – DAY

Kendall is hyping himself up for a deal. 'An Open Letter to NYC' by the Beastie Boys plays.

This is his routine when he needs to pep himself up – listening to this track and throwing punches at the back of the seat in front of him.

KENDALL
(*rhyming along*)
Brooklyn, Bronx, Queens and Staten
From the Battery to the tip of Manhattan
Asian, Middle Eastern and Latin,
Black, White, New York, you make it happen!

Boom. *The final punch connects very firmly and rocks the driver in front sharply.*

Apologies, Fikret.

The limo pulls up outside an investment bank's offices. He gets out onto the plaza.

NEW YORK. 8:30 A.M.

As he hurries to the doors, Kendall lights a red Marlboro. Takes one single drag which is all he has time for before entering, stubs it. Walks into the big lobby.

INT. INVESTMENT BANK – MEETING ROOM – DAY

Kendall is arriving outside the key meeting room. Nods to senior family advisor, and Chief Operating Officer, Francis Alfred (sixties), who is waiting for him.

KENDALL
Yeah?

Frank nods. They head in. A bunch of execs and advisors, including the CFO and advisor to CFO, Alessandro.

As he sits, Kendall attempts a bit of grandstanding icebreaking with Lawrence, the founder of the target firm, Vaulter.

Hey hey hey, man! Good to see you. So. Where are we? Are we ready to fuck or what?

There's a ripple in the room. Some smiles. The curse word doesn't offend. But nor does it land to make him the alpha male he'd like. On the other side of the table, Lawrence leaves Kendall hanging after his big entrance, listening to the words of an advisor and looking at his phone.

LAWRENCE
Yeah. Okay. Look. I'm really sorry. But it looks like there's an issue.

KENDALL
How do you mean, dude? I'm here?

> LAWRENCE

Yeah I'm sorry, but we've been looking at the offer, while you were in transit, I mean really looking at it.

> KENDALL

What, before you didn't have your glasses on? You were smelling it? Huh? I got the call.

Kendall looks at Frank.

> LAWRENCE

I'm sorry, but it won't fly – with my board.

> KENDALL

I was told it did?

> LAWRENCE

Yeah well it won't. Not this actual number.

> KENDALL

I came all the way down here, dude?

> LAWRENCE

Well, I'm sorry, 'dude'.

Kendall tries to sniff out what the issue might be here—

> KENDALL

You know I love what you do. That's been made clear? I'd love to keep you and your team in place, Lawrence? I love Vaulter.

> LAWRENCE

Sure. I just think bottom line, I can deliver a lot more value for our shareholders. Hope I haven't inconvenienced you?

> KENDALL

I see you. I see this.

Lawrence rises.

> LAWRENCE

We're grateful for your interest in our little outfit, but I think that's it.

INT. INVESTMENT BANK – CORRIDOR – DAY

Lawrence walks – Kendall catches up. But then—

LAWRENCE
(*whispers*)

You got the message? I am not letting you Neanderthals in to rape my company. Ever.

Kendall looks around, can't quite believe what he's hearing. But recovers his composure—

You're a bunch of bloated dinosaurs who didn't even notice the monkeys swinging by till yesterday. Well fuck you, daddy's boy.

KENDALL
(*water off my back*)

Oh what? Please.

They reach the elevator area. Their staffs catch up. Now Lawrence speaks loud enough that the last of this is certainly heard by the wider group—

LAWRENCE

I've got a track record from founding one of the most exciting new-media brands in the world. What have you got? Track marks from shooting junk?

His team and Kendall's react – mostly by avoiding eye contact, though it would be plausible for Lawrence to deny he intended for his talk to be 'public'.

But now he switches to public mode—

Thanks for coming down. Great to meet you. Sorry this isn't going to work out.

KENDALL

It's going to work out.

LAWRENCE

No it isn't.

Kendall can't think of a way to come back that doesn't sound ludicrous. Lawrence and team hang by the elevators. It takes a while longer than anyone would want. Silence. Then the elevator arrives.

Lawrence and his team head in. Elevator doors close. Kendall lets his guys assemble around him.

KENDALL

What the fuck? Frank. How did this happen? How can we sweeten this?

FRANK

You still want to pursue it?

KENDALL

Of course I want to pursue. I want to announce. This is part of the whole thing. Our offer is fucking good right?

Alessandro looks at a banker, then offers—

ALESSANDRO

You want to bump the offer another point?

Kendall looks at Frank. Alessandro sees a flicker of indecision—

You wanna call your dad?

Kendall looks like someone's punched him in the nuts but he refuses to react.

KENDALL

Do I want to call my dad? No I don't want to call my dad. Do you want to call your dad?

Is that a real question? From the length of time it hangs, evidently, yes.

ALESSANDRO

No.

KENDALL

Does anyone want to call their dad?

Silence.

No one wants to talk to a dad. Good. Okay, so, we've started so let's buy this fucking company? I'm pushing the bid to one-twenty. Okay?

ALESSANDRO

Okay.

Kendall's phone goes. He checks the incoming name. Nods for everyone else to head in to the elevator. Watches them pass. Then answers—

INT. LOGAN'S APARTMENT – OFFICE – DAY

Logan is in a chair at his desk. There are boxes with files in the room, still to be unpacked.

> LOGAN
> How's it going? Did you close?

At the sound of his dad's voice there's a quaver of tightness.

Intercut with:

INT. INVESTMENT BANK – CORRIDOR – DAY

> KENDALL
> I'm right in the middle, Dad.
> > *(full of inch-deep confidence)*
> Yes it's okay! We're not quite closed. I'm going to one-twenty.

Silence from Logan. Kendall waits, then isn't going to bite.

> So that's good. And are we still on for the announcement?

> LOGAN
> Uh-huh.

> KENDALL
> Great, cos obviously I'm soft floating to like Frank and Rava? And there's obviously gossip getting soft floated.

> LOGAN
> By who?

By Kendall.

> KENDALL
> By the ether. I don't know.

Logan gives a non-committal growl, taps on his mouse.

> Well look, happy birthday, old geezer! It's exciting. This is going to be great for you, Dad.

> LOGAN
> > *(not excited)*
> I'm excited.

Phone down. Logan clicks again.

> *(shouts)*
>
> Marcy!

Marcia is there.

> I thought this whole place was going to be ready? Have they
> fucked us on the internet because—? My emails—
>> *(mumbling to himself)*
> I'm going to call, Ellison or Gates because my emails are—

He opens a drawer.

> Pencil! Where's a—?
>> *(mumbled)*
> (fucking pencil in this whole new set-up, it's ridiculous!)

*He gets up and starts looking in random boxes for a pencil. Marcia
looks at his email account.*

> ### MARCIA
> I think it's all up, Logan?

> ### LOGAN
> I'm not getting anything. Who do they think I am? Uncle Fuck.
> It's not working, I'm not paying until—

The ding of an email.

> ### MARCIA
> I think maybe you just didn't get an email for like ten minutes?

> ### LOGAN
> Uh-huh.
>> *(that sinks in)*
> Okay.
>> *(finds a pen)*
> He's started floating. That wasn't the arrangement. He's offering
> one-twenty. He's got a hard-on.

Marcia takes that in.

> You don't walk around with a hard-on. Makes you look
> ridiculous.
>> *(mumbling to himself as he taps the keyboard)*
> Get it trapped in the eye of the fucking Halloween pumpkin.

She's got another preoccupation—

MARCIA

But the me thing? You're okay on the me thing?

LOGAN

I'm on it, Marcia, don't worry.

MARCIA

I mean not that I mind?

LOGAN

I do.

MARCIA

This is going to be great for us though. Did you see the brochure I sent? The Galapagos thing?

LOGAN

Oh, yeah? Great. Turtles, all kinds of disgusting shit. Terrific.

She has some envelopes.

MARCIA

A lot more cards? Presidents, prime ministers, royal crests.

He looks at a PDF of a paper on his screen, scrolling through the pages. Ignores the cards.

LOGAN

Just have Jan log them—
                    (gets up)
so I can see which fuckers have dropped me already.

She kisses him. He's a tough old bastard, and not of a generation to melt and kiss.

Marcia—

MARCIA

What?

LOGAN

Look I'm not about to spill my guts like some queer. But you know.
                    (looks at her, doesn't say it)
(I love you.)

> MARCIA

Thank you. I love you too.

Marcia exits. But he's already on the phone. Looking at a PDF of a front-page mock-up.

EXT. WASHINGTON, DC – UPMARKET SHOPPING STREET – DAY

This is a street of jewelers, fine-art dealers, boutiques with buzzers to gain entry.

Tom is scanning windows anxiously as Shiv (Logan's youngest) talks to an assistant, Sarah. Nearby they have a black Mercedes parked up.

> SHIV

I'll be back by Sunday night so I'll look at his speech with him then, okay?

WASHINGTON, DC. 9:15 A.M.

> SARAH

Okay but his office wants the poll numbers by the prekend.

> SHIV

By the 'prekend'? What the fuck's the prekend?

Tom is looking at a painting, but earwigging on Shiv.

> TOM

The prekend is Friday.

> SHIV

If he wants them by Friday can he not say Friday?

> TOM

Thursday lunch to Friday p.m. is the prekend.

> SHIV

Fine. Get Rennie to put them together. Okay?

Sarah says her farewell and heads off. Tom stares into a window.

> TOM

Ugh. This is a fucking disaster.

Shiv is looking at her phone, focussed on sending an email.

Shiv? Can you— I need to strategize my gift?

She comes over.

What can I give him he'll *love*?

>   SHIV
> I don't know, my dad doesn't really like – things.

>   TOM
> He doesn't like 'things'?

>   SHIV
> Not really, no.

>   TOM
> Ugh! It needs to say, I respect you, but I'm not awed by you.
> Start a fresh chapter. What says that?

>   SHIV
> A pen.

>   TOM
> A pen?

Is a pen the secret? The answer? She smiles, he sees she's fucking with him.

>   SHIV
> Tom, every gift he gets will mean an equal amount of nothing to
> him. Just make sure it looks like ten to fifteen grand's worth and
> you're good.

As they look at a watch in the sparsely merchandized window of an upmarket jewelers, Tom is still not quite convinced all will be well.

EXT. THEME PARK – DAY

Greg's POV: looking out through Doderick's wide eyes.

Inside, he's stoned out of his gourd. He's hot, he's bothered. He can't see out too well. Breathing hard.

In a wider shot we see Greg in his Doderick costume mimicking the cartoon character's loping walk.

A gang of kids on a birthday party are suddenly calling him over. One starts to cheerfully pull on his tail. Greg has to remain in character

21

and hop around playfully. Making a cheerful game of remonstrations, shaking a comedy fist at these pesky kids.

But inside he's getting dizzy.

From outside: the kids want to be chased. They're running round and round in circles—

Inside. Sweat. Disorientation. He's going in tighter and tighter circles. Man is he stoned! He can't see straight—

Until. Spin out. The world's moving fast round his head. Oh no! Uh-oh. Here it comes . . .

In a wider shot: we see Doderick bend double. A kid jumps on his back, taking the bend as an invitation. Puke starts to come out through Doderick's eyeholes.

Some of the kids back away. Some are kind of fascinated.

> KID AT THEME PARK
> Ewwww! He's puking out of his *eyes!*

Greg retches for quite a while. Another kid pulls his tail again, which makes Greg hiss—

> GREG
> (*quietly*)
> Fuck *off.*

Theme-park helpers rush to pull the incongruous figure out of sight. Greg is clawing at the costume head.

> THEME-PARK ATTENDANT
> (*on walkie-talkie*)
> Protein spill.
> (*to Greg*)
> Head stays on! Head stays on!

EXT. THEME PARK – DAY

Outside – in the thin winter light, Greg is on his cellphone. He's woken his mom, Marianne, in LA.

> MARIANNE
> Greg? Are you okay? How's it going?

GREG

Going great.

MARIANNE

Uh-huh, so why are you calling me at six-thirty in the morning?

GREG

Yeah, great but also – Mom, sorry but I screwed up. Well not me – but look, a, a – kid smoked a joint in my car.

MARIANNE

'A kid'?

GREG

Yeah. Some 'nutball' – a hitchhiker – I picked up, like an idiot because it was raining, and I thought they might get – sexually assaulted if I didn't, maybe, well more fool me! Because he – he gets in and before I can say anything, he whips out this HUGE doobie, and I'm like GET OUT, man. And he won't. He just aggressively smokes out this whole blunt, on my time, and I'm saying, 'No! I have an important first day at a management-training program of a leading theme-park operator' and he's just smiling this – stoned grin – and I can hardly see the freeway exit because of the dense plumes of toxic smoke and – and—

MARIANNE

Uh-huh?

GREG

And so, if you can believe it, the car smelt like skunk weed, and I guess I smelt like – well you can see from there, how I got implicated in this kind of tragic misunderstanding?

MARIANNE

Did you – tell them – who you are?

GREG

No. No. I thought – no. I didn't want to be an asshole. Or – get into it all. I don't know.

(*beat*)

I liked it. I'm sorry, Mom, I'm such a fucking screw-up!

MARIANNE

Okay. Listen to me, here's what you're going to do—

INT. WAYSTAR – KENDALL'S OFFICE BREAKOUT – DAY

In the meeting room off Kendall's office, the Waystar team are trying to figure out how to buy Vaulter. A selection of takeout containers are across the table. Frank is on the phone.

> FRANK
>
> Okay. Uh-huh.

Frank looks at Kendall who is all antsy—

> KENDALL
>
> What?

Frank is nodding.

> What do they say to one-twenty?

Frank puts his hand over the phone.

> FRANK
>
> They're not going to budge unless it gets to be a stupid number.

> KENDALL
>
> What's a stupid number?

> FRANK
>
> What's a stupid number?
>> (*beat*)
>
> A badillion? I don't know.

> KENDALL
>
> Because one-twenty is stupid.

Frank hangs up.

> FRANK
>
> Look, I think this is clearly about Lawrence. Should we look at his package?

Kendall spots a guy arriving.

> KENDALL
>
> Okay. Who's this? Is this news?

The room stirs.

> BUSINESS ALCHEMIST
>
> Hi, Kendall Roy?

KENDALL

Hello?

The business alchemist opens his briefcase.

BUSINESS ALCHEMIST

I was sent by – Roman. To burn some sage?

In there are bunches of dried herbs. Essential oils.

KENDALL

Excuse me?

BUSINESS ALCHEMIST

It's auspicious? I'm a business alchemist. It's a gift, from your brother.

He has a bunch of sage pulled out.

FRANK

Will it set off the smoke alarms?

BUSINESS ALCHEMIST

Not usually.

KENDALL

'Not *usually*'?

FRANK

Yeah, we're looking at a billion-dollar acquisition so I think we'll need a little more reassurance before we break it up with a building evacuation?

Just then, Roman Roy, thirty-eight, tanned and taut, ready to roll, arrives. Uppity and ready to shoot his mouth off.

ROMAN

Hey hey hey, motherfuckers!

KENDALL

Roman.

He goes to hug his brother. Roman nods to the alchemist.

ROMAN

My guy?

(*to the alchemist*)

Are you saging?

25

> FRANK
>
> We're just concerned about the alarm?

> ROMAN
>
> Right, bad juju. Maybe you should make a move, dude?

> BUSINESS ALCHEMIST
>
> I can use essential oils?

> ROMAN
>
> I think just fuck off thanks.
>> (*to the room*)
>
> How's it going?

The business alchemist starts to pack up his kit.

> KENDALL
>
> Good. Just finessing. You okay, man?

> ROMAN
>
> Of course I'm okay. Obviously I'm okay. Why do you ask?

Kendall motions: Are you okay back amongst all this?

> What here? Oh, man, I'm so over all this. I was a bad fit. I was never a corporate cock-suck anyway. Besides. I never got this high in the fucking building! They stuck me in LA with Old Father Time, we were the pool boys, right, Frank. Fucking banana cabana?

Frank smiles – about all the good times they (didn't) share.

> So. What's the bid?

Everyone looks around. Roman's overstepping the mark. He's no longer an insider—

> KENDALL
>
> Well—

He doesn't want to say.

> ROMAN
>
> What that's 'commercially sensitive' – I'm still on the board, bro!

> KENDALL
>
> Going one-twenty-five.

ROMAN

One-twenty-five! Fuck!?

KENDALL

What? High or low?

Roman isn't about to put himself out there by pinning down just what his skepticism implies—

ROMAN

Whatever! For Vaulter? Bit of content and a brand name?
(*laughs*)
Your funeral. You'll be captain soon enough.

Kendall looks round the room: Shush.

Oh c'mon, every intern on the Street knows you're stepping up. Congrats, man, congrats.
(*beat*)
So pleased to be out. The company was essentially a cage to me. Well, congrats. I ought to head.

He looks around and chuckles, and starts to exit.

Look at all this fucking bullshit!

INT. LOGAN'S HOME – DAY

Logan walks the unfamiliar rooms of his large new apartment. Caterers are arriving with drink and food. Marcia is directing operations.

In the walk-in wardrobe Logan sees a maid with a bucket of water rubbing at the white carpet with a sponge to remove the urine stain.

He doesn't acknowledge her but walks to the living area. He tries to sit down on a couch. This is almost a test for him. Can he 'sit on a couch' and 'relax' like a regular human being might?

He looks at a magazine story – 'The Heir with the Flair' – and its picture of his son Kendall. After a few beats of trying to read, trying to sip coffee, he's up.

LOGAN

Marcy, I'm heading out, as ordered.

MARCIA

Great, till one should be—

LOGAN

Fine – but just here – yeah?
(*motions to where he wants people*)
I don't want to get a fucking heart attack from the surprise.
Have them here. And not too loud. Just – a—

MARCIA

You want me to email you the exact details of the surprise?

They share a smile as he goes to exit.

INT. PRIVATE JET – DAY

Shiv and Tom are watching movies. Shiv looking at a laptop. Tom snaps open the expensive watch box. Hmmm. Is it okay?

INT. AIRPLANE – DAY

In another plane. Economy. Greg bangs his knees as he swivels to get comfy with insufficient legroom.

INT. WAYSTAR – KENDALL'S OFFICE BREAKOUT – DAY

The room is still full of tired advisors. Most people have finished but Kendall is still picking at breakfast. He reviews some papers as he eats from a second breakfast burrito, big bites. His appetites are not quite under control. He eats, pushes it away, then picks it up again and demolishes more.

Without knocking, Logan enters. He watches his son for a beat as others in the room clock Logan. Kendall notices the shift in temperature, looks up and, as ever, feels obscurely judged. He chews fast—

KENDALL

Dad?

LOGAN

How's it going?

Everyone sits up, adjusting not-too-unsubtly to the new centre of gravity in the room.

                    KENDALL
Fine. Good. Why are you—?
         (*shuffling Logan into a private space and volume*)
Are we okay?

                    LOGAN
Oh yeah. Yeah. I just have some paperwork—

                    KENDALL
Ahead of the announcement?

Logan lays papers on the table. Logan sweeps the room. Clocks Frank. Gives him a wink. Looks over at Alessandro, smiles.

                    LOGAN
For putting Marcy on the trust. Just bullshit. But I felt like checking in.

                    KENDALL
Oh. Because on my announcement, what's the precise timing on that?

                    LOGAN
Let's see how this goes and I can lay it out.

Kendall scans the headings on the papers.

                    KENDALL
Okay? So this is just the trust?
         (*whispering to keep this private*)
It doesn't affect me stepping up?

                    LOGAN
Nuh. I think I told you about—

Someone's cellphone goes. Kendall looks over. It's not news.

                    KENDALL
Dad – I'm busy, do I need to lawyer all this?

                    LOGAN
                     (*no*)
It's housekeeping.

*Logan hands him a pen. Beat between them. Can son trust father?
The father clearly wants this – and the son wants to be liked, to
demonstrate his trust—*

Logan is making an assessment too. Kendall takes the pen.

> KENDALL
>
> Fine. Marcy's fine by me. I mean the others, might not feel the
> same?

> LOGAN
>
> I'll deal with that.

Fuck it. Kendall is all in – signs.

> Okay. So – I'll see you in—?

> KENDALL
>
> Yeah look, Dad, on lunch. I really want to be with you but the
> deal—

He motions to the room: The deal, it's complicated.

> LOGAN
>
> If you need to stay, you need to stay.

A difficult balance. Kendall tries to read his dad.

> KENDALL
>
> I really want to be with you?

> LOGAN
>
> I appreciate it.

> KENDALL
>
> It's just, delicate. I mean they can handle it but—

Kendall waits for a hint. But Logan gives him no steer.

> LOGAN
>
> Son, your call. It's just – priorities. There'll be plenty more.

*True? Or passive-aggressive? Kendall sort of wants his dad to tell him
what to do, but doesn't want to ask for direction.*

INT. TAXI – NEW YORK – DAY

Greg in a decrepit New York yellow cab. ATN News is playing on the taxi television screen. A bit of promotional graphics play as a voice announces—

ANNOUNCER

ATN News is provided as a complimentary service in this taxi cab by Waystar Royco. ATN News: Trusted and True.

Then on screen – our anchors are behind a desk.

MALE ANCHOR

'The internet of things.' Ever wonder what exactly it means? Well what it *could* mean is your refrigerator getting transformed into a lethal weapon that could be turned against you.

FEMALE ANCHOR

That's one of the terrifying possibilities we'll be considering in the next hour as we take a closer look at the technology which is going to dominate the next one hundred years.

MALE ANCHOR

But before that, coming up in just a moment, we'll be giving you an update on all today's breaking news.

FEMALE ANCHOR

But first, we're talking immigration to our panel of experts and asking: After all the tough talk, is it finally times for action?

MALE ANCHOR

Yup, some congressional leaders are suggesting that recent strong rhetoric on illegal immigration is nothing but a smokescreen. And asking if it isn't finally time for the gloves to come off when it comes to undocumented workers?

FEMALE ANCHOR

Plus deficit talk. Is government borrowing getting so far out of control radical new measures need to be considered to curb it?

MALE ANCHOR

All that, coming up.

EXT. CENTRAL PARK – DAY

Logan walks, killing time, pretty slowly, through Central Park. Ahead is a security guy/driver. Behind, Logan's minder, Colin.

Logan is alone. Maybe shuffles his feet to be super-sure not to slip.

He sits on a bench and Colin hands him a wedge of newspapers – US, UK and Canadian. Five papers – all owned by Logan.

He starts to examine the pages, layout, pictures and choice of stories in each one.

He's on a quiet stretch of path. A young couple pass by. It's hard for them to tell what exactly he is? This elderly man with a big pile of papers. Hobo, or eccentric millionaire?

INT. WAYSTAR – KENDALL'S OFFICE BREAKOUT – DAY

Kendall has made a decision. He is about ready to leave – with Frank. Gives his final instructions from the door—

> KENDALL
> *Anything.* Any indication. Call me. Okay?
> (*beat*)
> And look, this is gonna get press-released, but – by tonight I'm going to be Chief Exec of Waystar.

They all knew.

> I just wanted you lowlifes to be amongst the first to know, okay?

> ALESSANDRO
> Congratulations.

> KENDALL
> Thank you. Okay. That leaks, you're all fucking fired!

He holds a serious face then winks – knows he's opened the gates to the story breaking. Smiles, heading out the door.

> Off we go let the trumpets blow
> Because the driver of the mission is a pro. The ruler's back!

EXT. LOGAN'S APARTMENT BUILDING – DAY

Logan is back outside his new apartment building. There is a gaggle of three photographers outside the building. Colin goes ahead, leaving Logan with one minder.

> COLIN
>
> Okay, guys – can we back off, private event?

They don't go. Colin takes out his camera phone. One by one starts taking deliberate snaps of their faces.

> Freelance? Could be getting colder out there, boys.

But they hold position. Colin looks over. He can't get rid of them. Logan comes over, puts a phone to the side of his face and lowers it so they can't get a decent shot, and heads in.

> JOURNALIST
>
> Mr Roy. Logan, you going today? Is that right?

> LOGAN
>
> Fuck off.

INT. LOGAN'S APARTMENT BUILDING – LOBBY – DAY

Logan marches in past the doorman's station up towards the elevators, where Greg stands, holding a small package.

Greg seems sweaty and shifty. Colin and the driver are suddenly threat aware. Greg doesn't know how to say hi to the uncle he's not seen for twenty years—

> GREG
>
> Hi. Hello there!

Colin stays on point while the driver backtracks to the doorman to check on the kid's status, but the doorman is sending a delivery guy away – round to another entrance.

> COLIN
>
> Can I help you, sir?

> GREG
> *(to Logan, weirdly)*
> I'm actually – I'm here to see you!

Logan doesn't like the look of the situation. Greg with his package and a weird intense smile, jerky move for a hug.

The old man has a sudden flash of concern. Steps away. Colin steps decisively towards Greg and pins him against the wall. Hard. Over the line of social propriety.

> COLIN

Can I see some ID?

He has hold of both Greg's arms. Ready to take him down.

> GREG
> (gabbled)

I'm Greg? Marianne's Greg? Your nephew? My mom called Marcia and I heard – I checked with the – the man and he called up and said it was all okay—

As Colin and Logan look over, the security guard/driver who is talking to the concierge gives a thumbs-up.

> LOGAN

Oh. Right. I didn't know you were coming?

> GREG

Yeah I'm— I think you did?

Colin releases. Logan looks around.

> LOGAN

Uh-huh. Are you (alone)—?

> GREG

I'm on my own. I hope it's okay. I wanted to say, many happy returns.

> LOGAN

Thank you. You okay?

Greg's shaken, but wants to make it all okay.

> GREG

Oh fine! Seriously, fine. I get it. I could have been anyone. An assassin. You could be dead now, or dying. But – yeah. Happy birthday!

INT. LOGAN'S APARTMENT – MAIN ROOM – DAY

Marcia is saying hello to Shiv and Tom. She's good at this stuff, playing the stepmom role.

Grace, Roman's wife, talks to Connor (Logan's eldest son). Roman greets Tom.

> ROMAN
>
> Hey, Global Tom! How you shaking? You still fucking shit up for us?

> TOM
>
> Ha! Still tidying up your mess, pal!

They hug. Joking, but not. Tom winces, over the shoulder. Did he go too far?

> ROMAN
>
> Sis. The pols still boring the living shit out of you?

> SHIV
>
> Yeah, you know, still burying the bodies and counting the cash.

> ROMAN
>
> Ha! Look at you.
> > (*looks at his younger sister*)*
> Walking around like you're an actual human person!

They embrace. Shiv sniffs.

> SHIV
>
> You smell good. What is that? Date Rape by Calvin Klein?

> ROMAN
>
> Yeah you wish!

Marcia gets a text message.

> SHIV
>
> 'You wish'?

---

* We never state the birth order of Shiv and Roman on screen in the show. After the pilot, as we discussed the characters in the writers' room, some felt the family dynamics suggested that Roman was likely the youngest child. That is sort of implied in 'Prague' (season one, episode eight) but never stated. But since Sarah is younger than Kieran that remains the canonical order for me.

> MARCIA

Okay! He's back! Folks, he's back! Can we – can you find somewhere?

Everyone starts to arrange themselves outside the elevator.

INT. LOGAN'S APARTMENT – ELEVATOR – DAY

Logan and Greg stand uneasily next to one another. Colin and the other security guy have stayed downstairs.

Greg doesn't know what to say.

> GREG

It's – a long way up.

Logan doesn't quite catch it.

> LOGAN

Ah?

> GREG

It's— We're going up?

Logan doesn't do small talk.

> LOGAN

Uh-huh.

> GREG

So great to be here. I thought you would have known. I hope it's okay?

> LOGAN
> (*blank*)

Sure. Good to see you.

Silence.

> GREG

I actually came because, I needed to ask something?

> LOGAN

Uh?

> GREG

Yeah um, I actually I think you know but I had some help, and I got on to the international management-training program? The theme-park tour? And – and – I was very into it? But I got sick. Out of – actually – out of Doderick's eyeholes and—

The doors open—

INT. LOGAN'S APARTMENT – OUTSIDE ELEVATOR – DAY

A beat, then the whole family spring out—

EVERYONE

Surprise!

Logan can't get this shit over quick enough.

LOGAN

Great. Excellent. Wonderful.

People crowd round. They take in Greg. He shuffles off to the side of the room with a sheepish smile. He might be a fixer or minder, it's hard to tell.

Okay, give me some room?

Everyone backs off – Shiv, Roman and Connor are first in line to hug. As they enter the main room of the apartment.

Connor, Primo! How are you?

Hug with eldest son.

CONNOR

Good. Excellent, Pa. Here you go.

He hands him a gift bag. Roman is coming in for a hug as Logan puts the package aside. Gives it back to Connor.

LOGAN

Roman, Romulus! Look at you, you look fantastic!

ROMAN

Happy birthday, Dad.

On to Shiv—

LOGAN

Siobhan. Sweetheart. Is Tom here?

SHIV

Uh-huh. Yup.

LOGAN

Oh well, never mind.

Tom and Logan share a smile as he shakes Logan's hand.

This is Craig, everyone, by the way.

He motions vaguely behind him.

Cousin Craig.

Greg raises his hand. Hi.

SHIV

'Craig'? It's Greg. No?

GREG

Yeah. Greg. Greg.
                    (*so why did he not say?*)
People have mistakenly called me Craig in the past so I answer
to both.

*Greg smiles and is accepted into the room. Tom presents his gift. A
watch in a box—*

TOM

Here. It's just a token of my very real and enduring admiration
and the hope that a new dawn might—

*Before Tom can hand over the watch, the elevator doors go again and
there are Frank and Kendall.*

LOGAN

Kendall? You came.

*And in that instant – if he could see it – Kendall would know he got it
wrong. Always business first. But they hug. Then Shiv gives Kendall a
hug.*

SHIV

Hey. Big day. Congratulations.
                    (*then whispered in Kendall's ear*)
You bastard.

But she smiles and he smiles back. Connor makes it over.

CONNOR

Congratulations. Good luck.

Roman eyes Frank – not so pleased. Logan gives Frank a handshake.

> LOGAN
> *(then to the room)*
> So, what's the news?

And then – Kendall's phone starts to buzz. He looks at the number, looks around—

> KENDALL
> Okay. I'm just gonna—?

Kendall needs privacy. Logan opens an arm, Kendall heads—

INT. LOGAN'S APARTMENT – STUDY – DAY

Kendall has headed to find privacy, Frank following—

> KENDALL
> Okay, we're good. Talk to me—
> *(into phone)*
> Is there word?
> *(hits a button, into phone)*
> You're on speakerphone.

Frank is all ears. But Roman has shuffled in too, behind.

Kendall is holding a hand up – this is private – but Roman listens anyway—

> ALESSANDRO
> *(off)*
> PPG Bank have got their nose in, might be rustling up another bid.

> KENDALL
> Ugh. Shit on my dick.

> ROMAN
> O-kay! Now the fucking's started! *Now* you're getting fucked!

> KENDALL
> I'll call you back.

Logan is out too now – with Shiv following. Logan looks at Kendall: What's going on?

Just a few final issues with the acquisition.

Logan looks at Roman: What's going on?

> ROMAN
>
> PPG are balls deep in him. Hustling up a rival bid.

> SHIV
>
> Okay!?

> KENDALL
>
> It's under control.

> ROMAN
>
> You know, I think the only thing worse for us than buying that piece of shit would be trying and losing.

Kendall looks at him.

> KENDALL
>
> Fuck off.

> ROMAN
>
> Well that's unnecessary!

> LOGAN
>
> You want the rival bid to go away? Banks are whores. Pay them and they'll fuck anything. So cut them in on our financing and—

> KENDALL
>
> Well, no because, there are rules—

> LOGAN
>
> Yeah the rules are for the – the people who like rules—

> SHIV
>
> Are you getting played, Ken?

> KENDALL
>
> Am I getting played? No I'm not getting played. I'm the puppet master. I'm all over this, like fucking – mayo. Now look, can we please clear the room please?

Kendall waves for them to leave him. Logan looks round. He physically winces at the prospect of leaving the negotiation.

Thank you. I'll be out, yeah? Thanks, guys. Great input.

As the family retreats, Frank leaves it a beat then whispers—

> FRANK
>
> People need to know you're the boss, Ken?

> KENDALL
>
> Uh-huh. I know it.

> FRANK
>
> This is your day. And not because he said eighty was retirement in some interview ten years ago. Because you deserve it. You did the MBA, you did the hard yards. China. But you might just need to push it over the finish line?

Kendall appreciates that.

> KENDALL
>
> I'm not losing this deal. We call PPG, offer to cut them in on the financing, if they make the other bid fuck off. Okay? It's Logan's idea.

> FRANK
>
> Great idea, Ken. Right idea.

> KENDALL
>
> Thank you.

INT. LOGAN'S APARTMENT – SITTING ROOM – DAY

POV: the picture of a lone tree over the mantelpiece.

> CALMING VOICE
>
> You are able to do anything. You are a master of the seas. If your final destination has been correctly determined, then all apparent diversions are but waymarkers of your route.

Greg has his iPod going. But summoning resolve as he lip syncs the words of his self-help recording to himself. He can do this—

INT. LOGAN'S APARTMENT – STAIRCASE

On the stairway, Shiv presents Logan with her gift.

> SHIV
>
> So, I brought you this. Happy birthday.

He looks at the book.

                              LOGAN

Oh. Thank you.

He's thinking. Flicks it.

This is? These are nice. These are nice houses – where is that?

                              SHIV

That's Vancouver?

                              LOGAN

I like Vancouver.

                              SHIV

That's our old house, Dad.

He leafs.

These are all our old houses? LA, yeah? Montreal. London?

                              LOGAN

Wow. The paper is very thick.

                              SHIV

Yeah. You like it?

                              LOGAN

Oh sure. Great. This is—
                    (*searches for the words*)
a quality item.
                         (*sets it aside*)
I want to look at this properly later.*

She regards the book going down.

So, go on, give me five. What's the news. What's happening?

                              SHIV

Good. Yeah. I want to talk to you about Tom. He thinks maybe
he might be ready for the parks, you know globally and—

---

* Shiv presenting Logan with a scrapbook of all the Roy houses got cut for time
in the edit, but I always liked it and we stitched it into 'Dundee' (season two,
episode eight).

INT. LOGAN'S APARTMENT – MAIN ROOM – DAY

They arrive back in the main sitting room. Connor is there. With his gift bag again.

> CONNOR
> Look, Dad, we should get this somewhere ambient.
> *(proffers the package)*
> You want to—?

> LOGAN
> Connor. How you going? How's the ranch?

> CONNOR
> Perfect. Light pollution is like zero so, that's nice, you know.

Logan pulls a Tupperware box out of a gift bag.

> LOGAN
> Wonderful.
> *(then)*
> What the hell is it?

Roman comes close. Looks in the box.

> ROMAN
> It's a – goo? Is it goo?

> SHIV
> *(re the gift)*
> Perfect.

Kendall is rejoining his siblings now.

> CONNOR
> Sourdough starter.

Logan looks at it, tips it around.

> ROMAN
> *(to Kendall)*
> *Amazing.*

> CONNOR
> I thought you might enjoy making something?

> LOGAN
> (*unenthusiastic*)

Uh-huh? Right?

> CONNOR

Fine. Forget it. I just thought you might like it?

> LOGAN

I do. I just don't know what the fuck it is.

> CONNOR

It's sourdough starter. To make bread, without yeast? The old way?

Marcia is there, looking at Logan: Don't be a dick.

> LOGAN

Oh, okay. Old bread. Thank you.

Logan smiles. Clocks Kendall, who checks his phone. The group disperses as Logan heads over to Kendall.

How are we looking?

> KENDALL

I'll keep you posted.
> (*then, musters all his nerve to remain 'casual'*)
Look, Dad, I just checked with Frank and the holidays mean the board might be hard to get together and it's all over the web, so I've scheduled a call for four? Then we can issue the release?

Logan rides this.

> LOGAN

Uh-huh. You did?

> KENDALL

Yeah. Is that okay?

Rava, Kendall's ex-wife, is arriving with their two kids. They're all still on good terms. Kendall looks over. Rava always makes his belly drop—

> LOGAN

You go on.
> (*then mumbled and off-hand*)
I'm not going.

Kendall doesn't know quite what Logan's referring to or totally hear as Rava approaches and he steps off towards her—

> RAVA

Sorry we're late.

He kisses her on the cheek. Respectful. Even slightly timid.

> KENDALL

No worries. You're not even. Twenty is margin of error.

> RAVA

And I got your message. That's fine.

> KENDALL

Yeah? It's just as it all goes through – next two weekends will be crazy. But then – once it's done, it would be great if—

He nods to the kids.

> RAVA

It's fine. Bank the weekends – spend them later.

> KENDALL

I don't want to fuck things up though. I can come up to you? And then – if you want we could grab dinner for the handover?

Or maybe more? Rava mentally flips through her schedule.

> RAVA

What like – two weekends. Ummm?

> KENDALL

No?

Rava hesitates.

Are you— Does that not (work)—? Are you doing (something)—? Are you seeing someone?

This is a bit over the line. She comes back dead straight.

> RAVA

Yeah. I am. And I'm just hoping this one won't leave coke smeared all over the kids' iPads?

Kendall deflates—

              KENDALL

Uh-huh. No. Fine. Yeah.

He looks crushed. She didn't want that.

              RAVA

Kendall, it's okay. I'm fucking around. You're good. Coronation day. You deserve it. Seriously. After everything. And I think you're going to be able to cope with this.

              KENDALL

Well, obviously I'm going to be able to cope with this.

So why did you say that?

              RAVA

Exactly. I know.

Do we shift focus to elsewhere in the room where Marcia intercepts Logan?

              MARCIA

Are we okay? Lunch in ten.

He nods. She hands him envelopes. Then Logan calls to the room—

              LOGAN

Hey, okay, listen, just two minutes before lunch? Kids. Can I get you, for two minutes?

              SHIV

Oooh a speech!

They filter towards the sitting room.

Greg meanwhile is screwing up all his courage. Ready to make an intervention. He marches over . . . full of resolution and tries to intercept—

              GREG

Er Uncle Logan could I get—?

              LOGAN

Not now.

              GREG
              (little bit of grit)

Sorry. I need your attention.

Logan looks at him.

About the— What I was saying, about the management-training program? I need to get back in.

                              LOGAN
You're out?

                              GREG
Yeah. I got, there was an issue – and so my grandfather said to come and talk and—

                              LOGAN
I'll do anything for my brother.

                              GREG
                              (relief)
Oh that's – that's nice and, I'm really going to give this one hundred percent and I would love to be able to move up and—

                              LOGAN
He just needs to ask.

                              GREG
Oh. My grandfather?
                              (deal-breaker)
Right? I think he doesn't like to—
                              (how to explain)
I mean you two don't, talk so much, right?

                              LOGAN
Anything. Just get him to ask me.

Logan smiles. Greg doesn't get it. Then he does get it – he's fucked.

                              GREG
Uh-huh. Hm. Right.

And Greg stays behind as the family head into the sitting room – Logan closes the door. Maybe Greg bangs his head on it in frustration.

INT. LOGAN'S APARTMENT – SITTING ROOM – DAY

Roman is joshing—

                    ROMAN
He wants some sourdough tips!

                    CONNOR
Hey. It was just an idea. What did you get him anyway?

                    SHIV
Money.

                    ROMAN
                 (to Connor)
Dude, he's gonna love it. He can let it rise while he does his
yoga?

Logan arrives.

                    KENDALL
Dad – are we—?

                    ROMAN
What's the deal?

                    LOGAN
Er – yeah. So.

Quiet descends.

On the family trust, that will decide the situation in the event of
my unlikely demise. I'm going to add Marcia to myself and you
four.

                    SHIV
Whoa? Okay?

                    LOGAN
With my seat also to go to her on my death—

Shiv sees things fast—

                    SHIV
What, which would give her, double voting weight?

                    LOGAN
Uh-huh. So I've got the paperwork for—

Kendall didn't know about the double-weight thing—

                    KENDALL
What so, Marcia will have two votes when you—?

ROMAN

If he—

KENDALL

Well no, Rome, it's not an if?

ROMAN

Well excuse me if I don't want him to (die)—

CONNOR

Well it doesn't matter what we want in this case, Rome?

Logan has three sets of legal papers for them.

LOGAN

Kendall's already signed up but if I can get you all to—

Kendall is leafing through the documents—

KENDALL

Two? Two votes. I don't think I was aware of that when I—

ROMAN

Read the small print, asshole!

Shiv is looking at her papers.

SHIV

This looks— I mean, yeah. But, I might need to talk to— You know, for all the implications?

Roman scans the papers.

LOGAN

Of course.

SHIV

Just to get the full picture?

LOGAN

Sure. Take a beat. But look, I love the bread – goo and the picture book, but this is the present I really want? So by four, good?

The kids are momentarily disorientated. In a matter of hours?

And also, I just mentioned this to Kendall, but despite the chatter, and all things considered I'm going to give it a couple of years.

SHIV

As in?

LOGAN

I'll stay in situ. As Chairman, CEO and head of the firm.

KENDALL

Dad, you what?

LOGAN

Well I just said, son, or were you not listening as usual?

KENDALL

But – I'm, you're not— *What*??

LOGAN

No big deal. I'm just staying on. We can discuss the details.

KENDALL

You *didn't* tell me.

LOGAN

We can announce you're in pole position. Pending events. A move up or some—

KENDALL

'Pending events'?

Roman and Shiv look freaked and shocked – but immediately, not necessarily completely against—

LOGAN

Okay, lunch! C'mon.

Logan heads out. Leaving the kids in shock and Kendall trailing—

KENDALL

Dad?

ROMAN
(*lightly, smiling at the drama*)

Oh fuck!!

Kendall turns, objecting to his levity of tone. His life has just gone up in smoke.

KENDALL

Well I don't know what you're fucking laughing about!

ROMAN

I'm not even laughing – what?

KENDALL

What the fuck? This is – this is going to be a shitstorm. He's going to blow the firm's credibility.

(*switches tack*)

Did he look okay by you?

SHIV

Oh come on! Ken. This is typical.

CONNOR

I'm out – okay, I'm not playing. Whatever you three say – goes. Goodbye!

Connor goes to leave.

SHIV

Con!

CONNOR

On the trust, I refuse to play. I don't want to engage. I'm water, I just flow.

And he's gone, Kendall goes to follow—

KENDALL

This doesn't stand, right?

Shiv shrugs.

Oh fucking *shrug*, you're fucking *shrugging* me . . .?

Kendall makes for the door. Clocks that Roman is messaging on his phone—

Are you messaging? What are you . . .

Kendall reaches for Roman's phone. With the elder brother's sense of ownership. Roman pulls it away.

ROMAN

Hey! What the fuck? Off the cloth, moth! Private! We're not fourteen, dude!

KENDALL

What are you—? Are you telling? This stays in here. This is a lockdown—

ROMAN

We all need advice, man—

KENDALL

Advice – what? You're gonna give a double vote to a power-hungry maniac who will do *fuck knows what* with it because she's got our dad's dick in some super-max pussy grip and she's juicing him before he croaks—!

ROMAN

Oh, dude, come on—

Marcia steps in.

MARCIA

Um, guys? Lunch is coming up—

Ouch – they make faces. Did she hear?

KENDALL

Sure thing.

MARCIA

Sorry, guys, I know you don't get to see each other much but we're nearly—?

They file past – back to the dining room. Kendall zooming past—

KENDALL
(*as he goes past*)
No fine, thanks, apologies—

MARCIA

Not at all. It's do as you please here. It's not like we're in a maximum-security penitentiary.

She hits the prison notion lightly. Its repetition could just be a coincidence. But an extra quarter of a second's eye contact suggests probably not as he looks back and she gives an impossible-to-read smile—

Kendall heads on to follow his dad.

INT. LOGAN'S APARTMENT – DINING ROOM – DAY

Kendall catches up with Logan. The dining room has a couple of staff setting up in there.

KENDALL

Hey. So you've fucked me?

LOGAN

I changed my mind, Kendall—

KENDALL

When? When *exactly*? Cos it feels like you fucked me.

LOGAN

I had doubts and then certain things caused me to rethink.

KENDALL

When? Like what? This is—

LOGAN

It's me. It's mainly me. But you – you're still— Three years ago you were still in the nuthouse.

KENDALL

Rehab. And, Dad, that makes (no sense)—

LOGAN

It's all good. I'm just worried – you might be soft, as yet.

KENDALL

Are you kidding? I'm battle-hardened. Fucking year in Shanghai.

LOGAN

I hear the guy from the website trash-talked you and you let him just come?

KENDALL

Not a website. And I was being professional!

LOGAN

I hear it played weak. Conflict-averse.

KENDALL

I wasn't about to get into a fucking big-dick competition.

LOGAN

I hear you bent for him.

                    KENDALL
What?

                    LOGAN
I hear you bent for him and he fucked you?

                    KENDALL
Well, no.

                    LOGAN
Thing is, you've probably read a lot of books about
management technique and this and that but you know what?

                    KENDALL
What?

                    LOGAN
Sometimes it is a big-dick competition.

                    KENDALL
That's it is it? I should have shouted at some guy? But I didn't?
So you've ripped up eighteen months of corporate strategy?

Logan shrugs. Almost mumbles—

                    LOGAN
And you never lawyered the trust change.

                    KENDALL
Oh, I *trusted* my father. That's a black mark?

                    LOGAN
It's an – an accumulation. You left the room. The deal.

                    KENDALL
To come to my dad's fucking birthday party? We don't know
how many more there'll be!

Logan doesn't like that. Kendall breathes.

So come on. When will you be ready? To step down?

                    LOGAN
I don't know – five?

                    KENDALL
Five *years*?!

LOGAN

Ten?

KENDALL

Ten!! Dad? Seriously?

Logan has reached the edge of what he feels he needs to do to placate.

LOGAN

It's my fucking company.

Kendall is full of rage now.

KENDALL

Yeah and you're running it into the ground. You spend all your time on costs – where's the vision? You're off the beat. Where's the growth? All our graphs go down. All of them.

LOGAN

That's why you're paying a billion dollars for a gay little website?

Weirdly, it is the repetition of 'website' that really pisses Kendall off—

KENDALL

It is *not* a fucking *website*! It's a portfolio of online brands and digital video content and it's part of a strategy to save us if you'll just let me—

LOGAN

Do you want to hit me, is that it?

KENDALL

For fuck's sake.

LOGAN

Are you going to cry?

KENDALL

You know I've been floated already? There's fucking paps outside. I'm getting asked for quotes?

LOGAN

Fuck them.

KENDALL

Yeah, course, 'fuck them'. Great media strategy, Dad, great business strategy.

Logan looks at him like: Yeah, maybe it is actually?

When the Street hears, when the board hears? *You* sold a very promising digital platform for buttons. You just fucking missed it, okay? Fine. Everyone misses things. But you gotta let me get our beak in. The world is—

LOGAN
(*interrupting*)

Yeah yeah. Everything changes. The studio was gonna tank when I bought it, everyone was gonna stay home with videotapes, then guess what – no, they wanna go out. Everyone told me no one wanted to watch network, except you make it zing and they do. You make your own reality. But once you've done it, then, apparently, everyone's of the opinion, it was all fucking obvious?

(*he's finished*)

Lunch!!

INT. LOGAN'S APARTMENT – BATHROOM – DAY

Kendall is in the fancy bathroom. Fast cuts as he—

Stamps on a tube of toothpaste so that it explodes.

Takes a hair-dryer, and smashes it again and again against the wall, until, eventually, it starts to crack and then smash and the two halves of it fall apart, spilling its electronic guts.

Screams in rage and pain into a white towel.

INT. LOGAN'S APARTMENT – LIVING ROOM – DAY

Logan looks over the shoulder of his grandson, Kay – Kendall and Rava's eight-year-old boy.* In the background everyone is gathering for lunch.

Logan watches the images on the iPad. The kid is watching an unboxing video on YouTube. He and his six-year-old cousin, Isla, are transfixed.

---

* Since they'd never been uttered out loud, we had the chance to choose more apposite names for Kendall and Rava's children after the pilot.

Logan can't put it together – he watches for a while.

Logan folds the cover over the iPad to kill it. Nods – lunchtime.

INT. LOGAN'S APARTMENT – BATHROOM – DAY

In the bathroom: the pathetic clean-up.

Kendall cleans up the toothpaste explosion. There's some left on his trouser leg he doesn't catch.

He takes the trash liner from a pedal trash can and carefully scoops up the broken parts of the smashed hair-dryer.

INT. LOGAN'S APARTMENT – MAIN ROOM/DINING ROOM – DAY

It's lunch. Head of the table is Logan.

Round it we have: Kendall and Rava and their two kids; eight (Kay) and fourteen (Gem); Frank; Greg; Connor; Roman and Grace and their six-year-old (Isla); Shiv and Tom; and Marcia.*

But everyone is eating in silence. Towards the end of the meal. Shiv – down far from Marcia – looks at Roman, Roman looks at Shiv. Tom smiles at Kendall.

Roman maybe gives Grace a nod, encouraging her to end the silence.

> GRACE
> Um, that was delicious.

> MARCIA
> Thank you.

> GRACE
> Not at all.

Shiv looks at Roman: I see you. Then she smiles at Marcia, friendly and warm.

---

* With time to consider how the family dynamic played after the pilot, we reconceived Roman as being in a relationship with Grace, not married, and Isla being her child, not his.

> SHIV

No, absolutely fantastic. The whole day. So thoughtful.

Next to her, Roman gives her a childhood look.

> ROMAN
> *(coughs, covering)*

Suck-up.

Shiv looks at him: Fuck off.

> *(very quiet)*

'Gee you're so great, Double-Vote-Power Mom!'

Shiv and Roman smile, laugh. He's caught her.

> SHIV
> *(coughs)*

Fuck you.

As Kendall eats he's self-conscious. Logan watches – monitors everything, table manners and portions included.

> CONNOR

And Greg, how's your mom?

> GREG

Oh good. I mean she can play the – the – nut-crusher, but she's *so* great.

Kendall is sent a message in his lap. Looks up, distracted.

> KENDALL

Oh that's good. That is good.

He gets a buzz in his lap. Logan nods to Frank. He stands.

> FRANK

Um, yeah, if you'll excuse me I think it falls to me, I guess, today to just say a few words. Um. Logan Roy. Born in Quebec* province eighty years ago today to a pop with a print shop and a few advertising billboards and a mom with a herd of cattle. He, of course, took over the advertising, Roger his elder brother

---

* After we'd shot the pilot, we altered Logan's birthplace. A more complicated story of Scottish roots and emigration felt more authentic.

the farm. Roger has been a considerable success winning any number of awards at county fairs!

Laughs. Not from Greg. During the speech, Shiv and Roman are exchanging text messages discreetly on their phones.

Logan of course has also made a decent way for himself over the last sixty years.

Generous, knowing laughs.

Fifth-largest media conglomerate in the world. Feared by the phony, loved by the true, a pal to prime ministers, a truth-teller to presidents. He's tough, he's wily, but he's always true to his word. I arrived to give him legal advice thirty years ago and never got out the door! Until today I'm proud to call him a friend. So, now, with his family around him, which means everything. Let's raise a toast. Logan Roy!

They all raise their glasses.

> ALL

Logan Roy.

Logan coughs from the head of the table—

> LOGAN

Okay. Thank you very much. Now, when we're done. It's time for the game.

> KENDALL

We're playing the game?

> LOGAN

Well, it's my birthday so yes we're playing the game!

EXT. LOGAN'S PARK AVENUE APARTMENT – DAY

Three cars are parked up outside with Kendall's Cadillac. The families each climb into one.

Greg is anxious to get a word with Logan. He lingers, looking for an opening.

As people climb into the cars – Greg edges towards Marcia and Logan—

                              MARCIA
You okay, Greg?

                              GREG
Sure – I'm not . . .

                              MARCIA
Wanna jump in with Frank or Connor?

                              GREG
Um. I think— Is there room in there?

Cars are pulling off. Logan doesn't fancy it, already getting in – but Marcia is not about to be rude—

INT. CAR – BACK SEAT – DAY

Greg is next to Logan, between him and Marcia. Colin and the driver up front.

Logan isn't used to riding with three across the back.

                              GREG
I'm sorry if it's a crush?

                              LOGAN
S'fine.

They ride in silence.

                              GREG
Yeah, I was just talking. To your brother? Grandpa.

Logan bristles.

                              LOGAN
Uh-huh.

                              GREG
He said, 'Happy birthday'.

                              LOGAN
Did he?

                              GREG
Well. No. I guess. Not.
                              (*beat*)
But he is aware it's your birthday.

> LOGAN

Uh-huh.

> GREG

But it occurred to me. Talking to him, and Mom, that having him with his seat on the – on the holding company, still, from historically. That must be suboptimal, in some ways?

Nothing from Logan.

But if I could – if he was willing to give his seat, eventually, to someone more – perspicacious. Who could learn the ropes, running say a theme park. Would that, maybe, be a win-win?

Logan looks at Greg.

> LOGAN

Running parks?

> GREG

Just learning. Just a little guy. Initially. Could that be—? You scratch my back . . . I wouldn't say I could scratch yours. It's too considerable. But – you scratch my back, I you know, not suck your— But. Is there an angle there perhaps?

Logan gives the tiniest of potentially assenting nods.

EXT. DOWNTOWN HELIPORT – DAY

The cars are pulling up. Three Bell 412 helicopters await. As Logan climbs out, Greg moves off, uncomfortable from having tried his power-move. Logan surveys the helicopters and their pilots waiting. Logan stops and whispers to Colin—

> LOGAN

. . . I don't like Lefty.

> COLIN

Which?

Logan turns aside to talk privately with Colin.

> LOGAN

Lefty.

> COLIN

Lefty?

The guy on the far left has a beard and is laughing, talking loud and macho into his cellphone/drinking a Red Bull.

Yeah? He's – he's a trusted— You've had him before?

> LOGAN
> I don't want him flying me.

> COLIN
> Uh-huh?

> LOGAN
> He's safe, I'm sure. But we had that bumpy touchdown on the Vineyard? He looks like a prick.

Colin gets the message.

> COLIN
> Not a problem – do you want me to – let him go?

> LOGAN
> He's fine. Just—

> COLIN
> You go Righty. Who shall I send in Lefty?

They look at the helicopters. Look at the family. Suddenly it feels like a judgment of Solomon.

> LOGAN
> I don't— Greg or Connor and—?
> (*doesn't like picking*)
> It's fine. You decide.

Logan walks off towards the right-hand helicopter.

Colin is left holding the baby. He knows it will all be fine, but now there is a bad vibe about the whole allocation. And what if something did happen? Shiv is heading over—

> SHIV
> Can we go? What's going on, Colin?

> COLIN
> Just jump into that bird, Shiv, thank you!

He motions to Lefty.

EXT. NEW YORK – DAY

Three helicopters take off and head up the East River—

INT. HELICOPTER – DAY

On the bearded pilot. He has an iPhone in his lap. He's glancing at a text/game. They're on autopilot.

In the back: Shiv reads the change of trust agreements. Across from her, Kendall watches. She looks up. He shakes his head: No.

She raises her eyebrows. Tom looks at Kendall. His two kids between them. And Rava who stares out to sea.

INT. HELICOPTER – DAY

Logan and Marcia are flying with Roman and Grace. Logan next to Roman. Logan looks at him then whispers—

> LOGAN
> So what you thinking, son?

Roman raises his eyebrows.

> On the thing?

Roman looks over at Marcia.

> She's really smart. She'd make good picks. Family first.

> ROMAN
> Oh sure. I'm sure.

> LOGAN
> So?

> ROMAN
> So? Well, you know. I guess, I want to do anything for you.

Logan smiles.

> But—

> LOGAN
> But, where's your cut?

ROMAN

No. God no. It's your firm, Dad. It's not 'what's in it for me'.
(*beat*)
But you know, what *is* in it for me?

LOGAN

I would love to get you back in?

ROMAN

Sure. Sure.

(*then*)

It was just tough last time. *Very* tough, with Frank over me, in LA.

LOGAN

Frank is important to the firm.

ROMAN

Oh sure. I understand. It's just, at the studio I had ideas, I'm quite an innovative thinker, but I found a certain amount of resistance?

LOGAN

Is this still the film thing?

ROMAN

No, what? *Robot Olympics*? It's not about one great idea. It was a culture. I think he was maybe threatened by my energy?

Logan nods through this bullshit.

LOGAN

So what would be your dream outfit?

ROMAN

Oh, I don't know. You know me, I think we should liquidate. Financialize. Who wants pipes and product. When you can float hot with pure cash?

LOGAN

Uh-huh.

ROMAN

But if not. I'd wanna run the show. But, till that opened up. Chief Operating Officer. But I guess, that's Frank?

LOGAN

Uh-huh.

Roman smiles. Logan looks away, considering.

EXT. LONG ISLAND – DAY

The three choppers make it down.

They are in a hard-bitten bit of grassland. The wind blows.

In the field there are some folk waiting under gazebos with softball equipment, and some stainless-steel flasks of coffee, soup and tea on trestle tables.

As the family make for the refreshments – some guys, and their young kids standing nearby with shovels and rakes, move out to re-clear a diamond and prepare it for a game.

EXT. TENT – DAY

As the family stand and watch the workers set up bases, Logan looks at his family. Allows himself a moment of reflection, pleasure. They're a pretty good-looking bunch.

Then, maybe spots the splatter of toothpaste on Kendall's trouser leg – what is that? As he homes in on Shiv—

LOGAN

How you feeling. We good?

SHIV

Yep, sure. I'm not totally against Marcia as a concept.
(*beat*)
And you know Tom would love to oversee the parks? He'd be good?

LOGAN

He would? Okay . . .

They smile at each other. A deal?

And for you. If things are getting shaken up, would you come inside?

> SHIV

Dad, I'm not just playing with the politics.

> LOGAN

No sure. Politics. Politics. Shiv, not to be crude, sweetheart, but politics is what comes out the asshole. Wouldn't you like to be up front, feeding the horse?

She can't help but smile a naughty smile.

> SHIV

My guy, he's got that Airforce One look.* So to come back, I'd want the top job.

> LOGAN

And if that was difficult?

She won't reveal her hand.

Overseeing everything outside the US – parks and all?

> SHIV

What, me Tom's boss?

> LOGAN

Yeah? Stepping stones.

She smiles: Maybe. Over in the field, Greg is making a phone call.

> SHIV

What's the long-lost cousin sniffing around for?

> LOGAN

Oh he screwed up. Needs help.

> SHIV

Are you gonna sprinkle some sugar in his bowl?

> LOGAN

I like him.

> SHIV

You like him?

> LOGAN

Kind of. He's scratchy. Hungry.

---

* Shiv's candidate became a woman as we wrote the first season.

(*provocative*)
I think he might fit at the parks eventually? Could Tom handle competition?

As Colin gets word that they're all set up, Tom intercepts—

TOM
Yeah so – just wanted to give this to you. And say 'happy birthday'.

He hands him the watch, in its box.

LOGAN
Thanks.

TOM
Yeah it's just a Patek Philippe. So.

They both look at the very expensive white-gold watch. Tom has a prepared line—

It's incredibly accurate. Every time you look at it, it tells you exactly how rich you are.

LOGAN
That's everything I look at, Tom.

Tom smiles, Logan walks on, even the box is irritating to him to have to carry.

Nearby, Kendall, on his phone, approaches Shiv – looking at her phone.

SHIV
My lawyer says it needs to be simple majority.

Kendall has been texting.

KENDALL
Same. So what are you thinking?

SHIV
Well – starting position is – I'm diluting my power and that's, probably a no, right?

KENDALL
Absolutely. My thing would be, why would we do this?

Roman arrives to check out the chatter.

Shiv's saying she's for no, on Marcia?

SHIV

Well – no, I said—

Kendall looks at her—

That's my *initial* position.

KENDALL

Oh, I thought—

SHIV

It depends.

ROMAN

Uh-huh, it *does* depend.

KENDALL

How does it depend?

SHIV

What the final situation is?

ROMAN

Plus, do you want to tell Dad no?

KENDALL

That's not a big deal.

SHIV

Yeah?? You'll stick the bottle brush up the Lion King's butthole?

KENDALL

As a group, we could just—

The other two are smiling at him.

Sure. I'd cram that shit right up.

SHIV

He'll put a kebab skewer through your eyeball.

KENDALL

Look my thing is – maybe it's a package. Here's the deal: we say no – all of us on the trust, full block. We say: stability. Stick to the plan. I take over – and we just – you two, under me – co-presidents?

> SHIV

Under you?

> KENDALL

Uh-huh.

> *(beat, looks at them)*
> But three. The power of three?

Shiv and Roman clock one another. They know what they think of that.

> SHIV

Interesting.

> ROMAN

Can we think about it?

> KENDALL

Of course—

> ROMAN

Yeah I thought about it, fuck you!

Roman laughs and walks off—

Shiv isn't so harsh but she laughs too, walks off too. A batting team is assembling.

EXT. LONG ISLAND – DAY

It's freezing. Greg is walking towards the outfield, Tom smiles, joins him in the walk.

> TOM

So I hear you're the new kid?

> GREG

Oh well I only just started to get into the business I'm not even—

> TOM

I've got my eye on you.

Could be good or – not so good?

> You need any help, advice— just, you know—

Greg is smiling into it.

don't fucking bother okay?

Greg's smile fades. Tom smiles.

Are you tripping?

GREG

Right? As in?

Greg looks at Tom a bit scared, then Tom breaks a smile.

TOM

I'm only razzing you, cuz! You're dreaming! Relax. Pals, yeah?

Offer him a high-five. Greg goes for it.

Would you kiss me, if I asked you? If I told you to?

GREG

Kiss you?

Greg is terrified. Doesn't know what to do.

I don't . . .

TOM

Your face! Haha! Fuck me, man. That was an expression. Pals!

Elsewhere: Kendall is about to be pitched to by Grace. But before she can pitch, his phone starts buzzing.

KENDALL

Oh – okay. Apologies. Hold it.

He answers. A boo goes up.

Uh-huh. Uh-huh. Okay.

End of call.

Okay. I'm out of here. It's the crunch. Frank, will you be linkman here? Dad, can I—

LOGAN

Of course. Everything okay?

Kendall waves away any concern. Everything's just great! He says farewell to Frank, Rava and the kids and makes for one of the helicopters in the distance.

From first base where he's waiting to run, Roman pipes up—

ROMAN

If Kendall's going we need one more to make it fair!

He looks round.

You wanna?

There's a kid, Tolly, watching with his Latino father, Pablo. Tolly looks at his dad.

PABLO

Sure?

ROMAN

C'mon. You're up. Relax. Can you hit a ball?

Tolly smiles.

Cos I'll give you a million dollars if you hit a home run, kid.

The boy smiles.

I don't know why you're smiling. Seriously. A million.

FRANK

Hey, I'll do it for a million!

Frank steps forward from his spot as backstop to take the bat from the kid – who pulls it away, still half-smiling, but unsure what game he's in with these adults, and wanting to keep his shot at the big time.

There's a mini cheer for the kid as he dodges Frank, who backs away smiling.

I'm kidding – you're good.

ROMAN

Grace, where's my—

He gets his checkbook.

SHIV

Rome?

There's a murmur of disapproval.

ROMAN

Oh you don't want him incentivized!

Roman scribbles.

One million dollars for a home run.

Roman holds out the check. The kid looks at his dad over with a couple of other workers, leaning on a shovel.

Pablo knows he should intervene. Or at least – contextualize this mad offer. But he doesn't know what to say, he smiles like it's all something of a joke. But, like his son, he doesn't know quite how much of a joke it is. He grins, fixed.

> LOGAN
> Okay. We okay?

The kid feels the world wobble around him. The centre of attention; of a grown-up game.

Roman waves the check. The kid doesn't understand much about the situation, but he understands a million dollars.

Grace pitches, not a tough ball. The kid is in a vortex of emotion and he swings hard for it – hits it and it spins out. Not a great connection. But lands between two fielders who react slowly, and he's off running. Running, he feels, for his life—

But as he makes it round first and second base the ball comes in to third. To one of Kendall's kids, Kay, who fumbles but catches and Tolly is – out.

Roman, one base ahead, who has made it round, boos.

> ROMAN
> Ah, man. You choked! You choked it!

He rips up the check into four.

> Still you tried. Here's quarter of a million!

He gives Tolly one quarter. Pablo smiles, like it's all funny, not horrible.

Logan talks to Colin (or another member of staff) and sends him off to look after Tolly to make sure there'll be no comeback – and hand over the watch.

EXT. LONG ISLAND – DAY

Kendall walks to the helicopter, on his phone. In the far background, we can see the family.

                    KENDALL
Yeah – hey it's just background for the story I heard you had
cooking? Yeah I know Kendall Roy. And he's saying Logan's lost
it. Kendall loves him but he's slowing down. Making bad calls.
Some major shareholders are worried. That's what I'm hearing
from people close to the family—
                    (*kidding*)
those disloyal fucks.

EXT. LONG ISLAND – DAY

Kendall's helicopter takes off.

EXT. DOWNTOWN HELIPORT – DAY

The helicopter is landing.

INT. INVESTMENT BANK – MEETING ROOM – DAY

*Kendall arrives. Lawrence is outside the main meeting room looking
at his phone – in the room are some of his team.*

                    KENDALL
Hey. Lawrence. Sorry the other offer evaporated. But we
fattened the goose nice now, right?

                    LAWRENCE
I hear it's a decent package.

                    KENDALL
The number is one-forty. Cash with a stock alternative.

Lawrence wasn't expecting it to be that high.

You're on our board. Take the stock and you'll own a nice piece
of us. Rockstar salary.

Lawrence can hardly refuse—

                    LAWRENCE
Well that is an appealing package.

Kendall is determined to claw back status. He comes in close.

> KENDALL

It is, yeah. It's appealing.

> LAWRENCE

You better play nice though. Because I'm the whole company.

> KENDALL

No. You're OFM. One Fungible Motherfucker. You think you're so fucking hip but all I want is the brand. The whole firm is just so much fairy dust. It just happens I want some today.

Lawrence is searching for a comeback.

> LAWRENCE

Well we'll see if I choose to—

> KENDALL

Yeah I think you're going to stick around. I'm going to stuff your mouth with so much gold. Non-disclosure agreement. Non-compete. I'm going to lock you in a golden cage, fuck you with a silver dildo and pay you so much you sing whatever song I want.

> LAWRENCE

Easy. You still need me to recommend this or—

> KENDALL

No, this is a deal so fucking good you have to take it, or we'll see you in court.

Lawrence considers.

EXT. LONG ISLAND – DAY

Logan is walking with Frank.

> FRANK

You wanted five?

> LOGAN

Yeah. Frank. I've been thinking if now isn't a time for a new role for you?

Frank catches something in Logan's demeanor.

> FRANK

Okay? As in. What sort of—?

> LOGAN

Light duties.

> FRANK

'Light duties'?
>> (*this is the code he's heard a bunch of times before*)

Are you kidding? Logan. Me?

> LOGAN

No one has as much respect as me for you, Frank—

> FRANK

Oh no. No, c'mon, fuck this—

Those are not good words to hear—

> LOGAN

It's a step up. The press release should be on your phone. Just proof it. You might want to add some color, it's quite dry.

Frank looks at his phone.

> FRANK

That's it? To *me*. That's it? After thirty (years)— Jesus Christ, man. Here?
>> (*what can he say?*)

You are what you do, Logan. You know that? In the end you're just what you do.

Frank looks him in the eye. Does that land, even a little?

> LOGAN

Yeah well, you'll get your nut.
>> (*calls over*)

Hey, kids?

He summons Connor, Shiv and Roman to ride with him.

EXT. LONG ISLAND – DAY

Logan's helicopter rises from the ground.

On Pablo and his son Tolly's faces as they watch it go up, up and away—

INT. HELICOPTER – DAY

Logan is looking at his kids. The envelopes of legal documents are there on their laps.

                    LOGAN

So. What you say, kids?

                    ROMAN

What's the Frank situation?

                    LOGAN

Frank's out of the picture.

                    ROMAN

Yeah? Fuck.

                    LOGAN

Frank's dead. Tom should be stepping up. Shiv's thinking about a new role. So, are we good?

                    ROMAN

Um? Shiv?

                    SHIV

Rome?

                    ROMAN

Um? Con?

                    CONNOR

I'm with these two. What they say goes.

Shiv looks at Roman.

                    SHIV

Our position is that this doesn't quite work for us. At present.

                    LOGAN

You what?

                    ROMAN

It's not sufficiently attractive. As a proposition.

                    LOGAN

Are you fucking joking?

                    SHIV

We get that. We do. We'd like to help. I'd love to help.

LOGAN

Then help.

SHIV

But – why would I? When— I mean— Giving *away* power. Why would I do that?

She looks at his face. A lot of reasons she might do that. But they're difficult to summon in this moment.

The chopper blades chop. The noise is great. The dying winter light is ebbing. And at that moment—

A blood vessel blows in Logan's head. And the blood seeps. And an extraordinary burst of pain shoots through his head – a super-migraine.

And he starts to lose control. His sense of balance goes and he tilts, oddly, unnaturally.

Shiv and Roman look at one another. What sort of weird reaction is this?

ROMAN

Dad? It's just a first position?

He keels over into Connor's lap.

SHIV

Dad? Dad.

ROMAN

Dad!

CONNOR

Dad?

Roman turns and shouts to the pilot.

ROMAN

Take us— Get us to a hospital.

EXT. HELICOPTER – DAY

The helicopter banks to a different destination as we hear over the wide shot of the copter the kids' shouts and cries.

                              SHIV
                             (off)
        Dad? Are you—?

                            CONNOR
                             (off)
        What's Dad—? Are you—?

INT. INVESTMENT BANK – MEETING ROOM – DAY

Lawrence takes a call. He looks away, covers the interaction. Talks in a corner.

                            LAWRENCE
        Uh-huh. Uh-huh. Uh-huh. Thank you.

Lawrence ends the call. He takes a breath. Closes his eyes. Big decision. Opens them. Turns.

        Kendall?

Kendall heads over. They meet for a whispered conference.

        You heard?

                            KENDALL
        What?

Clearly not. Kendall's phone buzzes – but he cancels.

                            LAWRENCE
        Deal. It's very exciting. I can't wait to join your board.

                            KENDALL
        I think you've made a great decision and I hope there's no hard feelings over all the cock-jousting.

                            LAWRENCE
        Nuh-huh. You win.

He shakes Kendall's hand.

                            KENDALL
        Fuck yes!

Kendall's phone starts going again.

LAWRENCE

Your dad just had a brain hemorrhage.

KENDALL

What?

LAWRENCE

I'm sorry. I'm sorry for you.

KENDALL

Are you? Is this—?

Kendall doesn't know what these words mean – is it grim trash-talk, or a mistake, or truth, or what—?

Lawrence goes to sit down. But first he leans in.

LAWRENCE

But you just invited me into your chicken coop. And I'm going to eat you all. One by fucking one.

Kendall is in shock. Answers his phone.

KENDALL

Hello?

Over Kendall expression as he talks to Shiv—

'What You Do to Me' by Blackroc/The Black Keys plays—

And we revisit our key players and contenders for the throne:

In the dying light: Frank Vernon, having a drink, thinking, out at the softball diamond on Long Island—

Shiv Roy, at the hospital, on the phone to Kendall, with Tom at her side—

Roman Roy, pacing the ER waiting room—

Lawrence walking back to his team—

Connor Roy in the emergency room, reading a magazine—

And finally, on a ventilator in the ICU, Logan, shallow breathing.

EXT./INT. QUEENS – AN APARTMENT – DUSK

On a special place on the table sits Tom's gift to Logan – the watch, still in its box.

Pablo, Tolly and Tolly's mom watch TV business news—

> NEWSCASTER
> As of tonight there is a degree of stockmarket volatility as Waystar Royco's Chairman is reported to be in a critical condition following a major medical incident today.

As the news plays on we—

Pull back on all the windows of a block of apartments. All the windows twinkling, the cacophony of media voices spilling out from TVs, laptops, smartphones, radios.

Episode Two

SHIT SHOW AT THE FUCK FACTORY

Written by Tony Roche
Directed by Mark Mylod

Original air date 10 June 2018

Cast

LOGAN ROY	Brian Cox
KENDALL ROY	Jeremy Strong
MARCIA ROY	Hiam Abbass
GREG HIRSCH	Nicholas Braun
SHIV ROY	Sarah Snook
ROMAN ROY	Kieran Culkin
CONNOR ROY	Alan Ruck
TOM WAMBSGANS	Matthew Macfadyen
FRANK VERNON	Peter Friedman
LAWRENCE YEE	Rob Yang
COLIN STILES	Scott Nicholson
RAVA	Natalie Gold
SARAH	Katie Lee Hill
MARIANNE	Mary Birdsong
PARAMEDIC ALEX LONG	Michael King
DOCTOR KENNETH WARNER	Justin Cunningham
NURSE CARRIE BUCKLEY	Mei Li
NURSE TERESA MENENDEZ	Margaret Ivey
DOCTOR QUINN ASHBURY	Austin Durant
DOCTOR RASHIDA JOHNSON	Gameela Wright
JESS JORDAN	Juliana Canfield
GERRI KELLMAN	J. Smith-Cameron
EVA	Judy Reyes
KAROLINA NOVOTNEY	Dagmara Dominczyk
KARL MULLER	David Rasche
DOCTOR THOMAS LEWIS	Marcus Ho
NEUROLOGIST JEREMY LIPE	Eric Pargac
WILLA FERREYRA	Justine Lupe
DOORMAN	Jorge Chapa
NURSE ELISA HIGHSMITH	Sarah Nina Hayon
JAI	Nikki Massoud
NEWSCASTER	Tanya Rivero
DOCTOR VAL MONTGOMERY	Jon Norman Schneider
JOYCE MILLER	Eisa Davis
DOCTOR TROY JUDITH	John Rue
FIKRET	Greg Harvey

TATSUYA	Jake Choi
PUKING GUY	Nick Fondulis
HALAL GUY	Justin Long
GREG'S TAXI DRIVER	Gary Curasi

DAY ONE

EXT. FDR DRIVE – DUSK

Logan's ambulance races, or crawls, through traffic.

INT. AMBULANCE – DUSK

*The paramedics work on Logan. Responsiveness tests: verbal,
tap, pinch, sternum rub, pupil test. His clothes are cut off as the
paramedics continue to work on him. Lifepack in use. They give him
an IV drip, oxygen, check his blood pressure. Shiv watches on, a mess.
One of the paramedics calls in to the hospital.*

PARAMEDIC ALEX LONG
We've got an eighty-year-old male, found with LOC. Vitals are
BP one-ninety over one-oh-two, pulse at ninety-four. Respiration
at twelve. Patient only responsive to pain is on high-con O2 at
fifteen-LPM. He's unstable. I've spoken to the daughter, she can't
tell me what meds he's on.

But they come to a slow halt.

SHIV
Why aren't we moving? Why the fuck aren't we moving?

PARAMEDIC ALEX LONG
We're in traffic. We'll get there.

EXT. HOSPITAL – DUSK

*Close on Logan as his gurney is met by the waiting team and taken
into hospital. We might see Shiv, maybe focussing on trying to
compose herself.*

DOCTOR KENNETH WARNER
Still unresponsive. Take eight vials and get them to the lab.

Intercut with:

EXT./INT. HOSPITAL – VARIOUS LOCATIONS – NIGHT

New York Presbyterian-style upscale hospital.

Logan, unconscious on a gurney, rushed inside the hospital by the medical team. Shiv follows.

EXT. HOSPITAL – NIGHT

A taxi pulls up at the hospital. Roman and Connor spill out and rush inside.

INT. HOSPITAL – ELEVATORS – NIGHT

Elevator doors open. Logan, on a gurney, is rushed out as doctors and nurses work on him.

INT. HOSPITAL – NIGHT

Tom and Greg hurriedly press the elevator button and wait. Tom stares off, the weight of the world on his shoulders. Greg looks with a bitten lip at Tom: This is bad.

INT. KENDALL'S CAR – NIGHT

In the back of his car, Kendall looking tense and sick.

INT. ICU – NIGHT

A medical team works on Logan. Marcia arrives, shocked to see Logan. Colin guides her away.

INT. KENDALL'S CAR – NIGHT

Kendall and Jess, Kendall's assistant, are being raced to the hospital. They hit traffic.

> KENDALL
> (to the driver)
> How long, how long does the satnav say? Which app is that?

(to Jess)
Cross-check, cross-check Waze and Google Maps and Apple Maps.

(to the driver)
I don't care about the traffic! Make it. Let's make it. Let's weave, man. This is my father.

He observes the traffic and tries to make a call on which lane is moving fastest.

Middle lane! My father's dying, let's get me there, let's do it.

Kendall takes a call.

Roman? What? Is he okay? Stop crying, buddy. Please. I can't understand anything you're saying, man. Seriously. You're going to make me cry. I'm there, I'm nearly there. I'll be there now, man, okay? Hang tight. I love you. Tell Dad I love him. Okay?

He's trying to make plans, but there are no plans to make.

(to Jess)
Oh fuck. Oh fuck. We need – we need. I don't know what we need.

JESS
Ken, we'll be there. We'll get there.

Kendall tries to sit back, breathe.

EXT. HOSPITAL – NIGHT

Kendall gets out of the car and rushes inside.

HOSPITAL EMPLOYEE
You can't park there.

KENDALL
(to Jess)
Talk to him.
(to the guy, as he passes)
My dad might be dying!

INT. HOSPITAL – ICU CORRIDOR – NIGHT

Tom and Greg arrive. Tom sweetly embraces a devastated Shiv. Colin is in the background talking to administrators.

TOM

Hey. Are you okay? Do we know anything? Are you okay?

SHIV

Yeah. No. Yeah.

TOM

What can I do to make this better? Tea? Call your mom?

SHIV
(*too fast*)

No.

TOM

Shiv, I'm human Siri, task me.

SHIV

Um, tell Sarah to get Dad's doctor. And research the best neurologists.

TOM

I will action that.

SHIV

Maybe I should? I should go through my diary with her, clear it out, and you won't know what's important . . .

TOM

Hey. I'm doing it. I've done it. It's already happened. Forget it.

His hands on her shoulders, holding her together. She looks at him. Broad shoulders. She nods.

Some medics hurry through with equipment. Tom moves away to make calls.

Shiv sees Marcia and Roman talking, looking over at her. Shiv, feeling guilty, wonders if she's being blamed.

NURSE CARRIE BUCKLEY

Sorry, you need to be in the waiting area.

*Nods but no one moves. They're lost in thought. Shiv approaches
Roman.*

> SHIV
>
> What were you and Marcia saying?

> ROMAN
>
> What?

> SHIV
>
> You were just – you were looking at me and talking?

> ROMAN
>
> She said, 'You're my favorite, don't tell Shiv.' What do you
> think? She asked what happened. So I told her.

Is he blaming her? Connor comes over. Paternal air.

> CONNOR
>
> It will be okay, I promise. I'm here.

> ROMAN
>
> Thanks, big man. Huge relief.

> CONNOR
>
> Hey come on? Just saying, lean on me.

Kendall arrives.

> KENDALL
>
> Hey. Where are we at? How is he?

A nurse passes by, to the group.

> NURSE TERESA MENENDEZ
>
> I'm sorry, we need this area clear.

> KENDALL
>
> I just arrived? I don't know where to stand, okay? Show me
> where to stand and I'll stand there.

Colin steps in to placate the nurse.

> CONNOR
>
> Wise elders, Ken. These people do an incredible job.

The family move into the ICU.

INT. HOSPITAL – ICU – NIGHT

Logan is being attended to by doctors. Marcia's with him. Kendall goes to see him, is shocked at what he sees.

> KENDALL

Fuck. What's the situation? Do we need to call anyone?
> *(re the medics)*

Are these people the best (people)?
> *(re the ICU)*

What is this – part of the hospital, is this the best – section?

> ROMAN
> *(to the medics)*

Excuse me, are we in the best part of the hospital? Sorry – but we need to—

> DOCTOR QUINN ASHBURY

The ICU is the ICU. This is the best place for him.

> MARCIA

I told the staff to take Rava and Grace and the kids away, and bring them in later, yes?

> SHIV

Should the kids see this?

> CONNOR

It's good. It's the cycle of life.

> ROMAN

Well he's not dying.

> SHIV

Nobody said he was dying.

> ROMAN
> *(indicates Connor)*

He did.

> DOCTOR QUINN ASHBURY

I'm sorry, could you give the team some space?

> ROMAN

Here's an idea. How about you worry about the medicine, not the fucking feng shui?

The doctor nods as they head out.

*Marcia stays. As the group of kids exit, Shiv looks back, at Marcia –
does this mean she cares most?*

INT. HOSPITAL – ICU CORRIDOR – NIGHT

The family congregate. Kendall calls to a passing nurse.

> KENDALL
> Can you give us a picture please, and we want to just check this
> is the highest care level available?

Maybe a flicker of acknowledgement but the nurse doesn't stop.

> Look. Do they know who we are? Do they know who he is?

> ROMAN
> Should we call Mom?

> SHIV
> No. What? There's a million people to call.
> *(then)*
> And she'll make it about her.

> CONNOR
> I think you should call. I mean, it's not like she'll come.
> *(a little bit scared?)*
> Will she?

But no one's listening to Connor. A doctor heads past.

> DOCTOR RASHIDA JOHNSON
> Folks. You need to wait through there—

> KENDALL
> Hey, I'm sorry, we're getting mixed messages. We have no clue
> what's going on.

> DOCTOR RASHIDA JOHNSON
> We'll be with you as soon as we have an assessment.

> KENDALL
> We need to know what's happening.

The doctor smiles, understanding.

There are hundreds of thousands of American jobs dependent on his wellbeing.

The doctor smiles as she moves off.

> SHIV
> *(after a beat)*
> 'Hundred of thousands of . . . '

Kendall can feel he pushed that one.

> KENDALL
> Hey, I'll say anything to get him the good medicine.

Colin comes to usher the family to an area he's secured—

INT. HOSPITAL – ICU WAITING AREA – NIGHT

The family are in a corner. Jess is on the fringes of the room.

> KENDALL
> So, look, what happened, exactly?

> ROMAN
> I don't know. It was freaky.

> SHIV
> We were just talking.

> ROMAN
> Yep, one second Shiv was hardballing Dad, the next he mumbled something and – you know.

> SHIV
> I wasn't hardballing him, we were talking. A brain hemorrhage doesn't come from some chit-chat?

> KENDALL
> It's definitely a brain hemorrhage? Is that what they said?

> ROMAN
> Someone said brain hemorrhage? Right?

> SHIV
> Did they? Or stroke?

> ROMAN
> Umm, the first – the ambulance guy?

CONNOR

A stroke is a hemorrhage.

KENDALL

Did someone say hemorrhage or is it just you who said it?

TOM

It could be an aneurysm?

KENDALL

Why aren't we chasing this?

CONNOR

Is there any—? Did Dad ever talk to you guys about cryogenics?

KENDALL

Are you insane?

TOM

I'll chase.

Tom heads off, not unimpressive. Shiv smiles at him.

KENDALL

We need to call Dad's doctor. And his neurologist. We need to be on this, now!

SHIV

We already called Doctor Judith. We dropped that we know half the board. Kendall, I'm on it. We are checking out names. We all are trying to do the best. Back the fuck off.

ROMAN
(*googling*)

According to this it sounds like a stroke.
(*googling*)

Could be an acute subdural hematoma.

KENDALL

Great, get in there and operate, Doctor Google.

Roman is going to respond but bites his lip.

CONNOR

He once talked to me about cryogenics.

(then, off their looks)
What, wouldn't that be typical, all the other billionaires are
strolling around with new bodies but not Dad because we were
too embarrassed to actually discuss it?

KENDALL
Let's just worry about keeping him alive till tomorrow, before
we worry about the next thousand years, yeah?

INT. HOSPITAL – ICU CORRIDOR – NIGHT

Greg is by a vending machine on a call to his mom.

GREG
I know. And on his birthday too. It's so shitty.

Intercut with:

INT. MARIANNE'S HOUSE – LATE AFTERNOON

*Marianne is sitting on her bed in her home in Bolinas, a hippy
Northern Californian town.*

MARIANNE
What's happening now? Are you staying at the hospital?

GREG
I guess. I think I've got a job, but I don't know. Logan said I did.
But Marcia was the only one there. And then he tragically, you
know.
(then)
Should I ask her?

MARIANNE
What sort of job? A good job? A blowjob?

GREG
I don't know. I can't believe he offered me a job and then he had
a brain hemorrhage, it's so unfair . . . Unfair for him, I mean.
And everyone. I have like twenty bucks. The world is so fucked
up.

> MARIANNE

I am not sending you any more money, Greg. Step up. Harvest an organ.

> (then)

And make sure. About the job. Because that side of the family, they'll spit in your face and charge you for moisturizer.

Shiv approaches the vending machine. Looks at it, confused – smiles at Greg.

> GREG

I know. I know it. They are.

Greg smiles at Shiv.

> MARIANNE

Just don't do or say anything stupid. I need to call your grandpa and let him know—

> SHIV

Do you have cash?

> GREG

Er. No. Not— Just—

He has one twenty-dollar bill. He holds it up. She takes it.

> SHIV

Thanks.

INT. HOSPITAL – ICU WAITING AREA – NIGHT

Close-up on: shots of Logan entering a business meeting. Pull out – it's a news package playing on Kendall's phone.

Roman, looks at it. Looks at Kendall.

> KENDALL

ATN obituary. They want us to okay it in case they have to run it?

Kendall shakes his head. Kneads his eyes. He can't believe where he is, what's happened.

> ROMAN

Is it nice?

> KENDALL

Made by his own news outfit? It doesn't say he was a prick. You wanna (watch it)—?

Roman walks away. But someone needs to. With a deep breath, suppressing the urge to weep or crumple, Kendall carries on.

In the background: another family (husband, kids, brother, maybe grandparents) wait for news about their mom. Maybe they're thinking about asking passing staff for information but are too timid to ask.

Off in the corner: Connor is on the phone.

> CONNOR

Well I'd love to see you. Yes, it's appropriate. It could hardly be more appropriate.

Kendall nods to Jess, who is nearby.

> KENDALL
> (re obit)

There's nothing in here about Mom, or Connor's mom. They need to be included.

Roman comes in from the corridor.

> ROMAN

PJ says Aziz Khan at the Mayo Clinic is the best there is.

Tom gets off his call. Shiv is returning with some Diet Cokes. Greg trails after her.

> CONNOR

I know a great hypnotherapist.

> ROMAN

Uh-huh, interesting. You think this is a good time to get him to stop biting his nails?

> CONNOR

I meant for *later*. For recovery. Roman.

> TOM

Sarah says Ann Wieman at NYU.

> KENDALL

That's not the name I have.

SHIV

Well it's the name I have.
(*to Tom*)
Tell her to call them.

Greg whispers, Shiv doesn't hear, no one hears – but we do—

GREG

(Was there any change at all?)

A doctor enters, everyone crowds round him. Marcia follows.

DOCTOR THOMAS LEWIS

Hi, I'm Doctor Lewis, the senior neurologist here— So. We've
done everything we can to stabilize Mr Roy—

KENDALL

And is he okay?

ROMAN

He's fine. It's a fucking power-nap. Medical siesta.

DOCTOR THOMAS LEWIS

I'm sorry, I can't tell you more until we know the results of the
CT scan, but we'll have those soon.

KENDALL

Doctor, look, ranked, what are the most likely outcomes?

DOCTOR THOMAS LEWIS

Right now I'm afraid all outcomes are possible. We'll know
more soon. I'm sorry. It would be misleading to say more right
now.

*He heads off. Marcia puts her head in her hands. Shiv hugs Marcia.
Greg watches him go.*

GREG

It's most probably a hemorrhagic stroke.
(*off their looks*)
I did zoology. Animals also have strokes. Even reptiles. So.

ROMAN

It's fine. He'll never retire and he'll never die.

Connor hugs Roman. Tom puts his arm round Greg's shoulder. Kendall stands on his own. Inadvertently left out. Jess takes delivery of an elaborate fruit basket.

> KENDALL
>
> Already? People are sending shit already?

> JESS
>
> It's from Lawrence.

> KENDALL
>
> Call him and tell him that is not fucking appreciated.

Gerri, Waystar General Counsel, lets Kendall's impotent fury subside.

> GERRI
>
> Can I get five? We need to talk to you.

Gerri and Eva (from ATN) head out, Kendall goes to follow.

INT. HOSPITAL – CORRIDOR – NIGHT

Kendall joins Gerri, Karl and Eva.

> GERRI
>
> Obviously the board, the nominating committee, has a plan in the event of Logan's incapacitation . . .

> KENDALL
>
> Do I need to hear this right now?

> GERRI
>
> You do. The guy's an ox, we know that, but—

> KARL
>
> The stock is not in great shape as it is and—

> KENDALL
>
> I am not thinking about the stock right now, okay?

> GERRI
>
> I know. I know.

> EVA
>
> Nor are we. Nor is anyone.

Beat.

GERRI

Nevertheless. If we carry on, on – the current trajectory in terms of his – consciousness – we need to announce a plan by around six-thirty before the markets open to avoid a lot of – funky chowder.

KENDALL

'Funky chowder'?

Kendall looks back, towards the family.

EVA

If you want to— We've set up through here?

Gerri heads off, expecting Kendall to follow. He does.

KENDALL

What have you set up?

GERRI

You're gonna want somewhere to – be. We spoke with a hospital trustee, just to make sure everybody knows who's who around here.

KARL

This isn't a war room as yet.

GERRI

But if we need one, it's available.

EVA

There's so much going on. This must be very confusing.

Kendall eyes her suspiciously.

In another part of the corridor Shiv is following Roman.

SHIV

Can't we just talk here?

INT. HOSPITAL – AUDITORIUM – NIGHT

Roman ushers Shiv into an empty room. It's a surprising space.

ROMAN

You know Connor's invited Willa down?

> SHIV

Ugh. Here? Why would he do that?

> ROMAN

I don't know. He saw an empty bed and it made him horny?
I have no idea.

Real reason for the chat—

But listen, so I was thinking – this must be tough on Marcia.

> SHIV
> (*sounds unlikely*)

Yeah? You're thinking that? What? Will she put all her
inheritance into gold, or oil?

> ROMAN

No, look I know the trust only comes into play if certain things
happen—

> SHIV

He's dead. Or brain dead.

Roman waves that away—

> ROMAN

But I was thinking, wouldn't it be nice for Dad to wake up and
for us all to have signed, like he wanted? A nice gesture?

> SHIV

And if he dies? We've signed over to Marcia, basically, the
power to choose the new Dad.

> ROMAN

So, for the record, you're declining to sign the change of trust?

> SHIV

'For the record'? What is this, McCarthyism? I'm not declining.
I'm just not – clining.

> ROMAN

Okay. It just seems a bit shitty. Under the circumstances . . .?

> SHIV

What circumstances?

> ROMAN

Well, you did make her husband's brain explode . . .

SHIV

Fuck off—

Shiv, furious, hits him hard. He instinctively pushes her back. She goes for him. A flurry of kicks and slaps. Intense. Vicious. Over in seconds. Then it stops.

Tom walks in. Can tell something weird has just happened. It feels like he might have just walked in on them fucking.

They stare at him. He backs out.

INT. HOSPITAL – ADMINISTRATOR'S OFFICE – NIGHT

Kendall walks in to an impromptu mini war room being set up. Maybe there are some random pieces of forgotten hospital equipment being moved out of the way by a hospital employee. Maybe an administrator is overseeing someone plugging in a printer.

Maybe some paper stuck on the wall where Karolina Novotney – Head of PR and Communications, perfectly, even somewhat impractically turned out – is making an action plan—

'Schedule emergency board meeting,
Draft press release,
Update key personnel,
Investor/press strategy post-announcement', etc.

Karl and Eva are there. Plus an assistant.

KENDALL

Jesus. Hi.

KARL
(*re the room*)
We've implied we might be making a totally unrelated donation to the hospital?

Kendall nods, taking it all in.

GERRI

There's a bathroom through there. I have Dewi and Asha from the nominating committee on the line.

Gerri hits a button on the landline and puts Dewi Swann and Asha Khan (male tech CEO) on speakerphone.

Kendall's here and you're on speaker, guys.

> DEWI
> (*on speakerphone*)
> Hi, Kendall, it's Dewi. So sorry about the news.

> ASHA
> (*on speakerphone*)
> Likewise. How's he doing?

> KENDALL
> Er – we don't know.

> GERRI
> As you know, our standing plan, in the event of Logan's . . .
> 'absence' is we separate his CEO and Chairman roles.

> DEWI
> (*on speakerphone*)
> You become acting CEO, Frank stays on as COO and steps up
> from Vice Chairman to acting Chair—

> KENDALL
> (*interrupting*)
> Look, my dad is my focus right now.

> GERRI
> Of course. It's just – there's a problem in terms of – you know,
> in terms of the optics if what happened between you two today
> gets out?

> KENDALL
> I don't know what you're talking about.

> GERRI
> Sure. Well—

> DEWI
> (*on speakerphone*)
> And then there's the problem with Frank?

> KENDALL
> As in?

> EVA
> Logan fired him. And promoted Roman.

KENDALL

Roman? Jesus.

ASHA

(*on speakerphone*)

So, in this, uhh, situation, with your father having you know, cast some doubt on you in a – in a way, and Frank, we just wonder if . . .

GERRI

It's a difficult position.

EVA

He didn't tell you about Roman?

KENDALL

I'm sorry, I can't get into this right now.

KARL

Of course. You're in no fit state.

Kendall, stung, senses Karl and Eva's maneuvering, looks around, thinks – even in the midst of all this he needs to clarify his position.

KENDALL

But here's my take. My dad got sick today. Right? I don't know, nobody knows when he started acting out of character, but he didn't seem great from the morning on, and, there's no paper on any of the moves made today, right, Gerri?

GERRI

Nothing meaningful.

KENDALL

It was words and words are – what? Nothing. Complicated airflow. So, if I was saying what *actually happened* today? It would be nothing.

Gerri looks at Karl and Eva. The phones buzz with static – are they going to buy this?

GERRI

Well that would certainly make things simpler from our point of view? And simple's good. Can you get the family behind it?

KENDALL

Yes.

> KARL

And Frank?

> KENDALL

Sure.

The room has come to a position.

INT. HOSPITAL – ICU CORRIDOR – NIGHT

Kendall, slightly energized. He gets out his phone.

> KENDALL

Frank? Pal. Listen, you've heard, right? Can I possibly get five?

INT. HOSPITAL – ICU WAITING AREA – NIGHT

Greg, Marcia, Connor are sitting. Silence.

In the background: the brother comes back with news about their mom. Bad news. The family collapse in grief.

Roman and Shiv enter. Maybe slightly for Shiv's benefit Roman gives Marcia a hug.

> ROMAN

We're here for you, Marcia.

Marcia puts her hands on his shoulders – some little motherly gesture that we sense Roman might be yearning after.

> MARCIA

It'll be okay.

> CONNOR

You know, the irony is for all we spend the US actually has the worst health outcomes of any developed nation.

> SHIV
> (*re Marcia*)

Easy. Yeah?

> CONNOR

Hey, don't shoot the messenger.
> (*beat*)
Because he would *not* stand a great chance of recovery.

Greg feels he should join in with the being nice to Marcia.

> GREG

I'm here for you too. This is so unfair, he's a good man – he let me come to his birthday lunch, he offered me a job . . .
> *(a split second looking for acknowledgment)*

He doesn't deserve this. If there's anything I can do let me know.

> MARCIA

Actually there is something.

> GREG
> *(shit)*

Great.

> MARCIA

Can you go to the apartment and get his bed things and slippers? With the dark checks. For if, for when he wakes up? You don't mind, do you?

> GREG

No. I'd be delighted. Not delighted . . . Happy. Willing.

He heads off.

> SHIV

Marcia, we can get the housekeeper, or the driver or Colin to—

> MARCIA

I don't need that fly buzzing in my face.

As Greg passes Tom, on his phone.

> TOM
> *(hissed)*

Don't fuck it up!

INT. HOSPITAL – CORRIDOR – NIGHT

Roman catches Greg as he goes, puts an arm round his shoulder, whispers to him—

> ROMAN

Listen, Greg, I need a favor. Dad wanted us to sign some paperwork today – it's in some envelopes back at home, I need you to bring it in. Don't look so worried, man! You can pretend like you've got a job working for FedEx?

Roman continues to explain as Greg looks anxious—

INT. HOSPITAL – CT SCAN ROOM – NIGHT

Logan, unconscious, is loaded into the CT scanner.

INT. HOSPITAL – CT CONTROL ROOM – NIGHT

Doctor Thomas Lewis and a CT-scan tech watch Logan enter the scanner.

> DOCTOR THOMAS LEWIS
> Better not fuck this one up. I don't want Logan Roy's newspapers going through my trash cans.

> NEUROLOGIST JEREMY LIPE
> Well then you shouldn't do so much meth.

> DOCTOR THOMAS LEWIS
> We still have to try to save his life, right? Even though he's a horrible person?

> NEUROLOGIST JEREMY LIPE
> I believe so. I think technically, that's the case.

They look at the scans.

INT. HOSPITAL – ICU WAITING AREA – NIGHT

Close-up on: a hastily but not-badly-put-together meme – the face of Logan pasted on to an animated figure, maybe Kenny from South Park. *Logan's head explodes and Kenny/Logan falls over.*

Wider: Roman returning, minimizes the meme in a window on his phone's Twitter feed. Shiv's there. Jess nearby on her phone.

> SHIV
> What are people saying?

ROMAN

Oh just rumors, 'taken to the hospital'. Some of Twitter says he's dead. A good deal of – of – rejoicing at our father's potential demise.

(to Jess)

Can you screengrab these fuckers who are saying shit?

Shiv listens to a voicemail from her assistant.

SARAH
(off)

Shiv, it's Sarah. Sorry, something's come up. Can I call?

Shiv turns her phone off.

In the background: the other family, still devastated, being asked to sign some forms.

Roman looks down the corridor, sees Connor greeting Willa (twenties, elegant, self-possessed). He nudges Shiv. They exchange a pointed look. Kendall arrives. His look says: Any news?

ROMAN

Scan. And the news is out.

KENDALL

Okay? Right. Well— So, um, listen, I don't want to even think about this but I just spoke to the nominating committee.

Shiv and Roman look at one another.

KENDALL

The thing is, that the plan is to announce that I take over from Dad. That's the plan.

Shiv's reaction is instinctive, almost involuntary.

SHIV

Well, no.

KENDALL

Excuse me?

SHIV

Let's not— We're waiting for the results of the scan, so it's a pointless conversation.

> KENDALL

Okay, well, let's talk about it—

> SHIV

I can't talk about it, I'm upset.

> KENDALL

Hey, I'm upset too!

> SHIV

Not too upset to go and fucking plot with the suits?

> KENDALL

Oh fuck you. I could – I could hardly hear them for the blood rushing in my ears and—

> SHIV

Isn't there a plan anyway, why do we even need to (talk about this)?

> KENDALL

Yes there's a plan – that's what I'm fucking telling you!

> SHIV

Well I'm not sure—

> KENDALL

Shiv, that's what we have to talk about, me and Frank will take over.

> ROMAN

Well Frank was fired, so?

> KENDALL

Okay, well let's discuss – and just see where we are and—

> SHIV
> (emphatic)

We're not doing this. If Dad dies I do not want to be talking about this shit when he dies.

> ROMAN
> (quietly)

He won't die.

Kendall, frustrated, walks over to Jess. His phone rings—

INT. HOSPITAL – ICU WAITING ROOM/EXT. WAITING ROOM
OUTSIDE AREA – NIGHT

Kendall answers his phone, walks outside.

> KENDALL
>
> Yes?

> ISOBEL
> *(through phone)*
>
> Hi, this is Isobel Silva at *The Mail*, I'm sorry to be in contact
> at this difficult time, but we've just emailed you the lede of a
> story – we're looking into the events of the last twenty-four
> hours and I wondered if you'd like to comment?

> KENDALL
>
> What events? What story?

> ISOBEL
> *(through phone)*
>
> How Logan Roy was going to make you Head of Waystar and
> then withdrew the offer and how his brain hemorrhage has
> created a power vacuum at the heart of the company. Did you
> have a comment on that?

> KENDALL
>
> Okay, I've got no comment. But off the record, yeah? You're a
> vulture. You're a fucking piece of shit, and I hope you've got a
> good contract cos if you ever need a job anywhere else in news,
> anywhere, I'll see what I can do to make sure you're fucked,
> forever. Goodnight.

Kendall breathes. Was that smart? Looks back inside to his family.

EXT. LOGAN'S APARTMENT BUILDING – NIGHT

A cab pulls up. Greg gets out. Beckons the doorman.

> GREG
>
> Hi? I'm really sorry but I don't have any money to pay for the
> cab?

> DOORMAN
>
> I'm sorry, sir, do I know you?

GREG

I was here earlier. I got assaulted a little? Can you pay for the cab, please?

(*off the doorman's look*)

She said she'd call, but maybe she didn't because there's an emergency and anyway I don't have any money, so could you pay for my cab, because it's an emergency? And I gave my last twenty to the family, for Coke? Bottles of Coke.

DOORMAN

Sir, I'm sorry, I don't know who you are.

Stand-off. Greg makes a decision. He goes back to the cab.

GREG
(*to cab driver*)

So, basically he won't lend me the money, so he owes you your money.

(*turning, to doorman*)

You better give me the money, dude.

(*to them both*)

Look you two need to figure this out, because basically, one of you guys hasn't got fourteen dollars, okay?

(*to doorman*)

Look, can you just call Mrs Roy?

DOORMAN

Can you?

GREG

I – I don't know her number?

The doorman's phone rings. He answers.

DOORMAN

Oh, hi, Mrs Roy.

Greg looks at the doorman. It's going to be okay.

INT. HOSPITAL – ICU – NIGHT

Tom brings Marcia a coffee. They both look at Logan. Tom smiles. The smile goes on too long. Awkward. Tom should retreat but he sighs. Wants to talk—

> ### TOM
> I'm so sorry.
>> (*beat*)
> So – weird.

> ### MARCIA
> I actually like hospitals. Lots of people don't, but they're safe.

Silence. They look at Logan. A bubble descends the IV drip.

> ### TOM
> Is that bubble okay?

> ### MARCIA
> I don't— I assume so?

> ### TOM
> The weird thing for me, is I was – I'd been intending to – talk to Logan and then, make a proposal.

He looks for a response from Marcia, can't read what little he gets.

> I've actually been meaning to ask for his blessing for a while, but now it's very difficult.

> ### MARCIA
> Right.

Tom watches the bubble head down towards Logan's arm.

> ### TOM
> I've been carrying the ring around for months!

> ### MARCIA
> You need to find the right time for these conversations.

> ### TOM
> Right. The weird thing I'm thinking now is, do you think Logan would still like to be asked?
>> (*then*)
> I know he can't reply. But would he appreciate the gesture? If he was told about it later? Or even in the case of the worst – would that be nice to have asked, his body?

> ### MARCIA
> Umm—

> TOM
>
> I guess my question is, I'd really like to ask her, but do you think Logan would be angry if I asked Shiv without asking him, even though it's hard to ask him because he's – you know?

> MARCIA
>
> You should do whatever you think is right, Tom.

He nods seriously. No help there. He watches the bubble for a long beat as it travels down the IV line. Then—

> TOM
>
> You know what, I'm just going to—
> (*calling out*)
> Excuse me!

A nurse heads in.

> Is this bubble, is it okay for a little bubble to go into him—?

> NURSE ELISA HIGHSMITH
> (*patronising*)
> All fine, it's not our first rodeo.

> TOM
>
> Thank you. Not entirely appropriate language. This is a human being. Not a horse.

INT. LOGAN'S APARTMENT – VARIOUS ROOMS – NIGHT

Greg enters. See the envelopes with the contracts on a hallway table and picks them up – tick! Checks out the place, checks out the skyline. He walks the stairs, feeling like half Goldilocks, half burglar as he explores the apartment.

INT. HOSPITAL – ICU WAITING AREA – NIGHT

On Shiv's phone, revolving anxiously in her hand. Buzzing.

In the background: the other family get ready to leave.

Tom returns, smiles.

> TOM
>
> Hey. Do you want to talk? Because I've got something—

SHIV
(*looks at her phone*)
Apparently I need to get a briefing.
(*dials, connects*)
Sarah? What's going on?

SARAH
(*off*)
I'm actually, I wanted, in case you needed me to be available—

SHIV
Sure, come on in.

SARAH
(*off*)
Fine – I'll be with you shortly.

Sarah rounds the corner.

Instantly, really. I wanted to be near.

She joins Shiv and Tom, glances at Tom.

SHIV
Sorry, Tom, could you give us a minute?

He gets up, trying not to look too dejected.

So?

SARAH
So – you don't need to get into this, I've got it, but so you know
the territory— Daniel called me.

SHIV
Joyce's husband?

SARAH
He said he thinks something bad could have happened? That
could hurt Joyce's campaign.

SHIV
Oh what the fuck now?

SARAH
He says there's been a hack on a dating site. Filthy Rich? For
married people who want to fuck around?

                    SHIV
Delightful. Was he on it?

                    SARAH
He says – it's complicated.

                    SHIV
Oh great. *Great*. Of course it is.

                    SARAH
I can handle (if you)—

Is Shiv eager for distraction? Something beyond family shit?

                    SHIV
I'll do it.

                    SARAH
Yeah because—

                    SHIV
It's fine. Get me this profile. Then talk to Daniel, ask him if
someone was being horrible, if someone was being shitty, what
the worst thing they could find was? Okay?

Sarah leaves. Roman appears, motions for Shiv to follow him.

INT. HOSPITAL – ICU CORRIDOR – NIGHT

*Roman catches Kendall. He's alone, watching the obit again, slumped
against a wall.*

                    ROMAN
They're gonna give us the results?

                    KENDALL
Okay. Fuck.
                    (*getting up*)
You okay, man?

                    ROMAN
He'll be fine. He's probably in there eating a fucking chicken
bucket and checking the market.

INT. HOSPITAL – ICU WAITING AREA – NIGHT

Marcia, Connor and Tom are with Doctor Thomas Lewis. Kendall, Roman and Shiv approach. Logan's personal doctor, Troy Judith, is also there.

> DOCTOR THOMAS LEWIS
> He's had a hemorrhagic stroke. A bleed in the deep right hemisphere put pressure on his thalamus and brainstem and that's what caused loss of consciousness.

> SHIV
> So, what? Do you operate?

> DOCTOR THOMAS LEWIS
> We don't do that for deep bleeds, especially in older patients.

> ROMAN
> He's not an 'older patient'.

> KENDALL
> Dude, he just turned eighty.

> ROMAN
> But physically, he's basically still in his seventies. And he's in great shape. Thirty years.

> DOCTOR THOMAS LEWIS
> The evidence is that operating in these situations isn't worthwhile.

> SHIV
> Well you can't do nothing.

> DOCTOR THOMAS LEWIS
> We're carrying out regular observations. Hopefully, we'll see an improvement soon.

> SHIV
> That's not good enough, right, Doctor Judith?

> DOCTOR TROY JUDITH
> It's an excellent department.

> SHIV
> *(to Doctor Lewis)*
> Well thanks for your input but you'll understand if we check
> our options – my assistant's spoken to Ann Wieman at NYU and
> we might move Dad there.

> MARCIA
> No.

Shiv turns to face Marcia: What?

> He stays here. He gets better here.

> SHIV
> Well, we can discuss.
> *(to Doctor Lewis)*
> We'll discuss and get back to you.

> MARCIA
> No. No discussion. I'm his next of kin, I'm his proxy – I'm in
> charge. Thank you.

A frosty, uncomfortable beat.

> DOCTOR THOMAS LEWIS
> Good. We'll move Logan to a suite in Greenberg. I'll show you
> the way.

*Everyone heads out. Shiv looks at Roman: Did you say something to
Marcia? Roman doesn't respond.*

INT. LOGAN'S APARTMENT – NIGHT

*Greg walks the public rooms. Sits on a couch. Maybe goes to a drinks
cabinet or a bottle of Scotch on the side and takes a sniff. Pours
himself something. But when he dips his finger – it's so strong! He's
not a Scotch man.*

Stealing stationery.

Skidding on shiny floor in socks.

Looking at the medals.

He plays himself at chess.

He studies a painting. Touches it. Worries his touch will be noticed. Wets his finger, dabs it. Blows on the saliva mark.

He looks at some family photos, lingers on one of Shiv.

He reads a huge coffee-table book of nudes/on architecture. *

EXT. STREET OUTSIDE HOSPITAL — NIGHT

Kendall is walking across the road.

> FRANK
>
> I'm sorry, Ken.
>
> (*then*)
>
> How is the old bastard?

> KENDALL
>
> Not great. He'll be fine.

> FRANK
>
> You okay, Kenny?

Hand on arm. Frank has known Kendall a long time.

> KENDALL
>
> Maybe. Yeah. Look, I don't know what the fuck I'm doing. I need to get back in there – this is nuts.

Kendall looks like he might head back.

> I'll call you.

Frank looks at him. Kendall thinks.

> Look, we don't know what's going on. He could be fine, he could not. Either way he's not going to be back tomorrow. So long story short: will you carry on as COO and step up on the board and—?

> FRANK
>
> Become Acting Chairman?

> KENDALL
>
> Yes.

---

* The script gave a few ideas for what Greg might do in the apartment. But Nick then improvised and we suggested some lines to go along with the action.

                    FRANK
No.

                    KENDALL
What?

                    FRANK
He fired me, Ken.

                    KENDALL
I don't know if he even knew what he was saying? If his brain
was working.

                    FRANK
His brain was working fine.

Kendall is buying some food from the stand.

                    KENDALL
Look, whatever else, there's no proof, legally, that yesterday even
happened . . .

                    FRANK
That's not the problem.

                    KENDALL
                (sensing something unsaid)
What's the problem?

                    FRANK
I just don't want to be Chairman.
                (fake modest)
I am just an attendant lord, here to swell a scene or two.

                    KENDALL
Look – this is a horrible day. But it could also be a, a – positive
day. Me and you? Yeah? Me CEO, you Chairman. We could do
great things together—

Frank shakes his head.

What do you need, Frank?

                    FRANK
A jazillion dollars in unmarked bitcoin. I don't have a price,
Ken.

KENDALL

Frank, I don't understand?

FRANK

Just— We'll talk. There's a lot of mess to be cleaned up, Kendall, but you can do it, son. You can.

KENDALL

There's nothing I can say to change your mind?

FRANK

I'm sorry about your father. And good luck, Kenny.

On Kendall – today is so fucking hard.

INT. HOSPITAL – VIP CORRIDOR – NIGHT

Greenberg 14 South: the luxury wing of the hospital – riverside views; wide, quiet hallways; high-end-hotel feel. The family head to Logan's new suite. Shiv and Roman hang back.

ROMAN

So I asked Greg to bring the change of trust—

SHIV

What?

ROMAN

—and when he brings them, we should sign them.

SHIV

I'm not doing anything without my lawyer.

ROMAN

Well I'm going to sign and I'm getting Connor to sign so that's going to make you look pretty fucking heartless when you don't?

Shiv looks like she might hit Roman again.

Oooh, scary look. You hit me again I will ask them to sedate you.

INT. LOGAN'S APARTMENT – LOGAN'S BEDROOM – NIGHT

Greg lies on the big man's bed. He's eating a big sandwich. Sniffs the pillow. His phone goes. Scares him.

> SHIV
> *(off)*
> Greg, did you find the contracts Roman asked for?

> GREG
> Yes, I'm on it, I have them!

Intercut with:

INT. HOSPITAL – VIP CORRIDOR – NIGHT

> SHIV
> I think you have the wrong ones.

> GREG
> Oh. Okay?

> SHIV
> That's possible. So—

> GREG
> Um. Right. What shall I do—?

> SHIV
> Look, there's a lot of confusion. Cuz, if you have any doubt, maybe you can't find them and that might be simplest?

> GREG
> Uh-huh? But if I do?

> SHIV
> Don't bring them.

> GREG
> Did he change his mind?

> SHIV
> No, I'm just telling you – don't bring them in.

> GREG
> Okay. So what's the chain of command here? It's— Are you the more senior sibling?

> SHIV

Greg. This is a favor I'd like you to do for me, and I'd like you to be discreet. It's simple. You stay for a while, you can't find them, you come back. Okay? Thank you.

She hangs up. Greg doesn't know what to do. He inspects a photo of Logan shaking hands with Boris Yeltsin.

INT. HOSPITAL – LOGAN'S VIP ROOM – NIGHT

Luxury surroundings, but ICU medical equipment. Logan, unconscious, breathes on a ventilator. Doctor Thomas Lewis performs responsiveness tests. Marcia and the family watch.

> DOCTOR THOMAS LEWIS

Nothing yet.

INT. LOGAN'S APARTMENT – WALK-IN WARDROBE – NIGHT

Greg opens the wardrobe to find multiple dressing gowns and pairs of slippers – several have dark checks. He's not sure which ones are the right ones. Ugh.

He's in a quandary over Shiv's request. Looks at the envelopes. He paces, then throws himself on the bed in an agony of indecision.

INT. HOSPITAL – VIP CORRIDOR – NIGHT

Shiv steps out of the bathroom. Sees Sarah at the end of the hallway talking with another junior political operative, Jai.

> SHIV
> (calling down to Sarah)

What?

Shiv walks to meet Sarah.

> SARAH

Um, we're good. We've been digging and I've got the situation covered.

> SHIV

It's okay?

> SARAH
>
> Shall we just do it tomorrow?

Sarah looks at Jai.

> SHIV
>
> It's fine, just tell me.

> JAI
>
> Okay there's a picture related to his profile. Embedded in some chat. You won't want to see it—

> SHIV
>
> If I won't want to see it, I need to see it.

Sarah flicks her phone – shows Shiv an image.

> Is that— What . . .? Is that . . . an asshole?

> SARAH
>
> It's his asshole.

> SHIV
>
> No. I can't— No. I'm not contactable tonight, okay? No.

Kendall returns from outside. He smiles as he passes Gerri, Karolina, Eva and Karl, who wait at a discreet distance. Gerri might subtly gesture to her watch.

Connor and Willa aren't around. Tom is but Kendall ignores him and approaches his siblings.

> KENDALL
> (*whispers*)
> Um, look, so I know you don't want to talk about this, but I'm just informing you Roman as a board member, and Shiv as a shareholder, I'll be taking temporary charge as CEO and Chairman. Frank is not interested in the position at present and therefore—

> ROMAN
>
> I'm sorry but even if we were talking about it, which we're not, it wouldn't necessarily be you, bro.

> KENDALL
>
> I'm sorry then who the fuck would it be?

ROMAN

I don't know. Anyone. It could be me.

KENDALL
(*laughs*)

Are you insane?

ROMAN

Dad just made me COO?

KENDALL

I don't think so, dude. Dad wasn't thinking straight.

ROMAN

Well, I think he was.

KENDALL

You, the 'Chief Operating Officer'? If that wasn't a sign he was loco in the coco I don't know what is.

ROMAN

I don't see it that way.

KENDALL

It was a position, Rome, he was playing you, do you even know what it fucking involves? He conked out midgame.

ROMAN

Are you saying I'm a dipshit?

KENDALL

No. Rome! I love you, man, but you're not a serious person.

ROMAN

Fuck you! He's alive, you're not the fucking boss—

SHIV

Look, hey, let's not throw our shit around. We're in the middle. This is why we just hold tight, no sudden moves.

KENDALL

Well we need to move. The markets are going to want to know who's behind the wheel. We need to control the narrative.

ROMAN

'Control the narrative'. You probably yell that when you cum.

> KENDALL

Fuck you. Everyone knows he's in the hospital, we have to say something.

> SHIV

But no one knows how serious it is, so we don't have to say anything.

> KENDALL

We're required to announce. There are rules, there are laws.

> ROMAN
> (*baby voice*)

Oh no, the law? We couldn't possibly break the law.

> SHIV
> (*calling over*)

Karolina, has a CEO ever been out of action and people haven't been told?

> KAROLINA
> (*approaching*)

Not that I can think of. There was Apple but—?

> SHIV

But can we drag our feet on this, till we figure out the moves?

Karolina doesn't know who the boss is – looks around.

> KAROLINA

Well, once we know, there's a duty to shareholders to let people—

> SHIV

But I don't know what we know! It's unclear. It could be flu, it could be an allergic reaction?

> KENDALL

Oh come on! Look at the fucking orchids! It's like we're being held hostage at the Honolulu Airport.

There are many cards and orchids now in the room.

> SHIV

But if we wanted to say – something, other than what is . . .

KENDALL

It's called a lie, Shiv. When you say the thing that's not. That's a lie.

KAROLINA

We need to make a holding statement. But of course I'm open to your suggestions on how we finesse it.

SHIV

Thank you. We'll make a decision shortly.

Kendall, frustrated, heads for a walk.

EXT. HOSPITAL – BALCONY AREA – NIGHT

Two a.m.-ish. Kendall paces, makes a calculation, calls Lawrence.

Intercut with:

INT. LAWRENCE'S APARTMENT – NIGHT

Lawrence's husband is asleep. Lawrence, adrenalized from the sale of Vaulter, is reading the coverage, replying to congratulatory emails on multiple devices.

KENDALL

Lawrence. How you doing?

LAWRENCE

Kendall—

KENDALL

Yeah so listen I'm just calling to issue a reminder. Your pecker's in my pocket, okay, Dickless Dickleby? I just got bothered by some piece of guttershit about my dad and what went down yesterday. I'm just making sure you weren't planning a move in that direction?

LAWRENCE

Well, Vaulter and all our satellite sites have editorial independence, as set out in our agreement—

> KENDALL

You know what that piece of paper is to me? Nothing. I'd jerk off on that paper and send it to you as a greeting card. You do what I say. Let others say what they want but we stay dark. You get me?

Lawrence keeps his cool.

So Simon Says: 'Fingers on lips, motherfucker.'

Kendall hangs up, nods. That was cathartic.

INT. HOSPITAL – VIP ROOM – WAITING AREA – NIGHT

Shiv and Roman are processing their talk with Kendall. They walk away from the waiting area and pace.

> SHIV

It's been a tough day for Ken.

> ROMAN

It has. I feel sorry for him.

> SHIV

And I don't want to talk about this now but the fact is, if he becomes Acting CEO, he'll end up CEO.

> ROMAN

Yeah, right, that's the flow.

> SHIV

And maybe we're happy?

Roman makes a 'maybe' face.

It's just a question of who would Dad want to be in charge—?

> ROMAN

That's right.

> SHIV

I tell you what he really *doesn't* need, is Dad waking up and going apeshit at him for trying to seize the company while he was unconscious?

> ROMAN

No, he does not need that.

                    SHIV
I guess, and I don't want to get into this, but I think we need to
just cut off the whole Kendall CEO thing. Because otherwise it
could get painful?

                    ROMAN
Well, I'm not looking for it but I guess I'm already COO so
another small step and—?

                    SHIV
It won't be you.

                    ROMAN
Because?

                    SHIV
Come on?

                    ROMAN
I don't know what that means?

                    SHIV
Yes you do.

                    ROMAN
It doesn't matter who does it, it's temporary, anyone will do.

                    SHIV
Sure. Anyone. Tom?

Roman laughs.

    Karl?

                    ROMAN
Prick. Eva?

                    SHIV
Cunt. Frank?

                    ROMAN
Basically dead.

                    SHIV
I mean it could be anyone. It's only temporary?

                    ROMAN
So who? Someone Dad trusts. Dad doesn't trust anyone. Apart
from Frank. And he fired Frank for shits and giggles. Gerri?

SHIV

I don't love Gerri, I don't even like Gerri, but I don't hate Gerri.

Beat.

ROMAN

I'll talk to her.

Shiv gets a text. From Sarah.

EXT. HOSPITAL – BALCONY AREA – NIGHT

Kendall paces. Checks the Vaulter site on his phone. There's nothing about Logan.

INT. LOGAN'S APARTMENT – BEDROOM – NIGHT

Greg watches a (non-ATN) TV news report about Logan's ill-health: 'Logan Roy, Waystar mogul, rushed to the hospital' while on the phone to his mom.

NEWSCASTER
(under Greg)

Logan Roy, CEO and Chairman of Waystar Corporation, has been admitted to New York Presbyterian Hospital after suffering an unspecified medical emergency. He is undergoing treatment and is currently listed as being in a serious condition. The Waystar board has scheduled an emergency board meeting and will make a statement in due course.

GREG

So what do you think I do?

Intercut with:

INT. MARIANNE'S HOUSE – NIGHT

It is Marianne's night-time, she's in bed.

MARIANNE

What did she say?

GREG

Roman said bring in the papers, Shiv said don't bring in the papers?

MARIANNE

I guess you need to decide which one of them is more important?

GREG

I guess – Roman's in the firm but Shiv seems like more . . . I don't know, bossy?

MARIANNE

Well, I don't know.

Greg makes a moan of agony.

GREG

And I don't know which slippers. Is checked the same as plaid? Cos then you have gingham. And tartan. It's a fucking criss-cross minefield.

MARIANNE

Fuck the slippers, Greg. You have to strategize.

GREG

I'm trying to strategize, Mom, with you but you won't strategize!

MARIANNE

Can you just – stay?

GREG

Just stall? Stalling doesn't seem proactive. Is stalling proactive?

MARIANNE

I don't know.

GREG

I'm trying to brainstorm with you, Mom. But you're not bringing anything to the table!

Greg stands up – looks at the papers.

INT. HOSPITAL – CAFETERIA – NIGHT

Shiv's at a table, Sarah and Jai bring coffees and a cookie. Shiv's looking at the asshole pic.

> SARAH
>
> I bought a cookie to split. I assumed we wouldn't be able to face a donut right now.

> SHIV
>
> Is it definitely his?

> JAI
>
> I mean, an asshole's like a fingerprint, isn't it, so we will be able to – tell, eventually.

> SHIV
>
> Is an asshole like a fingerprint?

> JAI
>
> Um, you mean because of the – the puckers?

> SARAH
> *(looking at phone)*
>
> The google on this is – it's, it's not one of those searches with a really binary sort of (answer) . . .

> SHIV
>
> Can we find out if an asshole has—?

Jai looks around. Behind them a group of junior doctors are chatting. Jai looks at them, Shiv shrugs, why not.

> JAI
>
> Hi. Excuse me, guys, quick question, and sorry to bother you but does an asshole have a fingerprint?

> DOCTOR VAL MONTGOMERY
>
> I'm sorry?

> SHIV
>
> Is every asshole unique?

> DOCTOR VAL MONTGOMERY
>
> Um, I don't know.
> *(to a colleague)*
>
> Do you know?

Shiv sees she's going to get nothing.

> SHIV

Thanks, guys!
> (*then*)

Someone fell asleep in asshole class . . .
> (*to Jai*)

Can we chase that?

> JAI

They're pretty anonymous, right? I mean, could you pick out yours?

> SHIV

Was the account in Daniel's name?

> SARAH

His credit card details are in there, anonymized so, it might not come out. But it might.

> JAI

Could we say the profile was set up by a friend? As a joke?

> SHIV

Who's the friend, what's their name, why, when, how, where's the card, it'd last like, three to five hours?

> SARAH

We could say he meant to take a good, old-fashioned dick pic and got the angle wrong?

> SHIV

'He's such a dick he couldn't even snap his own dick'? I don't know if that helps . . .

> SARAH
> (*gets a text*)

Joyce wants to see you. Do you have the time? Do you want me to say no?

> SHIV
> (*picking up phone*)

I don't know. I don't fucking know.

EXT. HOSPITAL – BALCONY AREA – NIGHT

Kendall waits. He checks his phone. An alert from Vaulter. Breaking news, a new story: 'Shit Show at the Fuck Factory'.

The little photo of himself with a red line through it, a photo of Logan. He heads inside, determined.

INT. HOSPITAL – VIP ROOM – WAITING AREA – NIGHT

3:30 a.m.-ish. Roman, Connor and Willa are hanging around. Tom approaches Shiv as she returns – he's brought her a coffee.

> TOM
> Listen, can I get a moment alone with you do you think . . . ?

Kendall enters.

> KENDALL
> Have you seen this?

He's surprised to see Willa nearby.

> WILLA
> I'm so sorry about your father.

> KENDALL
> Thank you. Could you give us a minute?

She moves off. Kendall looks at Tom.

> TOM
> Oh come on, I am not the same as her.

He looks at Shiv, who nods at Kendall – Tom can stay in the huddle.

> KENDALL
> (*shows them his phone*)
> Lawrence is running a story about how the company's in turmoil.

> SHIV
> Don't we own him?
> (*reads*)
> 'Shit Show at the Fuck Factory'?

KENDALL

Uncertainty, discord. That is not a good story. 'Family Gets Behind Other Member of Family', that's a good story.

SHIV

Fuck them. When Jobs was croaking, Apple didn't say anything.

KENDALL

We're in a hospital, Shiv. Everyone knows. We can't just prop him up and wave his hand and say he's fine like they did in the Politburo or *Weekend at* fucking *Bernie's*.

ROMAN

I like the sound of that.

KENDALL

Look you can't put a value on a human life. Except in our case you rather precisely can because when trading opens tomorrow we're going to drop like a stone. The only question is, what's the bottom? I think I'm the best option.

Tom steps in.

TOM

I just want to say – if you need me to go get coffee or sandwiches or step up from regional parks to run North America, I will, I can. That's just an offer on the table.

KENDALL
(*almost friendly*)

Fuck off, Tom.

SHIV

Fuck off, Kendall. Don't talk to Tom like that.

TOM

It's okay.
(*to Kendall*)
It's fine.

KENDALL

I was about to be announced, how can I not be the logical choice?

> SHIV

You were *going to be* announced, but then you weren't, Ken. Look, I hate to say this but the only thing we know for certain, for absolute certain, is Dad didn't want you to be boss. So if there was a list of the seven billion people on earth, you're one of the very few people we'd know for sure Dad did not want running this company.

> ROMAN

Dad fired you, man.

> KENDALL

He did not fire me. He said it was just going to take a little longer.

> ROMAN

He said that to be nice. What he meant was: You're not up to it, and it's going to be someone else.

> KENDALL

The board are offering this to me. I don't need your backing.

> ROMAN

Well you do kind of need it, really?

> SHIV

I think you do. Without it, after what Dad did to you, we could take any appointment to court.

> KENDALL

Jesus, Shiv, we're going to court now?

> SHIV

Hey, I didn't want to talk about this, remember?!

> KENDALL

Look, what have you got against me?

> SHIV
> (*with no conviction*)

Nothing.

> KENDALL

Nothing?

He looks at her.

SHIV

What, do you want me to actually say?

KENDALL

Yes.

SHIV

You lack killer instinct, you're wet, you're green, you're intellectually insecure—

KENDALL

Oh my god! Bullshit.

SHIV

You're not emotionally strong enough, you have addiction issues—

KENDALL

No, no. I've heard enough.

SHIV

I don't think all that. I'm just trying to be Dad's voice—

ROMAN

Bravo. It was an excellent impression.

CONNOR

I just want to say – I'm not getting involved.

KENDALL

Good!

CONNOR

But Shiv's right. I'm not saying I'd be a better CEO . . .
(beat)
That's unsaid.

KENDALL

Hey – pal – why don't you go make out with Willa?

CONNOR

Okay, you decide, I don't even want to know. I just observe. I'm a UN White Helmet.

KENDALL

Who else are you going to get?

> TOM

I think Shiv would do a great job.

> SHIV

Thanks, baby. No way.

> KENDALL

She doesn't work in the company and has no experience of the company and the markets would freak. But apart from that, I agree with you.

> SHIV

But we have options.

> KENDALL

Sure, you could all ask for morphine. So you can carry on in your painless dreamworld where the orchids dance and the company's run by a – hipster – fucking unicorn!

Kendall walks out and finds himself staring at Eva and the others and them staring back at him.

Shiv and Roman end up looking at Connor.

> CONNOR

Look, I don't want to do it.
> (beat)
Which is ironic because that probably means I'm actually the person best suited to do it.

Roman looks at his watch – he has a date. With Gerri.

INT. HOSPITAL – VIP ROOM – LOGAN'S ROOM – NIGHT

Doctor Thomas Lewis checks Logan's pupillary light responses. Marcia looks at the doctor, expectantly.

> DOCTOR THOMAS LEWIS

Response times can vary.

INT. LOGAN'S APARTMENT – DINING ROOM – NIGHT

Greg looks at the envelopes in front of him. His phone rings.

> GREG

Hello, this is Greg.

INT. HOSPITAL – VIP CORRIDOR – NIGHT

Roman is on the phone with Greg, making a quick call on his way to see Gerri.

> ROMAN

Greg, how are you doing?

> GREG
> *(too quick?)*

I'm not dawdling.

> ROMAN

Listen, you're at the apartment, right?

> GREG

Um, just—

> ROMAN

I know you're getting PJs and all that shit. Just, pick up a sweater maybe. Also. My dad's, okay?

> GREG

Okay, which . . .?

> ROMAN

Doesn't matter. Not something washed. Something he's worn, maybe, if you find one.

> GREG

V-neck or crew. I guess it doesn't matter, right?

> ROMAN

Just smell it. Okay. Jesus. I just want something that smells of him, okay. I just want that. Is that enough for you?

> GREG

Okay, dude. That's nice. Sorry. I'll . . . sniff some stuff.

> ROMAN

Just whatever. And don't tell anyone, or I'll cut your dick off. And don't forget those papers we talked about. And also – thanks. And fuck off.

INT. HOSPITAL – VIP-WING CAPPUCCINO BAR – NIGHT

Gerri and Roman are grabbing coffees.

ROMAN

So, Gerri. How you doing?

GERRI

Oh fine. This is where they brought Baird, so it's a little—

ROMAN

Baird?

GERRI

My husband. Shiv's godfather . . .?

ROMAN

Ohh. Does he – with the tortoise?

GERRI

Yeah.

ROMAN

Yeah. Of course! How is he?

He's clearly dead. Gerri doesn't spare him.

Yeah, no I do, I remember. Anyhoo thanks, for captaining us through this shitstorm. You do a good job, Gerri.
(*beat*)
You are a real good job-doer, my friend.

A beat of awkward silence. Roman nods.

Look, I'm not great at the whole corporate flirt, I'd rather just lube up and fuck, you know?

GERRI

I see.

ROMAN

Yeah – so, look, for me and Shiv the Kendall thing doesn't work, so we're thinking. General Counsel, you know where the bodies are buried, you probably buried them 'ha-ha', so, you'd have the family's support to step in and take the reins. Okay?

GERRI

Well that's a generous offer but I'm going to have to decline.

He wasn't expecting that.

ROMAN

Right. Can I ask why?

GERRI

Why don't I want the job that makes your brain explode?

ROMAN

Okay. But—
                (*this doesn't compute*)
Gerri, excuse me but I've always thought of you, and I mean this in the best possible way, as a stone-cold killer bitch?

GERRI

And you said you couldn't flirt . . . Shush now.

Roman looks at her: What? Karl comes over, he knows what this conversation is.

KARL

What are we talking about?

ROMAN

Tortoises and lube.

KARL

Great. Love all that stuff. Very happy to join in those conversations.

He puts a hand on Roman's arm.

INT. HOSPITAL – VIP CORRIDOR – NIGHT

Rava appears and approaches Kendall. He's surprised to see her.

KENDALL

It's nearly four a.m.?

RAVA

I couldn't sleep. Put the kids to bed and I felt like I was missing all the fun. So?

KENDALL

How are they doing?

RAVA

The kids. They're okay.

> KENDALL

Would you mind bringing them in tomorrow? Just so they can say their . . . their, hellos.

They head towards the closed door.

> RAVA

How are you feeling?

> KENDALL

Good. Yeah.

> *(then)*

I don't know. Calm then – then, yeah. How am I feeling? Fuck. Ask me another.

> RAVA

Jesus, what a day for you.

> KENDALL

Yeah. The nominating committee want me to be the big boss.

That's what he's always wanted. But this isn't the way—

> RAVA

'Yay.'

> KENDALL

'Yay.'

He looks away. Breathes.

Acting. But Shiv and Roman won't back me. Because of what Dad said at lunch.

> RAVA

Jesus, your family is so – fucked. I mean I'm sorry but—

She hugs him. He holds her tight. A long, long hug. She takes half a step back.

Is that— Kendall? I assume you're aware that you're prodding me?

He's got an erection.

> KENDALL

What can I say. Adrenalin. I don't know. It's just my body. I'm glad you're here.

RAVA

Yeah, I can tell.

INT. LOGAN'S APARTMENT – DINING ROOM – NIGHT

Greg gathers up Logan's things, decides to leave the envelopes, heads out. Then comes back, picks up the envelopes, stands, hovering, looking at the envelopes.

INT. HOSPITAL – VIP CORRIDOR – NIGHT

Roman returns – intercepted by Kendall.

KENDALL

So, man, look, I've been thinking and this is my vision: We go for it. Me and you.

Roman looks at him.

CEO and COO. Me and my Homey Romey?

ROMAN

I thought I was a fuckhead?

KENDALL

A dipshit, and you said that?

ROMAN

You said I wasn't serious.

KENDALL

It's been a long night. But seriously, me and you, bro. I can teach you—
(*not right tone*)
and you can, you know, teach me.

ROMAN

And Shiv?

KENDALL
(*working Roman*)
You know what Shiv's like. She's a daddy's girl. She wants to play it safe. We're the ones with the nuts to revolutionize.

Roman makes a calculation – yes, he could be on board for this, in which case—

141

                    ROMAN
Okay – I'm not uninterested.

                    KENDALL
Alright, then. Let's fucking do it.

Beat.

                    ROMAN
Only thing . . . Gerri turned down the top job. Does that mean
something?

Kendall looks at Roman: What's the angle?

                    KENDALL
Are you fucking with me?

                    ROMAN
No.

                    KENDALL
This your move. Scare me off?
                         (*but he is concerned*)
Who asked Gerri?

Now Roman is careful—

                    ROMAN
. It was mooted.

                    KENDALL
It was 'mooted'? By who? Fucking Moot-zart? The Count of
Mooty Cristo? Did you moot?

                    ROMAN
I'm just telling you what I know. So we trust each other.

Kendall looks at him. Zero trust.

INT. HOSPITAL – VIP CORRIDOR – NIGHT

Shiv waits. Tom's with her.

                    SHIV
I can't believe my dad's dying and I'm having to deal with this
asshole's asshole.

Tom squeezes her hand.

TOM

You know, there are men in the world who would never do this. And I'm one of them. To be clear. If that wasn't—

The elevator opens and Joyce emerges with two of her team, glad-hands some hospital staff who are big fans.

Connor watches, entranced. In his conscious mind: 'I want to do politics.' In his subconscious mind: 'I want to be liked.'

Joyce moves towards Shiv but is intercepted by Connor.

CONNOR

Connor Roy. Big fan.

They shake hands.

I mean I find your policy prescriptions laughable. But personally. Huge fan.

Connor exits. Joyce and Shiv share a warm embrace.

JOYCE

I'm so sorry about your father.

SHIV

Sarah's found us somewhere horrible.

INT. HOSPITAL – SMALL ROOM – NIGHT

Shiv and Joyce are in a small room with baby mannequins, half-mannequins and other medical training equipment.

SHIV

Joyce, I'm so sorry he cheated on you. You deserve better.

JOYCE

He didn't cheat on me.

SHIV

Oh? Okay. But – it was his credit card? And his laptop?

JOYCE

Someone stole them.

SHIV

Right? And did he report it?

> JOYCE

He has multiple credit cards and multiple laptops. He's a very
successful businessman with a number of enemies, any one of
whom could be targeting him or me for any number of reasons.

Shiv looks at her: Really, you're pulling that with me?

> SHIV

Joyce? What? If this comes out we're just saying it wasn't him?

*Joyce has been holding it together then: she explodes, punches a wall.
(A couple of staff passing by outside might clock the noise.)*

> JOYCE

Fuck fuck fuck fuck fuck. What should I do? This is just the
worst fucking day.

> SHIV

It's okay. We – we— Look, let's cool this off. Have you talked to
him?

> JOYCE

No. Yes. Kind of. If he fucks this for me, I will kill him. He's
in Portland. We Skyped. I thought there was someone else in
the room but it was my echo. It all went wrong. He's such a
fucking— I don't know. Do you trust him?

> SHIV
> (*beat, no*)

That's not my area, Joyce.

> JOYCE

You think I should leave him?

> SHIV

We're weeks out from a Senate Primary.

> JOYCE

So I'm stuck with him?

Shiv looks like: I can't say. Joyce is in pieces.

Would it be crazy, to – focus-group the – the scenarios?

> SHIV

Yes. Yes, Joyce, that would be fucking crazy.

(*arm round her*)
Look, we can manage this. And you know, you need to do what feels right. No one can judge you. Except the voters, of course.

INT. HOSPITAL – VIP ROOM – WAITING AREA – NIGHT

Marcia is in with Logan, Tom's elsewhere, Connor enters and sits with Willa. He gives her a gentle, almost romantic, right-on-the-edge-of-unacceptable, kiss.

ROMAN
Oh come on, man. Not cool.

INT. HOSPITAL – VIP CORRIDOR – NIGHT

Kendall passes a contemplative Shiv.

KENDALL
C'mon. Family get-together.

INT. HOSPITAL – LOGAN'S VIP ROOM – NIGHT

Kendall and Shiv enter. Kendall gives Willa a look. She leaves.

KENDALL
So, listen, I've asked Roman to be Acting COO—

ROMAN
Actual COO.

KENDALL
To my Acting CEO.

SHIV
And you said?

ROMAN
I said, why not?

SHIV
Snake.

ROMAN
Sis, please. I'm trying to bring us together here. I'm mediating.

> SHIV

Well I'm saying no.

> CONNOR

Me too.

> KENDALL

I thought you were a fucking White Helmet?

> CONNOR

Sometimes the peacekeeper has to go to shoot a maniac on the perimeter.

> KENDALL
> (to Shiv)

Why would you say no to this and yes to Gerri?

> SHIV

Gerri's been with the company for twenty years. Dad trusts her.

> CONNOR

Gerri's older, wiser, more mature. (Like me.)

> KENDALL

Yeah well, she doesn't want it.

> SHIV

And so in my opinion we should find someone else, temporary.

> KENDALL

Like who?

> SHIV

Someone neutral, anyone. Eva. What's he called, American Psycho? Or Karl?

> KENDALL

Karl? Yeah? You trust him?
> (lets that hang)

And what if it isn't temporary? What if he uses his position to make it permanent?

> CONNOR

He wouldn't do that?

> KENDALL

Wouldn't he? How do you know?

CONNOR

He's nice, he brought coffee.

KENDALL

Oh he bought coffee? Then we should definitely let him take control of the company?

They look over – can we see Eva with Karl?

ROMAN

Dude, Karl's not going to—

KENDALL

It's a gamble. It's either me and Roman and us as a family. Or it's Eva and Karl or some fuck-droid from the deep state of the company.

Shiv and Connor look unsure.

They could take the company out of our hands, and we'd never get near it again.

(*to Shiv*)

If Dad wakes up – and he's frail and he's looking at the endgame – do you want to be the one who tells him his family business isn't family-run anymore?

This looks like it lands with Shiv.

I mean, maybe you could get away with it? His favorite . . .

SHIV

Fuck you.

KENDALL

But maybe you wouldn't stay his favorite if you gave away the company?

Shiv rolls her eyes.

Look, we need a statement by six-thirty. So, you have to think, bullshit aside, who do you think, really, Dad would prefer?

INT. HOSPITAL – LOBBY – NIGHT

Greg, clutching Logan's stuff, walks through a throng of patients, waiting for care. Maybe a rich young twenty-something, worse for wear, throws up. Little bit bleak.

INT. HOSPITAL – VIP RESTROOM – NIGHT

Shiv is deep in thought.

INT. HOSPITAL – VIP CORRIDOR – NIGHT

Shiv emerges from the restroom. Tom stands in her way.

> TOM
> Stop. Look, there's something I have to say.

He gets down on one knee and takes out a ring.

> SHIV
> Tom, I'm not in the mood for fucking around—

> TOM
> Siobhan Roy, will you marry me?

> SHIV
> Are you serious?

> TOM
> I love you. And I wanted to do something to make all this better.
> *(starting to lose faith)*
> And I thought, while your dad's still with us, wouldn't that be nice? We can do a quick wedding.

She looks into his eyes.

> SHIV
> What is it about my dad dying in a – a – sterile environment that screams 'big romantic gesture' to you?

Tom looks lost.

> TOM
> It's – it's a horrible day. I thought this was something nice?

SHIV

Tom, you can't balance it out like that? I'm not gonna give you a – blowjob when your dog dies, yeah?

She looks at him.

TOM

Look, no, fine. I misjudged it. I get it. Bad call.

SHIV

No, I'm sorry. It's fine. Look. Why don't you do this again properly another time. Yeah? Let's not have this as the moment?

TOM

No, exactly. This isn't it. This didn't happen. Abort.

SHIV

Good.

TOM

Good.

SHIV

But so you know, sure, whatever.

TOM

Yeah?

SHIV

Sure. When it happens, yes.

Tom's delighted. He kisses Shiv.

Such a shit show.

TOM

What?

SHIV

My family.

TOM

Our family.

INT. HOSPITAL – VIP ROOM – WAITING AREA – NIGHT

Greg, pleased with himself, delivers the slippers to Marcia. He also has a sweater.

GREG

Hey hey hey! So I got the slippers!

MARCIA

Thank you, Greg. Just—

She motions for him to leave them on the table or sofa. Greg, deflated, heads off.

TOM

So you got the slippers. I guess that makes you Prince Charming?

GREG

I guess so.

TOM

So, you're saying you want to fuck Marcia?

GREG

What? No. Why would you—?

TOM

That's what you said—

GREG

No it isn't—

TOM

You said you were Prince Charming.

GREG

No, you said that.

TOM

I'm kidding.

GREG

Uh-huh.

(*changing the subject*)

How's Logan?

TOM

Well I don't think he's going to be wearing those anytime soon.

GREG

Oh, shit.

(*then*)
You know that he gave me a job?

TOM

What job?

GREG

I don't know.

TOM

Okay.

GREG

Do you know when I start?

TOM

No obviously I don't know, why would I know?

GREG

I don't know, I guess I thought you all talked. I thought people might have been talking about me, what to do about me?

TOM

Yeah, no, everyone's been talking about you the whole time.

GREG

I get it. Uh-huh.

TOM

Look, when you figure all that out, come in and see me – I'll look after you, okay?

Greg looks at him. Is he fucking with him?

Seriously.

Greg smiles a grateful smile. Until Tom turns away. Then the smile drops. He's not sure if he can trust Tom.

He walks off, looking back and finds—

Kendall, Shiv and Roman huddled. He hands Roman the sweater, which Roman tries to casually put aside.

ROMAN

Hey, cuz, you got the papers?

Greg is a surprisingly good liar.

GREG

What – oh, dang! Roman, shit, I'm sorry, bro. I was so caught up in the, I asked the doorman and then, I got up and then I was thinking about your dad. That is *so* dumb.

Roman shakes his head, he's busy.

The siblings move off. Shiv looks back and gives Greg a wink: Good work.

INT. HOSPITAL – VIP AREA – CONFERENCE ROOM – NIGHT

Kendall, Roman and Shiv enter.

GERRI

Okay, we're going to have to announce, where are we at?

Beat – Kendall looks at Shiv.

SHIV

While Dad is ill, the family proposes that Kendall should run the company, with Roman as COO.

CONNOR

I endorse this decision.

Maybe this is the first time we see Connor is there. They glance at him. No one cares what he thinks.

GERRI

Okay. I'll inform the committee of the family position, and board approval pending, we'll announce.

Gerri nods to Karolina. She and Karl go to make preparations. Eva looks at her shoes – not a good call.

Congratulations, Kendall.

KARL

Yes, congratulations.

EVA

You should get some rest.

ROMAN

Look forward to working with you, bro.

SHIV

Good luck. I have to say for the record, I personally believe this to be a total fucking disaster.

She leaves, knowing she's taken the wind out of their sails.

GERRI
(*quietly, to Kendall*)
Okay, good. Kendall, listen, we need to talk—

DAY TWO

EXT. HOSPITAL – BALCONY – DAWN

Gerri is with Kendall.

GERRI

Okay. There's really no nice way to say this, but your dad has slit our throats and we're now bleeding to death.

KENDALL

What is this?

GERRI

We have a huge debt problem.

KENDALL

What are you—? No.

GERRI

Three billion.

KENDALL

Fuck off. I'd know.

GERRI

No one knows. Me and Frank.

KENDALL

What about Dad??

Gerri smiles at his innocence.

GERRI

Yeah, your dad. Hence the debt.

KENDALL

What the— Gerri? What the fuck is going on? Was he secretly funding the war in Afghanistan – and paying LeBron James to lead the fucking infantry?

GERRI

'95, Logan needed cash badly for the studio acquisition. He took out a loan, through the family holding company—

KENDALL

Where it's hidden from view?

GERRI

The company's private and he knew that, besides Frank, none of the other board members would see what was happening. And he added the loan to the company's already considerable debt.

Kendall's already figuring it out.

KENDALL

Okay. Okay, we can deal.

GERRI

It's secured against Waystar stock – and when the stock hits one-thirty we've breached the covenant and they can pursue repayment in full. Which, if they went through on, would eviscerate us.

KENDALL

But they won't, they'll renegotiate, right?

GERRI

Well. That depends.

KENDALL

Uh-huh.

GERRI

The banks know the man they invested in can no longer function. As far as they're concerned you're just some guy. With hair. So, it's a question. Do they stick or twist?

Hangs in the air.

KENDALL

You're making it quite fucking hard to savor this moment, Gerri.

INT. HOSPITAL – ADMINISTRATOR'S OFFICE – EARLY MORNING

The war room is being packed up.

INT. HOSPITAL – RECEPTION AREA – EARLY MORNING

Staff share a joke as they start their shift.

EXT. NEW YORK STREET – EARLY MORNING

People head to work. It's busy, vibrant, energetic.

EXT. HOSPITAL – EARLY MORNING

Greg goes outside to get some air. Sees Kendall.

GREG

Hey.

KENDALL

Got a cigarette?

GREG

Sure.

He puts a hand to a pocket, hesitates.

I know it's a weird time. But I have some weed if you want to smoke a bone?

KENDALL

I've just been appointed head of one the biggest media companies in the world and I've also been in rehab for drug addiction and it's possible my dad might die at any second – so excuse me if I don't get stoned out of my gourd with you right now, cuz.

Greg nods.

But a cigarette would be great.

Greg hands over a cigarette.

GREG

Is he going to be okay?

KENDALL

I don't know.

INT. HOSPITAL – VIP ROOM – WAITING AREA – EARLY MORNING

Doctor Thomas Lewis is with Marcia, Kendall, Shiv, Roman and Connor.

DOCTOR THOMAS LEWIS

We had hoped to see a response by now. There's hope. But if we don't see one soon, that's not promising. What we do know is: he's stable. So, if you want to grab some sleep, this is a good time.

INT. HOSPITAL – VIP RESTROOM – EARLY MORNING

Marcia fights hard to keep the tears back.

INT. HOSPITAL – LOGAN'S VIP ROOM – EARLY MORNING

Logan looks pale but peaceful. Roman leans in to him.

ROMAN

Night, Dad. See you soon.

He leaves. Shiv bends down to Logan's face.

SHIV

Stay strong, Dad. Keep fighting.

She leaves. Kendall looks at his unconscious dad. Complicated emotions. He kisses him. Then whispers something to him.

Connor lingers. He whispers to Logan.

CONNOR

Dad, I think I've finally worked out who I am and what I'm doing with my life. There's a job I want.
(*beat*)
It's called President of the United States.*

---

* In the end, we held off the reveal of Connor's presidential ambitions until later in the season.

INT. HOSPITAL – VIP CORRIDOR – EARLY MORNING

Marcia exits the restroom, is surprised to see Greg right there, waiting for her.

> GREG
>
> Hi. Sorry, Marcia, it's just everyone's going home and I don't know where to go?

> MARCIA
>
> I don't know, Greg – a hotel?

Greg hesitates – wants to say he hasn't got any money, can't.

> GREG
>
> Of course. Right. A hotel! So simple.

He leaves, maybe doing a slightly weird curtsy as he goes.

INT. HOSPITAL – LOGAN'S VIP ROOM – EARLY MORNING

Marcia sits facing Logan, covers herself with a blanket.

INT. HOSPITAL – VIP ROOM – WAITING AREA – EARLY MORNING

Greg looks round, sneaks some fruit from a gift basket.

INT. KENDALL'S CAR – EARLY MORNING

Kendall looks out of the window – what the fuck do I do now?

INT. SHIV AND TOM'S CAR – EARLY MORNING

Shiv and Tom sleep as they're driven home.

INT. KENDALL'S CAR – EARLY MORNING

Kendall is asleep as he's driven home.

INT. HOSPITAL – CHAPEL – EARLY MORNING

Greg, asleep. Snores gently as someone tries to pray.

INT. HOSPITAL – LOGAN'S VIP ROOM – EARLY MORNING

Marcia fights to stay awake. Her eyelids flicker. Then close.

Opposite her, Logan lies unconscious. Dead to the world.

Until his eyelids flicker open for a second. Then shut again.

Episode Three
LIFEBOATS

Written by Jonathan Glatzer
Directed by Mark Mylod

Original air date 17 June 2018

Cast

LOGAN ROY	Brian Cox
KENDALL ROY	Jeremy Strong
MARCIA ROY	Hiam Abbass
GREG HIRSCH	Nicholas Braun
SHIV ROY	Sarah Snook
ROMAN ROY	Kieran Culkin
CONNOR ROY	Alan Ruck
TOM WAMBSGANS	Matthew Macfadyen
FRANK VERNON	Peter Friedman
LAWRENCE YEE	Rob Yang
COLIN STILES	Scott Nicholson
RAVA	Natalie Gold
SARAH	Katie Lee Hill
MARIANNE	Mary Birdsong
SOPHIE ROY	Swayam Bhatia
IVERSON ROY	Quentin Morales
JOAN	Lynne McCollough
BREX	Brock Yurich
LISA	Mandy Siegfried
GERRI KELLMAN	J. Smith-Cameron
KARL MULLER	David Rasche
JESS JORDAN	Juliana Canfield
POLK	John Ottavino
RECEPTIONIST	Helen Piper Coxe
EVA	Judy Reyes
KAROLINA NOVOTNEY	Dagmara Dominczyk
SARAH	Katie Lee Hill
DANIEL MILLER	Jason Butler Harner
MALE EXECUTIVE	Michael Cruz Kayne
STEWY HOSSEINI	Arian Moayed
PHOTOGRAPHER	Timothy Stickney
NATE SOFRELLI	Ashley Zukerman
SANDY FURNESS	Larry Pine
HIPSTER CLERK	Soojeong Son
MALAYA	Greta Quispe
BRAD KILMARTIN	Drew Lewis

DOORMAN	Jorge Chapa
FIONA	Sommer Blair
GLADHANDER 1	Riley Hansen
GLADHANDER 2	Michael Mulhearn

Under black, music: 'The Erie Canal' by The Charleston Trio.

DAY ONE

INT. KENDALL'S HOUSE – BEDROOM – PRE-DAWN

A high-end bedside clock turns from 4:44 a.m. to 4:45 a.m. A gentle bong would be just enough to wake Kendall, if he weren't already awake.

In the background, lights slowly rise in Kendall's obviously well-appointed bedroom; the traditional work song and the opulence clashing.

Kendall is up right away, iPhone on. Checking the business news – stock prices.

INT. KENDALL'S CAR – MORNING

A little later. From the back seat, Kendall looks at the empty pre-dawn streets flashing past.

The early-morning crew, construction workers. We pick up a street cleaner. Moment of eye contact while Kendall is stopped at the lights.

INT. BLACK FRAME – MORNING

A flip phone flashes bright. A hand reaches over, grabs it, kills the alarm. In the glow . . . Greg.

Reaching up, he turns on a reading light to reveal his home . . .

At $79 a night, you get a single bed amongst four others and that's about it. A light snoring continues from somewhere.

There's not even a closet, just combination lockers. On a hanger affixed to the bunk-bed frame, a suit.

The curtains are closed – all the other occupants (foreign students) are still asleep.

INT. POD HOTEL SHOWER – MORNING

It's not so bad. A see-through curtain. He can be seen by his fellow residents. While he showers, a nervous habit, Greg whistles.

EXT./INT. WAYSTAR – LOBBY – MORNING

Kendall walks into the lobby of the building. It's early and still very quiet. The night security staff are still in place.

INT. WAYSTAR – MORNING

Kendall is alone. The lights flicker on as he walks the aisles of the desks outside the executive suites.

He walks past his office, past a bunch of other private offices and there he is – outside his dad's office.

A breath. He walks in.

INT. LOGAN'S APARTMENT – LIBRARY – MORNING

The door to Logan's hospital at home. We hold on it – the blank exterior.

Outside is a medical orderly, scrolling on his phone, and Joan in charge of Logan's care at home. And nearby, the houseman. As Marcia appears – Joan snaps to attention, the orderly puts away his phone.

> MARCIA
> *(to the houseman)*
> Can you get me the Waystar stock price at close last night please?

> JOAN
> How is he?

> MARCIA
> Good. A little clearer. He tried to put on a sock.

Music continues under—

INT. WAYSTAR – LOGAN'S OFFICE – MORNING

Kendall prowls the room looking at everything afresh. The photos. Dad with Yeltsin, Dad with Reagan. Dad with first editions of newly launched papers, Dad with movie stars from the 1990s.

He looks at the chair behind the desk. Sitting in it would be too much, right? Instead he sits on the desk like it's a park bench. Closing his eyes he breathes in, as much as anything, to calm his own nerves.

INT. POD HOTEL – MORNING

Greg is standing in front of a mirror in a suit. From the ankles up, he's looking sharp, black suit, white shirt, dark tie. But the trousers fail to conceal his clashing, well-worn deck shoes.

His phone goes. Greg rushes to answer. The out-of-town student traveler wakes, looks at Greg.

Intercut with:

INT. MARIANNE'S HOUSE – MORNING

It's very early Marianne's time, she's in her bed.

> MARIANNE
> Hey. Are you awake?

> GREG
> (*whispering*)
> Mom. Obviously I'm awake.

> MARIANNE
> Are you stoned?

> GREG
> No! Obviously I'm not stoned. I haven't had breakfast, what kind of monster do you think I am?

The student traveler looks over and does a gesture – 'Do you wanna smoke a spliff later?'

> MARIANNE
> And you've got ideas, in case they want ideas?

> GREG

Mom, don't micromanage!

> MARIANNE

I'm not micromanaging. Have they given you an advance?

> GREG

It's my first day! And you kind of are micromanaging, Mom. Okay? 'To the moon and back, bumblebee' to you too.

He hangs up. Greg licks his thumb and rubs at a stain on his trousers. He licks his thumb again, thus tasting it. Weird. What is that?

EXT. STREET – MORNING

Greg outside in the big city on his first day of work.

INT. SHIV AND TOM'S APARTMENT – KITCHEN – MORNING

Shiv's ready for work, standing watching the ATN News on an iPad at the kitchen counter. There's a chyron that reads: 'Joyce Miller, NY AG & Senate Candidate: Police Need New Powers to Target & Destroy DrugDrone Menace'.

Tom enters, all ready for work. Waits for Shiv's attention.

> TOM

Okay! Just wanted to say goodbye.

He breathes: Big day, remember? Shiv's also monitoring Twitter.

> SHIV

Have you looked at the numbers? Poor Ken. He's like dysentery for the stock price.

Tom bends to his knees before her. She looks down: Not now?

You're walking into a burning barn.

He looks dead ahead – between her legs. Kisses the fabric of her suit pants. Nuzzles.

> TOM

Just paying – homage.

(*whispering ahead*)
What's that? You miss me? I miss you too! Maybe we should arrange a date when 'she's' not around.

He stands up, and gets businesslike.

SHIV

Weird.

TOM

You're weird! Okay!

SHIV

Tom, listen, will you come with me?

TOM

Ugh. I gotta stand firm on this one, baby. It's a huge-y, first morning stepping up?

SHIV

Tell them you went to see the big boss. Please? C'mon.

Shiv heads out. Tom is left in an ecstasy of indecision. Thinks – what should I do, stand firm or give in?

TOM

Arghhhhhh!
(*after her*)
Don't make me choose! It's a man's right not to choose.

INT. WAYSTAR – LOGAN'S OFFICE – MORNING

Kendall looks outside. The morning papers are being laid out outside Logan's office. Kendall FaceTimes Rava. Connects.

KENDALL

Thirty seconds?

Intercut with:

INT. RAVA'S APARTMENT

RAVA
(*over phone*)
I'm getting the kids ready.

> (*to au pair*)
Malaya, can you get him his cup?

KENDALL

Yeah, this is dumb but – bank call this morning. And I just wanted to ask—

RAVA

What bank – our old joint account?

KENDALL

Um, no, no, Rava! *The* bank. ICBC who've apparently bankrolled the old man for years— I said?

RAVA
> (*interrupts*)
Oh yeah, sorry. I'm just in a rush.

KENDALL

Yeah. Two minutes. Do I play hard-on or softcock? What's your read?

RAVA

Ken. Talk to your people.
> (*to the kids*)
Malaya, it's good to let him pour it himself, thanks.

KENDALL

You're just, you're always smart – and just . . . hard-on or softcock?

And he likes talking to her . . .

RAVA
> (*over the commotion*)
Ken, can't we do this later? But no one likes a softcock.
> (*then*)
Iver! No!

KENDALL

What's he doing? Let me:

Rava is with Iverson on Kendall's phone screen.

Hello! Ive – listen to me, you need to be cool with your sister. Alright? Remember your strategies?

Iver's put the phone down and wandered off. Rava reappears.

> RAVA
>
> We have to go. I can't do this now, Ken? Let's eat something sometime, yeah? Okay? I'm sorry. Why don't you ask Roman?

> KENDALL
>
> Roman? Rava? C'mon.

INT. CORE CLUB – PRIVATE ROOM – MORNING

Brex is stretching Roman out, post-workout. How tough is the stretch? Roman has new gym clothes on.

> BREX
>
> Out of ten?

> ROMAN
>
> A seven.

> BREX
>
> You're in decent shape. Little sloppy. But I can get you tight as a drum.

> ROMAN
>
> Okay well, I trust Pax. Pax says you're the best.

> BREX
>
> Pax is the best.

> ROMAN
>
> He's a prick. But he knows the best places. He's the only person I trust on food. So I thought, I should trust him on, like, the opposite of food.

He means Brex.

> BREX
>
> Only thing I'm gonna say, Roman. I take my shit seriously, that's why I have the reputation I do, so you got to be on board for this regime.

Okay, who's employing who . . .?

> ROMAN
>
> Dude, no need for the speech, I'm down.

> BREX

Five-thirty, every day is the regime.

> ROMAN

Serious as cancer. Seriouser. Fucking—
                    (*most serious thing*)
money cancer. I gotta check out. I'm rolling COO now.

> BREX

Uh-huh.

Brex works with lots of rich folk, isn't getting it.

> ROMAN

Chief Operating Officer. Waystar Royco. If it operates, I chief it.

Brex focusses on stretching Roman.

Five-thirty is perfect.

> BREX

That's a.m., yeah?

> ROMAN
> (*shit*)

Sure. Cool. Because the other five-thirty I'll be – being an agent
of change and you know, sacking people.

> BREX

How's that now?

Brex stretches him.

> ROMAN
> (*it hurts*)

A six?

> BREX

Bullshit. I can go four more?

It's hurting Roman.

> ROMAN

Argh! I think you popped something.

> BREX

Hahahah. Nope. Señor, you're done!

Brex sits up, laughs. Roman gets up and rotates his lower back, he's pulled a muscle and can't get it to feel right. Can't help feeling Brex hasn't 'got' how important he is.

INT. LOGAN'S APARTMENT – FOYER – DAY

Shiv and Tom exit the elevator. The houseman in a polo shirt is there to see her in. Marcia shouts down to the member of staff—

MARCIA
(*off; severe*)
Ask her to wait there.

SHIV
(*cheery*)
Hey 'she's' here!

Coming down the stairs is Marcia, she's following an occupational therapist, Lisa, upset, carrying a gym bag, being consoled and controlled by the lead carer, Joan.

JOAN
It's just something that happens. The morphine—

LISA
(*not fine*)
I know. I'm fine.

SHIV
Is everything okay?

MARCIA
(*with ease and sparkle*)
Lovely to see you, Siobhan. Tom?

TOM
I'm afraid I can't stay.

Lisa has left, Marcia takes Joan aside.

MARCIA
We will settle any outstanding fees and non-disclosure agreement with her.

JOAN
Really? She's good—

                         MARCIA
                    (with arm squeeze)
It's best.

Joan begins to action this on her phone.

We follow Lisa out into the elevator. Her phone vibrates – the bad news, and she maybe lets go and starts to cry.

INT. LOGAN'S APARTMENT – DRAWING ROOM – DAY

Marcia turns from manager to hostess as she heads into the drawing room and joins Shiv—

                         TOM
What's the (matter)? Marcia?

                         MARCIA
Nothing. Staff. So! Good to see you.

They realize they haven't kissed and do so. Once on each cheek.

                         SHIV
Likewise.

Shiv and Marcia compete to be aggressively polite.

Look, I know you said he wasn't great, but I was passing and I just thought, why not (drop by)?

                         MARCIA
                    (cutting her off)
Oh that's sweet. He's not seeing people right now.

                         SHIV
Sure, but I just thought I'd pop up even if he's grumpy—?

                         MARCIA
It's best you don't.

                         SHIV
It's okay, I'll take the earbashing!

                         MARCIA
                     (sweetly)
I'm afraid that's out of the question.

Shiv looks at Tom.

> TOM

Um. I mean, could you just see and check he hasn't, changed his mind?

> MARCIA
> (*a beat, then kindly*)

Of course. Let me go and ask.

Marcia heads back upstairs with a smile.

Shiv and Tom, left uneasy, make faces at one another.

In the hall, Shiv sees Joan talking to Richard, the houseman. She decides to act.

> SHIV

Hi? Shiv. Logan's daughter? Thanks so much for everything by the way.

Joan would rather not be invited into this interchange.

> JOAN
> (*guarded*)

That's quite alright.

> SHIV

Yeah well, much appreciated.

> TOM
> (*now fishing*)

And how does he seem today?

But Joan is loyal to her mistress upstairs—

> JOAN

Oh. You know.

> TOM

Yeah, we heard all about the sock?

They wait expectantly for something more from Joan, but there is no information forthcoming. Joan smiles and looks upstairs.

INT. WAYSTAR — KENDALL'S OFFICE — DAY

Kendall is with Gerri. They have lots of documents laid out.

They both look at a twin-screen Bloomberg terminal. A number, the Waystar price changes. 145.12. Goes down incrementally.

> GERRI
>
> It'll stabilize.

> KENDALL
>
> I know. I know it will.
> *(looks at some papers)*
> So, I've been thinking and I've got a new strategy for the call?

> GERRI
>
> Uh-huh?

Gerri is tense. Tries to read some of Kendall's notes upside down.

> KENDALL
>
> Hey. Don't look so fucking nervous. It's making me nervous.

> GERRI
>
> I'm relaxed!
> *(then)*
> It's just maybe a little late considering the gravity and the need to get the relationship right.

> KENDALL
>
> Absolutely. The new strategy is really just a refinement of all this great work—
> *(pats the files)*
> It goes—
> *(thinks)*
> Well the working title is: 'fuck you'.

Gerri tries to absorb.

> GERRI
>
> Uh-huh?

His phone buzzes. Kendall hits a button – speakerphone.

> JESS
> *(over speakerphone)*
> Hi, I have Mr Polk.

> KENDALL
>
> Uh-huh. What do you think?

GERRI
(*I think you're a fucking lunatic*)
I think – I may need a little more explanation before—

KENDALL
My dad's a bastard. They need to know I'm a bastard too.
Right?

He hits the button – to talk to Jess. Gerri looks concerned.

GERRI
Right but—

KENDALL
Great.
(*click*)
Hey, Mr Polk?

POLK
(*on speakerphone*)
Hi. Kendall, good to connect.

KENDALL
Likewise. Great. So? You wanna go?

POLK
(*on speakerphone*)
Er, sure, or why don't you go?

KENDALL
Um, well, we just wanted to make contact, given where we are.

POLK
(*on speakerphone*)
Uh-huh. We are concerned.

KENDALL
Absolutely. Now obviously, look, the main thing is we just
handle this very calmly because the last thing either of us want
is for this rather private arrangement my father made to cause
waves?

Gerri smiles: Yes.

POLK
(*on speakerphone*)
Oh absolutely.

>   KENDALL
> But I guess the issue is, we owe you three-point-two billion.

>   POLK
>   (*on speakerphone*)
> Three-point-two-five.

>   KENDALL
>   (*kidding*)
> Hey, I was rounding down!

>   POLK
>   (*on speakerphone; kidding*)
> We round up.

>   KENDALL
> Secured against Waystar stock which is undergoing some
> temporary turbulence due to sector-wide factors.

No comment. Maybe some shuffling.

> So – I guess what I'd like to know is what your position will be
> if we have a sustained breach of the stock price and we fall out
> of compliance with our debt covenant?

>   POLK
>   (*on speakerphone*)
> Okay, well, if the stock drops, we're entitled to ask for
> repayment in full.

>   KENDALL
> Uh-huh. Exactly. Technically. So what – what will we do here in,
> reality?

>   POLK
>   (*on speakerphone*)
> If it breaches one-thirty, you've broken the covenant and we will
> want repayment.

Kendall looks at Gerri: Oh please.

>   KENDALL
> Right – I know. But really?

>   POLK
>   (*on speakerphone*)
> Seriously.

> KENDALL

I get it. That's your starting position, but we will want to restructure, and—

> POLK
> (*on speakerphone*)

Look, here's where I'm at. We're not crazy about the media sector, we're not crazy about how your father has treated our relationship. And our position is to seek recoupment.

> KENDALL

Oh come on, man, fuck off.

Gerri winces.

Kendall looks at Gerri: It's fine. Long silence. The buzz of the phone line.

It's something of a stand-off. The moment holds. Is this okay? Eventually Kendall can't stand it—

Hello?

> POLK
> (*on speakerphone*)

Hi.

> KENDALL

Yeah? C'mon. Real world. Can we start to negotiate?

> POLK
> (*on speakerphone*)

That's our position. If the stock drops below one-thirty, you're in breach and we want our money back.

Kendall looks at Gerri.

> KENDALL

Fine, well let's keep talking—

> POLK
> (*on speakerphone*)

If you need to talk to me maybe it's better if we go through an intermediary. I'm not a particular fan of foul language and I don't like to be insulted. Thank you. Good morning.

End of call. Buzz. Eventually, buzz ends. Gerri looks at Kendall.
Kendall looks at Gerri.

Kendall feels the world rush in on him. He's the top guy. He made the
call. It was kind of a disaster. He can feel the sweat break out on him.
The table feels unreal to his touch.

> KENDALL
> Was that— I never (met Polk), is that typical of him?

> GERRI
> *(with a sigh)*
> Uggghhhh.

> KENDALL
> Give me a level?

Roman comes in.

> ROMAN
> Fuuuuuuuuck! That was brutal.

> KENDALL
> You were listening in?

> ROMAN
> Of course I was in! I'm COO.

> KENDALL
> *(to Gerri)*
> Are they for real. Would they squeeze us?

> GERRI
> Well obviously they could.

> KENDALL
> But why would they? They won't, will they?

> ROMAN
> Relax, bro.

He is swiveling his hips, feeling out his back.

> New trainer. It'll be okay.

Kendall's looking for somewhere for his anxiety and fear to blow.

                              KENDALL

No it fucking necessarily won't. If this became public. We could
nosedive. We could death spiral here.

                              ROMAN

Fine, dude, I was only trying to be nice, that was a fucking shit
show and you handled it like a moron is the truth.

                              KENDALL

Fuck off.

                              ROMAN

Fuck you.

                              GERRI

It's fine. Just— We need, next time, to have a more considered
strategy. I've got a portfolio of options?

                              ROMAN

I have a pitch?

Jess is there – Kendall nods to her.

                              JESS

Sorry, bunch of calls. Shiv is trying to reach you?

EXT. WAYSTAR/INT. WAYSTAR – LOBBY – MORNING

Tom and Shiv. Walk towards elevators.

                              TOM

Finally entering the Death Star!

                              SHIV

I can't fucking believe it. Can you? Fucking – where does she get
off?

                              TOM

Just can't help feeling this is a little like my mom's taking me to
my first day at Death Star school.
                         (*whispered*)
Such a sexy little mommy.

INT. WAYSTAR – MORNING

Greg heads to the reception desk.

> GREG

Greg Hirsch? I'm, I ah . . . believe I'm working here, as of today?

> RECEPTIONIST

Okay?
> (*checking her envelopes*)

Umm—

Greg looks around – smiles to his new colleagues as they pass.

I have no – record of that.

> GREG

Well I've definitely got a job, so?

> RECEPTIONIST

I'm sure. I just don't – have anything?

They smile at each other. Stand-off.

> GREG

Okay. Um? Then, what, should I just head on in and have a mooch about?

> RECEPTIONIST

Um, no.

Eyes to security.

> GREG

Okay. So, what do you suggest?

> RECEPTIONIST

Well what is your job title and who appointed you?

> GREG

Um, job— Not entirely sure per se.
> (*you did ask*)

And I was actually personally appointed by Mr Logan Roy?

Receptionist catches sight of his shoes, looks at him like he might be a crazy person.

Can we call Tom? Tom um—

> RECEPTIONIST

Last name?

GREG

His last— Weird, don't think I ever, Tom, Boss Tom—? He's in a relationship with my cousin, Shiv, Roy? Who's my cousin?

That lands with her.

I mean I think that's public knowledge. Although. Maybe, if you could keep that under your hat?

In the background, the elevator opens to let some executives out. There are Tom and Shiv. They spot Greg across the way. He spots them.

Tom? Tom? Hey!

He responds with a distracted but definite 'Hi'. The doors close.

The receptionist goes back to looking at her envelopes again. A little harder now—

RECEPTIONIST

Okay. Greg? Greg Roy?

There is a computer click, he's in the system!

GREG

I'm actually a Hirsch, not a Roy. But my mom was a Roy. So, I'm basically a Roy in all but name. As it were.

INT. WAYSTAR – KENDALL'S OFFICE – MORNING

Kendall is with Roman and Gerri. Looking at papers as Shiv heads in – she hasn't taken no for an answer from four layers of assistants—

SHIV
(to Jess)
I'll be two minutes, thanks.

KENDALL

No. No, Shiv— What?

SHIV

It's got weird, okay? I was over there and it's gotten very weird.

Kendall looks at Gerri who slides away.

ROMAN

How is he?

> SHIV

I don't know, he might have put on a sock.

> ROMAN

Well that's good, right?

> SHIV

Or he might be lying there dead, I have no idea.

> KENDALL

I can't do this now, Shiv.

Roman's feeling out his back.

> ROMAN

She thinks Marcia's poisoning him.

> SHIV

I do not. Apparently, he doesn't want to see us.

> ROMAN

What, not including me?

> SHIV

Why would he say that?

> KENDALL

Still pissed at you for not signing up to his corporate restructure? To make Marcia queen of the castle?

> SHIV

Well maybe *she's pissed*. Look did *you* see him over the weekend?

> KENDALL
> (*defensive*)

I heard he wasn't up to seeing people?

> SHIV

No one's seen him since we moved him home from the hospital on like Thursday?

> KENDALL
> (*to Roman*)

Rome – you saw him, right?

Roman is squeamish, didn't like seeing Dad weakened.

ROMAN

Sure. For like five minutes. He was – he was pretty – you know, it wasn't really 'him', him. There were tubes.

SHIV

But after that?

(*seriously*)

No one apart from Marcia has seen him for the better part of a week.

KENDALL

Four days is not a week.

SHIV

Okay for the majority of the week. And we're just accepting, the world is just accepting, this woman's word that he put on a fucking sock?

This hits with Kendall, the mention of the marketplace.

KENDALL

We don't want to rush the recovery.

SHIV

Right, cos you like playing boss?

(*cajoling*)

Ken, we need to know what's going on. Will you go over and see, please?

Kendall looks at Roman.

ROMAN

Should we take twenty?

KENDALL

Shiv, this is— I literally have something unmissable.

He checks his Bloomberg terminal, winces.

Later, I'll try later, okay?

SHIV

Okay.

(*re phone, his demeanor*)

Everything okay?

Truth as joke—

> KENDALL
> No, we're on the brink of total corporate collapse.

Shiv's off—

> SHIV
> (*'kidding' to Roman*)
> Uh-huh. That figures. Call me if we go Lehman will you? I might like some of these chairs.

INT. WAYSTAR – BIG BOARDROOM – DAY

Tom makes it in. He walks to his spot, looking around a full global heads of division Waystar meeting.

> TOM
> Hi, morning. Here to help fix the Death Star. 'Grill on the exhaust vent, guys, grill on the exhaust vent!'

> EVA
> (*why are you late, prick?*)
> I've got your back. I told them this won't be a habit.

We gets a sense of the scope of the organization, thirty-ish people:

The Head of Waystar Studios with five underlings: President of Movie Production; President of Marketing; President of Digital; President of International; President of Animation.

Head of Parks, Tom, greets Parks and Resorts divisional heads: President of Theme Parks; President of Resorts; President of Cruise Lines; President of Marketing; President of Americas; President of Europe/Middle East/Africa/Asia Pacific.

Eva, Head of Entertainment Networks (TV) (Eva is also there as Acting President of ATN); also there are: President of the Sports Networks; President of Entertainment; President of Owned Television Stations; President of Radio.

News and Information: split between a Head of Newspapers, President of Magazines.

President of Book Publishing.

President of Vaulter (Lawrence Yee).

President of Video Games.

Many of the divisional heads have strategy documents with them and a visual presentation prepared. There is an air of disquiet. All is not great at the company and everyone knows.

INT. WAYSTAR – CORRIDOR – DAY

Kendall is walking the corridor with Karolina, Roman, Gerri and Karl (CFO).

> KAROLINA
>
> My only concern would be, to brief this – meeting – is it a little – aggressive – for a temporary CEO?

Gerri agrees – she and Karolina have talked.

> GERRI
>
> That's a good point?

> KENDALL
>
> Yeah well we've got a very aggressive drop in our share price, so I think that's appropriate, good? So brief this wide and brief it fast, okay?

End of conversation.

> KAROLINA
> *(bad)*
>
> Good.

> KARL
> *(big mistake)*
>
> Great.

> KENDALL
>
> Good. And then I'll be doing the Vaulter shoot and we'll hopefully crystalize a new vibe, right?

INT. WAYSTAR – BIG BOARDROOM – DAY

They all head in. Heads turn. Feel the weight of the organization. Kendall's not bad at holding the room.

> KENDALL

Morning morning morning! Hey hey hey. My people. How's it going? Great to see you all. You know my brother and I, CEO and COO? Gerri and Karolina?

> ROMAN

Hey.

They are approaching their seats. Roman doesn't sit.

I'm going to stand.
> (*explains*)

Back. New trainer.

Kendall winces. Oh fuck, what an oddball. Plus, it's a weird status vibe having Roman stand as Kendall sits.

> KENDALL

So. Just wanted to get the group together early in my tenure to say: Yo. You're probably all wondering about my dad. He's doing okay.

Roman goes for water.

> ROMAN

Yowch—
> (*under his breath*)

motherfucker.

> KENDALL

We're hoping for a full recovery.

> ROMAN

He's like a thousand percent better though. He's like a bull in rhino hide.

> KENDALL

Uh-huh. Slow and steady.

> ROMAN

This morning he put on a sock. So.

> KENDALL

That's right. This morning he tried to put on a sock.

Bit of a weird silence – Kendall looks at Roman: Shut up, man.

And welcome to Tom Wambsgans who was managing resorts and is now sitting up with the grown-ups.

Tom tries to take the ball and run with it but it was a barely polite sidebar.

>   TOM
> Hey—

>   KENDALL
> So – what I want to discuss with you all this morning, is a new strategic vision.
>   (*pause for effect*)
> We have a great firm here. Multifaceted. Parks, cruises, et cetera. But at the heart, media: TV, movies, books and newspapers. And what we're fighting for is eyeballs. Eyeballs we sell to, eyeballs we crate up and auction to advertizers. And bottom line: we're losing. To monopolistic disruptors: Alphabet, Facebook.

>   ROMAN
> Internet. Fucking game-changer, baby.

Kendall suppresses the wince.

>   KENDALL
> But we are still, just – *just* in a position to leverage our brands into something in the new landscape. But if we don't, we're gonna be like the biggest fucking horse trader in Detroit, 1909, okay?
>   (*looks around*)
> We need a more dynamic strategy – let's call it, for the sake of clarity, the Strategy of a Thousand Lifeboats. Vaulter is a lifeboat. ATN Citizens is a lifeboat. There are no bad lifeboats.

>   ROMAN
> VR could be a lifeboat?

>   KENDALL
> VR's a bubble. But yeah, no bad ideas.

>   ROMAN
> Porn could be a lifeboat?

>   KENDALL
> Except that. That's a bad lifeboat.

(*chuckles*)

Hey – thanks, Rome. Look, this isn't a brainstorm, all I'm saying: Everyone's invited. I want all of you to be innovating, challenging, and bringing me a hundred lifeboats. Be bold, be disruptive! Okay? Because steady as she goes hits the iceberg?

On the group, Eva, Gerri. That was bracing. Not a bad performance—

ROMAN

Okay! Thanks, everybody! Woot woot!

INT. JOYCE'S CAMPAIGN OFFICE – DAY

Shiv arrives. She's pissed off and preoccupied thinking about her dad as she marches through—

SARAH

He's through there.

Shiv heads on past the campaign volunteers and paid staff into her private office.

SHIV

Hey Daniel. I understand you wanted to talk to me direct?

DANIEL

Yeah. It's difficult with Joyce right now, so I thought this might be better.

SHIV

Well, let's get right to it, shall we? What happened? What do we say?

DANIEL

Okay, so I've been speaking to a friend who's a lawyer and I've spoken to the PR people, at my publishers and I'm currently taking the view that I don't want to comment as regards to anything.

She looks at him. For quite a long time.

SHIV

Uh-huh. Fine. But between us, I don't have time for a lot of – tofu. Was it your asshole online, were you looking to fuck around, what's going on?

> DANIEL

I've been advised not to say anything publicly.

> SHIV

Yeah but we're not public and if this hack leaks Joyce is going to get fucked at a thousand miles an hour from every direction, so I need the facts?

> DANIEL

The facts are – complicated and I can't go into them right now.

She wants more.

Everything isn't as it seems. Is all I can say.

She looks at him. Incredulous.

> SHIV

'Everything isn't as it seems'? That's what I'm building my house on? What is that, your fucking Vegas magic show?

> DANIEL

That's it, for now, in terms of what I can say.

> SHIV

Okay well that's a huge waste of my time, and I can't speak for your wife but that's a fucking treehouse of dildos right at the heart of this operation, so thanks a million and goodnight.

Shiv is up and heading out—

> DANIEL

How's your father? I was sorry to hear—

> SHIV

I have no fucking idea. Goodbye.*

INT. WAYSTAR – BULLPEN – DAY

Roman and Kendall are outside as the big meeting room – bit of glad-handing after the meet. Tom grabs a back-slap as he retreats—

---

* The Joyce and Daniel storyline got largely pushed to episode four of this season.

> TOM

Great work, sir! Kudos! Here if you need a friendly ear, Lord Vader!

> KENDALL

Just get shit moving at parks yeah, Tom? It's stagnant. Shake that fucking tree, C3PO?

> TOM
> (*robotic moves*)

Shaking, bro! Shaking it big time!

Kendall walks, Roman at his side. Kendall is texting: Stewy.

> KENDALL

Fiona—
> (*to Fiona, confidential*)

can you send flowers to Rava? Nice but, y'know, not ridiculous. They should smell like flowers, not desperation.

Kendall makes it through. We could cut to a different space.

And Fi, talk to Jess – I might want to throw a couple of items up on the internal – not a big deal, coupla TED Talks. And a documentary on the *Epic of Gilgamesh*. First story. Because what are we, if not storytellers?

Kendall walks on through the slightly drab offices.

> MALE EXECUTIVE

Hey, Captain.

He likes the sound of that.

> KENDALL

Hey.

He turns to an assistant.

And let's get Carlo up in here. Those kitchens are a disaster. And maybe something fun. Not ping pong, but something, y'know. Throw some tags up in here. Not that. Skate park. Climb wall. None of these, right, but the essence?

Fiona nods. He's reached somewhere where Jess waits.

(*to Jess*)

Talk to me.

There is a beat of apprehension.

JESS

Down three points.

KENDALL

Ugh. Okay.

That slows his roll.

JESS

There's an AP headline: 'CEO tells staff Waystar headed for iceberg'.

KENDALL

Not iceberg! Lifeboats! Lifeboats not iceberg. Jesus? Karolina?

KAROLINA

That's what we're pushing.

KENDALL

The new regime shoot, Lawrence knows?

ROMAN

Yeah on that, 'the new regime'? Forgive me for whoring in but shouldn't I be in there as well?

KENDALL

Let's not muddy it.

ROMAN

And in that equation, I'm the mud?

GERRI

Okay, look I want to talk options to you, okay? I've got some thoughts that we've shared with Logan—

We're now at Kendall's office.

KENDALL

Interesting? Ideas that Dad didn't want. Sounds appealing. But no, thanks.

GERRI

Ken, these are modeled and thought through and—

> KENDALL

And rejected. Now if you'll excuse me, I'm going for a walk, I need some perspective.

INT. WAYSTAR – ROMAN'S OFFICE – DAY

We follow Roman towards his office. He nods to his assistant, the folks outside and then sits at his desk.

There are folders of material on the table and when he, slightly reluctantly, pushes his mouse – a million new emails in bold.

He feels oppressed by the magnitude of his role. Caged by the room. He gets up and prowls. He lies on the floor. Gets up. Walks around the room, closing the blinds and shutters so that he can't be seen from outside.

Then he goes and stands at the glass window – looking out and down on the city. He pushes his pelvis against the glass.

Focussing on making the space his own. Being in the moment. Owning the space, the city, Roman touches himself through his pants and then pulls his dick out and, boldly, defiantly, starts to beat off right up against the window – looking out at the city.

He's fucking the city. He's the boss—

INT. COFFEE PLACE – DAY

Kendall stands with Stewy Hosseini waiting for their coffees. Stewy, a man of large, insatiable appetites, of great intelligence, but scattershot focus, has been a pal since college.

Stewy is eating a cronut. Kendall scans the place, making sure no one's clocked him.

> STEWY

The thing about capitalism is, and I mean there are issues, but *fuck me.* I mean this is a piece of shit chain on a stretch of nothing and this – this is like the most fucking delicious thing that anyone has ever tasted.

> KENDALL

So, Stewy, listen, I could do with a read, from someone without a dog in the fight?

> STEWY

I wanted to ask you something too.

> KENDALL

This is tight, this is absolutely just us okay? Because a leak kills me.

> STEWY

About Rava. For a pal.

> KENDALL

Rava?

> STEWY

Yeah, it's a mutual friend, and like, is it cool? Or are you still hankering for a wankering . . .?

> KENDALL

I don't have time for this – I mean, who, who's asking? What?

> STEWY

I can't say, but they wanted to know if it was an issue?

> KENDALL

Like who? Fucking, Paul?

> STEWY

Fine, if you're asking I'm assuming it is an issue.

> KENDALL
> (*the public line*)

Yeah well, look, we're separated. Whatever. Free agents.

But his look suggests otherwise.

> STEWY

I get it.
> (*holds up a five*)

I'm having another. If you eat it fast enough you can actually burn off the calories. It's a loophole.

> KENDALL

So. When I took over, found out Dad took out a huge loan, a decade ago, secret, through the holding company?

This gets Stewy's attention.

> STEWY

Seriously?

> KENDALL
> (*nods*)

Secured against the family's stake in the public firm.

> STEWY

Oh fuck.

> KENDALL

Yeah. Now the stock is getting ready to breach and the bank
are—

> STEWY

Yeah I saw that price, brutal. Who's the bank?

Kendall's not saying. Stewy is trying to catch the server's eye.

Sounds like they have your dick strapped to the clapper of the
opening bell.

> KENDALL

I need a read.

> STEWY

Well, number one, you boost the price.

> KENDALL
> (*obviously*)

Uh-huh. Well I am trying. How's it going to play for us to
refinance elsewhere?

> STEWY

Honestly? Not great. 'Why won't your original bank step up?'
Not good. People don't love the sector. They don't love the firm,
it's ramshackle is the view, the fucking everything shop – and
they don't love—
> (*you, Kendall*)
the situation. It's tough.

> KENDALL

Uh-huh.

> STEWY

Plus the options for sounding it out? Without word spreading? Horrible.

Stewy takes a bite.

> Ugh. I'm so disgusting.

He bins the cronut.

> One thing occurs, just blue-sky. Wouldn't happen in a million years, but. What about we came in, my outfit, took the whole thing off the family's hands?

They start to head outside.

> KENDALL

Uh-huh? Well, obviously no, fuck off, how dare you, I'm so insulted, et cetera.

> STEWY

Of course. But you and Roman and Shiv. Do you all want to be in it, forever? You could all get fucking fucking, rich. Do anything. You can get into tech, Shiv can do consultancy, Roman can, I don't know, DJ for douchebags as they kill hookers in St Barts.

> KENDALL

Uh-huh. Thanks.
> > (*then*)
> It's Paul, right? Rava – it's Paul?

Stewy mimes zipped lips. Then slight nod.

INT. WAYSTAR – ROMAN'S OFFICE – DAY

Squeak.

A Kleenex wipes a splatter of cum off the window in Roman's office.

He can't do a great job. It's quite smeared. He makes a couple of attempts then uses a dab of saliva from his finger – but in the end – he leaves the swirl of smear and goes and opens his door.

> ROMAN

Okay! I am open for business!

INT. WAYSTAR — ADVENTURE-PARKS FLOOR — CORRIDOR —
DAY

*Tom is striding down the corridor towards his office with an
assistant.*

> TOM
> And can I get the senior team together tomorrow for a
> reorientation? I'm shaking the tree, folks!

*He spies Greg in the kitchen, looking around, trying not to feel like
the new kid at school. He takes a bag from his pocket and pops in a
few cookies.*

> Excuse me, Greg, are you kidding?

> GREG
> *(with a start, guilty)*
> Oh hey.

> TOM
> Greg, forgive me, but are we talking to each other on the poop
> deck of a majestic schooner?

Greg looks blank.

> No? Then why the fuck are you wearing a pair of deck shoes?

Greg looks down.

> GREG
> Oh, yeah? My credit card got maxed out? I'm living in a youth
> hostel on like (eighty dollars a day)—?

> TOM
> Jesus. How, squalid.
> *(noticing bag)*
> Dude, are you carrying dogshit?

> GREG
> *(re food)*
> No, it's – it's free, right? Is that cool? I mean, I don't want to be
> melodramatic but – my body is growing weak, due to – lack of
> sustenance.

> TOM
> But in a – dog-poop baggy?

GREG

Yeah I have a bunch from (back home).

TOM

Greg, that's disgusting.

GREG

Not really. They don't pre-poop them? They're just bags, really. It's just a mental barrier.

TOM

Pair of cap-toe Oxfords. Crockett & Jones. ASAP. Lucinda, can you figure out where we might put the talented Mr Greg?

His assistant jumps in to take Greg away.

INT. PHOTO STUDIO – DAY

Flash! Kendall and Lawrence pose with one another in front of a gymnast's vault. In between shots, an ongoing conversation.

PHOTOGRAPHER

Can I get you to do a kind of a – a like an arm wrestle, on the top there?

They rearrange so they are across from one another, and going to arm wrestle. As they smile for the camera.

LAWRENCE

So. How does it feel, man?

KENDALL

Feels pretty good.

LAWRENCE

Fastest falling stock on the exchange? One-three-four? Yeah?

KENDALL

Well, you know, I probably overpaid for you, so. Gonna hurt us.

LAWRENCE

I didn't sign up for the toilet.
                    (*then*)
I signed up for Logan Roy, major investment, global reach, not – Scrappy Doo and his thousand holey lifeboats.

                    PHOTOGRAPHER
Okay. Little cheesy? But 'Vaulter'. How about, Kendall, would
you like vault, like over Mr Yee here?

                    LAWRENCE
No.

                    KENDALL
No.

                    PHOTOGRAPHER
Fine. Okay. Then maybe just – bros? Hanging?

*Kendall and Lawrence share a look re the photographer. The
photographer chatters on as they arrange themselves.*

Bros pose. Let's go with the bros. 'These are the bros who
knows.'

                    LAWRENCE
I tell you what I wonder about you?

They arrange themselves, trying to out-status the other.

Could you even open a restaurant? Could you actually fucking,
do anything? Or are you just a name?

Kendall glances at him: Fuck you.

                    PHOTOGRAPHER
Good! How about another idea – 'verbal gymnastics'? Can you
give me a 'business conversation pose'?

Kendall's finished with this, takes his leave.

                    KENDALL
                  (*to PR person*)
They got plenty. Make it work.
                  (*to PR, as they walk*)
Tell him to take thirty minutes' worth of solo Lawrence shots
and then delete them all.

INT. WAYSTAR – ADVENTURE-PARKS FLOOR – GREG'S NEW
OFFICE – DAY

*Greg watches an HR Welcome video. The same one he watched at
the theme-parks management induction. But after the 'Feel It' logo*

*it cuts to a piece on the company's 'Respect yourself, respect others –
equalities and communities agenda'.*

*A deliberately diverse Benetton version of the company plays on
screen.*

*Greg leaves his terminal with the promo playing. Wandering the
office, we maybe notice every face we see is white.*

INT. WAYSTAR – BULLPEN – DAY

*As Kendall walks back in, we cut back and forth with Gerri, in a
tizzy.*

> GERRI
> (*over phone*)
> Kendall. Sandy Furness is here.

> KENDALL
> (*over phone*)
> What do you mean?

> GERRI
> He's here. In the building. In our offices.

> KENDALL
> The fuck? Who let him in?

> GERRI
> Security wasn't— And people were becoming aware . . . He's
> been very nice to everyone.

> KENDALL
> He can't do that. Fucking Pepsi doesn't just drop in to see Coke.
> Put him where no one can see him. South Tank. I'll be right
> there.

> GERRI
> Sharks are circling.

> KENDALL
> How are we looking?

He reaches Gerri.

> GERRI
> Down two more points.

On Kendall's face. The options are narrowing.

EXT. NICE ANONYMOUS-LOOKING HOTEL – DAY

Shiv heads in to the hotel.

INT. NICE ANONYMOUS-LOOKING HOTEL ROOM – DAY

Shiv answers the door to . . . Nate. A significant former boyfriend.
The air is heavy with a sense of shared history and mutual attraction.

NATE

Hey.

SHIV

Hey. Nathaniel.

She leads him in. He looks around the hotel room.

NATE

So. How've you been?

SHIV

Busy.

NATE

Uh-huh. Right. So? Is this—?

What is this – something sexy?

SHIV

It's work.

NATE

Okay. Of course.

Smiles form; him, then both.

SHIV

What?!

NATE

Fine. Just a simple work meeting on the bed of a four-star hotel
room.
(*then, as he looks around*)
If you don't want a cookie, Shiv, don't go down the cookie aisle?

SHIV

It's just private is all. The matter in hand.

Sounds like work—

NATE

Uh-huh, right? And, so how's it going working with Joyce, the long glass of tepid water from Albany?

SHIV

Good. How about you with that poor man's Fidel Castro? The senior senator from the state of 1975.

NATE

Zing!

They smile.

SHIV

Look. I just wondered if you could do me a favor?

NATE

Do I owe you a favor?

SHIV
(*smiling*)

Sure. Because I deigned to date you?

NATE

You *deigned*?!

They laugh.

SHIV

And I thought we were going to be friends?

NATE

Sure I want to be friends.

SHIV

I wondered if you could run a background check on someone?

NATE

That seems like it might cause some ethical issues because there's a world where my guy and your gal end up in the mud, wrestling for the democratic nomination and—

SHIV

It's not political.

> NATE

Oh, right?

> SHIV

I need background on someone off the record. Marcia.

> NATE

Marcia . . . the wicked stepmother?

Well that's interesting.

> SHIV

Occurred to me a few years too late, I really don't know much about her. Just due diligence.
> > (*defensive*)

Okay?

> NATE
> > (*thinks about it, then*)

Well, I do know a really horrible guy. And he's incredibly expensive.

> SHIV

Well, thank you. That sounds perfect. Can it all go through you?

She's done. Gets up.

> NATE

Uh-huh. 'Yes my lady.'
> > (*then, smiles*)

'Deigned'? Have you *seen* the women I dated after you?

She starts to head out.

> SHIV

Those women dated you *because* you dated me. It was like, 'Oh I guess he must have *something* . . .'

They smile.

INT. WAYSTAR – WINDOWLESS CONFERENCE ROOM – DAY

Kendall walks in alone. Is he going to be okay?

Sandy Furness stands to greet him. He's low emotion, apparently low energy. Wearing a blazer and slacks. Made his way in business on pure math. A robot, very well schooled in the way of the human.

KENDALL

Mr Furness! Kind of you to drop by.

SANDY

Not at all. I just came to say how sorry I was to hear about your dad.

KENDALL

Really appreciate it. That's kind.

SANDY

I know we've had our battles but he was one of the great visionaries of his generation—

KENDALL

Well, it's kind of you to do it in person when you could have just called, so. Thank you.

SANDY

I hope I didn't send the birds a-tweeting. What with all the uncertainty and whatnot.

KENDALL

We'll make sure people know it's just friendly.

SANDY

Great. And will you give your dad my best? Tell him I dropped by?

KENDALL

Sure. Maybe when that news is a little less likely to kill him.

Smiles. Knowing laughs. Kendall tries to wrap things up—

Okay well I appreciate this, you're looking great.

SANDY

Thank you. I eat babies.

Just before he goes—

And just to say, if I can give you any advice. I'm just watching the wheels nowadays so, you want to run anything by me, as an honest broker, use me. A mentor.

KENDALL
(*never in a million years*)
That is a very kind offer.

                    SANDY FURNESS
There's probably a million options with our two firms? Swaps,
acquisitions, cooperative interactions, smart stuff only a young
man like you can conceive of.

                       KENDALL
Oh, Sandy, you've been pretty smart. Smarter than the
regulators, anyway.

Kendall nods through the glass for Jess to interrupt them—

                        SANDY
Tell you what was smart, Vaulter. I don't care what the wise
apples say.

Jess comes in.

                       KENDALL
Jess, would you take Mr Furness down.

Sandy takes more time to get up than he'd like.

                        SANDY
Look at you. Right in the eye of the raging storm and cool as a
cucumber.

Kendall fights any reaction to this, the one thing he needed to hear.

Stay strong. Stay in touch.

*Kendall waits at the door, waving him off. Roman approaches, they
can still see him in the distance as they discuss—*

                        ROMAN
What happened?

                       KENDALL
He said I was dead in the water without him and tried to finger-
bang me.

                        ROMAN
What did you say?

                       KENDALL
I told him I'd rather eat my own shit.

Sandy gives a final wave – and Kendall back.

ROMAN

You heard?

KENDALL

What?

Shows him his phone.

ROMAN

It's over, bro. One-two-nine-point-eight. Clap hands, we're
fucked.

(*then*)

I think if this was a movie, the office would now blow up.

INT. WAYSTAR – KENDALL'S OFFICE – NIGHT

*Kendall and Roman, Gerri. They are looking for a way through. Long
evening of looking at the angles – they're all a little tired. Beat of
silence.*

KENDALL

You know sometimes you leave the party and you wonder what
everyone's saying about you?

ROMAN

With me it's usually – 'Who was that maniac who put a
watermelon on his dick?'

KENDALL

I know. I know what they say about me.

(*the Bloomberg terminal*)

That. That's how much people don't trust me.

ROMAN

Hey, it's me too, man. Don't leave me out.

Gerri's tired – summing up.

GERRI

I mean the truth is – we, we call their bluff which may not be
a bluff, and the debt becomes public and – we lose control. Or
we get the stock up, which we – can't, we can't magic that. Or
we pay the bank back. Which means – you know, to realize that
much cash? Stock sell-down. Which is horrible. There are no
good options.

Beat.

                    ROMAN
Can I suggest something?

                    GERRI
Uh-huh.

                    ROMAN
Can I suggest we all take our shirts off?

                    GERRI
Umm? Ken?

                    ROMAN
You know I beat off in my office earlier?

                    KENDALL
You didn't actually though?

                    ROMAN
You know, we can be a pair of little fucking worms wriggling around in here – do what the button-down fuckheads say. No offense, Gerri.

                    GERRI
Please. Go ahead. Masturbate your way out of this.

                    ROMAN
Seriously, man. They could write an algorithm to run this place. But that's not the answer.

Roman untucks his shirt and unbuttons.

Break shit up. Disrupt.

His shirt is hanging open now. Maybe he even takes it off.

Yeah?

                    GERRI
Ken? Tell him to put his shirt on.

                    KENDALL
I don't fucking know. I don't know.

Kendall undoes a button or two. As many as he can without feeling like a dumb-ass. There is something in what Roman says. He is feeling caged. Now he can breathe freer.

Kendall gets up. Walks around.

Okay. Look, so worst position, we sell down the stock. We survive.

Gerri pretends to puke. Kendall hops up on his desk. Does he stand on it? Or sit cross-legged. Whatever feels good.

ROMAN

Or. What about, next-wave shit. Prop-co op-co. Turn group finance into a profit centre?

GERRI
(skeptical)
Or go financial engineering. Full Enron?

ROMAN

Hey if you're gonna shit on every idea, I got places I could be.

KENDALL

I mean to get some cash in the holding company – sell the old outdoor ads? And for the share price, parks and cruises?

GERRI

Those are very profitable pieces of the jigsaw—

ROMAN
(rubs his eyes)
Poor Tom. Boo-hoo.

KENDALL

I mean sure but – what are we doing with them? Does that make a negative a positive?

ROMAN

Maybe we cut a title or two, from physical production. Newspaper-wise? Online only?

GERRI

That's a twenty-million solution to a billion-dollar problem.

KENDALL

But it's the right direction of travel. That feels right.

GERRI

Look, if you want stuff that will work for the price: lay-offs.

207

                              ROMAN
Yum yum, blood! See – shirt-off shit?

                             KENDALL
I guess it could be a package? Lay-offs, sell-offs.

                               GERRI
Structured retreat?

                             KENDALL
Well, yeah, but with a philosophy?

Beat. Okay?

                              ROMAN
I guess we should ask – or tell—

                             KENDALL
The sock-meister?

                              ROMAN
I mean we should at least *try*, right?

On Kendall.

DAY TWO

EXT. STREET – MORNING

Greg walking the streets the next morning.

INT. VINTAGE CLOTHING STORE – MORNING

Greg is at the counter of a vintage clothing store. A pair of black Oxford brogues on the cash desk. A hipster vibe.

                               GREG
Could I just check – are these ironic at all?

                          HIPSTER CLERK
Er, how do you mean?

                               GREG
I just— They look normal, but I've never— This isn't my usual domain and I need them for normal so I just wanted to check, they aren't ironical in any way or anything are they?

EXT. LOGAN'S APARTMENT BUILDING/INT. LOBBY – DAY

Kendall's car pulls up. Kendall enters.

INT. LOGAN'S APARTMENT – FOYER – DAY

On Kendall's shoes as they step out of an elevator. Classy, plain, black. Walking into something of a death sentence. He's got to tell his dad bad news.

He sees Rava, smart, ready to go on to work (management consultancy) with their nanny, Malaya, and their children, Iverson and Sophie, in the living room looking a bit doleful.

> KENDALL
>
> Hey, guys!

He gives his kids a big hug and kiss.

> (*to Rava*)
> Thank you so much for doing this here. I'm sorry. And –
> actually—
> (*sheepish whisper*)
> can't stay long.

> RAVA
>
> Apparently goes for us too. Aunt Marcia won't let us see
> Grandpa, right, kids?

They shake their heads. Marcia emerges.

> MARCIA
>
> Kendall!

She comes around and gives him a polite kiss on the cheek.

> KENDALL
>
> Is he okay?

> MARCIA
>
> He's improving. He's really improving.

Kendall feels the good news – with a minor chord of bad news.

> KENDALL
>
> Great! Because I probably need to let him know something.

MARCIA

But he's resting. I'm sorry. It's not a good time.

KENDALL

(*disappointed, but relieved*)

Oh, okay – well, it's just when my assistant called . . .?

MARCIA

(*you understand*)

She spoke with Joan, not me.

Rava nods to Malaya. Time to go. She gathers up the kids and starts heading for the elevator.

MALAYA

C'mon, kids.

KENDALL

Is this his request?

('*funny*')

The solitary confinement?

MARCIA

I'm absolutely guided by what he wants.

Hm? Kendall is torn. He would love a reason not to see him.

KENDALL

Well let him know, will you, I wanted to talk to him, keep him abreast of moves?

MARCIA

If you like you can tell me, and I'll pass it on.

He looks at her. Is this going to be the new world?

KENDALL

It's complicated.

MARCIA

Oh. Of course. Over my head.

KENDALL

We're – we're retreating. Tactically, and—

She looks like: That doesn't sound like a Logan move. He feels it in his bones . . .

> MARCIA

I'm sure you're doing the right thing.

Kendall turns. As he heads to join his family he's thinking hard. This isn't Logan's move, is it?

INT. LOGAN'S APARTMENT – ELEVATOR – DAY

In the tiny elevator, the kids play a word game with Malaya, while Rava and Kendall are squeezed in, face to face. He's thinking. Shaking his head.

> RAVA

She's being protective.

Kendall shakes his head. Laughing sardonically, he drops his head onto her shoulder. She doesn't mind.

> KENDALL

Right. She probably has his brain in a jar and she's working all night on his signature. For the new will.

Rava laughs. Kendall stares into her eyes. Rava checks to see how many floors left.

You get my flowers?

> RAVA

Tell Fiona, thank you.

Kendall smiles, shrugs. They stand there.

> KENDALL
> (*whispers*)

Listen, how about you let the nanny take the kids.

> RAVA

Uh-huh . . . ?

> KENDALL

Come back to the old place and we probably need to—

> RAVA

Yeah—?

> KENDALL

Y'know—

                         (*glances at kids*)
        negotiate.

This gets a suppressed laugh out of Rava. He remains deadpan.

                            RAVA
        You want to 'negotiate'?

                          KENDALL
        Yes. Like animals negotiate. Tough.

The elevator doors open.

EXT. LOGAN'S APARTMENT BUILDING – DAY

                          KENDALL
                         (*to Rava*)
        Have dinner with me? Tonight.

She's tempted. It's got the edge of a command.

INT. WAYSTAR ADVENTURE-PARKS FLOOR – CORRIDOR OR
CONFERENCE ROOM – DAY

*Tom's assistant is walking, with an assistant – gets to where Greg is
there waiting.*

                            TOM
        Hey buddy. Come on. First meeting with the senior management
        cadre.

                            GREG
        Uh-huh? Great. Great stuff.

                            TOM
        I'm gonna bad sheriff it, you cool to play the fuck-sock?

                            GREG
        Uh-huh? As in?

Another thought—

                            TOM
        I was looking through employee emails, which by the way is
        completely legal, but does my breath smell? Honestly?

GREG

Er. No. No, I mean it smells of – breath but—

Back on the meeting—

TOM

Too much drift in parks. Gotta shake that tree. I might punchbag you a little, that cool?

GREG

Oh sure. As in?

A friendly slap and Tom and Greg head in. Tom nods to the people he already knows.

TOM

Morning, people. New day. Great to see you all. So, I've got a number of new approaches, that I'd like to run through. But first, some of you I know, some no, and I just want to get a feel for the team and let you get a feel for me?

Smiles, nods.

So, to kick off. Here's a question. Here we are, off in the theme-park division, but tell me: If you could do anything, professionally, work anywhere, what would that be?

Picks one of the ten execs assembled around the table. Nods to him—

Yeah, go ahead. Can you intro?

BRAD

Um, Brad Kilmartin, global marketing.

TOM

Hey Brad, good to meet you, man. So? Dream gig?

BRAD

Um. I guess I've always wanted to work towards the creative sector in terms of— I could see myself, using my marketing skillset at a movie studio?

TOM

Sexy!

Everyone chuckles.

I'm going to do you a favor, Brad.

> (*a blessing*)
> You're fired. Follow the dream, man.

Brad assumes he's kidding. He's not.

                    BRAD

Heh. I mean—?

                    TOM

I'm sorry. This is the best division of the best company in the world. If you're not happy, it's probably best you move on.

Brad tries to compute.

If we aren't feeling it, how can we get millions of American families to? Huh?

Brad stares at Tom in disbelief. Laughs nervously.

                    BRAD

Are you serious?

Tom holds.

Jesus Christ?*

Tom's phone lights up and buzzes. He ignores it.

                    TOM

So, now, you—

Turns on Greg.

Yeah 'family man'? We all know why you're here. You silver-spoon piece of shit?

                    GREG

Hey?

                    TOM

So, you bringing any ideas to the table or are you an empty fucking vessel?

---

* We shot a version of this firing scene (inspired by a story recorded in James B. Stewart's *Disney War*), in both this episode and 'Vaulter' (season two, episode two), but neither made it to air.

> GREG
> (*choked*)

Um – um. Ideas?

> (*mind blank*)

Petting zoo?

> TOM

Excuse me?

> GREG

Like a scaled version, the biggest petting— It wouldn't be pathetic, could be kinda rad with an advertizing push? Kids love a (petting zoo). I know I did!

Tom's phone goes.

> TOM

Are you arguing from anecdotal? Because you better have numbers to back that up or I will tie your lanky limbs into a bow and turn you into a fuckable pretzel.

On phone:

It's Shiv calling. Tom gets up. Greg swallows hard – execs now looking at him.

Excuse me?

INT. WAYSTAR ADVENTURE-PARKS FLOOR – CORRIDOR – DAY

> TOM

Okay, well, it's hard. Well, I guess if Connor's flying in?

INT. WAYSTAR ADVENTURE-PARKS FLOOR – CORRIDOR OR CONFERENCE ROOM – DAY

Greg is looking out after Tom.

> GREG

He's actually a pretty great guy.

EXT. STREET – DAY

Kendall is walking with determination.

INT. COFFEE SHOP – DAY

Kendall is back with Stewy.

> KENDALL
>
> So. Stewy. You know how everyone hates you?

> STEWY
>
> Well, no. That's not something I'm aware of, no.

> KENDALL
>
> Oh sure, they do. Private equity, getting your meat hooks in, chiseling your profit? Like a vampire locust fuck.

> STEWY
>
> What is this? If I wanted to be insulted, I'd have coffee with my daughter.*

> KENDALL
>
> I've had an idea. How about instead of taking us over, you give me four billion dollars?

Stewy doesn't respond. Thinks. In the background, unseen by them, Greg is lining up for coffee. He tries to catch Kendall's eye.

> I stay boss. You stop raiding shitty companies for scraps. You *invest* in a blue-chip corporation. One that is currently undervalued because of some unfounded concerns about its leadership, i.e. Little Lord Shareplunge here? The story twists. Happy ending.

Stewy takes it in. Thinks, sees the angles, the possibilities and the problems—

> STEWY
>
> Okay, full disclosure: I have a hangover.
> (*off Kendall's look*)
> Bigger than normal. So, let's do this the way we did back in the day – head into the boardroom with some something-something and bash out a few ideas?

> KENDALL
>
> Not for me.

---

* We removed this reference to Stewy having a daughter in the edit – we got more of a sense of Stewy's character as we wrote more of the season.

                         STEWY
Uh-huh. How would you feel if I . . .?

                        KENDALL
Really? Man?

                         STEWY
What can I say. I'm Bacchus. I'm Type A.

INT. COFFEE SHOP – BATHROOM – DAY

*Stewy taps out a bump of coke onto his phone. Kendall looks the
other way. Doesn't care to watch.*

                        KENDALL
Are you done?

                         STEWY
No. Obviously – I don't generally take minority stakes in public
companies?

Sniff.

                        KENDALL
You're a parasite. How about for once you make things bigger.
With an old pal? Are you done?

                         STEWY
Yes. I couldn't begin to even think about this.
                         (then)
But if I could. To sell it, I'd need it to be voting stock?

                        KENDALL
As long as the family maintain control.

                         STEWY
Well, effective control.

Kendall looks not uninterested.

And I'd need a board seat.

                        KENDALL
I'd force it on you, dude. For the optics. Shit-hot new CEO has
some hot-shit new money for investment? New generation.
I keep the debt out of the news. Sisters are doing it for
themselves?

Stewy thinks.

> STEWY
> I'm not necessarily totally opposed to this notion.

> KENDALL
> That's right and luckily I speak Stewy. And that's Stewy for 'I have a raging hard-on for this.'

> STEWY
> How much?

> KENDALL
> And listen, tell Paul to stick to jerking off at the opera. Rava's still my wife.

EXT. LOGAN'S APARTMENT BUILDING/INT. LOGAN'S APARTMENT BUILDING – LOBBY – DAY

Shiv and Tom and Connor. She has a file.

> CONNOR
> You background-checked her?

> SHIV
> No need to tell Ken.

> CONNOR
> Is that legal?

> SHIV
> You don't need to know—

> CONNOR
> I mean could anyone do that on . . . anyone?

> SHIV
> First husband, you remember – Lebanese businessman. They had the high life in Paris, lot of parties, lot of pols and writers and also lot of slimeballs and fixers and shitbags and arms dealers. Oil guys—

> CONNOR
> And further back?

> SHIV
> Further back is complicated. No leads.

CONNOR

Right. Is that—?

TOM

It's weird.

SHIV

It is apparently a little weird and there are two possibilities.

Connor nods, go on.

Either, she came from kind of nowhere, Tripoli, Lebanon, turns up in Paris as a publishing assistant aged thirty-one and marries this guy, fine—

CONNOR

Or?

SHIV

A clean-up job. Someone sometime tidied loose ends, did a deep-clean, bleached Google. Tied everything off.

CONNOR

Why would she do that?

SHIV

Well – either, she didn't, and you're paranoid, or – there's another possibility, and I don't know what it is?

INT. LOGAN'S APARTMENT – FOYER – DAY

The doors open. Marcia is right there.

MARCIA

Hello. Hello, everybody?

SHIV

Yeah, hi. You know Connor, Logan's firstborn son.

CONNOR

Hi, Shiv, c'mon let's . . .

SHIV

And this is Tom, my, partner. And between them they are over twelve feet of we would like to see him please?

TOM

Good morning.

> MARCIA
>
> Are you going to force entry? Is that it?

> CONNOR
>
> Sorry I didn't realize this would be framed so aggressively –
> I mean this is just normal. Let's de-escalate?

> MARCIA
>
> He simply isn't up to visitors.

> SHIV
>
> Is this about me signing some pieces of paper or—

> MARCIA
>
> Shiv, please. It's a very difficult—

Marcia looks sad, tearful even?

> SHIV
>
> Oh, the fucking waterworks now is it?

Shiv goes to head upstairs.

> MARCIA
>
> Siobhan?

Marcia subtly steps across. Undeterred, Shiv starts to push past Marcia.

> SHIV
>
> I can't believe you would try to stop me seeing my father!

> MARCIA
>
> I can't believe you would try against his wishes!

Shiv heads up.

> CONNOR
> *(to Marcia)*
>
> Well it is nice to see you.

> TOM
> *(to Connor)*
>
> And how long are you in town?

CONNOR
(*to Marcia*)

I think she's really upset but it comes out as anger. Pretty much everything comes out as anger with her. You look well at least.

TOM
(*to Connor*)

She does look well. You also look well. Everyone looks well.

(*then*)

Apart from Logan.

INT. LOGAN'S APARTMENT – LIBRARY – DAY

Shiv opens the library door.

There's Logan in bed, remote control in hand, his face blank. Joan is there as well, she's set up a TV for Logan and is now hooking up a Blu-ray player.

Logan glances over to her, inscrutable. He turns his attention back to the TV – ATN News.

Logan maintains his focus on the TV. Shiv approaches Logan and gives Joan a nod of dismissal. Joan exits.

SHIV

Dad—? How are you feeling?

He mumbles something that might be 'good'. She stands by. Finally . . .

So, I wanted to come in.

Logan appears to nod.

Um. Tom and I are engaged and—?

Logan doesn't respond. She comes up to his bedside. He gives her a glancing look, then back to the TV.

LOGAN

Where's Frisk . . .?*

---

* The mention of Frisk the dog never made it to broadcast. Happily, because it let me have Caroline say in season three that she never had a dog when she was together with Logan.

Shiv takes a beat.

SHIV

The . . . You mean the dog?

LOGAN

Uh-huh? I love you.

SHIV

I love you too, Dad.
(*then*)
Mom took her to Italy. Yeah?

He keeps his attention on the TV. Hesitant, Shiv puts her hand on Logan's. He doesn't seem to register her. Then something breaks through.

With his other hand, his bad hand, he reaches across and places it on top of hers.

Shiv is relieved to finally have some affection returned. They hold like that for a good while.

Then Logan moves Shiv's hand decisively towards his crotch.

She pulls the hell away.

Shaken, Shiv backs her way out. Joan is outside the door.

On Logan, watching TV; a part of his brain knows something troubling just happened, the other part is asleep.

INT. LOGAN'S APARTMENT – OUTSIDE THE LIBRARY – DAY

Shiv emerges. Comes downstairs, gathers herself.

MARCIA

Everything okay?

SHIV

Uh-huh. Thank you. He's looking better.

MARCIA

The morning is not usually a good time. The morphine, he gets confused. He doesn't want you all to see him when he's not himself?

                              SHIV
    Uh-huh. Sure.

The others look at her.

    He wasn't himself.

                             MARCIA
    No.
                        (catches Shiv privately)
    And, Shiv—

                              SHIV
    Yes?

                             MARCIA
    I'm a private person. Not all of us are born into good ease.

                              SHIV
    Right?

                             MARCIA
    If you want to know anything about me, you can just ask me
    and I will tell you.

*As Shiv goes to the bathroom she might be wondering how Marcia
might know about her digging. We see Colin in the distance.*

INT. WAYSTAR — KENDALL'S OFFICE — DAY

Kendall, Gerri, around the speakerphone. Roman hangs back.

                             ROMAN
    I just thought we were doing our plan, man. Shirts-off shit?

                            KENDALL
    Retreat? Rome, this is a million times better, right?

Roman shrugs. Cut out of the action. The younger brother.

Then—

                              POLK
                        (on speakerphone)
    Good afternoon.

                            KENDALL
    Thanks for making time for us, Mr Polk.

                              POLK
                        (*on speakerphone*)
Not at all. And we've been looking at the terms we can offer
and I think you've seen what we put together?

                            KENDALL
It's a very brutal structure?

                              POLK
                  (*on speakerphone; winning hand*)
Well, these are the terms we think we can offer right now.

                            KENDALL
I mean the margin you're making, you might even say you
were— Well I mean blackmail is an ugly word. But so is getting
goat-fucked.

                              POLK
                        (*on speakerphone*)
I think we should keep things professional, don't you?

                            KENDALL
Uh-huh. Sure. And professionally, we're going to repay.

                              POLK
                        (*on speakerphone*)
As in?

                            KENDALL
We're good. Everything's golden. We don't need you. This can all
stay private and I'll be looking elsewhere for a banking partner
as we go supersonic. Goodbye.

                              POLK
                        (*on speakerphone*)
Um—

                            KENDALL
And fuck you.

Click. Beep. Kendall smiles at Gerri.

INT. RESTAURANT – DAY

Rava and Kendall. Kendall is looking at the wine list—

> KENDALL
> (*to the waiter*)
>
> I think, champagne for my friend?

> RAVA
>
> Ken? I can have water with you.

> KENDALL
>
> No, it's cool. I'll taste it on your tongue later.

> RAVA
> (*beat, looks at him*)
>
> Bit creepy?

> KENDALL
>
> Not suave?

> RAVA
>
> No. Nope. Have you been trying that a lot?

> KENDALL
>
> Oh, I thought that was— No wonder all the women I date keep throwing up in their soup.

> RAVA
>
> So – is this the Stewy money we're celebrating, I saw the news?

> KENDALL
>
> Well I'm not saying I'm the man but if there was a man, hypothetically, he might look a lot like me. I've solved the debt issue, with private equity money.

> RAVA
>
> Well I'm very happy for you.

> KENDALL
>
> Yeah, well, the thing is, all of that, it's made me think about – everything? And you know, here's where I'm at: I love you.

> RAVA
>
> Okay. Well.
> (*formally*)
>
> Thank you. Noted.

> KENDALL
>
> And – so—?

He motions: Are you going to reciprocate?

225

> RAVA

Ken?

> KENDALL

C'mon?

> RAVA

Well, okay. I'm not sure I love you.

How's he going to take that? Punch in the gut? He smiles—

> KENDALL

Yeah you do.

> RAVA
> (*sweetly*)

Fuck you!

> KENDALL

Look. You want us to live separately, we don't know why right now, but you say you do. Now that makes me unhappy. On the other hand, you claim – though of course I don't believe you – that us being together will make you unhappy. So. One of us is going to be unhappy. I just don't see why it has to be me?

He smiles. She smiles.

> RAVA
> (*drains her glass*)

Wow, I cannot argue with that logic. No, actually I can. Because it's the argument of a psychopath.

> KENDALL

At least let's flip for it?

There is an undeniable spark.

INT. KENDALL'S HOUSE – LIVING ROOM – NIGHT

They didn't make it to the bedroom. In Kendall's living room, they're having messy, straight-through-the-door, almost-falling-over-the-couch, then pants-round-the-legs, not-much-dignity sex. They know each other well.

In between – the argument might carry on, half kidding, half getting off on the rousing, jousting, tussle of the argument in amongst their pushy sex—

KENDALL

We are not breaking up.

RAVA

We fucking are. I'll do what I want.

KENDALL

Nope.

RAVA

Yes.

DAY THREE

INT. WAYSTAR – ROMAN'S OFFICE – MORNING

5:30 a.m. view of sunrise. Brex stands and waits, looking at the clock. Roman enters.

ROMAN

B-man!

Brex is impressed by the office.

BREX

Nice office.

He looks out the window. They clock the people in the street.

ROMAN

From up here, all the fucking ants, you can almost imagine they're people, right?

BREX

So, you wanna work out down here or? We can parkour it or take my car to the park?

ROMAN

Well here's the thing, Brex, I can't run today because my back has been fucked since Monday.

BREX

'Fucked' how?

                        ROMAN
I assume you're insured?

Brex is concerned.

I mean, I'm doing big shit, big big shit every day and so like
losing even a quarter of a percent of my operating capacity,
that has million-dollar implications. And I'm thinking, maybe,
test case, I throw three or four dozen white-shoe lawyers at
you and see what it would be like to actually physically destroy
someone?

That could happen. Brex is still: Who is this guy?

                        BREX
Dude. I don't know what happened, but I'm sure I can fix it.

Roman laughs.

                        ROMAN
Fuck you – look at you, are you okay? No. I'm just saying, you
need to take this seriously?

Brex chuckles.

                        BREX
Sure. Look – what— It could be a trapped nerve but most likely
it's just a muscle pull. You want to lie down?

Roman comes over, takes his jacket off. He lies on the floor.

I'm trained in deep tissue. Here.

*Brex makes Roman put his arms in the air. He presses pressure points
in his back until Roman moans.*

Okay.

*Brex pushes Roman to the floor, flat. Brex pushes on Roman's
back, pushing him to the floor with his knee against his back. It's
dominating and not unsexy. Eventually, Roman relents and the
pressure point is released. He groans heavily.*

                        ROMAN
Fuck you!

                        BREX
Yeah?

                         ROMAN
    Fuck you.

                          BREX
    Yeah?

                         ROMAN
    Fuck you!

INT. KENDALL'S HOUSE – BEDROOM – MORNING

Rava wakes with a start.

                          RAVA
    Okay. I have to go.

                        KENDALL
    What about Malaya, can't she—?

                          RAVA
    Iverson will freak out.

He watches her roll out of bed.

                        KENDALL
    Rava. Why don't we just do it all. Back together?

                          RAVA
    Let's talk later.

She puts on her dress, disheveled.

                        KENDALL
    That was nice, right?

                          RAVA
    Nevertheless.

                        KENDALL
    What? You know I'm clean.

                          RAVA
    Oh I know. Sure.

                        KENDALL
    And everything else, that was just the rest of that?

Okay, if he wants to do this—

> RAVA

Look. I don't know. Maybe it's seeing you doing so well at the— I don't know, it's like you're moving on and that makes me feel okay about moving on too?

She goes to use the bathroom – her old bathroom.

> KENDALL
> (*calling through*)

Hey, no. That's bullshit. I'm not moving on. Rava? It all comes down to work and family. That's all I want. That's the secret sauce.

He follows her.

> RAVA

I got a lawyer. He's nice. Let's make it all really really nice, yeah?

We stay on Kendall. Fuck. His phone buzzes. Caller ID tells us it's Marcia.

> KENDALL

Marcia. Everything alright?

> MARCIA
> (*off*)

Your father would like to see you.

INT. LOGAN'S APARTMENT BUILDING – LOBBY – DAY

The doorman recognizes Kendall.

Kendall talks on the phone to Lawrence as he heads into the elevator—

> KENDALL

It gives us options – I'm not going to finance you at the same levels as ATN – Lawrence, but it's a start. The rest is up to you— It went to ATN already. Sorry, I gave them that— We'll make it official soon enough.

INT. LOGAN'S APARTMENT – FOYER – DAY

Kendall steps out of the elevator into the apartment. The houseman is there, guides Kendall up—

INT. LOGAN'S APARTMENT – LIBRARY – DAY

He walks into the library. And there's Logan watching ATN News. This is the first we've seen him sitting up in a chair. He's still wearing a robe and PJs.

> KENDALL
>
> Hey. Look at you. Sitting up. Fucking watching the news!

> LOGAN
>
> Huh. Getting better.

Logan looks at him, blanks out again.

Kendall leans down, gives him a hug but doesn't know whether to include a kiss. There's not much give from Logan.

> KENDALL
>
> It's good to see you.
>   (*trying to lighten the mood*)
> Probably your first bit of downtime since the womb, right?

Logan keeps his eyes on the TV. Kendall surmises correctly Logan has seen or heard the news about the private equity partnership.

> You understand, after you went down, the stock tanked. You should be flattered, I guess.

Logan looks at Kendall.

> We had some pretty shitty options. But I found us a private equity solution so. I tried consulting but—

Logan flashes him an eye.

> Karolina says there's positive analyst noise. People like the shape of this.

Kendall wants congratulations.

> We're at thirty-six percent. Effective control. Plus a war chest to make some moves. We're – we're in good shape, Dad. Keep getting better. I got this.

Logan says something—

> LOGAN
> (*very quietly*)

Yafuginidit.

Kendall looks perplexed. Kindly leans in.

> KENDALL

Dad, can I get you something?

Logan wets his lips, concentrates everything he can on this phrase which he hisses low and only just audible but with sufficient clarity for us to hear—

> LOGAN

You are. A. Fucking. Idiot.

Kendall takes it like an electric shock. Logan refocusses on TV and resumes watching ATN.

What can he do? Kendall knows he carried them from crisis to calm.

We stay tight on Kendall's face.

'Walking on Sunshine' by Katrina and the Waves plays. *

He has a long walk out of the library to let all his resentments percolate.

One last look back at Logan before he closes shut the library's heavy oak door – the boundary line between Logan's diminished world and the rest of it.

INT. LOGAN'S APARTMENT – ELEVATOR – DAY

Kendall walks on and down . . . into the elevator. On his face as he descends. And out into the sharp wind of a New York day.

---

* 'Walking on Sunshine' was a working title for this episode and we always liked the idea of going out on the song. But when we tried it in the edit, it felt forced. Indeed, as I collaborated more and more with composer Nick Britell through post-production on the first season, it became obvious that the song suggestions I'd initially included were redundant. Often, they were far too direct or arch, and his score worked much better than 'needle-drop' moments. The sole surviving one is at the end of episode six – 'Which Side Are You On?' – which I'd imagined for so long for that moment that I couldn't quite let it go.

EXT. LOGAN'S APARTMENT BUILDING – DAY

Cold. The cabs and traffic pass Kendall by. His car and Fikret are there. Collars up. Onwards!

EXT. CENTRAL PARK – DAY

Close-up on Greg's Oxfords. They're a little big, the shoes slip and slide a little as he walks through the park to work. Greg bends down to tie one tighter.

He is doing his thing. He passes another business guy. The big man in the city! He walks with more confidence.

The next guys he spots are . . . on a bench—

Stewy and Sandy sitting together and chatting discreetly. A way off, Sandy's driver, keeping an eye on them a discreet distance back.

Greg clocks them – smiles at Stewy. He recognizes someone in New York City!

But Stewy doesn't see. He's deep in conspiratorial conversation . . .

Episode Four

SAD SACK WASP TRAP

Written by Anna Jordan
Directed by Adam Arkin

Original air date 24 June 2018

Cast

LOGAN ROY	Brian Cox
KENDALL ROY	Jeremy Strong
MARCIA ROY	Hiam Abbass
GREG HIRSCH	Nicholas Braun
SHIV ROY	Sarah Snook
ROMAN ROY	Kieran Culkin
CONNOR ROY	Alan Ruck
TOM WAMBSGANS	Matthew Macfadyen
FRANK VERNON	Peter Friedman
COLIN STILES	Scott Nicholson
GRACE O'HARE	Molly Griggs
SARAH	Katie Lee Hill
GERRI KELLMAN	J. Smith-Cameron
JOYCE MILLER	Eisa Davis
DANIEL MILLER	Jason Butler Harner
JAI	Nikki Massoud
KAROLINA NOVOTNEY	Dagmara Dominczyk
STEWY HOSSEINI	Arian Moayed
DOCTOR TROY JUDITH	John Rue
WILLA FERREYRA	Justine Lupe
EVA	Judy Reyes
JESS JORDAN	Juliana Canfield
JOAN	Lynne McCollough
KARL MULLER	David Rasche
LUCY	Christine Spang
ROLAND	Michael Crane
KAREN	Phoenix Carnevale
ANNA NEWMAN	Annika Boras
MARK RAVENHEAD	Zack Robidas
STEPHANIE	Susan Blackwell
ELEVATOR GUY	Omar Soriano
TELEPROMPTER OPERATOR	Vin Knight
ERIN	Zoe Chao
BILL	Mark Blum
KELLY	Bebe Browning
WAITRESS	Pearl Rhein

WAITER	Peter Evangelista
DANCER	Lloyd Boyd
JEANE	Peggy J. Scott
DANCE TROUPE 1	Charisma Glasper
DANCE TROUPE 2	Kassandra Cruz
DANCE TROUPE 3	Zoe Hollinshead
DANCE TROUPE 4	Ehizoje Azeke
DANCE TROUPE 5	Gabriel Hyman

DAY ONE

INT. ROY PRIVATE JET – BEDROOM – EARLY MORNING

Handel's Water Music *plays over the following:*

Kendall's POV on waking: plush interior, crisp cotton of the bedsheets.

A face comes into focus – the smile of a stewardess with coffee and juice.

Kendall sits up, smells the coffee. He's on a plane. He raises the blind to reveal the fluffy clouds. Life is good for a young CEO. Scribbles a note on a piece of paper.

EXT. ROY PRIVATE JET – EARLY MORNING

The jet cuts through the clouds.

INT. LOGAN'S APARTMENT – STUDY – EARLY MORNING

The music plays on – now filling the room from a Sonos set-up. A six-foot-by-six-foot square has been masking-taped onto the floor.

Marcia watches Logan, walking with a stick, aided by stroke rehabilitation specialist, Joan. There is also a fit young orderly there to help with the physical therapy.

> JOAN
> Okay, that's right – along the edge. Good! That's good!

> LOGAN
> Don't patronize me. Walking's not good. It's fucking normal.

> JOAN
> I'm not, that is good, Mr Logan!

                              LOGAN
          I need a sit-down! Chair!

Joan looks at Marcia. But Marcia is tough—

                             MARCIA
          Come on.
                         (*re the orderly*)
          If you are not well enough for the charity dinner maybe I go
          with this handsome young man?

Logan's reached a corner.

                              JOAN
          Okay and this is trickier, this is the proprioception.

Logan has to sidestep along the next side of the square.

                              LOGAN
                         (*re music*)
          Turn it off! It's like being inside a fucking commercial.

*Marcia coolly takes the Sonos control and stands at the furthest
corner of the square, places it on a stool for Logan to get if he can
walk there.*

INT. ROMAN'S APARTMENT – BATHROOM – EARLY
MORNING

*Roman, in a nice suit, no tie yet, admires his reflection. Mouthwash.
Grace comes in, from her bathroom. She puts her arms around him.
He's suddenly stiff.*

                              GRACE
          You look good.

                             ROMAN
                         (*naturally*)
          Uh-huh. Thank you.

Her hand goes to his crotch.

                             ROMAN
          Gracey? I'm trying to clean my fucking teeth here?

Still physically close.

GRACE

Did any more PRs get back about wearing my new pieces to the ball?

ROMAN

I don't know. They're not my fucking private army of little dollies I get to dress. I'll chase, okay?

He looks at her. Is she looking a bit put out?

This is why it doesn't work when you stay over. There are five bathrooms. Why are you in this one? And now I want to fart and I'm not, I'm physically not farting because you're here? I'm feeling kind of oppressed?

She leaves.

EXT. AIRPORT — EARLY MORNING

Kendall heads down the stairs of the Roy private jet towards a waiting car.

INT. ROMAN'S APARTMENT — BATHROOM — EARLY MORNING

Roman locks the door. That touch has got him turned on. He unbuttons and prepares to beat off. Flicks on a picture on his phone. A picture . . . of Grace, a sexy selfie she sent him once. But then, up pops—

A text alert. He reads it. Intriguing.

INT. SHIV AND TOM'S APARTMENT — KITCHEN — EARLY MORNING

Shiv and Tom, in their kitchen. TV on rolling news. Both looking at their iPads and phones and eating.

SHIV

So, I'm going to speak to Connor to confirm table arrangements? We're hosting basically the same table as last year plus Joyce and Daniel, that okay?

> TOM

I didn't go last year, Shiv?

> SHIV

Yeah you did. Remember? Racist Belgian GS guy and his wife who tried to kill herself?

> TOM

Shiv? I *think* I'd remember our first Roy Endowment Creative New York Ball together! I was crunching parks numbers like gravel granola?

> SHIV

Yeah?

> TOM

Honey, growing up I used to look at the pictures of the RECNY in Mom's old *Vanity Fairs*?

> SHIV

Uh-huh?

> TOM

And now – a little boy from St Paul is going. With the most beautiful gal in the world!

Shiv smiles – lovely. Ding.

> SHIV
> (*interrupting*)

Ugh. Fuck.

> TOM

What is it?

> SHIV

It's happened.
> (*dialling*)

It's the inevitable asshole.
> (*connecting*)

Okay, where did you get it?

Intercut with:

INT. ROMAN'S CAR – EARLY MORNING*

Roman's got an iPad with an email open and the image on there.

> ROMAN
> It's quite a haunting image, isn't it? The eye almost seems to follow you around the room?

> SHIV
> What is this?

> ROMAN
> You know your future senator? Apparently, this is her husband's asshole.

> SHIV
> What? Fuck off. Can you prove that? How will you prove that? Do assholes have fingerprints?

> ROMAN
> He posted it himself. With the words, 'Check out my asshole.' On a website called Filthy Rich. For married people who want to fuck around.

> SHIV
> Has everyone got it?

> ROMAN
> Um – just us I believe right now. Leak to ATN. My pal thought I'd be intrigued.

> SHIV
> Okay, well, bring it on.

> ROMAN
> Umm feisty!

> SHIV
> They're not going to run with it?

---

* This is where we ended up hitting the Joyce–Daniel–Shiv political scandal story, rather than including in episode three. Located here, it played more through a Roy family prism.

> ROMAN
Way below my level, Shiv.
> (*then*)
But my guess is, why not, a little? It's dirty, it's weird. And
it's evidence of precisely the sort of disgusting liberal metro
butt-love that makes our viewership angry enough to buy
pharmaceuticals.

> SHIV
It's not even a story, Roman. Her *husband*? That's— It's unfair.

> ROMAN
Oh it's worse than that, Shiv, I'd say, it's – it's – malicious.

> SHIV
Days from a special election? I mean, we're ahead but this
could – this could have an effect.

> ROMAN
Uh-huh. Would you actually say, it's like we're 'partisan
surrogates subverting the democractic process which underpins
our whole way of life'.

> SHIV
Okay, well thanks for the heads-up and fuck you very much.

> ROMAN
> (*cheerfully*)
Yeah, well, I hate to be the bearer of bad news!

Shiv starts to type a text. Sends—

INT. JOYCE AND DANIEL'S HOUSE – KITCHEN – EARLY
MORNING

*Joyce and Daniel are having breakfast. Their eleven-year-old daughter
is eating pancakes.*

Her phone dings – incoming text.

His phone dings. Then buzzes. He cancels.

Her phone dings again.

His phone dings then again.

He looks at her. She's read Shiv's text. The dings suddenly become incessant.

Soon they are both beeping and dinging and then the home phone goes.

She looks at him. A little nod. He realizes what's happened – the story's broken.

At the kitchen table he puts his head in his hands.

This is the last breakfast like this for a very long time. He looks at Joyce. Their daughter. She looks at him: We should talk.

They head into the hallway. We stay on the child, the voices are muffled and low outside.

INT. ATN – NEWSROOM CONTROL ROOM – MORNING

A studio director, vision mixer and journalist in the background. Meanwhile, news editor, Roland, is talking to Eva, the Head of Network.

ROLAND
What do we call it? 'An intimate body part'?

EVA
Sounds like his dick?

ROLAND
Or just – 'his anus'?

EVA
'Anus' – at breakfast? That's a juice-dropper. Lot of people gonna spill a lot of OJ.

ROLAND
'A very private part of his body'?

EVA
Makes it sound like he has an internal VIP area.
            (*looking at monitor, re anchor*)
She needs to get more sleep.
                  (*to anchor*)
You sleeping okay, Karen? Yeah? You sleeping on your face? I'm kidding you look great.

> MARK
> (*over comms*)

How do I look?

> EVA
> (*not unfriendly*)

F-I-E. Fuckable in an emergency, Mark.

INT. KENDALL'S CAR – DAY

Kendall looks between paperwork and the screen in front of him.
He's on the phone. In between his call with Rava we catch key words
from the ATN News report running—

> KENDALL

Hey, Rava? Did you make a decision yet?
> (*listens*)

Well, no it's not CEO arm-meat. Rava, this is a big night for me.
I'm making Dad's Wasp Trap speech.
> (*listens*)

Fine. I just kind of assumed your 'hopefully' was a yes.
> (*curt*)

Yes you said 'hopefully'. I remember—
> (*listens*)

I'm not trying to be anything. I know you, 'hopefully' implied a
yes, you know what a big deal this is for the family but if you've
changed your mind that's cool just don't try to tell me . . .

> KAREN
> (*on TV*)

Just days before New York special senate election, Joyce
Miller, the hotly tipped Democratic candidate, is red-faced this
morning after the hack on blue-chip-affair website FilthyRich-
dot-com. Not only was Miller's husband apparently hunting
for extramarital liaisons online, it appears he went on to share
photos of a *very intimate body part*. Now it's seven-thirty a.m.,
Anna joins us with her Wall Street Breakdown.

Rava's hung up.

> KENDALL
> (*to himself*)

Ugh.

He looks at the TV. Anna Newman smiles. Kendall likes her.

> ANNA
> *(on TV)*
> Thanks, Karen. Yesterday's market continued to move into
> positive territory. The S&P technology index led the way higher,
> up two-point-five-five percent. The index notched its best day
> in six months and is up nearly twenty percent on the year. The
> S&P 500 is having a harder time of it but still remains up seven
> percent on the year. Adding to positive sentiment was second-
> quarter GDP numbers that showed the US economy maintained
> a brisk pace of growth, at a two-point-eight percent annual rate,
> despite concern over a dip in the construction sector.

INT. SHIV'S KITCHEN – DAY

Shiv is on the phone to Connor.

> SHIV
> Connor, I'm just wondering if we should slide Joyce and Daniel
> and me off our table, and out of the front row, and the heat?

Intercut with:

INT. RECNY BALL LOCATION – DAY

Connor is in the middle of a huge hall.

> CONNOR
> Well if I move Joyce plus two that's a huge hole at table three.
> Right in the Chairman's Golden Circle. Do you want a gaping
> hole there? It's like having the front teeth knocked out of
> Waystar?

> SHIV
> And she's coming through the service entrance.

> CONNOR
> Can you put this in an email?

> SHIV
> Can you write it down? I'm sorry, it's a crisis day.

CONNOR

Yeah well I haven't finalized the name for the signature cocktails, so I know how you feel!

SHIV

Right and I don't know if she's bringing Daniel or— That seat's in limbo. That's a limbo seat, okay? I'll confirm closer to the time.

CONNOR

It's tomorrow, Shiv? You're murdering me right now, you know that?

SHIV

Listen, thanks for jumping on this whole thing. With Marcia busy with Dad.

CONNOR

Well that's very kind of you to say. And it's cool. No sweat whatsoever.

As they finish the call, the event planner, Stephanie, is there with a folder.

CONNOR

God help us! Right, Stephanie! What genius event planning are you going to dazzle me with today?

STEPHANIE

Okay, well I wanted to show you, this is how I would generally display the seating plan?

She has some copies of a previous room layout—

CONNOR

Uh-huh. Good. No, I don't like that at all.

STEPHANIE

Right? And this would be how we'll set up for the step-and-repeat?

CONNOR

Yes, we'll need to revisit all this. It doesn't work for me. Nope.
(*then, sighs*)
You know what Napoleon called Marshal Ney, Stephanie?

      STEPHANIE
No.

      CONNOR
    (addressing the guys wheeling chairs)
'The bravest of the brave'. The bravest of the brave. That's what
we have to be here, people!

INT. WAYSTAR – DAY

Kendall strides in from the elevator.

*An assistant is there with his coffee. Jess also meets him as he heads
into his office—*

      JESS
How was LA?

      KENDALL
Great. They're all fucking nuts, but great. Can you get on to
Lance about my speech? Can we get one of the late-night guys
to cook me up a bit?

      JESS
A bit?

      KENDALL
A selection of jokes and riffs.

*Gerri is nearby. Joins him as they head into Kendall's office. Gerri's
tone is different. Air of distance and professionalism.*

      GERRI
You're going to do a joke?

      KENDALL
What does that mean? I was fucking king of the *Lampoon*.
Kicked their distribution into shape too.

*Kendall looks at her and, as he does so, his eyes flick to his dad's
office – across the way.*

*He can make out bodies – movement in there. Kendall is alive to it
immediately.*

      JESS
Kendall, I've pushed everything this morning because—

> KENDALL

Who's that in my dad's suite?

> JESS

Because your dad wants to see you?

Kendall looks at Jess: What the fuck?

I'm guessing you didn't know?

> KENDALL

No, I didn't know. But—

He looks at Gerri – starts making a calculation right away – can he trust her?

Great news. I'm delighted. Right? Did you know?

> GERRI

No but it's great.

> KENDALL

Oh sure. Shouldn't he have told you? Listen, I'll just get straight and go and see the old – fucking—
>   (*what?*)
Goat.

Never said that before . . . Kendall's roll has been bumped. He almost seizes up as he heads into his office and collects himself to go see his dad.

INT. MODEST HOTEL – CORRIDOR – DAY

Joyce is coming through a hotel corridor with her aide, Simonetta, and Erin (campaign manager). Simonetta walks alongside them. It's a long corridor.

> ERIN

Tough morning?

> JOYCE

Yup. Yes.

Erin waits.

A lot of things he told me were the case – about this – now the transcript of the messages has leaked. They were maybe not the case.

ERIN

Uh-huh. Sure. Okay.

JOYCE

What's everyone doing in there?

ERIN

Um, just – basically, strategizing?

INT. MODEST HOTEL – LARGE SUITE – DAY

Inside the hotel room.

The team – Jai, social media manager, and Sarah, Shiv's assistant – are just thumbing through timelines and news reports. Jai and Sarah are sitting close. Shiv looks at her phone—

SHIV

Fuck.

JAI

Ugh. You see—?

Jai passes Shiv an iPad. Sarah is looking at something else.

SARAH

Oh. Urgh.

SHIV

You've seen the annotated transcript?

JAI

It's not a transcript it's a chat log. Date stamp. IP address. Not much wiggle room.

SARAH

Urrghh.

The door opens and everyone springs up. Joyce walks in, led by Erin, followed by Simonetta. Silence. Smiles.

SHIV

Hey!

JOYCE

Uh-huh.

Tight smiles all round. Silence.

JAI

He's let you down, Joyce. He's a dog. He's filth. He's scum and
I wish he was dead.

JOYCE

He'd actually like to come in later and say sorry to everyone?

No one knows what to say for a moment.

JAI

Okay. Well, that would be nice?

Everyone shares a look.

JOYCE

Shiv? Shall we?

*Shiv and Joyce huddle up in semi-private with Erin and Sarah. As the
rest of the team busy themselves with scrolling.*

SHIV

So, we need to issue a statement and as planned just move the
conversation back to your issues.

JOYCE

I want to get into this. Why I'm getting this crap.

Shiv and Erin look at each other: No.

ERIN

Sure, but just tracking the cycle for this, what people will be
asking is: It's an ass pic, is he gay?

Joyce moans slightly.

JOYCE

He's not gay.

They look at her, more please.

The full chat I think proves right, that, that he probably likes—

SHIV

This is just for background.

                        JOYCE
He likes a finger up his – anus and that's why he posted—

                        SHIV
A straight finger – a hetero finger?

                        JOYCE
Yes.

                        SHIV
Nothing else?

                        JOYCE
What do you mean—?

                        SHIV
Anything else? In terms of what went up there? Any surprises?
Because first it's a finger, then it's a fist, then it's a dildo shaped
like Richard Nixon?

                        JOYCE
Fuck this. A man wouldn't get this. Let's say that? Why can't
I say that? A straight white man's wife does this, does he get
hurt?

                        SHIV
Agreed. But for us, now, this isn't going away. I think you need
to talk to your husband.

                        JOYCE
It isn't going away because ATN won't let it go away. So maybe
you should talk to your father?

A stand-off.

INT. WAYSTAR – DAY

*We're on Kendall's shoulder as he walks, his ears fizzing. Out of his
office and round past the nearby desks.*

He smiles tightly at the assistants and execs he passes.

INT. WAYSTAR – OUTSIDE LOGAN'S OFFICE – DAY

Kendall strides through. Lucy stands, Jeane doesn't.

Kendall can see Logan's baseball cap. It grabs his attention.

INT. WAYSTAR – LOGAN'S OFFICE – DAY

Kendall heads in, he's planning to try to carry this lightly. Logan, looking smart, sits at his desk, on a call. Logan has ATN on.

> LOGAN
> I don't like 'intimate body part'.
> > *(listens)*
> Uh-huh. Your call, Eva. She tried to regulate every fucking sector in New York as AG, turns out she can't regulate her own husband. If we don't call out this frigid little – phony who will?

> KENDALL
> Hey, Dad! What's all this?

Logan gestures Kendall to sit as he ends his call. He hangs up. Looks at Kendall.

Kendall goes round to – what – to make contact, it's not easy. His dad is immobile and he doesn't know what to do, kiss, hug or pat—

> KENDALL
> *(cont'd)*
> I didn't know you were coming in? Did Gerri?

> LOGAN
> Do I need permission?

> KENDALL
> Hey, screw you! You okay?

Logan has post-stroke problems.

> Are you well enough to be in? Did you use the chair?

> LOGAN
> *(vague)*
> Chair?

> KENDALL
> The wheelchair, Dad.

Logan grunts, points. The wheelchair is there in the corner.

> LOGAN

Just making sure you weren't selling any more of the company from under me.

> KENDALL

Oh, you wanna get into that?

Nothing back.

You put a hole in us by taking on a shitload of debt, Pop?

Is Logan on it or not? He looks glassy-eyed.

But – look, this is great to see you.

Beat, is Dad okay?

So what's the plan? Do you want to schedule a catch-up every so – often, so you can, you know, keep up to date?

> LOGAN

You're lining up acquisitions, is that right?

> KENDALL

Good. Because, you know, things are cooking. Fucking, brave new world.

> LOGAN

Cuh. Nothing new under the sun.
> (*then*)
I was informed, you're doing my ball speech, is that correct?

> KENDALL

I was told you suggested it?

> LOGAN

Yeah I was told the mailman's prick tasted of toffee apple, but I didn't believe him.

> KENDALL

What, you don't want me to—

> LOGAN

Good luck to you. The Sad Sack Wasp Trap. One time a year anyone fucking likes us. Knock yourself out.

> KENDALL

You'll be missed. We'll raise a glass. You sure you're okay? Why don't you get a briefing and head home? Yeah?

> LOGAN

Uh-huh.

With a pat on his dad's shoulder, Kendall heads out. Gerri is there outside.

> LOGAN
> (*cont'd, calls out*)

Gerri?!

Gerri smiles at Kendall. Kendall winks at her, Gerri smiles but doesn't wink back.

INT. WAYSTAR – OUTSIDE LOGAN'S OFFICE – DAY

Kendall heads out. Lucy and Jeane exchange a look. Jeane's phone rings. It's Logan.

> LOGAN
> (*off*)

I need to take a leak. Where's the guy?

INT. WAYSTAR – DAY

Logan is wheeled by a medical orderly. Lucy is at his side.

> LUCY

You should have got the private bathroom put in.

> LOGAN

Waste of money. And close the blinds in there. I'm not a fucking zoo animal to be watched.

INT. WAYSTAR – DAY

As Kendall looks across towards Logan's office.

> KENDALL
> (*on phone*)

So. Dad's back.

Intercut with:

INT. WAYSTAR – ELEVATOR/BULLPEN/ROMAN'S OFFICE –
DAY

*Roman is on the phone, in the elevator, then walking in to the office,
greeted by an assistant.*

> ROMAN
>
> Back where, what? Back in the chair?

> KENDALL
>
> Back to check in. I hope he's okay. It's fast, right? But good.

> ROMAN
>
> 'Good'? You'd love it if his brain fell out the back of his head!

> KENDALL
>
> Roman, Jesus, man, no. I'm just scared in case he—

> ROMAN
>
> You're scared in case he's going to push you out and your plans
> for you – know, Uber for news, Facebook for cats? Fucking
> open-plan office you on a dance platform jerking off idea gloop
> into – 'think boxes'—

*Roman walks into his office and there is – Frank. WTF. He has his
feet up on the coffee table, reading a report.*

> ROMAN
> *(cont'd)*
>
> Got to go.

He hangs up and puts his phone away.

> FRANK
>
> Roman.

> ROMAN
>
> Frank?

> FRANK
>
> Good morning.

> ROMAN
>
> Well correction – it's not a good morning from my POV because
> you're here, and I hate you.

> FRANK

Oh, come on, kid.

> ROMAN

What the fuck is going on?

> FRANK

Your dad asked me to come back.

> ROMAN

The fucking, the – the Weasel Prevails.
> (*'witty'*)
That would be a good name for your autobiography – if they did books by, jerks.

> FRANK

So I've come back.

> ROMAN

You're pathetic.

> FRANK

He apologized.

> ROMAN

Sure, man. He didn't apologize when he hit our au pair with a car.

> FRANK

He wants me to show you the ropes.

> ROMAN

It was her fault, for being too short he said.

INT. WAYSTAR – ADVENTURE-PARKS FLOOR – DUSK

Tom and Greg watch Tom's predecessor, Bill, make his way through the office, being warmly greeted by ex-colleagues. He is getting clapped and the tables are being banged. Tom commentates.

> TOM

And here he comes. Bill. 'The Best Boss That Ever Lived'. It's like Mandela fucked Santa and he gave birth to *Bill*.

> GREG

Have you heard about Logan? He came in apparently.

> TOM
> (*no*)
> Uh-huh, I knew, but I couldn't say.
> (*in Bill's direction*)
> Come on, you genial old shitbag, get in here already, before it's time for *me* to retire.

Bill finally arrives.

> BILL
> Tom. Sorry about all that.

> TOM
> No problem, Bill! I just hope I can eventually inspire similar affection.

They head into a meeting room.

> This is Greg. New guy I took under my wing when I started—

> GREG
> I'm actually—

> TOM
> He doesn't need your life story, Greg.

> BILL
> So, thanks for everything. But listen, before I do the final photo. There's a thing I need to mention. Just us.

Greg looks at Tom, asking to stay. Tom looks at Bill, thinking – 'What the fuck is this about?'

INT. WAYSTAR – ADVENTURE-PARKS FLOOR – TOM'S OFFICE – DUSK

Bill closes the door on Greg, then cracks open a laptop and clicks and types.

> BILL
> So. Look, I've turned off the Wi-Fi, and this is air-gapped. I'm creating a Word document for you, and then I'm going to print it because I don't want anything in my handwriting.

TOM

I think *someone's* been watching a few too many spy movies since they retired, eh, Bill?

BILL

Hahahaha! Yeah! Maybe!

Tom stands behind Bill to look at the screen.

This is the number of a set of storage files in the depository. And they're— The subject is— It's something, that— It's not a big deal. But it – it just needs to be handled. And you're in the family.

(*points*)

So, this – is the name of the legal office that is the intermediary? This is the person outside the firm we used as a firewall to deal with blowback on NDAs?

Tom tries not to look rattled.

TOM

Uh-huh?

BILL

It's *not* a big deal, Tom.

TOM

Right. But – what is it Bill?

BILL

Okay. Look, you've got two viable options. I can tell you everything, and that's fine. Or, I can not tell you. And you can not know – and you stay clean out of the – death pit. And that's fine too.

TOM

Uh-huh?

BILL

So, the nice news is, both ways, everything's fine? Just keep the nuclear rods cool, and nothing's going to blow.

TOM

Well that's – that's a really reassuring image, Bill.

A knock at the door – a staffer, Kelly, comes in.

KELLY

Photographer's ready . . .

BILL

Terrific! Thanks, Kelly!

Bill's all smiles, up. Leaving Tom anxious.

INT. WAYSTAR – KENDALL'S OFFICE – DUSK

Roman comes in. Kendall's looking over documents, thinking.

ROMAN

Okay. You need to tell Dad to back the fuck off.

KENDALL

Hello? Did we have something scheduled?

ROMAN

He's rehired Frank to babysit me and I don't need a babysitter! Especially one I don't get to fuck.

KENDALL

Seriously? Frank?

ROMAN

Yeah. I mean, you're CEO, can he even do that?

KENDALL

It's, I don't— It's a question.

ROMAN

You need to tell him to butt out. We're running the show. Go back to bed, eat some soup. Get better.

Kendall thinks.

KENDALL

Look. Relax. The dinosaur's having one last roar at the meteor before it wipes him out. It's, expected.

ROMAN

And what do I do with Frank?

KENDALL

I'll talk to Frank.
                    (*needs him on-side*)
But, look, you're doing a great job.

ROMAN

Thank you. Thank you. That's good to hear. Because it's a big job.

KENDALL

I know it, bro. Tell me about it.

ROMAN

If you want I could help you – we could tag-team it on Dad's speech – at the Sad Sack Wasp Trap?

KENDALL
(*no way*)

Um, I guess, I mean it is a CEO thing, so, I think maybe, I mean I have a whole thing prepared, with jokes and so—

ROMAN

You're doing a joke?

Kendall looks at him.

Fine. Who you taking?

KENDALL

No one. Rava's busy.

ROMAN
(*translating*)

Doesn't want to.

KENDALL

So, I'll probably— Maybe I'll fly solo?

ROMAN

What? How does that look? CEO can't get an ugly sister to go to the ball?

KENDALL

Sure. I'll take something. A head on a stick. A cauliflower with lipstick.
(*then*)
I mean know who I'd like to take? Anna Newman. From ATN?

ROMAN

Oh yeah, I'd fuck that in a minute. Ask her.

KENDALL

Not cool. I'm her boss.

ROMAN

What a pathetic beta-cuck.
(mocking impression)
'Would it be "cool"? Cos I got something secret in my pants, would it be okay to show please, or is that a trigger-warning, baby?'

KENDALL

You're a walking fucking lawsuit.

ROMAN

No. I'm honest, I'm just like, 'Yeah I like your face, can I come on your face?' which is why I am drowning in pussy and you're not even fucking your wife. I'm sorry. Them's the facts.

INT. WAYSTAR – ADVENTURE-PARKS FLOOR – TOM'S OFFICE – DUSK

Tom sits on the floor of his office, shirtsleeves rolled up, papers laid out. He's reading fast, looking ill and sweaty. There's a knock on the locked door.

TOM

No thank you please leave me alone thank you!

DAY TWO

INT. ATN OFFICE – DAY

Shiv is in with Eva. Eva doesn't want to be there, but it's Logan's fucking daughter . . .

SHIV

So. Look, I want you to call off your dogs.

EVA

Uh-huh.

SHIV

Because this obsession with Joyce – it's out of line. It's sitting very high in your half-hour.

                              EVA
Uh-huh?

                              SHIV
And it's vindictive and it's – it's actually it's bad for democracy.

                              EVA
Uh-huh.

                              SHIV
So?

Shiv waits for a response: Are you going to engage? They stay silent.
Who's going to speak first?

Are you going to respond?

                              EVA
I think it's important to remember that I'm not the one taking
pictures of my asshole here.

                              SHIV
Are you running this because you think my dad likes this shit?

                              EVA
                        (*with a twinkle*)
Oh he doesn't put that kind of pressure on his people.

                              SHIV
Look. Okay. We are where we are. If I could get you some nasty
little tidbits on other folks I know, could you ramp this down?

                              EVA
We're not the only ones running this. It's a hugely popular story.

                              SHIV
But you're leading it, Eva. You had a ten-minute sexpert segment
on how to keep your man happy in bed, on a *news channel*?

                              EVA
Okay. You've said your piece and I've listened so—

                              SHIV
No. I'm saying, as her strategist, this level of attack starts to
reflect on your professional judgment and you should think
about the future because this is the old world and things will
change – in the world, one day.

A threat.

> EVA
>
> You know I wouldn't let any other strategist in the building let alone in my office?

> SHIV
>
> Well, I'm very grateful.

> EVA
>
> So when we're talking professional judgment? Good to bear in mind that only you're here because your name matches the one carved on the building?

Shiv feels diminished.

INT. LOGAN'S APARTMENT – STUDY – DAY

Morning. Logan's working out, walking the box.

> LOGAN
> *(to Joan)*
> So, you've done this for a few old—
> *(loses the word)*
> vegetables?

> JOAN
>
> And we step along, good—

> LOGAN
> *(testing her)*
> Did you do Ollie Sirrett? After his?

> JOAN
>
> I don't really discuss that sort of thing.

She passed his test. She's seen it all.

> LOGAN
>
> Uh-huh. And how many of us go back to normal?

> JOAN
>
> I like to think I can get you better and better every day.

> LOGAN
>
> Bullshit.

                                            (then)
                        Here's a question. One to keep—
                                    (where's the word? best he can do—)
                        lock.
                                    (a real worry, made light)
                        Can they test me? Can they, get a doctor in to see if I'm—

                                        JOAN
                        Impaired?

                                        LOGAN
                        A sad case. Have you heard of that?

                                        JOAN
                        I'm a rehabilitation specialist, Mr Roy. Not a lawyer.

Logan scowls and redoubles his efforts.

Karolina arrives with a review of the day's media for him.

                                        LOGAN
                        Morning? Personal first, then – the corporal.

                                      KAROLINA
                        Corporate?

He nods: That's what I said.

                        Um. Okay. Well, personal, nothing much. Pre-ball piece. We got
                        profiles of endowment recipients and that's all great? And one
                        little piece on your health. But I don't think you (need to hear)—

                                        LOGAN
                        Say!

She knows he won't like this.

                                      KAROLINA
                        'Kendall Roy will give the traditional address at the RECNY
                        charity ball tonight in a sign that even after recovery from
                        his stroke Logan Roy is intending to wind down from public
                        duties.'

                                        LOGAN
                        Where did they get that? Who gave them that?

                                      KAROLINA
                        I don't know.

> LOGAN

Well here's an idea: Find out, or find some other prick to pay
you a million a fucking year.

INT. LOGAN'S CAR – DAY

*Connor and Logan ride together. Colin up front. Logan is still
stewing.*

> CONNOR

Handling the ball, it's just not a big deal for me, that's the thing
that's so nice.

> (*it's a huge deal*)

It is not a big deal.

> LOGAN

Winding down. Winding fucking down? I'm winding up!

> CONNOR

I had six hundred quail that were not sourced to my liking and
I just had to make the call?

> LOGAN

Uh-huh?

> CONNOR

So I just did it. I trashed six hundred quail. No biggie. Sourced
six hundred others. Done.

> LOGAN

Uh-huh.

> CONNOR

It's just funny. Being in charge? Y'know when I think, how –
years ago, I'd be at the table between you and Mom? And we'd
look down and there'd be the mayor – and all the names of old
New York and you'd whisper, in my ear – 'that Astor used to be
that and he ran this, till he snafued that and he's porking her,
she's a slut and' – it was just a – very lovely time.

> LOGAN

Your mom loved all that. Fucking Wasp Trap.

> CONNOR

What I was actually wondering about the Foundation, since I'm doing all this organizing, is would it be a good way in for me?

> LOGAN

To?

> CONNOR

To national affairs? Like maybe in your absence. I could do the speech – not Kendall?

> LOGAN

I've jerked him around enough.

> CONNOR

Or. Maybe— What would you think if I took over a little on the Foundation? Could we pivot it away from sick kids and contemporary dance towards tax reform and the abolition of the US postal service?

> LOGAN

Uh-huh?

> CONNOR

You know, to be frank, everyone's dancing anyway, and a lot of charities cater for – sad sacks – and god knows I love them – but what about lending a hand to stimulate free enterprise.

They pull up outside Waystar. An orderly and a wheelchair. Connor leans over and pats Logan's arm. Colin opens the door and checks Logan is ready to go.

INT. WAYSTAR – DAY

A senior management meeting is breaking up. Karl and Frank are there. As people head out, Jess is there to brief Kendall.

> JESS

Stewy is here – I've got him South Tank in case you want to keep it on the DL . . .?

Kendall nods to Jess – but he's got an eye out, he wants to catch Frank. As he passes, catches his eye—

> KENDALL

Hey? So, why, Frank?

They round – a private conversation.

FRANK
(doesn't want to talk about it)
Oh, what no biggie. Why'd I come back? Thirty years he's
probably fired me forty times.

KENDALL
(bullshit)
He never wrote the press release before?

FRANK
I don't know. Big house, Ken. Big mower. Mower needs gas.

KENDALL
Money? Any fuckhead can turn a few million a year, Frank.

Okay. Frank owes him this.

FRANK
(whispers)
Look. Here's where I ended up. I could be humiliated in public –
fired – or I could be humiliated in private and come back.
I should have told him to fuck off but it's my life. I'm kind of
invested in the narrative?

Tom is looking to get in. Coughs. Kendall is eager to move on—

TOM
Kendall, I wondered if I could grab five—

*He'd really rather not. As they walk, Kendall is thinking about three
other things.*

KENDALL
Uh-huh?

TOM
Yeah it's something – something you don't know about and you
maybe probably don't want to know about?

*Something goes off in Kendall's brain. Parks. Cruises. Best not to
dig . . . After a beat he gives Tom some advice.*

KENDALL

You know what my dad used to say? He'd say he loved all his employees. But he particularly loved the guys who ate the shit for him and he never even knew it?

TOM

Got it. Then excuse me while I get myself a knife, a fork and a side salad.

Kendall smiles at Tom: Fuck off.

INT. WAYSTAR – DAY

Kendall arrives to greet Stewy. Acting calm and in control.

STEWY

Hey, man! So I heard your dad was back in?

Kendall tries not to look rattled.

KENDALL

Yup, he made it in. Which we were all delighted about—

STEWY

And what's the story?

KENDALL

No he's great. Likes to remind us he's still alive! Great to get his take. But he needs *a lot of rest.*

Just then, Logan opens the door, on his feet.

Dad? Hey. Just talking about you.

LOGAN

Uh-huh?

Stewy stands and extends his hand.

STEWY

Mr Roy. Logan. It's great to see you.

Logan stares at him, then Kendall.

LOGAN

So you're the little guy who owns such a big chunk of me?

> STEWY

Hahahaha.

> LOGAN

Excuse me barging in. Just, Gerri told me you have a meet with Opalite Data later? Just to say, I like it, buy it. Okay, Ken?

> KENDALL

Okay? Good thought. I'll come find you and we can discuss.

Frisson in the air. Stewy looks at his shoes.

> LOGAN

Sure. But if I don't see you. I want it.

> KENDALL

Okay. It's not necessarily the best option in the sector (so we can discuss)—

> LOGAN

I want us into data mining. Buy it.

They're both intensely aware of Stewy.

> KENDALL

Dad, it's a really flooded sector. Lot of hustlers. Lots of bullshit. It's a gold rush.

> LOGAN

Yeah. And who wants gold?
> (*beat*)
Make them an offer they get excited about. Make them an offer they tell their wives about that night.

> KENDALL

Great outdated sexism, Dad, but I'm sure you're all over the data mining.

Logan zones out a little. Collects his thoughts for a beat.

> LOGAN
> (*mumbled*)
Matched with an aged wife.

Is it a joke? Stewy smiles, indulgent.

> KENDALL
>
> You okay. Dad, should I get someone? You shouldn't be here, you know.

> LOGAN
>
> Fine. I just . . . need a piss.

Slight cringe in the room at Logan's oversharing.

> KENDALL
>
> Great, well thanks for sharing, old guy!

Logan leaves, feeling humiliated. Kendall smiles apologetically at Stewy.

> Still recovering.

> STEWY
>
> And like technically – without being too reductive, Ken, like, who is in charge, right now?

> KENDALL
>
> Me. I am. Legally and effectively.

INT. WAYSTAR – CORRIDOR – DAY

Logan hurries down the corridor. Ignores the chair. Uses the wall to steady himself. But instead of going all the way to the bathroom he stops at Kendall's office.

Nods to the assistant and enters.

INT. WAYSTAR – KENDALL'S OFFICE – DAY

The blinds are down. He makes it to the corner.

What's he doing? Bending and releasing pressure, and then – fumbling for a zip.

Logan undoes his fly.

And in the corner of the room . . . he pisses over Kendall's floor.

INT. WAYSTAR – ADVENTURE-PARKS FLOOR – OUTSIDE
TOM'S OFFICE – DAY

*Greg has a spot at a desk within sight of Tom's door. Tom is emerging
from a meeting with his private attorney.*

> TOM
> Okay. Thank you, Rick. Thanks for that. Really useful.

*Greg smiles. Tom looks like: Fuck off. Then, thinks, nods for Greg to
come in.*

INT. WAYSTAR – ADVENTURE-PARKS FLOOR – TOM'S
OFFICE – DAY

Tom is closing the door.

> TOM
> So listen, Greg. It seems I have been exposed to a virus.

> GREG
> Oh, right?

> TOM
> It's a deadly virus. And now I'm fucked, forever.

> GREG
> That sounds – bad?

> TOM
> It is bad. And I kind of need to share it – but anyone I talk to,
> I effectively kill.

He opens a file and shows Greg.

> That's the death pit, Greg. Take a look.

> GREG
> Right, I just don't know if I'll like it in the, the death pit?

Tom points, making Greg look at the file.

> TOM
> You're family.

> GREG
> (*reads for a beat*)
> It's – complicated?

TOM

Kind of. But not really. For a number of years, there was an unofficial company policy on our cruise lines that if a serious criminal incident took place we would, if possible, sail not home, but to a Caribbean or South American port where there were, so to speak, 'friendly authorities' and we could minimize the incident to avoid negative PR.

GREG

Incidents like—?

TOM

Theft, sexual assault, rape, murder.

GREG

Uh-huh. The bad ones.

TOM

There's hundreds here. Head of cruises himself, Lester used to go on 'entertainment tours' meeting the dancers and extending the contracts of the ones who'd suck him off. Everyone we could we paid off. But there's emails, there's correspondence. This could all blow. Who knows if the NDAs will hold — it's a time bomb.

GREG

So what are you going to do?

TOM

I don't know! And anyone I ask for advice, I make complicit. Because if you know about this, you should tell! But you can't! Or you spread the virus!

INT. WAYSTAR — DAY

Logan returns to Kendall and Stewy.

LOGAN

Okay, Ken. Why don't you grab the Opalite Data material and we can take a view?

KENDALL

Well as I explained, Dad, I think they're kind of snake oil salesmen. They're the people who – you buy a refrigerator and their algorithm is sending you thirty ads for more fridges? Great algo!

LOGAN

Yeah well, you're the business genius who sold me out to this
fucker, so I'd love Stewart's thoughts.

KENDALL

I'll get Jess to—

LOGAN

It's thirty fucking seconds' walk away, son?

*Kendall hesitates, but knows a disagreement would look bad. He
leaves. Logan smiles.*

INT. WAYSTAR – KENDALL'S OFFICE – DAY

Kendall walks into his office.

Something weird. He looks around.

What is it? A smell or – something?

KENDALL

Jess? Has anyone—?

She comes to the door.

He goes over to the corner – a wet patch.

JESS

Your dad popped in for like two minutes?

Kendall looks up to the ceiling, no leak.

*He leans down, goes to touch, curious, then as he puts a finger to the
wet patch pulls his hand back – he's come in contact with something
primal and revolting . . .*

KENDALL

What the Jesus fuck!

INT. WAYSTAR – DAY

*Kendall enters, silent, holding on to his incomprehension and rage, on
the verge of saying something.*

LOGAN

So I think we're buying. Good with you, Stewart?

Kendall holds the file out to his dad. Logan doesn't even pretend he wants to see it now. They lock eyes. His dad smiles. Challenges Kendall to say something.

Stewy senses something odd.

Kendall shakes his head, it's not going to be a winning move to start the conversation with Stewy there . . .

> STEWY

You're the boss.

> LOGAN
> (*to Kendall*)

All good?

Kendall wants to throw it in his father's face, but he can't. He puts the file on the table.

And, Stewy, you going to the Sad Sack Wasp Trap tonight?

> KENDALL
> (*off Stewy's look*)

He means the RECNY Ball.

> STEWY

Oh, sure, I'll be there. Will I see you there?

> KENDALL

Nah, I'm afraid—

Logan rises.

> LOGAN

I'll be there.
> (*fuck you*)
I thought I might as well go since I'm paying for it anyway.

INT. WAYSTAR – KENDALL'S OFFICE – DAY

Frank, Roman, Gerri and Kendall are in Kendall's office, looking at the wet patch.

> FRANK

You're sure it was him?

KENDALL

You think a lot of people come in here and take a piss?

GERRI

Maybe someone spilt something?

KENDALL

Yeah maybe the massive fucking ice sculpture I forgot about melted? It's urine.

ROMAN

This isn't a false flag is it? Did you piss on your own floor?

Gerri and Frank exchange looks.

KENDALL

Why the fuck are you looking like that. What if people knew? Gerri, you have to talk to him.

GERRI

What do you want me to say?

ROMAN

Well first, let him know where to go peepee and poopoo.

KENDALL

He came *in*. He was *talking* to Stewy. I mean, what's he going to do next? Start jizzing in my coffee? Take a dump on my iPad?

FRANK

He's still in recovery mode.

KENDALL

If he thinks he's okay to come back, he should talk to you, Gerri, and the nominating committee and set a date, right?

GERRI

Well, technically but I guess it's a gray area because—

KENDALL

He says he's coming tonight.

ROMAN

You're kidding?

FRANK

Okay, well that's a concern, because obviously, with major investors and press on hand?

Frank looks at Gerri.

> KENDALL
>
> What if he freaks out? What if he falls asleep in his soup? What if he starts shouting – racist comments.

> ROMAN
>
> Just another Saturday night, baby.

> KENDALL
>
> We have a fiduciary duty not to let the company look – nuts?

> GERRI
>
> And what did you do, Kendall – when he did this?

> KENDALL
>
> What did I do?

> GERRI
>
> Yeah, how did you respond?

> KENDALL
>
> I – I didn't want to humiliate him.

Everyone sees that Kendall did nothing.

> We need a game plan. Frank? Gerri, you need to tell him, he's sick, he can't run the company. Yeah?

They look at one another.

INT. RECNY BALL LOCATION – DINING AREA – DAY

4 p.m. A lavish-looking Cipriani space with a big screen above a stage area. The crew is setting up the space. Chairs are wheeled. Tables are having their tablecloths steamed. Servers polish a mountain of silverware. Bartenders set up the bar, with high stack of glassware racks on dollies.

At one of the large tables that already has linen, Connor looks at Stephanie, looks at the seating plan.

> CONNOR
>
> I just hope this seating plan holds. If it does, look out Middle East cos I can fix anything!

INT. LOGAN'S APARTMENT – BEDROOM – DAY

Logan is being prepped for the ball. He is half-dressed, braced in a corset. A make-up artist touches up his face. Doctor Troy Judith is with Marcia and Logan.

> DOCTOR TROY JUDITH
> This would be the third shot I've given you in a month?

> MARCIA
> He feels he needs to be there.

> DOCTOR TROY JUDITH
> *(to Logan)*
> You're only meant to have three a year. No wonder you're not sleeping. You're risking long-term nerve damage and—

> LOGAN
> Jab. Not jabber. Shut up and shoot up.

Doctor Judith shakes his head, then opens his briefcase.

INT. ATN STUDIO – DAY

Eva is watching an assistant unroll a delivery of not particularly elegant jewelry. Maybe feathers? Some anchors and correspondents have been called over.

> EVA
> Now this is just a nice offer vis-à-vis the event tonight, if any jewelry at all catches your eye this is all designed by Grace O'Hare, exciting new designer, and it's just a complimentary offer via our PRs to wear anything that works for you to the RECNY Ball tonight. Come on, pick something and let's get going . . .
> *(to one woman)*
> It all suits you. Everything suits you. Just take some.

The presenters finger it unenthusiastically.

INT. SHIV AND TOM'S APARTMENT – BEDROOM – DAY

Tom and Shiv getting ready. He's worried.

TOM

Sweetheart? Can I talk to you for a minute? I could really do
with some advice. Have you got time?

She looks at him, busy, texting on her phone.

SHIV
(*no*)

Uh-huh.

TOM

So, look, I don't want to get you into all this but – well, Bill
told me as part of the handover – where some of the bodies are
buried? But they're not very well-buried bodies. And they're not
really bodies. They're zombies, that might rise up from the dead
at any moment. And kill me.

SHIV

As in—?

TOM

I don't— Maybe you don't want to know?

She does a political shrug. Best not to know . . .

SHIV

Uh-huh?

TOM

But I'm worried if it does comes out – and it's kind of bound
to come out – and it's, while I'm in charge – I'm dead. Because
I know and I'm not doing anything. But if I do do something, I'll
have to, you know, do something?

He looks at Shiv. She returns his gaze.

I'd like to, not carry the can, obviously, but also do the right
thing? Maybe?

SHIV

And what's the right thing?

TOM

What I'm thinking is, as soon as possible, a press conference.
Get everyone in – tell all the top execs and law guys. And we go
public. Outside investigation. Disinfectant of sunlight. Pin the
rap on a tight group of naughty, rotten apples?

> SHIV

Sounds brave.

> TOM

Uh-huh. Right.
> (*then*)

And that's – good?

Her phones goes.

> SHIV

Look, can we circle back? I need to talk to Joyce.

She takes the call.

INT. JOYCE AND DANIEL'S HOUSE – DAY

> JOYCE

So, I missed your call, what's the news?

> SHIV
> (*on speakerphone*)

Yeah. Look, I know it feels huge to us but it started the day as item three, end of day, I think it will be item five.

> JOYCE

They're not going to drop it?

> SHIV
> (*on speakerphone*)

I can't stop it. Your husband's asshole is the gift that just keeps on shitting. We just have to hunker down, keep focussed, ride the cycle.

> JOYCE

Or, other option, I go after them?

> SHIV
> (*on speakerphone*)

I don't think that's a good play.

> JOYCE

Is that you saying that as you? Or as the daughter of a media mogul?

> SHIV
> (*on speakerphone*)
It's me saying that.

> JOYCE
Uh-huh. And so – how can we – how can we stop this?

> SHIV
> (*on speakerphone*)
Well – definite end, just as a fact, to kill this for now and 'the future' is if you leave him?

> JOYCE
Uh-huh? Okay.

> SHIV
> (*on speakerphone*)
But I can't advise on that?
> (*beat*)
So, see you – both – later?

> JOYCE
> (*dryly*)
Yeah. Looking forward to it.

Joyce looks to where in the house Daniel's presence is.

INT. RECNY BALL – LOBBY – NIGHT

6:15 p.m. Montage. The VIP guests being photographed on the step-and-repeat:

Kendall and Anna Newman – the reporter from ATN Kendall was watching – pose for shots.

People check in at a table with assistants with iPads. There's some horrible jewelry around on ATN anchors we saw earlier.

Roman energetically showing off, Grace trying to smile despite being upstaged.

Stewy and his date greet other guests.

Tom and Shiv. Tom enjoys the space. Looks up. Shiv is texting, looking back to the entrance.

EXT. SERVICE ENTRANCE – NIGHT

Down in the bowels of the building, Logan and Marcia's car pulls up.

There are a couple of security and medical. Colin supervises as they get Logan out and into a wheelchair.

INT. SERVICE CORRIDOR – NIGHT

Logan is pushed along the shitty corridors by a medical guy. Accompanied by Colin and Marcia. They reach the elevator. Marcia looks at Logan. He stares into space, vacantly.

> LOGAN
> I don't know if I can do this.

> MARCIA
> *(looks at him)*
> You can. *Vas-y.* Fuck them.

INT. RECNY BALL – RECEPTION AREA – NIGHT

6:30 p.m. The non-VIP guests have arrived and the cocktail hour has begun. Guests mingle and chat happily. Smiles, hugs, laughter.

But in the corner Connor is with Willa. Connor's noticed something about a table setting and stops a waitress.

> CONNOR
> Excuse me, what the hell is this?

Connor motions to the table setting.

> WAITRESS
> A glass?

> CONNOR
> Every glass should be at three o'clock. *This* is nothing.
> *(moves the glass slightly)*
> *This* is something. Check every glass! Unbelievable.

They approach the cocktail entrance area. Willa looks around.

> WILLA
> Why is no one standing in that half of the room?

CONNOR

Oh god. The room is growing lopsided! Let's lead them – like
sheep. Willa – lead them over, corral them!

Willa and Connor move to talk to people.

WILLA

Hey, guys – there's plenty of room over here.

CONNOR

Come and enjoy the space, guys! Acres!

As Stephanie passes, Connor corners her.

CONNOR

The signature cocktail is too avant-garde! The servers are
creating bottlenecks! They put pesto in the gin! It's a disaster!
There's no flow! The evening is congealing, Stephanie! There's
no flow!

Stephanie heads off.

Kendall is with Anna, from ATN, they look at a RECNY sign:

KENDALL

Yeah my dad's first wife thought she was gonna, you know,
empty the ghettos and get everyone into ballet when they started
this thing. So patronizing.

ANNA

Heh, right.

Not much back.

KENDALL

A couple of kids who got into New York City Ballet still send us
cards at Christmas though so I guess that's nice or whatever?

ANNA

Wow, that's nice.

Even less back.

KENDALL

Yeah it's dumb, but it's cool.

INT. JOYCE'S CAR – NIGHT

Joyce is being driven.

We adjust to reveal – her husband sitting next to her. They are weary of the turmoil. He smiles at her.

Text from Shiv. She reads it. 'If you're bringing him, try this . . .' We don't see the next text.

> JOYCE
> (*addressing the driver*)
> Okay, change of plan. We're going in the front.

INT. SERVICE ELEVATOR – NIGHT

Clank. Clunk. A big scratched and smashed freight elevator.

Logan in his chair. With Colin and Marcia. A huge guy operates it. A bag of fruit hangs incongruously.

> LOGAN
> So how many presidents you had in this contraption, buddy?

> ELEVATOR GUY
> Three, sir. Two former, one serving.

> LOGAN
> Who'd you like?

> ELEVATOR GUY
> I heard good things of them all, sir.

> LOGAN
> Uh-huh, very fucking diplomatic.

They share a smile – Logan can do this stuff well.

EXT. RECNY BALL – ARRIVAL AREA – NIGHT

Joyce and Daniel pull up outside and Joyce lights up for the small waiting press pack as she steps out.

She is smiling. Couple of shouted questions: 'Have you forgiven him?' 'How many women, Mr Miller?'

>   JOYCE
> I was going to use the, ahem, back entrance but I thought,
> maybe not tonight?

*Laughs. Jai smiles. Joyce smiles at Shiv – she's at the top of the stairs.
Daniel has the fixed grin of a man on the way to his execution.*

INT. RECNY BALL – BACKSTAGE CORRIDOR – NIGHT

*Logan is wheeled. Colin walks ahead of him. When they arrive within
sight of the ball, Logan lifts himself up out of his chair.*

INT. RECNY BALL – AUDIO-VISUAL AREA – NIGHT

*The teleprompter operator is spinning through the text. Connor is
running a check, adding last-minute changes he's been handed.*

>   CONNOR
> Good. Good. Good.
>   (*points*)
> Is that too wry? About our good works? I mean is it, like, snitty?

>   TELEPROMPTER OPERATOR
> Well there's all this? Like three pages of – about you, and the
> family, and the good works and the big hearts, and on and *on*
> and *on*.

Connor looks at him – is he overstepping the mark?

>   CONNOR
> Excusing you but I didn't ask for editorial comment—
>   (*looking as he scrolls*)
> And then it's into Kendall. Okay. And he's all blah blah
> blah – hold on, pal. What's that? 'Surprise Logan retirement
> announcement'??

>   TELEPROMPTER OPERATOR
> Yeah that came through late. He said he'd freelance that?

Connor considers.

INT. RECNY BALL — NIGHT

7:20 p.m. Cocktail hour continues. Gerri appears near Tom, who is talking to Greg. Gerri smiles at Greg.

TOM

Where you sitting, Greg? In the basement? Or out by the dumpsters? Tell me you're at least in this time zone?

Greg catches Gerri's eye and slips away.

GERRI

Hey! Tom, so, look, I hear you're thinking about holding a little press conference?

TOM

You know about that—?

GERRI

I don't know anything.

Tom tries to scope her out.

TOM

Right, it's just I think —

GERRI

Tom, you need to shut up. This isn't the time to get your conscience out and shout 'Oooh, look at me, I cannot tell a lie, I'm a good little boy, look at my ding-dong.' Okay?

TOM

I don't think that's a fair characterization of—

GERRI

Do you know who the sin-cake eater was?

TOM

Um, no—?

GERRI

He'd come to the funeral, and he'd eat the little cakes they laid out on the corpse, he ate up all the sins, and you know what, the sin-cake eater was well paid, and so long as there was another one who came along when he died, everything worked out.

(*smiles*)
So this may not be the best situation but there are harder jobs.
And you get a fuckload of cake.

TOM
And can I ask where you heard about this?

Gerri deadpans and Tom keeps nodding—

GERRI
Tom, it's tough to have to tell you this way but I'm in a sexual
relationship with your mother. And she talks in her sleep.

—until he realizes it could only be one person: Greg.

INT. RECNY BALL – DINING AREA – NIGHT

*7:30 p.m. People are sitting down for dinner. In the background, the
guests are having wine, water filled. Marcia and Logan are discreetly
seated at the top table. Near the stage. Connor approaches.*

CONNOR
Hey, Dad? Dad?

LOGAN
Ugh?

CONNOR
How you going?

Logan nods.

Yeah. Just wanted to check in on something? Just to check
you were – aware of Kendall announcing your retirement this
evening, I mean I'm sure you were but I wanted to triple-check?

LOGAN
What?

CONNOR
Yeah, is that – right?

Logan thinks.

LOGAN
No.

> ### CONNOR
> No? Is it a mistake? Cos Kendall's going to read it, it's on the teleprompter.

> ### LOGAN
> Change of plan. Kendall's not speaking. I'm speaking.

Connor smiles. As the MC's opening remarks begin in the background, Connor spots with distress Marcia trying to butter Logan's roll. The butter is hard and the roll tears.

INT. RECNY BALL – KITCHEN AREA – NIGHT

Connor bursts in, yelling at a senior server.

> ### CONNOR
> The butter's too cold! The butter's all fucked, you're fuckwads and you've fucked it! There are rolls ripping apart out there as we speak. It's like granite! I'm a laughing stock!

Stephanie is talking to someone else.

> ### STEPHANIE
> Connor, there are always some issues when you serve this many people but I think, on the whole, it's going very well.

> ### CONNOR
> Complacent! You're fired!

He leaves.

INT. RECNY BALL – NIGHT

7:51 p.m. Dinner continues. The salads are cleared. The appetizer course has arrived. On stage in the distance, a man in a suit is presented with a plaque from a woman in an evening dress.

Greg glances over, bored but politely engaged. He's about to dig into his food. Tom comes over to Greg full of rage.

> ### TOM
> Hey, you lump of fucking turducken.

> ### GREG
> Hi, Tom?

                    TOM
Did you squeal?

                    GREG
What?

                    TOM
Did you bitch me out, pig-man?

                    GREG
As in?

                    TOM
You bleated – about the press conference?

                    GREG
No.

                    TOM
Yes you did.

                    GREG
No I did not.

Tom leans in, aggressively—

                    TOM
Yes you did, you filthy piece of shit. I should drag you into the
kitchen and have them boil you until you're sterile—

*As he gets very close, Greg instinctively pushes Tom away. A shocked
beat.*

Oh my god, Greg, did you just touch me?

                    GREG
Tom, I'm sorry but your spittle was actually like—

                    TOM
This is extraordinary. What are we going to do about this? Are
these assaults going to be ongoing?

                    GREG
No.

                    TOM
And you're telling me you didn't do it?

GREG

I promise. I swear to god.

TOM

Then who the fuck did, Greg? Ah? Because I only told you?

*Greg shrugs. Tom looks around. Through the crowd he spots . . .
Shiv! Shit, no? Could she have done? Shiv cuts through to Kendall—*

*Polite applause from the audience. The man steps down with the
plaque. The MC calls a new, identical-looking man in a tux to the
stage.*

*Meanwhile, from the other side, Roman approaches Logan. Everyone
wants the king's ear.*

ROMAN

Dad, I don't want to shit-talk Kendall.
          (*stage whisper, wise-crack voice*)
'He's not up to the job'—
                    (*normal voice*)
but I think I speak for everyone when I say it's great to see you
back.

LOGAN

Thanks, son.

But Roman is scared. He can't really do confrontation.

ROMAN

But – one thing, and I don't mind, it's fine. But I wanted to say –
Frank is what to me now?

LOGAN

He's – Vice Chairman and your general advisor.

ROMAN

But why?

LOGAN

Why? What's the situation with the park numbers?

ROMAN

How do you mean—?

LOGAN

Attendance is good but occupied-room nights are down on last
year. Why?

ROMAN

Well, I'll press Tom?

Logan looks at Roman.

What? I've been waiting for Tom to get his feet fully under the
table—
(*then*)
The guy is a bit of a flake is the truth. But leave it with me.
When are you coming back in again?

LOGAN

You need to soak up Frank's experience.

ROMAN

Uh-huh, but what does that mean?

LOGAN
(*snapping*)
It means do what he fucking tells you.

Connor passes, leans in.

CONNOR

So sorry about the butter, guys.

Roman stalks off – humiliated.

*We follow him through the crowd as he burns with the sharp pain of
his father's disregard.*

INT. RECNY BALL — NIGHT

*8:25 p.m. The entrees have been dropped, but many are hardly
touched. During the meal, a pause from speeches, but a RECNY
slideshow scrolls through various good deeds.*

*Kendall and Anna are sitting, smiling around them. Awkward air. Shiv
passes behind Kendall and whispers in his ear.*

SHIV

Nice one, bro.

KENDALL
What?

SHIV
Fucking the talent?

KENDALL
Hey, come on, what?

SHIV
ATN are fucking me, you're fucking ATN. It's a literal fucking clusterfuck.

Shiv moves off. Kendall looks at his dad. Then at Anna.

KENDALL
Everything okay?

ANNA
Yes. I'm having a lovely time, thanks.

KENDALL
Is there anything I can do to put you at ease?

Anna looks over and catches a glimpse of Eva, smiling encouragingly at her. It might make her feel a little queasy.

ANNA
I'm having a wonderful time, really.

KENDALL
And you'd tell me if you weren't?

ANNA
(*fuck no*)
I'm a reporter, I report. Absolutely.

They share an awkward smile. Connor passes.

CONNOR
So sorry about the butter.

KENDALL
What?

CONNOR
And just so you know, apparently, Dad's going to do the speech, so late change of plan. Hope that's 'cool'?

                    KENDALL
  Excuse me?

Kendall gets up.

                    CONNOR
  Yeah he just said. So. I guess that's put a spoke in quite a few
  wheels!

                    KENDALL
  Con. He's in no fit state. Is he okay? I mean this could be, does
  he know where he is?

                    CONNOR
  Oh he knows. Uh-huh.

Gerri is near, passing.

                    KENDALL
  There's like, pension funds, there's analysts, there's major
  investors. This is fucking high-risk.
                    (*spots Gerri*)
  Gerri?!

She heads over.

                    KENDALL
  Dad wants to talk? Gerri?!

                    GERRI
  Okay. I did not know that.

                    KENDALL
  When he opens his mouth anything could come out. Drool, anti-
  Semitism, fucking silk handkerchiefs tied together. If he fucks up
  publicly we have a major problem. You need to talk to him.

Kendall looks at Gerri.

INT. RECNY BALL – NIGHT

*From afar, Kendall watches as Gerri approaches Logan. Kendall gives
her the thumbs-up. Gerri smiles back: Wish me luck! Kendall can't
hear anything Gerri's saying as he leans in.*

                    GERRI
  You good?

> LOGAN

I'm good.

> GERRI

Great. Good luck tonight. You're gonna knock it out of the park.

> LOGAN

Thank you.

Gerri retreats. Kendall looks over: How did it go? Gerri gives Kendall a shrug: What can I do? I tried.

INT. RECNY BALL – NIGHT

8:45 p.m. On stage MC Mark Ravenhead is making a speech in praise of the many good works of RECNY.

We follow Roman, pissed off and humiliated, as he says cold hellos and exchanges meaningless bonhomie with people until he returns to Grace, where she is getting topped up by an attractive male waiter.

> ROMAN

Hi, don't mean to intrude?

Roman smiles at the waiter who goes to move off.

Hold on, buddy.

Roman drains his glass, then holds it out.

Thanks?

The waiter tops him up. Then goes to move on. Roman gets him to wait with a finger.

> GRACE

It's still early, Rome?

> ROMAN

Well thank you, Grace, you delightful speaking timepiece.

The waiter catches Grace's eye then looks away, awkward. Grace smiles back, awkward.

> ROMAN
> (cont'd)
>
> Dude, if you like her that much why don't you ask for her fucking number?

Waiter smiles, difficult moment.

> GRACE
>
> Rome?

> ROMAN
> (to waiter)
>
> You clearly want to, right?

Waiter tries to laugh.

> (to Grace)
>
> Do you want to give him your number?

Grace isn't going to be bullied.

> GRACE
>
> Yeah I want to give him my number.

> ROMAN
>
> Dude, ask for her fucking number?

Tense moment. Roman waits. Nowhere for the waiter to go.

> WAITER
>
> Can I – get your number?

Roman likes the violation.

> ROMAN
>
> Okay! Here we go!

Grace writes down her number and gives him it.

> Okay? Thank you, everyone's happy!

INT. RECNY BALL – BACKSTAGE – NIGHT

Connor is walking, geeing-up the performers, back-slapping Mark Ravenhead. On stage, a speech in praise of RECNY's good works is being made.

Connor greets the members of a dance troupe that has received a grant. They're a group much more racially diverse than the guests.

CONNOR

Good luck. Bon chance! Best foot forward. You can do it!

He stops as outside the performers are being introduced. Connor is standing next to a young man.

Good luck. Nervous?

DANCER

Not too bad.

CONNOR

Uh-huh. Uh-huh. I had a thing, with the butter. But, seems to be okay.

(*smiles*)

Where you from?

DANCER

Er Bushwick?

CONNOR

Indeed. Yes indeed. Well, wonderful. Great effort.

(*thinks*)

Connor Roy. People have a lot of preconceptions about me too. It's difficult, I mean, not like— I imagine everything is for you but—

DANCER

(*what?*)

Right.

CONNOR

I actually have an idea that social equality could be effected by a total eradication of federal support. Just people like you and I, doing it together, fighting it out, without, all the – bullshit, that's holding you back. You know?

The troupe are ready to go on.

DANCER

Okay. This is me.

CONNOR

Great. Break a leg, my friend!

The dancer grimaces – wrong words.

INT. RECNY BALL – NIGHT

As the dancers dance, Shiv is talking to Logan.

> LOGAN
> So I'm sorry to hear your friend was getting crucified all day?

> SHIV
> Oh you heard that? I'm surprised you heard that, given that it
> had so little to do with you.

Shiv smiles. Logan doesn't mind this. He likes a game.

INT. RECNY BALL – DINING AREA – NIGHT

*The rich white diners are enjoying the performance. We pick up some
of the reactions to the show:*

*Frank giving it dutiful consideration. Maybe Frank stealing a glance
in Logan's direction—*

Kendall smiling in silence next to Anna. Looking at Logan—

*Shiv, enjoying the show, taking Tom's hand. Tom looks at her, bit
scared—*

Roman, looking bored and drunk and resentful and twitchy—

Logan leans to Marcia, holds up a cheese knife—

INT. RECNY BALL – DINING AREA – NIGHT

*9:20 p.m. In the background, dessert plates are begin cleared. The
dinner is over, people are standing and chatting. Connor is cutting
through the crowd. A few people throw compliments his way as he
passes.*

> FRANK
> Good job tonight, Con! Best event of the fall.

> KARL
> Terrific evening.

(*leans in and whispers*)
You really showed it to those cystic fibrosis fuckheads.

CONNOR
(*nonchalant*)
It's all about the charity, not about me, folks.

INT. RECNY BALL – KITCHEN AREA – NIGHT

Connor bursts in.

CONNOR
We fucking nailed it! Everyone! You're all amazing and I love you!
(*to Stephanie*)
Stephanie. My rock. We did it. We just landed this thing on the Hudson.

He gives her a big hug.

INT. RECNY BALL – DINING AREA – NIGHT

9:26 p.m. Time for the finale/closing speech. Logan ignores everyone on his table and focusses on the small cards Marcia's written some remarks on.

Mark looks to Logan and nods: Ready?

MARK RAVENHEAD
Ladies and gentlemen. It gives me *profound* pleasure to introduce to you, on this most auspicious of occasions—

Roman feigns a loud obvious yawn.

(*genuinely heartfelt*)
In a change to advertized attractions. The man, the legend, Logan Roy!

Applause. Logan's POV. He stands. Looks around – a sea of expectant faces. Down at Marcia, nodding, smiling. A long pause – he's lost for a moment. Then he snaps out of it.

Logan starts to walk the short distance to the podium with difficulty, trying to flash smiles to the guests, Marcia is at his side.

                              MARCIA
    You okay?
                              (*then*)
    Keep going.

He is flagging. He grunts a response.

    Just get to Dan. Then pretend to talk.

Daniel gives Logan a hug.

Over with Tom talking to Shiv or another guest—

                              TOM
    Oooh! Elvis! I thought we were getting the support act!
                              (*then*)
    He's kind of milking the walk?

Kendall is near Stewy. Kendall watches with concern.

                              STEWY
    There's forty billion dollars of market cap waiting to see if he
    can make it.

Kendall looks at him.

    What? If he falls, I could lose several of my houses.

Back with Logan, Marcia and Daniel. Marcia leans in.

                              MARCIA
    Now? Come on. Come on!

Logan nods. Grits his teeth. Walks on . . .

*Kendall watches intently. Is his dad going to make it? Does he want
him to make it? Half of him wants him to fall, badly, half wants him
to triumph over the doubters in the room.*

                              (*quietly*)
    Nearly there.

*He walks towards the podium. Makes it up. Catches his breath.
Looks to autocue.*

LOGAN

Evening. Gonna keep this brief. Thank you for coming. Thank you, to those that supported me through my recent, health – nonsense. Head cold.

Few laughs.

So – yes. Congratulations to all the grantees, amazing, work.
(*dry*)
Huge fan of contemporary dance.
(*laughs*)
In personal news. Someone took advantage of my being in the hospital.

A couple of looks between members of the family. Does he mean Kendall?

To propose to my daughter.

Some looks towards Tom who suddenly looks very anxious.

So I'd like to take this opportunity to welcome her fiancé, Tom Wambsgans, to the family.

Applause. Tom, surprised and momentarily delighted, to be publicly recognized by Logan.

Welcome to the family, Tom.

Shiv smiles. Logan smiles. Tom feels the weight of the family bearing down on him. But he feels the welcome embrace he's always wanted from them. Maybe Shiv even puts her arm round his neck and pulls him to her to give him a kiss. Tom looks at Gerri. He smiles. He's in.

Shiv fixes him with a look that says, 'Are we okay?' Tom gives her a look back that says, 'Yes.' But maybe there's a tiny hint of fear or uncertainty there?

It's so important that children are encouraged and supported. Everything I've done in my life has been for my children.

Roman and Kendall exchange a knowing look. That's bullshit.

And I'm proud of the way they've pulled together during my recent . . . issue. Kendall in particular.

All eyes on Kendall. He was not expecting this.

Well done, Ken. And tonight I have one last announcement . . .

> ROMAN
> (*whispers*)

He's retiring? He's a lizard?

Kendall can't help but lean in.

> LOGAN

I'm officially announcing . . . I'm back. You better believe, I'm back! Full time. Better than ever!

A huge round of applause. A standing ovation. Maybe Logan's eyes happen to find Kendall's in the crowd?

Kendall stands up and joins in, trying to hide his humiliation, knowing all eyes are on him. He smiles at people around him.

> ANNA

Great news! Right.

> KENDALL

It's great.

Marcia smiles at Logan. He looks at her with pain in his eyes. She looks concerned. He gestures it'll be okay. Maybe we see him fast-forward through the autocue. We know he's cutting it short. Bailing out.

Logan is ready to go, Marcia approaches.

> LOGAN
> (*gritted teeth*)

Get me out of here!

Marcia holds Logan as they shake hands and say goodbyes and Logan makes it away from his speech-making spot. As they make it through the crowd, a friend catches Marcia's attention for a moment – and checking he's okay, resting a hand on a chair back, she leaves Logan's side for a moment.

> KENDALL

And what was that?

> LOGAN

Went well, I thought.

KENDALL

What the fuck is wrong with you, Dad?

LOGAN

I see you. I spied you fucking out, son. Don't try that again.

KENDALL

I have no fucking idea what you—

LOGAN

Retire me? Shoot me like a dog in the street. I heard about your little speech?

KENDALL

What do you— I was going to do one fucking joke about how you'd never retire?

Beat. Logan can't accept that.

LOGAN

Bullshit.

KENDALL

Why didn't you just talk to me?

Logan won't engage.

I've no idea where this has come from, Dad?

Logan can't engage.

LOGAN

Huh.

Logan knows he should wait for Marcia but he's an impatient bastard and for a beat tries to walk towards the exit alone.

The cameras and attention, post-speech, are still on him.

As he goes to make off, Logan's bad leg buckles and he starts to stumble.

Kendall clocks it and has a moment to make his decision. He's aware of the cameras, the guests and he . . . adjusts to offer an arm, a hand to Logan so he's steady and doesn't go down.

It's instinctive. He can't not protect his father.

In the aftermath, Connor swoops in, grabs his dad, helps him sit down. In the crush, maybe Logan has clocked what Kendall did, maybe not? Still Connor is there, feeling he made the key intervention.

>   CONNOR
> You're okay, Dad. You're okay.

Logan, exhausted and disorientated, straightens up.

After a beat they try to make it through the crowd. Logan pats Connor's hand.

>   LOGAN
> You did well tonight . . . Connor. I'm proud of you.

Connor's waited for this his whole life, wells up slightly.

>   CONNOR
> You know. You pull off a night like this and you realize, people are just people.

>   LOGAN
> Uh-huh?

>   CONNOR
> 'I can no longer obey,' Dad. 'I have tasted command and I cannot give it up.' A certain artillery cadet by the name of N. Bonaparte?

Beat. Logan just stares at him as Marcia approaches.

>   MARCIA
> There you are!

>   CONNOR
> Hail to the chief, Dad?

As Connor points to himself, Marcia swoops in and guides Logan. Kendall takes the other arm.

INT. RECNY BALL – NIGHT

Kendall returns to Anna. He's fizzing with irritation and a certain freedom.

KENDALL

Hey.

Anna smiles politely at Kendall. Kendall can't take it.

So look, Anna. Can I just ask? Is there – something – going on here?

ANNA

As in?

KENDALL

Like, I don't know, is there – an atmosphere, did I say something to offend you?

ANNA

This has been a lovely evening. I was so glad to come.

KENDALL

Uh-huh. Thank you. So am I crazy? I feel like I'm on a date with an app, like there's invisible bubble wrap?

She makes a decision. Maybe she can trust him enough to come clean.

ANNA
(*sighs*)
Look. Off the record? Off-off? You seem like a nice guy.
(*off his look, yes*)
Eva told me to come.

KENDALL

Well asked. I asked her to just, ask your people.

ANNA

It's fine. I'm just seeing someone. But you're the boss.

KENDALL

What? No I'm not that guy? Okay?

ANNA

Yeah. Sure, no.
(*then*)
I mean you actually are that guy, right now but – sure.

KENDALL

What did she say, Eva?

ANNA

Nothing.

(*beat, why not?*)

To make sure you had a 'really good time'.

KENDALL

Was she joking?

Anna looks at him. He really doesn't get it.

ANNA

Eva? Oh sure. Okay? And I'd prefer it if you didn't say anything?

KENDALL

Well – I think I should (say something)—

ANNA

Please don't. Okay?

KENDALL

Sure.

She heads off. Roman watches her go and approaches Kendall.

ROMAN

Dude? This is our charity. How much a plate? You've got to get at least a blowjob. That's the law.

KENDALL

That's not the law.

ROMAN

Well it's the ethical code. I hate to say this, but she has behaved rather unethically here.

Kendall is pissed off. He spots Eva a way away. From a distance we see him head through the crowd. He knows he's not meant to say anything, but his mix of frustrated feelings are going to come out. We see them chat briefly, Kendall is frustrated and Eva knows it. She smiles tightly as Kendall lays into her and leaves.

She watches him go. Then turns to her colleague.

EVA

We might be looking for a new Wall Street correspondent.

INT. SHIV AND TOM'S CAR – NIGHT

Shiv and Tom are in the back seat. She smiles at him. He smiles back at her. Bit scared, not sure whether he can trust her anymore.

INT. RECNY BALL – NIGHT

As people are leaving, Gerri moves through the crowd. She passes Greg. Very discreetly presses his arm.

>   GERRI
>   (*whispers*)
> Good kid. Smart move. Keep talking.

>   GREG
> I aim to please, ma'am.

Gerri smiles and moves on.

INT. JOYCE'S CAR – NIGHT

Joyce's phone goes.

>   JOYCE
> Hey, Shiv. Uh-huh. Uh-huh. Well I'm glad you thought it went well. I'm glad Twitter is so positive about the joke. No I'm sure it was a great evening. You did great. Everything is great.

End of call. Joyce and Daniel travel in silence.

> Her opinion is we're okay.

>   DANIEL
> Oh great, well in that case I'll sleep soundly tonight.
>   (*then*)
> I mean it is only an opinion and you know the thing about opinions? Everyone's got one. In that respect they're like—

Joyce smiles a rueful smile.

INT. ROMAN'S APARTMENT – BEDROOM – NIGHT

In the bedroom. Grace is looking at photos online. Of people, ATN folk and others, wearing her stuff.

GRACE
God. AP photos. Some people just don't know how to wear jewelry.

Success. She gives him a kiss. This could be the start . . .

ROMAN
Did you tell him to call?

Just then her phone starts to buzz on vibrate. The waiter.

Roman is ready to kiss Grace but instead, takes the phone as it buzzes and moves it to her crotch, pushing it tenderly.

The phone buzzes away. This is how they're going to get off tonight—

INT. KENDALL'S CAR – NIGHT

A shitty night. Kendall's playing 'The Ruler's Back' by Jay-Z.

EXT. LOGAN'S APARTMENT BUILDING – NIGHT

The car pulls in.

MARCIA
Well, you did it.

Marcia looks over to Logan who is asleep. Two members of staff wait with a wheelchair and blanket. As the car stops Logan begins to stir. The door of the car is opened.

MARCIA
(cont'd)
No. Don't wake him. Drive. Keep driving. I want him to sleep. Just keep driving.

The car door is closed and the car drives away. Driving into the night.

As they pull away, Jay-Z plays on.

Episode Five

I WENT TO MARKET

Written by Georgia Pritchett
Directed by Adam Arkin

Original air date 1 July 2018

Cast

LOGAN ROY	Brian Cox
KENDALL ROY	Jeremy Strong
MARCIA ROY	Hiam Abbass
GREG HIRSCH	Nicholas Braun
SHIV ROY	Sarah Snook
ROMAN ROY	Kieran Culkin
CONNOR ROY	Alan Ruck
TOM WAMBSGANS	Matthew Macfadyen
FRANK VERNON	Peter Friedman
RAVA	Natalie Gold
KARL MULLER	David Rasche
GRACE O'HARE	Molly Griggs
MARIANNE	Mary Birdsong
SOPHIE ROY	Swayam Bhatia
IVERSON ROY	Quentin Morales
ISLA	Noelle Hogan
GERRI KELLMAN	J. Smith-Cameron
WILLA FERREYRA	Justine Lupe
EWAN ROY	James Cromwell
BREX	Brock Yurich
YOUNG EXECUTIVE 1	Aaron Albano
YOUNG EXECUTIVE 2	David Robert Moore
CHRIS	Michael Braun
GRETA	Taylor Ortega
AMIR	Darius Homayoun
OFFICE KEEPER	James Michael Brown
UBER DRIVER	Ricky Garcia

DAY ONE

EXT. QUEBEC COUNTRYSIDE – EWAN'S HOUSE – DAY

Greg trudges through thick snow. A large ranch in the distance. He struggles up a long lane. A ranch-hand is clearing snow/blowing leaves with a small snowplow/leaf blower.

Greg knocks on the door. Ewan opens it.

> GREG

Hey hey hey!

Greg embraces him. It's awkward.

> EWAN

Uh-huh uh-huh. You're late.

> GREG

Well, like ten minutes, Grandpa? Happy Thanksgiving!

> EWAN

Not for the Indians.

Ewan goes inside to grab an overnight bag.

> GREG
> *(here we go again)*

No, sir . . .
> *(half to himself)*

That's actually anti-racist and also racist. Which is kind of cool but also really not cool?
> *(to Ewan)*

So, shall we grab lunch then hit the road? I gots the old rumblin' tum.

Ewan walks out and bangs the door.

> EWAN

No. Let's go before it snows.

On Greg watching him walk past: this is going to be hard.

INT. WAYSTAR – KENDALL'S OFFICE – DAY

Frank passes Kendall's door.

> FRANK
> Ken? I think your dad might 'appreciate your input'?

He gives him a look – red alert. Kendall is right up.

> He's thinking big?

They share a look – that can be a problem. Kendall looks over to Roman, waves, he might be useful too—

INT. WAYSTAR – LOGAN'S OFFICE – DAY

In Logan's office. He's with Karl and Gerri. Frank and Roman and Kendall enter.

> LOGAN
> Oh, look out, folks, here come the 'top minds'!

> KENDALL
> Hey, what you got cooking?

> LOGAN
> Really no need, gentlemen, Frank wanted to fold you in.
> (black mark, Frank)
> But you should know probably my thinking in terms of – things.

> KARL
> There's a potential opportunity for some acquisitions and consolidation.

> GERRI
> Packet of local TV stations.

Kendall and Roman: Ugh. So depressing.

> KENDALL
> Local TV stations?

> ROMAN
> No one watches TV, Dad.

Logan nods to Gerri – tell them.

> GERRI
>
> TV is where the majority of people get their news. And more people watch local than any other kind.

> ROMAN
>
> Yeah. But not really.

> KENDALL
>
> Maybe raw numbers, but the demographic? I mean for Waystar, is it a good 'look'?

Logan lets 'look' hang there in its superficiality.

> LOGAN
> (*deliberately camp voice*)
> 'I don't know, Kendall, you tell me.'

> KENDALL
>
> Look, I can see short term we make cash but (in terms of a strategy where)—

> LOGAN
>
> You know there's this fancy new business theory, son? It's called, 'make more than you spend and you're King Cunt'.

Kendall looks down. How can he argue with this shit? Frank tries to help—

> FRANK
>
> These channels, they're not exactly cash fountains?

> KARL
>
> We like the scaling opportunities and the bargaining power.

> LOGAN
>
> I like putting the knife in the rival canoes. We're the number-five media conglomerate in the world . . .

> KENDALL
>
> Yeah, I'll get the T-shirt made.

> LOGAN
>
> Time to be number one.

Kendall looks around: Is this for real?

> KENDALL

That's great but it's unrealistic.

Logan doesn't like that: Don't fucking talk to me like that, son.

> LOGAN

And I want to look at a broadcast network. And I want to see what other news operations we can sweep up.

> KENDALL

Oh, Dad! C'mon?

> LOGAN

Why shouldn't we do all the news?

> ROMAN

Do all the news? Well, Kim Jong Pop, because that's not how things work in this country.

> KENDALL

You sure do love telling people what to think, don't you?

> LOGAN

Fuck off. People come to us because we don't try to sell them on anything. No packet of fucking bleeding-heart United Nations Volvo gender-bender horseshit.

> GERRI

The strategy eventually would be that we'd support a range of news brand perspectives.

> KARL

Bud. Miller. Corona. Becks. All the different beers are owned by one big bastard who wants to get you drunk.

> KENDALL

The politics on this would be horrible. Justice, FCC. Antitrust. We'd be tied up for years—

> LOGAN

Nah. TV's getting fucked, it's gotta consolidate.

Kendall gives up.

KENDALL

Look. Fine. I don't want to make this a thing – you like local TV, great, you're smart. I just hope it doesn't mean we can't pursue diversification and innovation.

Roman has been zoning out – having spotted an ad on the back of a magazine for a movie, The Biggest Turkey in the World.

LOGAN

Of course. India. China. You know how many fucking people there are in Indonesia?

Roman's clicking on links, through from Rotten Tomatoes to reviews. Logan looks at him.

ROMAN

What? Sure. Who doesn't.

Logan carries on looking.

More than you'd think. A billion?

LOGAN

Roman, you're a moron.
(*to Kendall*)
I think you should get into all that for us, Kendall.

KENDALL

What?

LOGAN

Get back into that, over there. Vice-President Global and Digital. Out of Dubai, wherever. China, India.

KENDALL

Excuse me, are you serious?

LOGAN

Meeting's over.

Logan looks away. Kendall walks out, shaking his head – looks back: We'll talk about this later.

Logan starts pouring himself a coffee from a pot on his desk.

He pours and keeps pouring. The cup fills, overfills, spills out onto the table. Logan seems oblivious.

> ROMAN
>
> Dad? Dad!

Roman looks at Frank. Logan keeps pouring.

> Dad! What are you doing? Are you okay? Stop, Dad!

Logan keeps pouring. Then comes to his senses and stops.

INT. GREG'S RENTAL CAR – DAY

Greg is typing the New York address into Waze on his phone.

> GREG
>
> Yeah. The long drive. I get it. Mom had a friend who was scared
> of flying? He actually died in a traffic accident. But he was on
> a bike. And heavy meds. So. But this is cool. We got this whole
> time to – talk about – whatever.
>> (*going fishing, gets nothing*)
>
> Business. The future. Corporate structures? Or just – let the
> country music play?

> EWAN
>
> No music. No chatter. Keep your mind on the driving.

Trip estimate: twelve hours. Greg swallows hard.

EXT. WAYSTAR – DAY

*Kendall is out on the street. Up against the big building he's a small
figure as he smokes a cigarette and watches the people go by. What
can he do?*

INT. SHIV AND TOM'S APARTMENT – KITCHEN – DAY

*Tom has a bowl of granola with blueberries in it. But he's not eating,
he's staring into it. Shiv comes on down.*

> TOM
>
> Sorry, got a kind of an important meeting.

Tom is still a little wary of Shiv.

> Nothing to worry about! Just – work. So yeah, couldn't sleep.

SHIV

Yeah nor me.

TOM

Sometimes I thought I was asleep and I actually wasn't. It was weird. But you looked like—

SHIV

It's not a competition, Tom. I was up till three-forty, actually, writing pros and cons of sticking with Joyce, on her PAC, and you were snoring like a hog. So?

Shiv hands him a big envelope.

TOM

Well my nasal strip fell off. What's this?

SHIV

The prenup.

TOM
(*brightens*)

Ooooh! Okay!

SHIV

Yeah?

TOM

Yeah. It means it's really happening? We're getting married!

SHIV

That's a very romantic way of looking at a prenup.

TOM

You know what, I'm not even going to look at this. Just show me where to sign.

SHIV

You have to look at it, Tom.

TOM

Honestly, honey, I'm not from money, you're from money. I don't want to look at it. I hereby comply.

SHIV

I don't want you to *comply*. That's not the basis for a healthy relationship.

TOM

Fine. Look, as a gesture of my love to you, I will have my lawyer look at it. But I want you to know, in my head I already signed it.

INT. WAYSTAR – ELEVATOR – DAY

Kendall in the elevator. Two younger executives are in there, one smiles at him. Knows who he is.

YOUNG EXECUTIVE 1

I hear your father is much better.

KENDALL

Yeah it's great.

Kendall smiles a tight smile. Pause.

YOUNG EXECUTIVE 1

Just to say though. Down in the 'Pig Sty' we're all huge fans of your stuff. The innovation.

This catches Kendall's attention. No biggie.

KENDALL

Thank you.
                    (*longish beat, can't resist*)
Like what?

YOUNG EXECUTIVE 1

Oh everything. Data storage. The digital guys I know were all popping. Not to sound cheap but the whole breakfast cereals thing?

YOUNG EXECUTIVE 2

The bircher muesli was off the hook. That shit was crazy. Were you involved with that?

The elevator arrives. Kendall is not about to indulge these low-level folk but he is a little proud, nods, steps out.

INT. WAYSTAR – ADVENTURE-PARKS FLOOR – TOM'S
OFFICE – DAY

*Tom is pacing anxiously as Chris, a loyal apparatchik from the
previous regime, gives a report.*

CHRIS

So, I met the guy. 'Sylvester'.

TOM

'Sylvester'. And did you use a fake name?

CHRIS

I think Sylvester is his real name.

TOM

What? Who's called Sylvester? Really?

CHRIS

Yeah. He's – he's just— We pay him. He's normal, he's legit. He's
on the record. He says it's easy.

TOM

Okay. Because I'm worried. You know, after the Iranian
revolution, the students taped back together the shredded
documents from the US embassy?

CHRIS

He asked a lot about the digital deep-clean? And I said that was
good. Emails and servers. Nice and general. Not specific. But
that of course we'd wiped the specifics.

TOM

Great. But how does this part work?

CHRIS

We shred. Then some guys come in when we're quiet, he
suggests right away, tomorrow, Thanksgiving and 'it's possible'
they'll dispose of all the unwanted material.

TOM
(*worried*)

It's 'possible'?

CHRIS

They definitely will. We just need someone to shred and to sign
out the materials from the document depository – and that

321

name could – that's a name that could draw heat, were things to go – bad?

Hm. Incriminating?

> TOM
> Well I can't do it obviously. Thanksgiving. Could – you?

> CHRIS
> Er. I mean. I could? It's just. It's— You know, the task in hand is a little—

Illegal.

> TOM
> No, sure. Absolutely.

> CHRIS
> You want someone you can trust. But who is, not 'expendable'. That would be horrible.

> TOM
> Oh no sure. Totally. I get it.

Tom thinks.

INT. GREG'S RENTAL CAR – DAY

Greg answers his phone (the call comes through the speakers). It's Tom.

> TOM
> (*on speakerphone, over-friendly*)
> Hey, buddy. What's up? Am I going to see you in the office any time soon?

> GREG
> Uh, not that soon. I'm driving down from—

> TOM
> (*a little bit curt*)
> Uh-huh. So what's your ETA?

> GREG
> About twelve hours? I'm in Canada.

> TOM

Excuse me? Canada? Canada with the healthcare and the ennui? Why's that, cock-sock?

Greg tries and fails to move the call from speakers to phone.

> GREG

Yeah. I'm just bringing my grandpa—

> TOM

Greg, fuck your grandpa.

> GREG

You're actually on speakerphone, Tom?

> TOM
> (*beat*)

Well I shouldn't be, Greg.

> GREG

Sure got it.

> TOM
> (*beat*)

Sorry, Grandpa!

> (*then*)

Well, hurry up, Greg, yeah? I have a job for you. And I'm being nice cos I'm on speakerphone but if I wasn't on speakerphone I'd be being, shall we say, somewhat less agreeable? Yeah?

Tom hangs up. Greg can feel his grandpa judging him.

> GREG

It's good. Rough and tumble, Grandpa. I call him a dicky too. He's actually pretty lonely and afraid, I guess. Like we all are.

INT. WAYSTAR — OFFICE GYM — DAY

Brex and Roman are tussling. Maybe Brex is sitting on Roman's thighs and holding them high up. It's sweaty and charged as Roman exclaims with each sit-up.

> ROMAN

Fuck you.

323

> **BREX**
> Yeah, you can't do it can you?

Sit-up.

> **ROMAN**
> Fuck you. You fucking, piece of shit.

> **BREX**
> You're a piece of shit, come on, come on, you fucking dirtbag.

Knock knock on the door.

> **ROMAN**
> No!

Knock knock. Brex gets up and off.

> (*shouting*)
> What the fuck. I think I've made it pretty fucking clear I need a modicum of space once every twenty-four hours!

Nothing.

> Fucking come in, my heart rate's dropping like a stone anyway!

A scared gym worker pops her head in.

> **GRETA**
> It's your brother, he absolutely insisted. I didn't know . . .

Kendall bustles in.

> **KENDALL**
> Is it true? About the coffee?

Brex and Greta withdraw. Neither Kendall or Roman 'have time' to acknowledge them.

> **ROMAN**
> What, Dad?

Roman waits for the staff to leave.

> Sure. He just kept pouring. It just went everywhere. It was like he didn't even see?

Kendall is excited and shaken at the same time.

KENDALL

Jesus. He's not right.

ROMAN

Local TV, local news? Here's a local news story for you:
'Elderly Local Man Doesn't Notice He's Getting Butt-Fucked By
Google'.

KENDALL

I am NOT going back to Shanghai. I *saved* the company when
he was sick.

ROMAN

Did you hear the way he talked to me? That was the tone, whole
time I was at the studio.

Kendall sees the angles, the offer of alliance.

KENDALL

So fucking patronizing.

ROMAN

Who knows how many people live in Indonesia? I mean who
even cares? Fuck Indonesia. It sounds like a medical condition.

KENDALL

When I— When one of us eventually takes over what's going to
be left?

ROMAN

How many people live up your ass, Father Dickmas?

KENDALL

The firm's being run by a compulsive hoarder. It's this big old
ugly spooky house and he's all caked up in the middle covered in
fucking moldy newspapers, with the local news blaring, feeding
Wonder Bread to raccoons.

ROMAN

You gonna do something.

KENDALL

I should.

> ROMAN

You should. And the only way he'll respect you is if you try to destroy him. Because in your position, that's exactly what he would try to do.

> KENDALL

Yeah. I can't do that.

> ROMAN

Obviously. So. Have fun in Shanghai!

EXT. WILLIAMSBURG STREET – WILLA'S BUILDING – DAY

Connor, carrying a bunch of large exotic flowers from the fanciest Manhattan florist, stops at an apartment building, buzzes.

> WILLA
> (*on door phone; surprised*)

Hello?

A resident of the block is heading out. Gives Connor a look.

INT. WILLA'S APARTMENT – DAY

Willa's at her door, dressed up.

> WILLA
> (*surprised*)

Oh wow!?

> CONNOR

You look incredible. Special delivery!

He hands over the flowers.

> WILLA

Oh? Enormous flowers!

> CONNOR

So?

He gestures: Aren't you going to invite me in? She wasn't expecting him.

WILLA
(*as if she'd forgotten*)
Oh what, sure. Yeah.

INT. GREG'S RENTAL CAR – DAY

Greg is driving. He wants to raise something.

GREG
Heh. Yeah. Heh.

No response.

So, yeah, work's going okay I would say. Yep, working hard.

EWAN
One of the symptoms of an approaching nervous breakdown is the belief that one's work is ever so important. Bertrand Russell.

Greg nods at the wisdom.

GREG
Ha! Yes indeed. Yes, sir. But I tell you what I sometimes think – I know you're very busy with the ranch and your readings and research but I sometimes wonder if you wouldn't, one day be interested in like, giving up your seat on the board and just – *seriously chilling* out. Like really relaxing you know?

Ewan looks at him.

EWAN
Life is nothing but a competition to be the criminal rather than the victim. Bertrand Russell.

GREG
Uh-huh. I don't have a Bertrand Russell quote because this is the first time I've heard of him. But I do have this quote: 'Just putting it out there.' It's a good quote. I don't know who said it.

INT. WILLA'S APARTMENT – DAY

Willa's place is nice.

CONNOR
(*slightly uptight*)

So, tomorrow's going to be great. Just a fun day relaxing with family. So I thought we should spend a few hours tonight discussing strategy, key alliances, the whole 'invisible chess game'?

WILLA

Oh, Con. I'm really sorry I can't do anything tonight, I have a prior engagement.

CONNOR
(*heartbroken, realizing*)

Oh? Right. No problem. I just thought we had two nights, tonight and tomorrow?

WILLA

I thought it was tomorrow and Friday?

CONNOR

Hm. Well could I have tonight as well, on top?

WILLA

You can have it however you want it, kiddo! No, no, I'm kidding.

CONNOR

I mean, considering the misunderstanding can't you cancel?

WILLA

Well no, my – friend's – a theater producer so?

Connor looks downcast.

But you've got me all day tomorrow?
(*then*)
And I've got you.

INT. GREG'S RENTAL CAR – NIGHT

The car is pulled over. Greg waits while Ewan pees.

Greg rummages in the glove box, finds something that looks like candy. He licks it. Ach. Ewan gets back in.

GREG

I think I just licked an air freshener. I thought it was candy. Do you think I'll be okay?

INT. LOGAN'S APARTMENT – FOYER – NIGHT

Logan enters. He looks frail but happy. Marcia is there to greet him. A staff member takes his belongings.

MARCIA

How was it? How are you feeling?

LOGAN

Great.

They kiss.

MARCIA

So I have some news. Ewan is definitely coming, for Thanksgiving.

LOGAN

Ewan? Bullshit. Why?

MARCIA

Why? Well, he asked and said he'd like to come and I said yes.

LOGAN
(*looks at her*)
You're a pretty good liar.

MARCIA

It's not good to have rifts in the family.

LOGAN

It's not a rift. He just lives in Canada. And is a prick.

MARCIA

Uh-huh? How long since you spoke?

LOGAN

We send him a fucking birthday card don't we? Not that I get any thanks.
(*walks*)
Think I need some physical therapy.

MARCIA

Of course.

She starts to lead him towards the equipment. He heads upstairs.

LOGAN

The other kind.

INT. KENDALL'S HOUSE – BEDROOM – NIGHT

Kendall can't sleep. He gets out of bed. He puts on music: 'What You Do to Me' by Blacroc/The Black Keys. It plays over the following:

INT. HOTEL ROOM – NIGHT

Connor sits on the bed, next to a tray of room service. He has his feet up on the couch and is watching reruns of The Joy of Painting, *shoveling fries into his mouth, depressed.*

INT. UPSTATE NEW YORK STATE HOTEL/MOTEL ROOMS – NIGHT

Ewan, in his room, is asleep.

Next door, Greg, in his room, is trying to construct a sandwich from stuff in the mini bar. Peanuts between Pringles.

INT. KENDALL'S HOUSE – BASKETBALL COURT – NIGHT

Kendall is working out solo. Skipping. The music blasting out from some high-end speakers in his basketball court workout area.

After a final set – he collapses. Listens to the loud music. Smiles to himself. Something's going to happen. It's not going to be the same forever.

DAY TWO

INT. LOGAN'S APARTMENT – DINING ROOM – DAY

Thanksgiving. Staff (in polo shirts) move silently and efficiently, preparing for a huge Thanksgiving meal. Classic dishes but here, elegantly, sublimely prepared in beautiful dishes. A bowl of fresh cranberries gleams. Marcia watches, eagle-eyed.

A family heirloom carving set is set at Logan's place.

INT. KENDALL'S HOUSE – KITCHEN – DAY

Kendall and Frank in Kendall's big clean kitchen. Kendall is by the espresso machine. But he has no coffee.

> KENDALL
> Look, you didn't come back out of love for my father. So I guess what I wanted to ask was, what's your plan?

> FRANK
> Ever heard of loyalty?

> KENDALL
> Sure, wasn't he one of the Seven Dwarves?

Frank looks like: Come on.

> No? A rapper. Was he a part of the Wu-Tang Clan?

Kendall is looking for coffee.

> I'm sorry, I gave everyone Thanksgiving off.
> (stops hunting)
> So, look, Dad's not well, right? The business decisions are not cogent, they're old-man shit. But that's his call in some ways you know, but he pissed on my fucking floor? What if that got out? No one wants to say it, but we can because we basically love him, but he's not okay. What about he wakes up one night fucking calls – Bezos and sells us out for a dollar?
> (beat)
> I just want what's for the best.

Frank looks at him, scopes him out.

> FRANK
> Ken, I'm an old man.

> KENDALL
> He's sick. Do you think the real Logan would want us to stand by and watch while he throws it all away?

Frank gives him a long look.

                              FRANK
    Talk more.

INT. SHIV AND TOM'S CAR – DAY

Shiv and Tom together in the back of their car, their driver up front.
Tom holds a can of cranberry sauce. He is on his cell.

                              TOM
    Happy Thanksgiving, Mom. I know. I'm sorry. But we'll see you
    at Christmas—

Shiv looks like – don't think so.

    or New Year.

Shiv makes a 'maybe' face.

    Maybe. But listen, thanks. Thanks for all that. No, I understand.
    Love you too.

He hangs up. He smiles. They drive in silence.

                              SHIV
    Is there a problem?

                              TOM
    No. No. It's fine.

Beat. He smiles tightly. Hums tunelessly.

                              SHIV
    What is it?

                              TOM
    Nothing, it's just my lawyer says—

                              SHIV
    You mean your mom says?

                              TOM
    She's a highly respected attorney in the Twin Cities?

                              SHIV
    Sure, so what did your mom say?

> ### TOM
> She says the prenup is a little bit—

> ### SHIV
> What?

> ### TOM
> 'Unconscionable'.
> (*pause*)
> I mean, that's a legal term. I don't care—

> ### SHIV
> Fine. We'll change it.

Beat.

> Guess I just got Wambsganned, huh?

> ### TOM
> What can I say? She's a hard-ass.

Tom looks relieved.

> ### SHIV
> I tell you what is unconscionable. Cranberry sauce in a can.

> ### TOM
> I know, but your dad loves it!

INT. KENDALL'S HOUSE – KITCHEN – DAY

Frank and Kendall discuss the arithmetic of the firm.

> ### KENDALL
> So, there's Roman, me, you, who'd stand up against him—

Frank gets out a pen and paper and starts totting up. Still no coffee.

> ### FRANK
> Don't you have the pods?

> ### KENDALL
> The pods? Three grams of coffee in six grams of packaging? The
> inventor of those is basically Oppenheimer.

Frank scribbles.

                              FRANK
        Ewan is never there so he won't vote.

                            KENDALL
        And even if he did, he hates Dad. How about Gerri?

                              FRANK
        Gerri? You're dreaming.
                    (*he has a list, considers*)
        But I think – yeah, if – there's no Ewan. Looking at the numbers,
        yes, you know Asha, Stewy, Roman, Lawrence you can firm up a
        couple of doubters. Yep – it's definitely possible?

                            KENDALL
        No CEO has ever survived a successful vote of no confidence,
        right?

                              FRANK
        You know, honestly, I think he might be looking for a way out?

                            KENDALL
        That's the spirit, killer. So, are we doing this?

                              FRANK
        Don't ask me. He's your father.

                            KENDALL
        I'd be doing it for him.

Kendall thinks. Then shouts:

        Carla! Where do we keep the fucking coffee beans?

Frank looks at Kendall: No staff? Carla appears.

        Skeleton staff.

INT. LOGAN'S APARTMENT – FOYER – DAY

*The apartment is beautifully decorated with fall arrangements
and Thanksgiving decor. Shiv and Tom prepare themselves to see
everyone. Last application of lipstick? Tom keeps his tinned cranberry
behind his back.*

                              TOM
        I mean, do we even need to have one?

> SHIV

Yes, my mom and dad's divorce was horrible. I just don't want more . . . mess.

> TOM

But we're not going to divorce.

Shiv thinks . . . no?

> SHIV

Uh-huh? You write a will, don't you? Even though you're not expecting to die?

Marcia comes to greet them—

> TOM

I am expecting to die, Shiv. Sorry, maybe I should have mentioned that when we first started dating.

> MARCIA

Happy Thanksgiving!

> TOM
> (*to Marcia*)

Happy Thanksgiving!

Marcia escorts Tom and Shiv. They head through from the foyer to the living room as Greg and Ewan arrive.

Marcia welcomes them warmly.

> MARCIA

Ewan. Happy Thanksgiving! I'm so happy you came!

She takes his hands. She's giving him her full charm.

He was asking for you when he was in the hospital.

> EWAN

Must have been the drugs.

She smiles – smoothing out all the edges today.

> MARCIA

He's tough I know. You're a pair of noble stags who can't stop butting heads!

She pats Greg's arm warmly, with meaning. She is grateful.

Thank you for driving him down, Greg.

                    GREG
Are you kidding? Great to spend some quality hours with you
Gramps! And how, may I ask, is Logan?

                    MARCIA
Oh you know. But together, Ewan, we will cheer him, yes?

                    EWAN
Well, that's not up to me.

Ewan moves away to the bathroom.

INT. LOGAN'S APARTMENT – ELEVATOR – DAY

*Roman and Grace ride with Grace's daughter, Isla. Roman looks at
his phone.*

                    ROMAN
The Thursday box office is trickling in and it's *killing*. How is
that possible?

                    GRACE
It's possible because, people are idiots.

They arrive and doors open.

INT. LOGAN'S APARTMENT – FOYER – DAY

Marcia is there to greet them.

                    ROMAN
                 (*to Marcia*)
Happy Thanksgiving to my favorite stepmom.

He kisses her.

Remember. No tongues, Mom!

                    MARCIA
                 (*forced smile*)
Welcome. Grace. Isla.

*Marcia has a Thanksgiving present for Isla. As they move inside
towards the living room, Roman looking at phone—*

ROMAN

It's just depressing is all.

GRACE

Rome, that's why it's hard to succeed – because how can geniuses, like us, figure out what morons, like people, will like?

He looks at her: Hm. Really?

INT. LOGAN'S APARTMENT – ELEVATOR/FOYER – DAY

Frank and Kendall look at one another.

FRANK

Yeah. You, me and Roman? So long as everything else went our way? Vote of no confidence and kaboom.

KENDALL

It doesn't need to be horrible, right?

FRANK

Sure. He tells the world he's decided, following his illness, it's time to step down?

KENDALL

I mean it will be fucking horrible.

The doors open. Marcia is right there. Kendall and Frank switch to saying warm hellos.

EXT. LOGAN'S APARTMENT – BALCONY – DAY

Greg is looking at the view. He has snaffled a number of breadsticks and he is eating them furtively. Roman comes out on the balcony.

ROMAN

Hey. What are you up to?

GREG

Nothing.

ROMAN

Are you smoking weed?

GREG

No.

337

                    ROMAN
Do you want to?

                    GREG
                    (*yes*)
No.

                    ROMAN
Watch the door.

Roman takes out a joint and lights up. He takes a big puff as Greg watches closely. He offers it to Greg.

                    GREG
                    (*reluctantly*)
No . . . I shouldn't. Tom might want me to—

                    ROMAN
Come on. Don't be rude. It's the weak sauce, Greg.

Greg takes the joint.

INT. LOGAN'S APARTMENT – FOYER – DAY

Kendall and Frank are in the foyer with Marcia. She's giving Frank some sugar.

                    MARCIA
Frank. Thank you for coming.

                    FRANK
Not at all. Kids are in Denver anyway. We're meant to alternate, but it never seems to be my year. I like to think it's all about the stuffing.

She gives him a pat on the back and rub as Kendall hands her a can of cranberry sauce.

                    KENDALL
For Dad.

                    MARCIA
Thank you. Kendall – say hello to your uncle Ewan.

Kendall looks through the foyer and spots Ewan in the lounge.

> KENDALL
> (*shocked*)

Ewan's here? Uncle Ewan?

> MARCIA

Yes. Isn't that nice.

EXT. LOGAN'S APARTMENT – BALCONY – DAY

Roman and Greg are with Grace, who is smoking.

> GRACE

Oh my god! This is so strong.

> GREG
> (*anxious*)

Is it?

> ROMAN

Oh yeah. You think I smoke schwag? Yeah, you're gonna be *incredibly* high.

> GREG
> (*screwed again*)

Oh, *man*. No.

> ROMAN
> (*looking at phone*)

Fuck!

> GRACE

What?

> ROMAN

The Biggest Turkey. Now they think it's going to set a fucking record for Thanksgiving box office.

> GREG

That's us, right? That's ours?

Roman glowers, then heads inside. Greg looks at Grace as she gives him the joint. Greg tries not to smoke it.

> GRACE

It's not a good film, Greg. When he was at the studio, he tried to stop it. But he got overruled by the jerkies.

GREG

Oh right. Although I guess it has made Roman and everyone more money?

GRACE

That's not the point.

GREG

No, of course. No?

Tom comes out. Greg quickly tosses the joint over the side.

TOM
(*to Greg*)

There you are!

Grace clocks him, no thanks – passes, waving her empty glass.

GRACE

Need more booze!

GREG
(*to Tom*)

Happy Thanksgiving.

TOM

How was the trip? I hear Grandpa Ewan's quite the character?

GREG

Oh, he's okay. Eventually I found an economics podcast he liked to shout at.

TOM

Uh-huh uh-huh. So listen. I actually need you to go into the office today. That cool?

GREG

Could it wait till tomorrow because I just drove all the way from . . .

TOM

Has to be today.

GREG

But no one will be there?

TOM

Exactly. Greg. Listen to me.

Greg feels stoned.

What do you want to do?

> GREG
> I was hoping to just eat some turkey and . . .

> TOM
> With your life? Where do you want to be in five years' time?
> What are your hopes?

Greg is cagey – does Tom know something?

> GREG
> I haven't really . . .

> TOM
> What are your fears?

> GREG
> Well, I mean, you don't mean just spiders . . . you mean—

> TOM
> You and I have had our bumps, Greg. But I want you to trust
> me. And I want to be able to trust you. Yes?

Greg smells he's about to get fucked.

> GREG
> What do you want me to do?

> TOM
> I have absolutely no idea.
> > *(then)*
> It has nothing to do with me. And we never had this
> conversation.

> GREG
> Okay? I mean I am going to need a little more detail, man,
> because—?

Greg feels very high.

> TOM
> You just need to go to the office. Sign out some boxes, do some
> shredding and meet some lovely guys?

GREG

Oh what? Is this the thing?

Greg looks worried.

TOM

Why are you making this a big deal, Greg? It's not a big deal. A chimp could do this, Greg! A little chimpanzee!

INT. LOGAN'S APARTMENT – FOYER – DAY

Connor and Willa arrive, with Gerri behind them. Marcia is icily polite with Willa.

MARCIA

Welcome, welcome.

CONNOR

Happy Thanksgiving.
(*introducing*)
This is . . .

MARCIA
(*sweetly but not sweetly*)
Yes, Willa. I heard you were coming. But I didn't believe it.

WILLA

Happy Thanksgiving! I hear this is Logan's favorite?

She hands over tinned cranberry sauce.

MARCIA

How kind. More. Excuse me? Gerri!

Gerri's brought macarons. Air-freighted from Paris especially.

Gerri? No? From Arnaud Larher? Oh, no, too kind.

GERRI

Well, we can't all bring cranberry sauce!

MARCIA

What would we do without you? You are so good to us. It doesn't go unnoticed.

As they move away, Tom is coming in from the balcony. He joins Kendall and Shiv to react to Willa's arrival. While Gerri clocks Greg and they exchange a look at some distance.

KENDALL

He brought her to Thanksgiving?

SHIV

Do you think she charges overtime for holidays?

KENDALL

It's not cool, man, one day that's a story?

TOM
(*disappointed*)
Oh, did they bring cranberry sauce too?

KENDALL

Forget it. You can't get him anything. Last Christmas. I thought I'd had an idea, new MacArthur biog. He got seven copies.

Shiv and Tom move off towards the living room. Frank appears at Kendall's shoulder.

FRANK

So what the fuck is Ewan doing here?

KENDALL

Plan is a big reconciliation.

FRANK

That would fuck your numbers.

They both look over at Ewan in the lounge.

Whose idea was it?

KENDALL

Marcia, I think. You figure she's on maneuvers?

FRANK

Your dad's suddenly all about changing the trust? She invites me *and* Gerri to Thanksgiving?

INT. LOGAN'S APARTMENT — BATHROOM — DAY

Marcia enters and locks the door. She leans over the sink, looking exhausted and strained. She makes a call.

> MARCIA
> (*in French*)
>
> Amir, where are you?

> AMIR
> (*on phone; in French*)
>
> I'll be there in five minutes.

INT. LOGAN'S APARTMENT — LOUNGE — DAY

Ewan is standing alone, drinking a glass of milk. Studying a display case of Logan's medals.

> KENDALL
>
> Hey. Good to see you, Uncle Ewan. It's been too long.

> EWAN
>
> Uh-huh. Likewise I'm sure. So, where's my kid brother?

> KENDALL
>
> Dad? Resting, I guess.

> EWAN
>
> I drove five hundred miles and he can't come downstairs?

> KENDALL
>
> Yeah, I guess he's still pretty sick. So.

Ewan looks at him, waiting for more.

> I mean, he's up and about. But he's . . . not really . . .
> (*cautiously*)
> quite his old self?

No response.

> (*a little bolder*)
> He's actually acting kind of . . . strange.

> EWAN
>
> Like inviting me for Thanksgiving?

Kendall smiles.

> KENDALL

It's good to see you. I've missed you, Uncs.

He leans in and puts an arm round. Calculated? But also real.

INT. LOGAN'S APARTMENT – LIVING ROOM – DAY

Roman and Grace (a bit stoned) take glasses of champagne from a member of staff. Shiv joins them and takes a glass too. Grace is zoning out. Roman nudges her.

> GRACE

So, how's it going? So sorry about your – woman, Shiv.

> SHIV

Joyce? She won, Grace. She's a US senator.

Roman shakes his head: You're embarrassing yourself.

> GRACE

No I don't think so – because—

> SHIV

I'm pretty sure. I was there. I was up for seventy-two hours. It was kind of a big deal for me? I've been asked to be senior advisor.

> GRACE

Oh. Well, congratulations?

> SHIV

Thanks.

> GRACE

You did a great job because she's quite – unlikable.

> ROMAN

Well that's true I never liked her.

> SHIV
> (*interested/annoyed*)

Oh really. And why's that?

> GRACE

I guess, kind of you know, kind of phoney. Kind of scary.

> ROMAN
> (*funny voice*)
> 'She want to take all my lovely money!'

> SHIV
> Uh-huh. That's, interesting. I mean too fake *and* too real?

> GRACE
> Yeah. It's weird. I guess she just comes off as a sort of a – bitch? You must hear that a lot?

> SHIV
> Yeah, I mean, not usually from family on Thanksgiving . . .

Roman nods to Grace.

> ROMAN
> This is what you're dealing with, Shiv. This is heartland right here.

Roman makes a not-so-flattering face re Grace.

> SHIV
> You don't think she has a sort of, presidential quality?

> GRACE
> Fuck no.

INT. LOGAN'S APARTMENT – FOYER – DAY

Amir arrives. Marcia hugs him closely.

> AMIR
> *Maman! Veuillez excuser mon retard.*

> MARCIA
> *Je suis content que tu sois là.*

Greg and Tom watch from the lounge.

> GREG
> And who's that?

> TOM
> I think – Marcia's son?

They're both weighing up the angles. Roman comes over – via the living room and foyer – slaps Greg and Tom on the back.

GREG
(*gesturing to Willa*)
And who's that?

Connor and Willa are in the den.

ROMAN
With Connor? Oh, that's his whore.

GREG
The woman talking about theater?! Does he know?

ROMAN
Of course he knows. He pays her to suck his cock.

Connor heads to the living room. Willa clocks them talking about her.

GREG
No way!

ROMAN
I actually introduced them at a party a few years ago. She wasn't a call girl then. Well, you could call her. She just hadn't figured out she could charge.

GREG
Oh, man, she's coming over.

TOM
(*looks at phone, to Greg*)
Okay, soldier. You ready? Just getting the deets!

Tom types a message discreetly. Moves away.

WILLA
Happy Thanksgiving!

ROMAN
Happy Thanksgiving.

Greg smiles, fixedly.

This is my cousin Greg. He's very excited to meet you. Would you excuse me?

Roman heads off to get a drink.

GREG
Hi.

> WILLA

Hi.

Pause.

Happy Thanksgiving.

> GREG

Yes.

Pause.

> WILLA

Sorry, did I interrupt something?

> GREG

No. No! We were just . . . We weren't talking. About anything.
We were just . . . talking about the theater.

> WILLA

Do you like theater?

> GREG

No. Not really. I mean, I haven't seen a lot. But of the stuff
I have, not really.

Pause. Head nods.

So, here's a question. Would you rather be trapped in a
swimming pool with a shark or in a cage with a tiger?

> WILLA

Um, maybe in a swimming pool with a shark. You?

> GREG

Yeah. Same.

*Greg nods sagely. Good choice. But he has no more. Tom comes over.
Taps his watch. Puts his arm round Greg, the walk of doom. Greg
smiles farewell at Willa.*

*Tom whispers instructions to Greg as they pass Amir in the lounge/
foyer doorway.*

> TOM
> (*to Amir*)

Hey man!

(*shakes*)
Good handshake. Firm. I can already tell I'm going to like you.

AMIR

Okay. Well, I like your handshake too, I guess.

TOM

And I've shaken a lot of hands. A *lot*. Handshake buddies! Okay you!

(*to Greg*)
Okay. These are the file numbers. This is the room number. You good?

Tom gives a slip of paper to Greg in the foyer. Greg looks scared.

INT. LOGAN'S APARTMENT – LOUNGE – DAY

Roman has returned to Willa now.

ROMAN

Shame I wasn't on a percentage?

WILLA

I'm sorry?

ROMAN

Because I introduced you. I'd be a rich man by now! Oh. That's right. I am anyway.

Connor comes over. Connor can sense the atmosphere.

CONNOR

May I 'cut in'?

ROMAN

What? I was ironicizing. I just think it's better to be honest about this stuff, we're all just raking the green, baby.

CONNOR

That's enough.

Connor takes Willa aside in a corner of the lounge.

WILLA

Nothing I can't handle.

CONNOR

Listen, Willa, here's the thing. I hate the 'jokes'. And I hate the atmosphere – and I've been thinking. And I have an idea.

Willa waits.

You're such a great person. Such a great writer-producer. I want to help you. With your career and . . . really the financial aspect isn't a concern. I can fund your work and—

WILLA

How do you mean?

CONNOR

I mean, I'd like us to be kind of . . . 'exclusive'? You'd get to stop hanging out with other – people – and you'd have more free time for theater?
                    (*pause*)
What do you think?

WILLA

Well it's obviously intriguing.

CONNOR

And if you wanted you could live with me in New Mexico?

WILLA

No.

CONNOR

Of course. I mean—

WILLA

I mean I need to be in the city for my work?

CONNOR

Well that works too! Look we can discuss the details. But it's just great you're open to this – this—
                    (*doesn't want to say deal*)
this opportunity, for progression. It's intriguing!
                    (*then, leaning in*)
It's so intriguing it's kind of making me horny, is it you?

INT. LOGAN'S APARTMENT – LIVING ROOM – DAY

Marcia is gathering people up for the meal. Approaches Kendall.

MARCIA

Should we keep on waiting indefinitely for Rava and the kids before we eat?

KENDALL

They're on their way but . . . please, go ahead.
(*looks at phone*)
It's hard for her, you know, her stepdad is very demanding so—

MARCIA

Of course, it's just a shame they couldn't be with us for the whole day.

KENDALL

How about Dad? Will he be joining us at all?

MARCIA

He'll be right down.

He looks at her. Could she ever be an ally . . . ?

KENDALL

I'm worried about him, Marcia.

MARCIA

I'm worried about you.

She reaches out and touches Kendall's cheek tenderly.

When I see you, you always look so tired. We both just want you to be happy.

KENDALL

Well I am happy. Mission accomplished. Don't worry about me.

MARCIA

(*smiles, unconvinced*)
Shiv's found something she loves. What do you really want to do?

KENDALL

It's clear what I want to do.
(*then*)
And what do you want to do, Marcia?

MARCIA

Oh, just to look after your father. That's all.

KENDALL

Uh-huh? Yeah?

Logan starts to make it down the stairs, looking relaxed. Marcia goes to him from the living room.

MARCIA

Logan! Look who's here!

Ewan makes his way from the lounge, through to a spot where he can see Logan. Ewan greets him.

LOGAN

Well, Ewan.

EWAN

Logan.

LOGAN

How was the journey then?

EWAN

Extremely long. You look terrible, I must say. 'Haggard'.

LOGAN

Thank you, I've been extremely unwell.

An awkward beat. Marcia steps in.

MARCIA

Alright. Everyone! Food's ready. Please!

INT. WAYSTAR – LOBBY – DAY

Greg enters the Waystar building.

There are a couple of security guards – skeleton staff – but it is largely empty.

INT. LOGAN'S APARTMENT – DINING ROOM – DAY

Everyone gathered around the beautiful table. Staff have placed classic dishes around them. It's family style. Grace, Tom dig in. The Roys hesitate. Oh, are we serving ourselves?

352

> MARCIA
> (*smiling*)
> Go ahead please, we're eating 'family style'.

> ROMAN
> Oh, 'family style', what almost like we're a family?

A moment. The turkey is presented. It's huge, beautiful. Oohs and ahs. Logan makes a ceremonial cut. His hands shake and the cut is ugly, jagged. Everyone claps. Kendall and Roman exchange glances. It's whisked away back to the kitchen.

Marcia looks at Logan with meaning.

> LOGAN
> So. How's the ranch?

> EWAN
> Well why don't you come and see for yourself sometime?

> MARCIA
> Thank you, what a kind invitation.

Marcia's greasing the wheels. Frank and Kendall watch them uneasily.

> LOGAN
> Any *squirrel* issues.

He's clearly poking at something.

> Huh?
> (*beat, looks at Ewan*)
> When we were kids, my uncle used to get us to kill the squirrels. I'd throw them in the trash but Ewan used to bury them with Palm Sunday crosses for headstones.

> GRACE
> That's sweet.

Roman looks like: What? Is Grace going to giggle?

> LOGAN
> One time, Ewan had been watching them tanning hides at a ranch. Tell them what you did.

A chance of connection?

                         EWAN
I decided to tan a squirrel's hide.

Roman and Grace start giggling.

                         SHIV
And how do you do that? Pray tell?

                         EWAN
Skin it. Wash it, dry it. Then you use the oils from the brain to
tan it.

                         ROMAN
Bullshit!

                         EWAN
Every animal has a brain big enough to tan its hide.

                         GRACE
Naturally.

                         EWAN
You basically cook the brain into a kind of soup. Then you
mash it . . . .

                         GERRI
I'm glad we're having this conversation while we're eating.

                         SHIV
I must write down this recipe.

                         GRACE
I think it's in Gwyneth's Goop book.

                         EWAN
Then you rub the brain soup all over the hide. Put it in the
freezer. Stretch and soften it. Then you smoke it.

                         ROMAN
You smoked squirrel? Grace, didn't you try that?

Roman and Grace giggle.

                         CONNOR
And then what did you do with it?

                         LOGAN
Used it as a blanket for his teddy bear.

> WILLA

Did one of the serial killers do something like that? I mean yours sounds cute.

> LOGAN

Took him about a week all in all. But you tanned that tiny hide.

> EWAN

I did. Till Aunt Vee threw away the blanket and she threw away the bear. Never been able to hang on to anything, have I, Logan?

An awkward pause. Frank and Kendall exchange a look.

At that moment, Rava enters, looking a little flustered. With her is her daughter, Sophie, looking grumpy and out of sorts.

> RAVA

Hi, hi, sorry we're late— Happy Thanksgiving! We're on the turkey trail.

> KENDALL

Hey? Where's Iverson?

Rava looks like: Come on.

> RAVA

He's outside. He's just having a . . . moment, guys. Sorry.

Kendall and Rava exchange a look, he goes to join her.

I'll stay sitting with him.

> KENDALL

It's fine. I will.
> (*quietly, looking at his watch*)
I thought we were in first position?

> LOGAN
> (*calling over*)
Don't go out there. Get him in here! He needs to be told.

> RAVA
> (*calling over*)
He just needs some time. Transitions are difficult.

> KENDALL
> (*quietly to Rava*)
Maybe we should tell him to come in? Few more boundaries?

Rava looks pissed off and heads out. Kendall follows.

INT. WAYSTAR – CORRIDOR TO BOX-FILE STORAGE ROOM –
DAY

Greg walks.

INT. WAYSTAR – OUTSIDE OF BOX-FILE STORAGE ROOM –
DAY

*Down in the bowels of the building. Greg is at the counter of a desk
which is in an area where packages are maybe received and cargo
comes in and out but also that gives access to document storage.*

> GREG
> Er – these are the boxes I need?

He has a slip of paper, slides it over.

> OFFICE KEEPER
> Okay. Pass?

Greg gives it to him, he writes down Greg's details and the file numbers.

> GREG
> And you presumably, you keep that. Obviously. The record of
> who got what, when?

> OFFICE KEEPER
> Uh-huh.

> GREG
> And that record? Where does that information go?

> OFFICE KEEPER
> No idea.

> GREG
> (shit)
> Cool. Great. Who cares, right?
> (then)
> Just asking cos. In terms of sharing it with third parties? I just
> like to keep pretty a tight handle on my data!

INT. LOGAN'S APARTMENT – FOYER – DAY

Rava and Kendall sit with Iverson, who is sitting on the bench under the stairs, totally focussed on lining up small pieces of Lego.

> RAVA
> Man. Your dad. Fuck *off*.

Kendall tries not to mind this pop at his family.

> KENDALL
> I know.
> > (*beat*)
> I guess, he had it pretty rough. Different generation.

> RAVA
> Uh-huh, go back, I've got this. I'm sure it's my fault anyway.

> KENDALL
> I wasn't saying that, Rava, fuck, I was just saying maybe Iver would like to feel where the line is sometimes?

Marcia appears.

> MARCIA
> Come on, your food will get cold.

INT. WAYSTAR – BOX-FILE STORAGE ROOM – DUSK

Greg's in a room with a shredder and a photocopier, on the phone to Tom.

Intercut with:

EXT. LOGAN'S APARTMENT – BALCONY – DUSK

Tom on the balcony.

> TOM
> Why are you calling me? Do not call me. Is there a problem? Don't tell me if there's a problem. Don't tell me anything. Your phone shouldn't even be on.

GREG

I signed at the depository for the document crates? And I'm in the room, Tom. Is that okay?

TOM

Well you know what to do?

GREG

But is it okay? Because it feels like a Watergate scenario. And I never studied it but I believe I am correct in saying they all got fucked.

TOM

It's okay. Greg! Of course it's okay. It's a job.

Greg opens a box, goes to the shredder. Reads the paper he's about to shred.

INT. LOGAN'S APARTMENT – DINING ROOM – NIGHT

Thanksgiving lunch is breaking up. Night has fallen.

WILLA

So Logan, when do we get to see the famous medal collection?

Connor smiles at her proudly.

ROMAN

Oh, god, please no. Wait. Did someone pay you to say that?

LOGAN

Maybe some other time?

WILLA

My dad was a naval officer. I'd love to see them?

Grace feels outgunned.

GRACE

Me too. Might inspire a jewelry piece. I mean, medals are basically jewelry but for killers.

Roman winces.

LOGAN

Everyone take note, this was not my suggestion.

INT. LOGAN'S APARTMENT – LOUNGE – NIGHT

The kids have gone to watch a movie, but the adults have followed through – Logan is at a cabinet.

> WILLA
>
> And are they expensive?

> LOGAN
>
> Varies. This is a Victoria Cross.

> GRACE
> *(to Roman)*
> You should collect something like this. It's nice to have a hobby.

> ROMAN
>
> Uh-huh, you see me stamp collecting? I guess I could show you my rusty sheriff's badge?

Grace smiles.

> Shiv's got a big collection of pictures of those.

> SHIV
>
> Yeah yeah yeah.

> LOGAN
> *(shows another medal)*
> This is a World War I 16th Canadian Infantry medal.

> WILLA
>
> Uh-huh?

> LOGAN
>
> Now, of course the Assyrians wore medals before the Romans but this is Roman and—

> WILLA
>
> And excuse my ignorance, but did you win any of these?

> EWAN
>
> Ha! Of course not, he's never served.

> WILLA
> *(reaches out for one)*
> Is it okay if I—?

LOGAN

Maybe don't touch. This one did cost rather a lot.

EWAN

Not as much as it cost the man who won it.

LOGAN

I collect them out of respect.

EWAN

Oh I'm sure.

LOGAN

Look, fifty years ago you volunteered for a war because you wanted to impress the town slut and no one's ever allowed to hear the end of it.

TOM

I thought Canadians only fought on ice!

Logan and Ewan stare at him.

EWAN

Thirty thousand Canadians fought communism in Vietnam.

LOGAN

Yeah, thank you, thank you, thank you, what do you want, a medal?

EWAN

Kept us free.

LOGAN

Viet Cong coming up your drainpipe in Ottawa were they?

EWAN

Free to pump your poison. Carnival barker for all the oil wars we didn't need.

LOGAN

Did you even fire a gun? Didn't you end up cleaning grill for the catering corps?

If we see Kendall we might clock he is quite enjoying the growing rift. Whereas Marcia feels the day falling apart—

MARCIA

C'mon now, please—

                              EWAN
They should send you the bodies.

                              LOGAN
'Bear any burden, stir any gumbo.'

                              EWAN
I don't have any of your channels in my house. I see them at the
place I go for noodles. And I'm frankly embarrassed.

                              LOGAN
Bullshit, you don't have them because you're bitter.

                              EWAN
Climate change! The blood of billions on your – hands.

                              LOGAN
Yeah yeah, you got your fucking nut, Captain Cautious.

                              EWAN
Everything isn't about money, Logan.

Logan smiles: Yes it is.

Have you ever heard of ethical considerations?

                              LOGAN
Uh-huh.
                          (*with malice*)
Ever heard of a begging letter?

                              EWAN
One fucking letter? I got a thousand acres, you got the rest of
the world.

                              LOGAN
Oh yeah, big man, big brother, wouldn't eat a blueberry till
they'd been weighed and written in the ledger? Little Miss Prim.

                              EWAN
You can't say who I am, you are not the arbiter of what's true!

                              LOGAN
Yeah yeah. Heard it all before.

                              EWAN
I was told you were ready to apologize.

> LOGAN

For what?

Ewan gets up.

> EWAN

You're all liars. You've lied to me and you've humiliated me.

It takes him a long time to get up and out, the moment threatens to become comic.

> ROMAN

But apart from that have you had a nice time?

> LOGAN

Are you trying to leave dramatically, Ewan?

> EWAN

You may have dragged my grandson into your filth but you won't drag me.

> MARCIA

I'm so sorry.

Ewan heads out. Kendall watches him go.

> ROMAN

I can't think why we don't invite Ewan every Thanksgiving.

Kendall thinks for a beat, follows.

INT. WAYSTAR – BOX-FILE STORAGE ROOM – NIGHT

Greg has lots of papers, ready to shred. He's on the phone.

> GREG

I mean, I don't know what I'm doing. But if I did, it could be really serious.

> MARIANNE
> (*over the phone*)

You don't know what you're doing?

> GREG

What, really?

> MARIANNE

Yeah, really.

                              GREG
Well yeah really I know what I'm doing, obviously. But I think if
it came to court or something I could get off by saying I'm like a
'goofy dolt'?

                            MARIANNE
Yeah I think so.

                              GREG
Well don't assent so readily, Mom?!

                            MARIANNE
I'm just agreeing with your idea, Greg!

                              GREG
The thing is – even if I play the, the, hapless jerk—
                    (*he's written down the details*)
You know the Sarbanes–Oxley statute? 'Obstruction of justice'?
'Spoliation'? I could get fined up to a quarter of a million
dollars. Or twenty years in jail. I don't have a quarter of a
million dollars, Mom.

                            MARIANNE
Well, son, you need to figure this one out? Okay?

                              GREG
D'you think, Mom? D'you think I need to figure it out??
                              (*then*)
I've fallen down a well here and you're shouting, 'You're inside
a well!' Jesus!

He's left anxious and alone.

INT. LOGAN'S APARTMENT – FOYER/ELEVATOR – NIGHT

Kendall catches Ewan getting into the elevator.

                            KENDALL
Hey!

                              EWAN
I knew it was a mistake. I'm going.

                            KENDALL
Can we talk?

Ewan jabs the elevator button, Kendall steps in. Heading down.

EWAN

You can try. He lies. And he thinks he's telling the truth. It's infuriating.

KENDALL

Yep.

EWAN

All I ever got was a mouth full of garbage.

KENDALL

He's tough. He is tough. There's something in there, but he's tough.

EWAN

I thought nearly dying might have changed him?

Beat. Kendall decides to go for it.

KENDALL

I think he has changed. I don't think he's himself at the moment.

Ewan listens. Right?

He's a lot sicker than he's letting on.

EWAN

Uh-huh?

Ewan scopes him out.

KENDALL

He's erratic, he's making bad decisions. I'm serious. If he's not careful he's going to destroy the company.

They reach the ground floor. Ewan looks thoughtful. The doors open. They start to step out.

EWAN

And you have a plan?

KENDALL

I'm considering. Look. I never got a chance to know you, Ewan. But I liked you. I'm going to say something now. And I'm, I'm putting my prick in a cigar-cutter here. But at the next board meeting, there's going to be a vote of no confidence. I mean, do you have confidence, in him?

No response.

So. What do you say?

                                        EWAN
My brother is an ex-Scot, ex-Canadian, ex-human being. But he's my brother and I won't betray him.

Ewan stops stock-still. Maybe even sits on the bench in the building foyer.

                                     KENDALL
Okay. I get it. Let's talk?

Ewan shakes his head. Needs to think.

INT. WAYSTAR — BOX-FILE STORAGE ROOM — NIGHT

Greg, still stoned, has a system going. He's shredding. But every now and again he takes a page – photocopies the page. Then shreds the original. Puts the photocopy on a pile near his bag. It's a good system.

                                        GREG
                      (*singing quietly, stoned to himself*)
Greg's getting it done.
He's not having fun.
But he's getting it done.

INT. LOGAN'S APARTMENT — KITCHEN — NIGHT

Tom finds Shiv.

                                        TOM
                           (*re the earlier bust-up*)
Do you think it's all going to be okay?

                                       SHIV
This is no way our worst Thanksgiving.

Tom takes that in.

                                        TOM
So apparently your lawyer is talking to my lawyer.

> SHIV

You mean your mom.

> TOM

Yeah. She's got all excited about bumps and tiered share option tie-ins for my sperm count et cetera and I'm just saying no no, but she noticed re infidelities there's no—

> SHIV

Yeah we don't need to do that.

> TOM

Cos that's not going to happen.

> SHIV

Right. And if it does. You know. We're both grown-ups.

> TOM

Yes.

(*pause*)

Meaning?

> SHIV

I don't know. Nothing's going to happen. But, things happen. We both travel.

> TOM

I don't travel that much?

> SHIV

Yeah, well, anyway, point is – shit happens.

> TOM

Does shit happen?

> SHIV

No. Not to us. No. But yes shit happens. That's why we have the expression, 'Shit happens'.

Shiv sighs, looks him in the eye. As Roman appears nearby.

Tom. I have not cheated on you. Because I love you.

> TOM

Thank you.

He smiles a big smile.

She leaves. The smile fades a little. Roman is there. How much has he heard?

ROMAN
I believe her. Do you believe her? Of course, she does coach professional liars for a living. So you do have to factor that in.

INT. WAYSTAR – BOX-FILE STORAGE ROOM – NIGHT

Greg puts the (now empty) big plastic orange storage boxes onto a shipping dolly.

Thank god that's over. The four or five sacks of shredded paper he puts on another dolly.

Tucks a file of the juiciest documents into his bag.

INT/EXT. WAYSTAR – LOADING BAY – NIGHT

Greg waits. A van pulls up. Greg greets the guys who are there to take his sacks of shredded material.

GREG
Thanks, guys. Thanks! Just another bunch of corporate materials. Headin' for an extra shreddin'!
(*then*)
Happy Thanksgiving! You're doing a great job! Really proud of you! Have a good one, guys!

INT. LOGAN'S APARTMENT – ELEVATOR – NIGHT

Kendall stands next to Ewan in the elevator. Kendall eyes Ewan, nervously.

KENDALL
Uncle Ewan – what have you got in mind? Because I have to say, I was only kicking some notions around? Nothing is set, so I hope you're not going to make a big deal of this?

He wonders if Ewan is going to tell Marcia what he said.

INT. LOGAN'S APARTMENT – FOYER – NIGHT

As Ewan and Kendall exit, Kendall doesn't know what he's going to do. He halts him in the foyer.

> KENDALL
> I'm only thinking—
>> (*quietly*)
> It's for his own good, for everyone's good.

> EWAN
>> (*quietly*)
> You know it'll kill him. Is that what you want?

> KENDALL
> Of course not. I want him to be able to relax.

Gerri is nearby – in the living room. Kendall can't see.

> EWAN
> Right. What a son. Lovely.

He moves off decisively towards the lounge. Logan comes into view. They regard one another. Kendall fears the worst. Ewan announces—

> Forgot my stick.

He goes and collects it or someone brings it, as Greg arrives and steps out of the elevator.

> We're going. Come on, Greg.

> GREG
> Oh, okay? It's just, I only just got here and – tomorrow I'm kind of busy. I have stuff to, they need me here, basically. I'm kind of important . . . and pretty hungry so—

> EWAN
> How am I meant to get home?

> GREG
> Uber?

> KENDALL
> I'll call one of our guys.

Ewan considers.

> EWAN

This whole family is a fucking nest of vipers. They're wrapping themselves round you and they're going to suffocate you.

Ewan retreats to the elevator.

> GREG

Pretty sure that's boa constrictors, Grandpa. Zoology.

The doors close. Logan looks around full of anger. He spots Iverson.

> LOGAN
> (*to Iverson*)

Okay. You, enough. Get in there now.

Iverson jumps up and goes in.

> (*to Kendall*)

See?

Roman is there watching too and, as others drift away, he hears the sound of children and Grace's voice, laughing. He listens, starts to head upstairs.

INT. LOGAN'S APARTMENT – TV ROOM – NIGHT

The other kids (Sophie, Isla) are watching a screener of The Biggest Turkey. *All the kids have Marcia's presents, identical, unwrapped. They don't want these beautiful wooden toys, they are intent on watching TV. Grace is watching too.*

> ROMAN

What are you doing? Who put this on?

> KIDS

Gracie.

> ROMAN

Why are you laughing?

> ISLA

The big turkey just ate the family's corn.

> ROMAN

And you think that would happen? But how did it even get from Colorado to eat the corn?

(*beat*)

Exactly, that's a big plot hole right there. Enjoy the movie, kids. Grace?

The kids all stare at him and Grace as she gets up and goes out.

INT. LOGAN'S APARTMENT – LANDING – NIGHT

Once Roman and Grace close the door:

> ROMAN

Assholes.

> GRACE

Hey that's—

> ROMAN

What the fuck, Grace?

> GRACE

It was just there. I'm sorry. It's actually pretty good?

> ROMAN

Yeah? Is it. Is it? Really?

> GRACE
> (*don't bully me*)

Yes.

> ROMAN

Well look. Fine. But I think we have irreconcilable differences, so. I think we need to have a talk.

> GRACE

What talk?

> ROMAN

What talk? The 'I'm sorry – insert name here – it's just not working. I hope we can always be blah, let's keep in blah, I'll never forget such and such . . .' That talk.

> GRACE

Oh right, that talk? The 'why do we only fuck once every six months' talk?

> ROMAN

Yeah fuck you. You got plenty.

Roman walks off.

INT. LOGAN'S APARTMENT – LOUNGE – NIGHT

Greg gets in, starving.

> TOM

All good?

> GREG

All done.

> TOM

I don't want to know and don't ever tell me. But well done.
Here.

Tom hands him a glass of champagne.

> GREG

Thanks, man.

> TOM

Welcome to the family.

They clink glasses. Greg smiles. Looks over at Gerri.

*Kendall looks at Frank: What did I miss? Marcia gets a whisper from
a staff member and announces.*

> MARCIA

Okay, everyone. Ready for pie?

*They are ushered back towards the dining room. Grace is there,
drinking and looking pissed off. As they go, Tom tries to break the
tension.*

> TOM

Hey listen, I have an idea. We should do what my family do at
Thanksgiving . . . ?

> ROMAN

Fuck the turkey?

> LOGAN

Go to other people's dinners?

> TOM

We go around and say what we're thankful for?

There's an unenthusiastic response from everyone in the room as they settle down.

MARCIA

Very well. Yes. Let's do that. You go first, Tom.

TOM

I can't go first. I need to go last because . . . I'd like to go last.

MARCIA

Okay. I'll go first. I'm thankful to have the family all together.

She smiles at Amir and at Roman.

ROMAN

I'm thankful I wasn't born a Siamese twin.

AMIR

Because?

ROMAN

What, you would? To be like fused to someone by the chest. Or to have two bodies and one head. C'mon. Gross.

SHIV

Yeah I guess I am thankful for that. And I'm thankful for this delicious food.

Everyone echoes the sentiment.

KENDALL

Yeah me too. The food. Amazing.

GREG

I'm thankful that Uncle Logan is feeling better.

Everyone wishes they'd said that.

TOM

I think we're all thankful for that. That goes without saying.

RAVA

Me? I don't know. I'm thankful I'm not in a refugee camp I guess, this is better than that.

ROMAN

And so say all of us!

Amir is next, looks at Logan.

AMIR

Well. Can I say?

Logan nods.

I'm thankful for the opportunity to head up animation in
Europe and I hope to turn around an underperforming division.

Kendall and Roman look at one another. Classic.

ROMAN

Well I'm thankful you told us about that, Dad?

FRANK

I am thankful for, uh okay, for my two boys . . . And while work
has often kept me from seeing them as much as I'd like, I –
I have been able to provide for them and their education.

GERRI

I'm thankful for Frank not oversharing.

CONNOR

I'm thankful to have Willa here.

WILLA

And I'm thankful to be made to feel so – welcome.

Awkward silence.

TOM

And *I'm* thankful that I'm going to be marrying into one of the
most – interesting and vital and—

He was going to say this, and it's not true but he persists.

kind and loving families in the world!

ROMAN

Let's hold him down and cut out his tongue.

MARCIA
(*re Iverson*)

Please?

CONNOR

Well since we're talking families. I have a little announcement!
Willa and I are pleased to announce I have asked her, and she
has agreed that we are to . . . take the next steps.

Silence.

> LOGAN
>
> You're not getting (married)—?

> CONNOR
>
> No, we're . . . we're, going steady.

> ROMAN
>
> You're 'going steady'? What are you, nine?

Grace is next, people look at her.

> GRACE
>
> Me? Oh I'm thankful for all the love Roman has shown to me and for never being selfish or self-centred or egocentric or neurotic or unfaithful.

Awkward. Marcia jumps in.

> MARCIA
>
> Okay, a game? Shall we play a game. Let's gather the children!

INT. LOGAN'S APARTMENT – BATHROOM – NIGHT

Tom is coming out of the bathroom. Willa is there. They whisper—

> TOM
>
> Congratulations on your 'next steps'.

> WILLA
>
> Thank you.

> TOM
>
> I'm interested to know what 'next steps' actually means. Is there a greeting card I can buy that says, 'Congratulations on *next steps*'?

> WILLA
>
> Your good wishes are all that's necessary.

> TOM
>
> Is there a ceremony? Or is it more of a financial arrangement?

Willa looks at him.

> WILLA

Hey, listen. At least I'm only getting fucked by one member of this family, yeah?

She heads back into the dining room—

INT. LOGAN'S APARTMENT – DINING ROOM – NIGHT

The game is just starting. Kids are there too now—

> ISLA

I went to the market and bought a pony, a big fat hen and this . . .

She hands a can of cranberry sauce to Grace, who is sitting next to her.

> GRACE

I went to the market and bought a new hat, a pony, a big fat hen and this.

She hands the can to Roman.

> ROMAN

I went to the market and bought a crack pipe . . .

The family objects.

What? What? Okay, okay, I bought a gimp suit . . .

More objections.

Fine. I bought a potato, a new hat, a pony, a big fat hen and this.

It's Logan's turn. He is handed the can and suddenly looks very tired.

Come on, Dad, what's it going to be? A hot dog. China. Immortality. Huh? The soul of the nation?

Logan hesitates. Marcia sees his eyes flash with worry.

> MARCIA

You went to market and you bought?

> LOGAN

I went to market and I bought.

There is a pause. Kendall watches with interest.

Local TV.

> ROMAN

Okay. Local TV and . . .

> SOPHIE

Can he buy that?

> ROMAN

Dad gets to buy whatever he wants. So, come on, Pop – 'and'—

> LOGAN

What . . .?

> ROMAN

Clock's ticking. Time's running out.
> (*prompting*)
Local TV, and what did I say?

Logan looks around, confused. Frank pretends not to notice. No need to help.

> LOGAN

Um . . .

> SHIV
> (*whispers*)

A potato.

> ROMAN

Cheating! Come on, Dad!

Logan's POV: the others giving him clues, or trying to misdirect him, or making random comments, all talking over each other – a confusing cacophony.

Kendall watches his dad.

> LOGAN

Big . . . turkey?

> SHIV

Don't mention that in front of Roman!

Everyone laughs. Logan is confused. He looks at everyone laughing, annoyed. Iverson comes to take the can from his hand.

IVERSON

You lose. Grandpa loses! You lose, Grandpa! You lose.

Logan raises his hand to stop him. He strikes Iverson. It's not clear if it's in anger or confusion or an attempt to keep the can everyone seems to be fixated on.

Everyone leaps up. Iverson is crying. Everyone speaks in a rush over one another—

KENDALL

What the fuck are you doing?

LOGAN

Are you alright?
(*then*)
I hardly touched him, it's the shock.
(*then to Iverson*)
Relax. Relax, boy!

KENDALL

He can't relax, can he?

LOGAN

Get him a mirror, get him a mirror!

KENDALL

We're not doing the mirror, let him cry!

Kendall leads Iverson away.

INT. LOGAN'S APARTMENT – FOYER – NIGHT

Kendall is by the front door, comforting Iverson. With Rava.

KENDALL

Are you hurt? Did he hurt you?

RAVA

Yeah?

KENDALL

I can't believe it! He's a fucking monster. They're monsters.

INT. LOGAN'S APARTMENT – LOUNGE – NIGHT

Outside closed doors, Marcia is leaving Logan sitting.

She and Amir are talking in French. Shiv approaches. Amir smiles and moves off.

> SHIV
> I don't think Dad meant it?

> MARCIA
> He would never physically harm another being.

> SHIV
> But Amir. That's hard, it must have been nice for you him being down at Wharton? Tough on you him going to Europe.

> MARCIA
> Life is hard.

> SHIV
> Uh-huh. Still, at least you've got some skin in the game now, ah?

> MARCIA
> I don't concern myself with business, Siobhan. I leave that to you clever kids.

She smiles and heads off.

INT. LOGAN'S APARTMENT – LIVING ROOM – NIGHT

Kendall looks out of the window, drinking a glass of water. Gerri approaches.

> GERRI
> So, what was Ewan talking about earlier, Ken?

> KENDALL
> I don't know. Everyone's pretty upset. Don't take any notice.

> GERRI
> Why was he so mad at you?

He tries to laugh it off.

> KENDALL
> Oh I don't know. It's just the usual family hatred you get at Thanksgiving. You know how it is.

GERRI

Listen, are you planning something?

KENDALL

Yeah. I'm planning on going home and taking some Advil.

He massages his temples. Kendall looks at Gerri. She has him cornered.

GERRI

I love your dad. Personally I'll always be there for him. He's a great man.

KENDALL

Yeah well, no one can argue with his record. You know he used to give us a mirror, when we were kids, to show us how 'dumb' we looked crying?

Gerri's not doing emotions.

GERRI

But my job, I work for Waystar, not Logan Roy. Are you thinking of a vote of no confidence?

Kendall isn't saying – deep in other thoughts.

Because if you are. I've spoken with Frank. And, I've seen all I need to see.

Kendall looks at her in surprise.

INT. UBER – NIGHT

Ewan is in an Uber, heading back to Canada.

UBER DRIVER

Well I've looked into it but I'm afraid from Oswego you're going to need to call a Canadian Uber. Do you have the app on your phone?

EWAN

My telephone is at home screwed to the wall.

He leaves it in the lap of his driver as he looks out of the window.

INT. ROMAN'S APARTMENT – BEDROOM – NIGHT

Roman reads reviews. As Grace packs up her few bits of stuff from his apartment and heads out, he hardly looks up.

INT. WILLA'S APARTMENT – NIGHT

Connor and Willa are in bed, spooning. Connor looks happy.

CONNOR

Thank you for today. I love you.

WILLA
(not sure what to say)

That's – that's a what a lovely thing to say.

INT. SHIV AND TOM'S APARTMENT – BEDROOM – NIGHT

Shiv is in bed. Tom climbs in, he has a nasal strip on to help with his snoring.

TOM

Hey hey hey! Captain Spooner coming in to spoon!

SHIV
(not excited)

You know what. I don't think I can do it?

TOM

What?

SHIV

Joyce's PAC. I just don't think she's the one. I'm not sure I can take her all the way?

TOM

Yeah. Smart. I was never sure about her.

SHIV

You were never sure? Then why the fuck didn't you say anything?

TOM

It's not a biggie. I don't like any pols, Shiv.

Beat.

SHIV

This bed isn't a king is it? We need to get a bigger bed.

It's pretty big.

It's so airless in here, I can hardly breathe.

TOM

You can have some of my air!

He breathes near her.

SHIV
(*changing the subject*)
Could you move over? That's too close.

As she moves, or pushes Tom, she accidentally elbows him hard in the face.*

TOM

Oh fuck, my eye.

SHIV

Oh shit, Tom. Sorry. But you were right over on my side.

INT. ROMAN'S APARTMENT – BEDROOM – NIGHT

Roman looks at his phone. Tutting at the figures.

INT. WILLA'S APARTMENT – NIGHT

Connor sleeps like a baby. While Willa thinks about her life.

INT. SHIV AND TOM'S APARTMENT – BEDROOM – NIGHT

Shiv fidgets, while Tom touches his painful eye and feels sorry for himself.

INT. UBER – NIGHT

Ewan drives through the night, looking at the darkness, really seeing the darkness.

---

* This cut scene is the origin story for Tom's black eye in episode six. Once we had to cut this scene for time, we decided to leave the explanation ambiguous.

INT. LOGAN'S APARTMENT – BEDROOM – NIGHT

Logan is sitting on the bed while Marcia undresses him.

> LOGAN
>
> I went to the market and bought a potato, a new hat, a pony, a big fat hen and this.

> MARCIA
>
> That's right, Logan.

INT. KENDALL'S HOUSE – BEDROOM – NIGHT

Kendall lies awake, thinking – I'm going to do this.

Episode Six

WHICH SIDE ARE YOU ON?

Written by Susan Soon He Stanton
Directed by Andrij Parekh

Original air date 8 July 2018

Cast

LOGAN ROY	Brian Cox
KENDALL ROY	Jeremy Strong
MARCIA ROY	Hiam Abbass
GREG HIRSCH	Nicholas Braun
SHIV ROY	Sarah Snook
ROMAN ROY	Kieran Culkin
CONNOR ROY	Alan Ruck
TOM WAMBSGANS	Matthew Macfadyen
FRANK VERNON	Peter Friedman
LAWRENCE YEE	Rob Yang
COLIN STILES	Scott Nicholson
KARL MULLER	David Rasche
GERRI KELLMAN	J. Smith-Cameron
EWAN ROY	James Cromwell
JOYCE MILLER	Eisa Davis
STEWY HOSSEINI	Arian Moayed
JESS JORDAN	Juliana Canfield
KALFU	Tremayne Rollins
NATE SOFRELLI	Ashley Zukerman
AIDE 1	Esther Chen
AIDE 2	Bret Lada
WAITER	Wayne Stephens
SARITA SHENOY	Surina Jindal
RICHARD	Richard Vernon
TATSUYA	Jake Choi
ILONA SHENOY	Jacqueline Antaramian
PILOT	Julian Wheeler
DRIVER	Dave Bobb
PAUL CHAMBERS	David Patrick Kelly
DEWI SWANN	Robert S. Gregory
DATU	Mihran Slougian
JEANE	Peggy J. Scott
SARAH	Katie Lee Hill
ASHA	Bisserat Tseggai
NOAH	Tom Weiss

DAY ONE

INT. KINGS THEATRE – BACKSTAGE – NIGHT

Stewy and Kendall wait in a long corridor, cement and nondescript, equipment and gear in evidence. There are a couple of folk from the record label. A couple of friends of the artist. Stewy sips a beer, Kendall a sparkling water. Jess is further away. There's noise from down the corridor.

> STEWY
>
> Dude, this is impressive. I'm impressed. You hooked it up for once.

> KENDALL
>
> Okay here we go. Here we go.

Now the artist they've just seen on stage, Kalfu, is heading down the corridor with his entourage. He passes, smiles at Kendall and Stewy, not recognizing them but clocking their air of self-importance.

> STEWY
>
> Great show, man. Way fucking great.

> KENDALL
>
> You're imperial. This is imperial right now. Imperial.

> KALFU
>
> No doubt. Thanks, gentlemen. Good looks. Much obliged, gentlemen.

Kalfu gives them friendly but non-committal smiles. Not quite knowing how much time to give them, but as his head turns and we clock it, his smile fades – who are they?

Stewy looks at Kendall as Kalfu heads off into a green room.

> STEWY
>
> Do we – follow?

> KENDALL
>
> Be cool. Be cool, Stew.

> STEWY
> I am cool. I'm fucking cool.

Kendall doesn't know quite what to do.

> KENDALL
> Jess – will you?

They watch as Kendall's assistant, Jess, speaks with a bouncer at the door to the green room.

> STEWY
> He's your boy huh?

> KENDALL
> So, listen, can I talk to you about something?

Jess returns.

> JESS
> He's decompressing apparently. But he's really keen to connect?

> KENDALL
> He's 'decompressing'? What, from his journey to the bottom of the fucking pop-rap ocean?

> JESS
> But the label has a room for us?

Jess leads them down the corridor. There are acolytes and hangers-on waiting around.

Kendall says hi to people as he goes.

> STEWY
> (to Jess, whispered)
> Maybe remind him he owns the firm that owns the firm that owns the label that pays him, yeah?

INT. KINGS THEATRE – BACKSTAGE LOUNGE – NIGHT

Kendall eyes Stewy as they head into an otherwise empty room that's been held for them. (Maybe it's nicer and different to the corridor, or maybe it's similarly shabby.) It's got some party lights and a good spread of booze and snacks. Including some shrimp around a pot of nondescript dip.

Occasionally passing by are women, and entourage of Kalfu, heading towards the fun in the green room. Noise in the distance.

STEWY

Um, shrimp!
(*takes one*)
Served in la spew. Warmed in an airless box for six hours, and served with – is this – goo?
(*dips and eats*)
It is. Delicious goo.

Kendall decides. Now is good.

KENDALL

I need to ask you something, but once I've asked, I'll have asked, and while it's not a big deal, it's delicate?

STEWY

Dinner and a show. And now I have to blow you?

KENDALL

You give toothy head. Everyone at school said so.

STEWY

So what is it? You've fucked the company?

KENDALL
(*smiles*)
I haven't fucked the company. I have something to tell you.

STEWY

Scientology?

KENDALL

Look, we're friends. I can trust you, right?

STEWY

No.

KENDALL

Sure, but on money stuff I can trust you?

STEWY

No.

KENDALL

Good, look, I know, deep down, I can trust you. Which is why
I'm going to tell you this . . .

STEWY

Uh-huh?

KENDALL

I have a collection of Victorian dolls and I hump them and cry
into their hair.

*Kendall smiles, he can do the funnies too. Needs to project confidence
now.*

STEWY

Uh-huh?

KENDALL

What? You look so serious. No you're going to want in on
this and on the right side because – we're calling a vote of no
confidence in my dad.

STEWY

What the *fuck*, man!

KENDALL

It's the best way forward right now.

STEWY

Oh my god. Holy shit, this is terrible, you're going to fuck the
company and I'm going to lose all my fucking money!

KENDALL

Relax. It's just cleanest. He's, he's – lost it. He's going to
Washington tomorrow. To piss away our political capital and
cement us in a dying sector.

STEWY

You think you can win?

KENDALL

Of course. It's finished. Not even close. I'm informing you, not
courting you.

STEWY

Cos I'll have to work with whoever's left?

KENDALL

Right – with me. So – we good, can I count on your vote for
Team Future?

He offers a handshake.

STEWY

Look. I can promise you I'm intellectually and morally and
emotionally totally behind – whoever's going to win.

*Smiles. Kendall looks confident, big smile. The future's bright. Jess
knocks and enters.*

JESS

He says he'd love you guys to join the party. Very sorry not to
get you in right away. Crossed wires.

STEWY

Okay! Now he's realized! Now he knows!

KENDALL

Stewy, you staying?

(*to Jess*)

Tell him I had to go, and he'll be shooting his next promo on a
fucking flip phone.

*He smiles – it's not true, shit-talk for the room – slaps Stewy on
the back, projecting 100% confidence, but under the confidence,
Kendall's working hard.*

DAY TWO

INT. ROY PRIVATE JET – DAY

*Logan and Marcia and Karl are on the plane. Logan looks dissatisfied
and shifts in his seat. He has a phone in his hand that he's prodding.*

Karl and Marcia shift in their seats.

MARCIA

What's the matter?

LOGAN

Nothing.

(*then*)

Fucking Wi-Fi on this phone. How much do we pay the crooks for this crap?

Karl gives eyes to Lucy, an assistant, who comes over to look.

(*then it works*)

Okay. No it's okay I was on the wrong fucking thing—

He's tired, grumpy. Karl looks at Marcia.

KARL

You want to take five before we get in?

MARCIA

Do you want a cookie?

LOGAN

It's not my blood sugar. I'm pissed I have to come to him like a fucking FedEx guy. Why can't he come to us?

MARCIA

Well, I suppose, he is the president?

LOGAN

Fucking Californian shrunken little raisin. Seen ten of them. He's basically an intern.

(*then*)

And you're okay on this, Karl? On the law?

KARL

Sure thing. Sure. Gerri walked me through it too so—

LOGAN

Wish she was here not you.

KARL

Well thank you. She needs to stay in the city for board-meeting prep.

LOGAN

It's a joke, Karl.

Logan throws his phone at the wall suddenly.

LOGAN

It's gone. It's fucking gone! Call Microsoft, call Gates, we should run one of these outfits, this is all fucking bullshit!

MARCIA

Give him a cookie.

Marcia nods to Lucy to get him a cookie.

EXT. STREET/RITA'S 24/7 DINER – DAY

Kendall walks the street. He pumps himself up. Got to show a positive face on this . . .

INT. RITA'S 24/7 DINER – DAY

Kendall enters. Gerri and Frank are at a booth. He approaches – Roman is ordering—

ROMAN

—and I'm guessing, if I say, cortado with almond you're going to look like I'm some kind of jerk, right, here in 1982 or wherever we are?

Kendall raises eyebrows at Gerri re the venue as he sits.

GERRI

I'm just concerned we don't bump into anyone?

FRANK

So. How did it go with Stewy?

KENDALL

It went great. He's in, naturally.

FRANK

Okay. Well. That's – great?

KENDALL

So we're all good.

Gerri and Frank are nervous. Exchange a look.

FRANK

Uh-huh. Shall I just run it once more, before we open our kimonos in public?

Kendall shrugs, sure, if you like. Frank nods to Gerri. She begins to write down names onto a napkin.

GERRI

So. Givens. Logan. Soon as the vote's proposed, he's recused.
Out of the game. Kendall, Roman, Frank three votes in favor.

FRANK

Asha. Your pet. That's good?

KENDALL

Rock solid. Already floated and noted.

GERRI

Paul, Dewi and Datu are old guard. They'll go Logan.

KENDALL

Yeah well, sure. I mean— But sure.

GERRI

Uncle Ewan? He's still a possible, right? Could you try again to
stoke the resentments?

ROMAN

Oo! Lady Macbeth, getting her little fucking screwdriver in?

GERRI

It's not a fucking teddy bears' picnic, Roman? It's a massacre.

KENDALL

Could do, if we wanted, just, is he unpredictable?

FRANK

Let's not poke. Hasn't voted in years. Count him out. Won't
come.

GERRI

Fine. Ilona?

ROMAN

She's a thousand years old. What has she got, something
disgusting?

FRANK

Cancer. It's quite a common ailment. You might have heard of
it? She's not attended for three quarters – which you'd know if
you had?

ROMAN

Alright, Captain fucking Prickle. Do you need to jerk off?
Because I'm getting a lot of rage here.

Kendall looks at the napkin.

> KENDALL

Looks good?

> FRANK

Got to be tough on ourselves, guys?

> GERRI

I think if you called, explained, she could be another one for Team Kendall?
> (*off Roman's look*)

And Roman.

> ROMAN

Didn't you go on a date with her daughter? You could rekindle the flame. Flash the wang, splooge us to victory?

> KENDALL

Could? Could. Don't want to spread the news too wide?

> FRANK

Lawrence?

> KENDALL

Logan would sell Vaulter for parts. Lawrence would be crazy not to vote with me.

> ROMAN

Except he hates you?

> KENDALL

Bluster. He's my bitch.

But Frank, after a beat, puts him down as 'unknown':

<u>*Predictive Board Vote of No Confidence*</u>

<u>*Against (3)*</u>	<u>*Unknown (3)*</u>	<u>*For (5)*</u>
Logan (Chair, non-voting)	*Lawrence*	*Kendall*
Paul*	*Ilona**	*Roman*
Dewi*	*Ewan*	*Gerri (non-voting)*
Datu*		*Frank*
		Asha*
		Stewy

395

> GERRI

Three for Logan, five against, three unknowns.

Gerri and Frank exchange looks. Still scary. Kendall looks at Roman across the table and, when the others aren't looking, gives him a bit of older-brother sugar, makes a silly face from childhood. These old fucks!

> ROMAN

Oh c'mon, this is bullshit. We push, Lawrence is ours. Ewan could be ours. Ilona could be ours. Gerri can't vote but she can talk for senior management. This is done, there's being cautious and there's being fucking time-wasters.

> FRANK

If you want me to do this. Got to look worst-case. Lawrence, Ewan, Ilona, all in play.

> GERRI

Uh-huh. I mean, just. One more makes us sure winners?

> KENDALL

Sure. We hit Lawrence. Okay?

The waitress brings Roman's coffee. Roman balls up the napkin, drops it in.

> ROMAN

Great.
> (*to Frank*)

Care to drink the evidence?

INT. SHIV AND TOM'S APARTMENT — KITCHEN — DAY

Tom's in the mirror, delicately dabbing his black eye as he speaks on the phone.

> CHRIS
> (*on speakerphone*)

I had a call. The nuclear reactor has been sealed off. We're in the safe zone. It's all good.

> TOM

Great. Great. Thank you. And goodbye. Goodbye forever!

Tom hangs up. Approaches Shiv who is concentrating. Sigh of relief. Kisses her, maybe drops to his knees before her.

I have just been given the all-clear.
> (*to her crotch*)
Yes, O beast of the southern wild!

Shiv is distracted. Watching a YouTube section of one of Joyce's most famous addresses. It's her bravura performance, like Cuomo in '84 or '92 nominating Clinton. Obama's 2009 Inaugural.

Joyce is speaking at a podium, at a rally. The speech plays under what follows:

> JOYCE
> (*on iPad*)

. . . Three men own half of the wealth in America. You know what. That's not a great system. That is not okay. That's not luck, and is certainly not the almighty intervening. That's a system we have built, or a system we have allowed to exist. While we also allow some of the children of our nation to grow up in poor housing, attending poor schools with parents working two or three jobs for wages which are falling because more and more cream is floating to the top.

> TOM

I can finally breathe. Honestly I feel like this nine-hundred-pound gorilla has finally stopped fucking me.

> SHIV

Uh-huh? This the thing I don't want to know about?

> TOM

Uh-huh. And now it's gone. Poof! I think I'm good. Greg. Me. The circle's tight.

> SHIV

And you can trust Greg?

> TOM

Greg's a disciple. He's Matthew, Mark, Luke, John, Paul, George and fucking Ringo all rolled into one.

Tom's thinking – hoping that's true. Shiv continues getting ready. Shiv stops the speech.

SHIV

I don't know. Ugh. I just I – I don't fucking know! Do I stick with her?
(*re iPad*)
Is that a president?

Tom looks non-committal.

TOM

Now I hate to be Groomzilla but can we talk venues? Because I really like Lake Como but I'm worried about fog?

SHIV

I know one thing: people don't change.
(*looks at Tom, and at Joyce*)
Candidates don't change. You plump and primp and re-present but if you think you're going to change them, fundamentally? Forget it.

TOM

So shall we just go very, old-New York classy?

SHIV

Uh-huh, um, on that I kind of had a shitty call with my mom? And to smooth things, I said we might go to England, for the wedding.

Tom doesn't like it.

TOM

You what?

SHIV

Yeah. Is that a biggie for you?

TOM

Excuse me? Shiv? What the fuck?

SHIV

Tom. It's just the wedding. The planners will figure it out.

TOM

'Just the wedding'? Shiv?

SHIV

Tom. I can't do this right now. Okay? I'm thinking about work. I'm looking forward to it, I just can't get into it all. And it might need to be in England but maybe not. Okay?

Tom tries to contain his strong feelings.

TOM

Okay. Fine. Let's talk about it tonight. Let's cuddle up here in our PJs and talk it all out over a Thai and a Gewürztraminer, yes?

SHIV

Uh-huh? Okay. Okay. Let me think.

She heads out.

EXT. RITA'S 24/7 DINER – DAY

The plotters emerge from the diner. Two cars await nearby.

ROMAN

Okay. So I take Lawrence, you firm up the others?

KENDALL

It's okay, I got him.

ROMAN

I know the guy, I see him at every fucking fakers party and phoney soft opening I go to. We're two peas in a metrosexual think-pod.

The three others look at each other. Can anyone trust Roman?

Hey. Are we doing this? Are we running a fucking company together, or what? Just because I like a joke doesn't mean I'm a fucking clown, and just cos you look like a fucking statue doesn't mean you're cool?

Gerri isn't about to engage. Frank looks at Kendall. Kendall needs to keep Roman on-side, he's volatile.

KENDALL

Rome, it's delicate . . .

ROMAN

Oh the delicacies? The little nuances I couldn't possibly—

(interrupts himself)
Lawrence hates you.

KENDALL

And he likes you?

ROMAN

Actually, yes. People like me. I look like a matador and everyone
wants to fuck me. I see him around. Trust me, this one is mine,
okay?

INT. CAR – WASHINGTON, DC – DAY

Logan and Karl are in the back of the car. Logan is fidgeting.

KARL

You okay?

LOGAN

Why? Do you wanna fucking make out with me?
(then)
Course I'm okay. I just want this nailed down.

KARL

Gerri says we have multiple indicators he wants to be
sympathetic to our expansion.

LOGAN

D'you think, Karl?
(after a beat)
He waves this through, he gets hundreds of local TV stations
most amenable to talking about what a fucking great guy he is.

KARL

He just has to be prepared to take a little political heat is all.

LOGAN

Four more years. We're Procter & Gamble of news.

Logan looks out the window, big dreams.

EXT. PENN STATION – DAY

Shiv is outside the station, leaving a voicemail.

> SHIV

Nate, it's Shiv. Thanks for meeting up at such short notice. I'm getting on the Acela now. See you at – at – the old place?

She hangs up. Excited but guilty. Takes a deep breath, makes another call.

Tom, hi! Listen, I'm going to DC. To see Joyce, yeah? I think I've got to do this thing full-on or pull the ripcord, yeah. Get some perspective. Do you mind?

Intercut with:

INT. WAYSTAR – ADVENTURE-PARKS FLOOR – CORRIDOR/
MEETING ROOM – DAY

Tom is walking the corridor. On the phone to Shiv.

> TOM

Sweetheart, no fine. If you need to think about your commitment to Joyce then do it, go. Go to Washington. I get it. I do. Slide her under the X-ray machine, baby!

Tom passes Greg in a meeting room. A meeting breaking up. Lots of cruise and theme-parks materials on the table. People are exiting, Greg was keeping notes. Tom waves. But Greg eyes Tom warily as he gives a little wave back. Tom stops as he passes the entrance then doubles back.

> TOM
> (cont'd)

Hey, man.

> GREG

Hey.

Greg has been burned so many times that he is a little like a beaten dog with Tom. He burrows his head into a laptop.

> TOM

Everything okay, Greg?

> GREG

Oh sure.

                    TOM
Good. Because you know you can talk to me about anything?

                    GREG
Oh? Thanks. Fantastic – resource.

Tom can see he's failed to make a connection. The last people filter out. Tom perches near Greg, he looks up nervously.

                    TOM
Okay, listen. Shiv's going to Washington. How about tonight I – take you out?

Greg doesn't say anything.

No?

                    GREG
What? For real?
                    (*beat*)
I thought you were going to say, 'take you out . . . and beat the shit out of you' or 'take you out and put a bullet in your dumb fucking head' or something else, you know, funny.

                    TOM
No, Greg, I'm not some beast!

Tom smiles. Greg smiles back. Unclenches a little.

                    GREG
Well, I actually did finally get paid and I was thinking of maybe going to . . . have you ever visited the California Pizza Kitchen?

Tom laughs quite hard.

                    TOM
Oh dear lord, no.

                    GREG
It's pretty delicious, Tom.

                    TOM
No it isn't, Greg. I mean it might taste delicious to you, but it's not.

                    GREG
Right. I mean they make a Cajun chicken linguine, just how I like it.

TOM

Well it's not how you're supposed to like it. Look, you probably have quite an undereducated palate. But come out, I'll teach you. I'll show you how to be rich. It'll be fun!

Greg nods and Tom pats him on the back and heads off.

INT. WHITE HOUSE – HALLWAY – DAY

Logan and Karl are escorted by an aide.

AIDE 1

It'll be just along the hallway here, Mr Roy.

LOGAN

Uh-huh. I've been here before.

They arrive in a very nice holding area some way from the Oval Office.

AIDE 1

Someone will be with you shortly.

Logan turns to Karl.

LOGAN
(*he likes it really*)

The whole fucking song and dance.

Another aide comes out to meet them.

AIDE 2

Mr Roy, I am so sorry. But the president passes on his sincere apologies, he's currently dealing with a matter of Homeland Security. He's sure you'll understand, but he's going to need to offer an alternative face for this discussion.

LOGAN

'An alternative face', what the fuck does that mean? I could drop my pants and show you an alternative face, how does that sound?

Aides retreat.

EXT. WASHINGTON, DC – AIRPORT – DAY

Logan and Marcia and Karl walk across the tarmac from the car to the jet. Logan's on the phone, furious. Marcia has an aide with her carrying shopping bags from fashionable boutiques.

> LOGAN
> (*on phone*)
> Have I been snubbed? Find out if I've been snubbed.

> KARL
> I don't think you've been snubbed.

> LOGAN
> (*on phone*)
> Is this a snubbing? Just fucking find out.

He hangs up.

> KARL
> It really might be a Homeland Security issue?

> LOGAN
> Maybe. Or maybe it's the new 'can I get out of gym class, I'm on my Homeland Security Period?' bullshit.

> MARCIA
> Why would he invite you down?

> LOGAN
> To snub. To distance! He thinks this old buffalo is getting taken down, well *fuck him.*

INT. WAYSTAR – KENDALL'S OFFICE – NIGHT

Kendall and Roman in Kendall's office. Kendall is looking over papers. We hold on him. The night before the board meeting. Roman is looking at his phone. They look at one another – but never quite catch the other's eye. Frank arrives – summoned.

> KENDALL
> Hey. One detail, Frank – do we need to slip something in the agenda to cover the vote?

FRANK

Er, sure, it's in. Under the 'Matters for Discussion': Presentation by Management focussed on Performance Issues?

Kendall nods.

And, what's the word, numbers?

Kendall is annoyed by Frank's constant numbers paranoia.

KENDALL

Rock solid. Okay?

It's not.

And final nail. Roman's having dinner with Lawrence.

FRANK

Uh-huh. Uh-huh.

ROMAN

Relax, old man. Relax. Tomorrow we storm the castle.

Frank smiles uneasily and departs.

Using your dome as a battering ram.

Tom is passing as Frank goes, Roman clocks him.

I'm sorry, Wambsgans, but do you have a black eye?

Tom comes in to Kendall's office.

TOM

You should see the other guy!

ROMAN

Who, the guy who jammed his dick in your eye?

TOM

Let's just say – I was in *bed* with Shiv.

KENDALL

And what – she punched you?

TOM

No, it can just get a little hot and heavy. A little freaky-deaky.

ROMAN

Oh, man, that's our sister!

> TOM

So, what's going on? Clue me in.

> KENDALL

We'd just finished, buddy.

> ROMAN

Yeah, and I've got to go eat some fucking – elk or something.

Roman leaves. As he goes, Kendall leans in and whispers in his ear.

> KENDALL
> (*whispered*)

Bag him, yeah? I need him. We need him, brother.

Roman heads off. On his face. He didn't realize it was quite so important.

> TOM

Okay, well, later. I'm gonna show the country cousin how to live in the city on under ten thousand dollars a day!

Kendall stops him. Time to sprinkle some sugar.

> KENDALL

Hey, Tom, just to say, I know you've been eating a lot of shit for me that I don't even know about, and I appreciate that.

> TOM
> (*can't deny it*)

Well, hey. Gotta be done. I just keep on chowing down.

> KENDALL

And I want you to know. I like you. You're Team Kendall, man. Lot of stuff going down, but you're on the team, okay?

Tom is overcome with gratitude. Fixes Kendall with a look.

Do me a favor. Keep your ear to the ground, let me know anything you hear won't you?

> TOM

You got it, brother.
> (*then*)

You got it.

Kendall pats him on the shoulder and exits. Tom watches him go, suddenly feeling ten feet taller.

INT. HIP NORDIC RESTAURANT – NIGHT

Roman is with Lawrence, and his partner, Tatsuya. Their food arrives. He proposes a toast.

ROMAN

Here's to us!

LAWRENCE

To us.

TATSUYA

Yes. To us.

ROMAN

Look at you fucking guys! If you ever have room for a threesome, let me know!

TATSUYA

We'll put you on the waiting list.

This is a big deal for Roman, feels the pressure from his brother. He's in the arena alone.

ROMAN

So look, Lawrence. I need to ask something. But – are we cool? Do we have a level? We can see each other?

LAWRENCE

We can see each other, sure.

ROMAN
(*meaningfully*)

And we're disrupters, yeah?

LAWRENCE

Uh-huh?

They're smiling – kind of flirting.

ROMAN

Right? We don't fear change. We eat change, yeah?

LAWRENCE

Sure. I eat change.

ROMAN

Cool, cool. So.

Roman looks at Lawrence.

Can I say something? What would you say if I told you there was going to be a vote of no confidence? Tomorrow. Kick out the old man, in with the new guard. Romey and the Homey.

LAWRENCE

You and Kendall are thinking of killing your dad? That's kind of Greek tragedy.

ROMAN

Hey, not cool. Did I say I'd fuck Marcia? No.
(*then playful*)
Although, I definitely would. But that's probably Phase Two.
(*then, smiles, looks at plate*)
I have to say, I am very pleased they dug up this particular cache of fermenting organs. Delicious.

INT. WASHINGTON, DC – GEORGETOWN RESTAURANT –
NIGHT

Nate arrives. It's a weird choice. A place they used to go. Shiv had plans but her wires are fizzing with contradictory thoughts.

SHIV

Hey hey hey!

NATE

Sorry I'm late.

SHIV

No worries.

NATE

So. This place has changed?

SHIV

Um. Yeah. I don't know. I mean we've changed. Everything changes.

NATE

What is this? Shiv Roy goes soulful? It doesn't suit you. It's like you're wearing a turtleneck and a stick-on mustache.

SHIV

Yeah. Well. I do have feelings.

That hangs. That's been an argument between them before.

> NATE

So? Congratulations on Senator Miller.

> SHIV

Thank you.

> NATE

I mean, not exactly the fucking Southern strategy getting a bunch of Jews, blacks and media-studies professors to vote in a Democrat in New York State but still—

> SHIV

Fuck you, you've seen the numbers.

> NATE

Yeah, there's a number of ways of analyzing—

> SHIV

I did a fucking good job. In the teeth of a scandal. This point in the cycle? I knocked it out of the fucking park. So here's to me.

She drinks. He drinks.

Thank you. How's everything in the People's Republic of Gil Eavis?

> NATE

Amazing.
> (*beat*)

So. Go on. What is this, Shiv?

> SHIV

Okay. Well I want you to think about joining us. Me and Joyce—

> NATE

Okay? Why?

> SHIV

I need a piece of shit on the team. Like a real amoral fucking knifeman.

> NATE

Well thank you.

409

> SHIV

The team I'm assembling. We're good on strategy, but in terms of rat-fucking and oppo-research, shit-stirring, muck-raking. We need a bit of edge.

He looks at her: Ouch.

I'm just being honest. We can be honest, right?

> NATE

Sure.

> SHIV

This is long-term planning. You know? For now, it's the PAC. But I'll maneuver her chief of staff out, take the top job, we go White House. I'll run things, you could take a nice role. What do you think?

> NATE

I think, is it a good idea? You and me?

> SHIV

Why?

> NATE

Well, historically speaking, we've found it quite hard not to fuck each other?

> SHIV

We're grown-ups.

> NATE

Yeah.

> *(looks at her)*

Yeah?

INT. CHEAP NOODLE PLACE – NIGHT

Greg and Ewan have each got a very heaped bowl of shitty-looking, wormy black bean noodles. Greg's trying not to fill up on food before his expensive dinner.

> GREG

It's great to see you. At such short notice.

EWAN

Shush. Finish.

GREG

Well, I've eaten most of them, Grandpa?

EWAN

Your mother says you don't have any money.

GREG

Well, until recently, but now actually my pay came through and I'm incredibly rich?

EWAN

Well I'm sure you'll be very happy. She told me to feed you. So: finish!

GREG

Honestly, I think my stomach might have shrunk during, during my period of poverty?

EWAN

The waste in this city is repellent. Finish it.

Greg eats.

GREG

And how come you're in town if I may ask?

Ewan looks at him. Decides – why not?

EWAN

Well, you're a grown-up, allegedly, so here's what grown-ups do. Kendall's going to call a vote of no confidence in his own father at a board meeting.

GREG

Right.
(*beat, eats*)
I mean, that sounds like a huge deal? But is it just procedural?

EWAN

It's an extraordinary act of wanton selfishness in keeping with everything I've come to expect from this nest of rats.

GREG

Right. Right. And are you going to tell Logan?

Ewan is slightly relishing the coming apocalypse.

> EWAN
> I am keeping my snout out of the trough. And my advice to you is: paddle your own canoe.
> (*then*)
> C'mon. I paid for that, eat!

INT. WAYSTAR – KENDALL'S OFFICE – NIGHT

Kendall is looking at papers. His phone goes, the caller ID tells him it's Marcia.

Intercut with:

INT. LOGAN'S APARTMENT – FOYER – NIGHT

Marcia, in a beautiful dress and necklace, is about to head out.

> KENDALL
> . . . Yes?

> MARCIA
> Kendall. I was just wondering, if you aren't busy, if maybe it would be nice to join your father for dinner?

Kendall's eyes widen. Does Logan know?

> KENDALL
> Did he ask to have dinner with me?

> MARCIA
> He's home alone. I have something unmissable and it's the first time, since – you know I leave him.

> KENDALL
> Just him and me?

> MARCIA
> Is it a bad time, have you got something planned?

> KENDALL
> Uh. No, of course. Um, I'm around.

> MARCIA

Merci beaucoup. I've left a little steamed fish. Thank you.

Kendall hangs up. Is he about to walk into a trap?

INT. EXPENSIVE POP-UP RESTAURANT – NIGHT

Tom and Greg at a table in an exclusive, high-end secret-supper-club-type establishment. Greg is picking at his starter.

> GREG

'Ummm.'

> TOM

Exactly. When I had their monkfish I thought I was going to shit, puke and cum all at once.

> GREG

Sounds – delicious. Although I actually don't have much of an appetite?

> TOM

Well you better find one quick. Because this is one of the most exclusive pop-ups in the city and we're having the full tasting menu.

> GREG

Uh-huh?

Greg eyes the wine list nervously.

Why aren't there any prices on the wine list?

> TOM

Because they're obscene.

> GREG

Okay?

> WAITER

Gentlemen, wine?

> TOM

Now, Greg? How would you handle this?

Greg peers with the light from his iPhone. And acts as sophisticated as possible.

GREG

Um, er, could we get – a – a maybe a – the pinot grigio, perhaps?

TOM

So, couple of little tips for you. Ask! Only hicks pretend to know. Display your ignorance. It's his problem not yours.
(*to the waiter*)
Two glasses of whatever will go perfectly please.
(*as he leaves*)
Why should we worry? If we don't like it, it's his fucking problem!

GREG

Okay?

TOM

Look. Here's the thing about being rich: it's fucking great. It's like being a superhero only better. You can do whatever you want, the authorities can't touch you and you get to wear a costume but it's designed by Armani and doesn't make you look a prick.

A new dish is placed before Greg. Yet more food!

INT. KENDALL'S CAR – NIGHT

Kendall is in the car, anxious. Practicing a nonchalant smile. What the fuck is going on? Maybe nothing is going on? Or maybe this is the end of the world?

INT. HIP NORDIC RESTAURANT – NIGHT

Lawrence has just posed Roman a question—

LAWRENCE

Here's the thing. If I was going to come in with you I need to know – what's your vision?

ROMAN

It's me and Kendall. Romey and the Homey. We storm the castle. We're the fucking French New Wave—

LAWRENCE

Not Kendall. *You*. What's *your* vision?

Roman's feet to the flames. He falls straight back on schtick.

> ROMAN

My vision? Is like all the kids, all the black ones and the brown ones and all the white ones they all, get together and do wind power. And fuck, or something.

> LAWRENCE

Uh-huh?

Lawrence looks at him, losing faith.

> ROMAN

Look. You know what. I ended up in a bookshop the other day and I just started to laugh?

> LAWRENCE

Uh-huh?

> ROMAN

Yeah, I looked at all the books cramming up all the walls and I just thought, you know, about the olden days, all the fucking monasteries and the bibles and the sermons and the 'did Jesus say this? Or mean that?' and all the wars and what-have-you. All *gone*. No one gives a fuck.

> LAWRENCE

You're saying. We're going post-literate?

> ROMAN

Oh, people are gonna read, but the old world it's gone. Papers gone. 'News' gone. Channels gone. Big man gone. 'Tune in to ABS at nine o'clock to get told what to think.' No. Over. It's all about the morsels, man, feed me the fucking tasty morsels. Keep me interested. That's where we're headed. Tasty morsels from groovy hubs. We need to be in the hub club.

> LAWRENCE

Yeah?

Roman is right on the edge of being convincing.

> ROMAN

Look. I'm dumb but I'm smart, okay? I'm too dumb to fix our whole company. I've got no attention span. This is the most interesting thing that's happened in my whole life and I'm thinking about six other things. But I'm fucking smart enough to see what needs changing. And I'm smart enough to spot the people who can help, *Lawrence*. So, are you in?

                    LAWRENCE
Well. I'm on the side of change.

Roman's phone goes. It's Kendall in his car. Roman walks away with a wink.

Intercut with:

INT. KENDALL'S CAR – NIGHT

                    KENDALL
So, listen, Marcia's asked me to have dinner with Dad?

                    ROMAN
Fuck. He knows. Does he know?

                    KENDALL
I don't know.

                    ROMAN
He knows. Don't go. It's going to be horrible. He'll chop your dick off and stuff it in your mouth.

                    KENDALL
Well it's either tonight, or tomorrow, but he's gonna find out, bro, so I'm going.

                    ROMAN
Did he mention me?

Roman looks over at Lawrence and his husband. Gives them a less relaxed 'it's all fine'.

                    KENDALL
What did Lawrence say?

                    ROMAN
                    (beat)
He's in.

                    KENDALL
For real?

ROMAN

Yes, for real. Fuck you.

KENDALL

Great. Thanks. If you don't hear from me assume we're good.

ROMAN

Sure. I'll assume that. Or that you can't talk because your mouth is taped up and full of severed dick.

INT. EXPENSIVE POP-UP RESTAURANT – NIGHT

Greg and Tom are finishing their plates. Greg's stuffed. But already they are being approached by a waiter carrying two small bowls, each containing a small fried object.

GREG

Oh Jesus, what now?

TOM

Ortolan.

GREG

What—

TOM

It's a deep-fried songbird. You eat it whole.

Greg looks down at the delicacy in his bowl.

GREG

Tom, are you fucking kidding me?

TOM

Be cool. This is a rare privilege. It's kind of illegal!

They're handed large white napkins. Tom seems to know what he's doing. Greg's less sure. Looks to Tom for a prompt.

(re napkins)

For the head. The exact purpose is debated. Some say it's to mask the shame. Or heighten the pleasure.

Tom drapes the napkin over his head, obscuring his face. Greg leaves it a beat.

417

>   GREG
>
> Really, man?

He follows suit. Tom and Greg sit at the table, white-linen napkins draped over their heads. Tom reaches down and takes the bird. Crunches into it.

>   TOM
>   (*from under napkin*)
>
> My god. *So* good.
>   (*then*)
> Did you eat it yet, Greg?

>   GREG
>   (*from under napkin*)
>
> Not yet, no.

>   TOM
>
> Eat it, Greg.

Greg takes the bird. And bites into it. Crunch.

>   (*from under napkin*)
>
> Yeah?

>   GREG
>   (*from under napkin*)
>
> I mean, I guess?
>   (*then*)
> It's quite crunchy? And wow. That's a rather – unusual – flavor?

>   TOM
>   (*from under his napkin*)
> It's that brainy, gamey hit, my friend.

Tom and Greg remove their napkins and hand them to the waiter.

> Thank you.

Tom holds out a fist to Greg.

> Songbird bros.

>   GREG
>
> Songbird bros.

Tom smiles. He feels like maybe he's just made Greg complicit in something. Tom gestures to the waiter for more wine. Greg eyes him.

What is this? Are you, are you trying to seduce me, Tom?

TOM

Hahaha! Yes. I am! Hahaha. Because the things we've done, the things we've seen. We're in this together, right?

GREG

Oh okay. Is that what this is? The *thing*?

TOM

No. No, man, no. Well, I mean, look, we have a bond, but also – I recognize myself in you.

GREG

You do?

TOM

Sure. I was an outsider once. A young guy from St Paul, alone in the big city. And it was hard. You have to know where to go and what wines to drink and what suits to wear and you have to wear this hard shell but really we're little nudie turtles.

Beat.

GREG

Okay, can I level with you, because if I have to eat any more songbirds I'm going to barf. My grandpa already bought me dinner.

TOM

Your grandpa's – in New York? What for?

GREG

Well – okay. Look, here's something, that – he – he – he he's come down for this vote of no confidence in Logan tomorrow? Did you know about that?

TOM

Are you serious?

GREG

He's come down especially to vote. That's kind of a big deal, right?

Tom excuses himself, gets up.

INT. WASHINGTON, DC — GEORGETOWN RESTAURANT —
NIGHT

Post-meal.

> NATE
>
> Here's my thing. You say you want me, but really, you don't.

> SHIV
>
> Ooh, it's exciting when you know more about me than I do!

> NATE
>
> You want me for my edge? Why? Because she's not edgy
> enough. I can't fix her. I'm just a guy. You should be working for
> a winner like Gil.

> SHIV
>
> Right. You know I am actually a considerably more successful
> political strategist than you?

> NATE
>
> You can only work with what you've got and what you've got
> is – bluurgggh.

He's hit a nerve.

> SHIV
>
> I've been grooming Joyce for three years.

> NATE
>
> I've looked at her, from our side and she – she kind of appeals to
> everyone.

> SHIV
>
> Exactly.

> NATE
>
> Which is a little like appealing to no one? She's nice. She's just a
> very nice person.

> SHIV
>
> What a horrible thing to say.

NATE

Look, you know how you're marrying that guy, that corn-fed
basic from hockey town?

SHIV

Tom's a great guy.

NATE

Sure. 'Great guy'? And you work with the nice black lady? What
are you trying to prove?

SHIV

You're such a fucking prick.

NATE

You should be with some exciting bastard like me?

SHIV

I tried playing with you, you broke.

NATE

And you should be working for some fucking winner. Like Gil.

SHIV

Gil's a strong flavor.

NATE

That's the way we're going. Flavor. To the max. Extra cheese,
extra chilli.

SHIV

And what does an amoral mercenary like you see in him?

NATE

Even Gandhi carried a gun. Look, I want to shake shit up.
I think things.

SHIV

Oooooh.

NATE

Plus. He's a winner. Take a look at your banknotes, Shiv. Not a
lot of black ladies on them? Don't shoot the messenger, I'm just
saying, why make it hard on yourself? What's wrong with the
average white band?

INT. LOGAN'S APARTMENT – ELEVATOR – NIGHT

Kendall rides the elevator. Nervous. Sweaty palms. Swallowing hard. Trying to breathe deeply but it's hard because of the tightness in his chest.

The elevator arrives. He steps out.

INT. LOGAN'S APARTMENT – FOYER – NIGHT

Kendall looks round. Richard, the houseman, is there.

> RICHARD
> Your father's on a call in the den. He asked if you'd wait a moment?

Kendall looks panicked. Who's he on a call to? He can't bear the tension. Has to do something. He steps in to the bathroom, closes the door. His phone goes—

INT. EXPENSIVE POP-UP RESTAURANT – NIGHT

Tom stands away from Greg.

Intercut with:

INT. LOGAN'S APARTMENT – BATHROOM – NIGHT

> KENDALL
> Tom, can this wait till tomorrow?

> TOM
> You're gonna want to hear. Ewan is in town. He knows and he's come to vote.

> KENDALL
> Who's your source?

> TOM
> *(so Greg can hear)*
> Can't reveal my sources.
> *(so Greg can't hear)*
> But it's Greg. Greg is my source. We're having dinner. He just saw Ewan.

> KENDALL

Fuck! Seriously? Fuck! Okay, Tom, you do not breathe a word of this.

> TOM

No way, hombre. My lips are sealed.

> KENDALL

Alright. Thanks, Tom. I appreciate it. Big time. I won't forget this.

Tom's delighted with the approval.

> TOM
> (*this is a big deal*)

Not a big deal. Team Kendall.

Kendall looks anxious.

Tom hangs up, crosses back to Greg.

Greg. It's happening. The troops are taking Saddam's palace. This time tomorrow, you and me . . .
> (*makes the calculation*)

I could be like . . . the third most important man in the company.

INT. LOGAN'S APARTMENT – FOYER – NIGHT

Kendall waits, takes a deep breath. The houseman leaves the den, indicates Kendall can go in.

INT. LOGAN'S APARTMENT – DEN – NIGHT

Kendall walks in. Logan has a Big Mac underway. On nice china. Fries and ketchup. There's a burger for Kendall too.

Kendall watches him. Logan watches Kendall watching him.

> KENDALL

Hey, Dad? Should you be eating that?

Logan fixes him with a look.

> LOGAN

You're not the boss of me.

Kendall sweats – what does that mean? He swallows hard. Logan smiles. Kendall sits.

> KENDALL
>
> Did you want to talk? Marcia said you wanted to see me?

> LOGAN
>
> She's got her own game going on.

> KENDALL
>
> What does that mean?

> LOGAN
>
> You know what it means. You've got your game going on.

Kendall's heart stops.

> I've got my game.

> KENDALL
>
> What's your game?

> LOGAN
>
> Everyone's got a game.

Beat. Kendall can't stand the tension. He'd rather know. Even if he's going to hate what he hears.

Logan eats some more.

> LOGAN
>
> So. What's going on, what's the action? What's the story?

> KENDALL
>
> What's going on?

> LOGAN
>
> You heard about my meet? You heard if it was a snub?

> KENDALL
> *(realizing Logan doesn't know)*
>
> What? Oh, yeah. I heard. It's tough to read. I heard real security alert? But who knows. You know what I think of the whole endeavour.
> *(beat)*
> I still think if you changed your mind that could be great for everybody . . .

Is there a way for Kendall to avoid tomorrow?

       LOGAN
  I'm not discussing that.

Silence. They watch TV.

  Thank you for coming though.

Kendall nods.

  And, so, you know, the thing with Iverson. That was an
  accident. You try to be a good dad.

       KENDALL
  Thank you.

INT. EXPENSIVE CLUB – NIGHT

*Tom and Greg are shown out of the club into the VIP lounge, or to
an area some distance off from the club. They look down/over/out at
the party raging below.*

       GREG
  I think I deserve a beer!

Greg goes to head off.

       TOM
  No need. It's bottle service. I ordered vodka.

       GREG
  I mean, okay?

He sits with Tom.

  And this is – what you do is it? You like come to the club and
  then you come to another bit where the club, sort of isn't?

There is some ceremony about the delivery of the bottle.

       TOM
  Uh-huh, drink up. It's two thousand bucks a pop.

       GREG
  . . . Why?

*Tom points to the attractive VIP bottle-service girl who pours their
gold-leaf vodkas with a smile.*

> TOM

Financial self-harm. It hurts a little to let you know you're alive.

They down a couple of shots.

Come on, Greg! We're celebrating!

They raise their glasses.They clink glasses and the gold leaf twirls round in them.

> GREG

Is this gold leaf?

> TOM

Drink the gold, my friend. Then later, you and I will take a twenty-four-karat piss!

INT. KENDALL'S CAR – NIGHT

Kendall's on the phone with Frank.

Intercut with:

INT. FRANK'S HOUSE – STUDY – NIGHT

Frank is in his study.

> FRANK

Does he know? I heard he might know?

> KENDALL

I don't think so. No. I don't think so.

> FRANK

Any news?

> KENDALL

Er, we have Lawrence.

> FRANK

Okay. That'll make me sleep easier, if I can sleep, which I won't.

> KENDALL

I'm just going to call Sarita and check Ilona's out of the action.

> FRANK

Do we need—? You not worried that could stir things—?

KENDALL

Just to cover all the bases.

(*beat*)

Frank. Listen, is this? Is this – objectively, horrible? Is it time to—? Should we hold off, should we see what develops and then we can put this together next quarter or—?

FRANK

Ken. You've put this together. It's hard enough to get five fucking people together on the same night for dinner. You think you can do all this again next time around, then go ahead, hold off.

Kendall doesn't speak, the silence is telling. He can't back down now.

Strength. Good strength, my young friend, you're a good kid. You are. Night, Ken.

EXT. STREET – NIGHT

'Black Steel in the Hour of Chaos' by Public Enemy plays. Kendall, stepping out of his car, moves towards his house. He pulls out his phone.

KENDALL

Hi Sarita. Sorry to call so late. I was just – thinking and—

SARITA

Nice to hear your voice.

KENDALL

Well it's nice to hear your voice. Yeah. Yeah. I – I felt bad and I wanted to check in on your mom. I assume she can't make it to the board meeting right, sadly?

INT. WASHINGTON, DC – HOTEL ROOM – NIGHT

Shiv and Nate are still drinking on a couch in Shiv's nice hotel room.

NATE

So tell me more about Mr Potato Head?

SHIV

Tom. He's amazing. He's great.

NATE

Okay? Great.

SHIV

It is great.

NATE

Well I'm pleased.

SHIV

But he is great.

NATE

You're convincing me, Shiv, you are, it's the constant, sort of weary repetition I think?

They drink.

I've called Gil to let him know you might be available.

He looks at her.

SHIV

We're not going to fuck tonight, right?

NATE

You know I'm getting married too?

SHIV

Really? Car model or failed actress?

NATE

Ouch! There she is. Welcome home, Shiv. She's actually a French doctor.

SHIV

I'm kidding of course. That's nice.

NATE

I mean. We could do other stuff? Theoretically.

They smile.

SHIV

I'm getting married in March.

NATE

I'm getting married in May.

SHIV

Well, it's not a competition.

NATE

Sure but only one of us is getting married in lilac season and it's not you.

She smiles.

Look. I have to say – I feel quite— I mean, could we masturbate in separate rooms? That's quite – modern?

SHIV

Oh no, come on, Nate.

NATE

Look, or, for old times' sake, last one, absolute last one – I could just – the old traditional – simply – stick it in?

SHIV

Right, 'Romeo, Romeo, why don't you come up here and stick it in?'

Nate laughs.

A French doctor? She sounds too nice and interesting for you.

NATE

Oh, she's not that nice. Deep down she's status- and money-obsessed like you.

She smiles.

SHIV

I think this is nice. This is like being friends right?

Nate gets a text.

NATE

Okay. Gil's interested. He's very interested, Shiv? I think you should do this? You're hot.

Shiv smiles.

You're so hot right now.

The mix of everything has got pretty heady. He puts a hand on hers.

>   SHIV
>
> Nate, but shall we be good people?
>
>   NATE
>
> I'd like to – but—?
>
>   SHIV
>
> Would that be nice? To wake up tomorrow and be like, phew,
> maybe I'm not a piece of shit?
>
>   NATE
>
> I did text Brigitte with a pretty high-level lie about why
> I wouldn't be home tonight? Seems kind of a waste?
>
>   SHIV
>
> You could stay here? We could try?
>
>   NATE
>
> Not to – all night? Jesus Christ, Shiv.
>
>   SHIV
>
> It would be the single greatest feat of fortitude in the history of
> human existence.
>
>   NATE
>
> It'd be like Lincoln delivering the Gettysburg address, with a
> hard-on.
>
>   SHIV
>
> They'd build statues of us.

She looks at him.

DAY THREE

EXT. KENDALL'S HOUSE – EARLY MORNING

*Kendall is let into his car by his driver, Fikret. They exchange
greetings.*

INT. WASHINGTON, DC – HOTEL ROOM – EARLY MORNING

*Shiv is trying to sneak out of the hotel room, leaving Nate – who's
slept on the couch but is awake. Phone by his side. Just before she
goes he takes her in—*

                              NATE
Hey, Shiv. You do know you're amazing, right?

                              SHIV
I guess.

                              NATE
Come meet Gil. He's not a pipe dream, Shiv. He's going to go all
the way.

Shiv's heard enough, she turns to go.

                              SHIV
We were good. We were really good.

                              NATE
You're a blond beast. You should have whatever you want.

Shiv smiles, thinking.

EXT. FRANK'S HOUSE – MORNING

Frank is climbing into Kendall's car. Kendall is nervous, covering.

                             FRANK
Hey? Still all good?

                            KENDALL
Still all good. Tight, but, you know, all the variables swing our
way?

*Kendall's phone rings. He clocks the name. Alarm. He answers,
speakerphone.*

                            KENDALL
Sarita?

An older voice, Ilona's, emerges:

                             ILONA
                       (*on speakerphone*)
Hello, Kendall?

                            KENDALL
Ilona?! You're up? How are you? Did you get my gift?

Intercut with:

INT. LONG ISLAND HOSPITAL – ILONA'S PRIVATE ROOM –
MORNING

Ilona with Sarita in the background.

>   ILONA
> Yes, so my daughter told me you don't want me voting in
> today's board meeting is that right?

>   KENDALL
> No, no. That's not it at all. That's— Can I explain?

>   ILONA
> Well, I'm letting you know, I'll be dialing in.

>   KENDALL
>   (*tries to control the alarm in his voice*)
> Okay, well there's some context and – there's some issues.
> I know— Look, could I come and talk it through?

>   ILONA
> I'm going to dial in.

Beat.

>   KENDALL
> I'll be there in an hour. We need to talk. Thanks, Ilona!

Frank looks at Kendall as he hangs up. Fuck.

>   FRANK
> You're going all the way out to her? Is there time?

>   KENDALL
> I can make it. Fikret, call Jess. I think I have to go. I need to see
> what's in her eyes. And she needs to see what's in mine.

EXT. NEW YORK – MORNING

The helicopter flies from Manhattan towards Long Island.

EXT. HELIPORT – MORNING

Kendall gets out of helicopter to awaiting car.

INT. LONG ISLAND HOSPITAL – ILONA'S PRIVATE ROOM – LATE MORNING

Kendall is with Ilona. Sarita stands in the doorway. They've been talking for some time but now Kendall has dropped the bomb.

> KENDALL
> Look, Ilona. He was a great man. But you know he was also a bully and a— Well he had many faults. When he was doing great work everyone was happy to ignore it. But he's putting us in a nosedive. It's time to look to the future.

Ilona thinks about this. She might not disagree with him.

INT. LOGAN'S APARTMENT – MORNING

Logan gets dressed for his board meeting. Marcia gives him a kiss. They look sweet. They look happy.

INT. ROMAN'S CAR – DAY

Roman looks out of the window at the city. He feels pretty alone.

EXT. LONG ISLAND HELIPAD – DAY

Kendall returns to the helipad. He's surprised to see the helicopter is not fired up.

> KENDALL
> Are you ready? Let's go.

> PILOT
> I'm sorry, Mr Roy, skies are closed. There's a temporary flight restriction. Possible terror threat.

> KENDALL
> No. I need to go, pal. I'll pay whatever fine they hit us with. Let's go.

> PILOT
> Can't do it, sir. FAA would pull my license.

Kendall thinks.

> KENDALL
>
> What do you need to take off right now? Anything. Whatever you lose financially, I'll make up in perpetuity.

> PILOT
>
> I don't think anything would make up for us getting shot down by an F-16.

On Kendall – fuck. Very bad.

EXT. AIRPORT/INT. CAR – LATE MORNING

Kendall jumps into the car-service car that has taken him from the hospital to the airport.

> KENDALL
>
> How long to get to the city? Financial District.

EXT. LOGAN'S APARTMENT BUILDING – MORNING

Logan walks to his waiting car. He smiles at his driver.

> LOGAN
>
> Morning, Colin. Good day for the race.

He has done this joke many many times—

> COLIN
>
> Uh-huh. What race, sir?

> LOGAN
>
> The human race!

INT. MARRIOTT HOTEL – MORNING

At the modest self-service breakfast buffet that comes for free with a room. Ewan takes a croissant in a napkin. A coffee from the urn.

Where there are a few papers by the door he takes a copy of his brother's New York tabloid and drops it in the recycling.

INT. CAR – MORNING

The car has come to a standstill in the Battery Tunnel. It's backed up. Kendall's on the phone with Gerri.

                    KENDALL
I'm on my way. The traffic's stopped. I need you to stall.

Intercut with:

INT. WAYSTAR — BOARDROOM — MORNING

                    GERRI
It's a bad line? I can't hear you?

                    KENDALL
Gerri? Can you, we're going into a tunnel. Stall.

He stops. No bars. Kendall pounds his seat.

                    (to driver)
Is your phone working? Can I get a motorcycle courier?
Something. Can you call your office?

INT. WAYSTAR — BOARDROOM — MIDDAY

*The hand on the clock on the wall is inching towards noon. There are
bagels and fruit and coffee displayed.*

*Gerri comes off the phone with Kendall and tries to look nonchalant.
Gerri texts Frank. Frank comes over.*

                    GERRI
He's in traffic.

                    FRANK
Oh what? Are you fucking kidding?

                    GERRI
He says how long can we hold it?

*Paul Chambers and Dewi Swann chit-chat in the corner, comparing
medical procedures, completely unaware of what is to come.*

                    PAUL
Boston Scientific. It's the Cadillac of stents, my friend.

*He bangs his chest. Lawrence stands by the window. Roman comes
by, friendly.*

> ROMAN

Hey, man, so how are we feeling?

> LAWRENCE

Good. Nice to see the war criminal.

Roman gestures to Datu, looking intimidating already seated in the corner.

> ROMAN

Fucking nice guy. Lovely guy.

They chuckle. Lawrence continues to assess the room.

We good? We solid?

> LAWRENCE

I heard Logan started on time even when he was airlifted in from Aspen with the shattered femur?

Asha seems nervous. She makes eye contact with Roman. Walks behind him.

> ASHA
> (*whispered*)

Where's Kendall??

INT. CAR – MIDDAY

The car's gridlocked in the Battery Tunnel. Kendall is bursting with energy, opening the window, peering out.

> KENDALL

What is going on? What?

> DRIVER

They're evacuating five blocks each way from the Stock Exchange. Gridlock.

INT. WAYSTAR – BOARDROOM – MIDDAY

The clock ticks to noon. The room hushes. Logan arrives.

Roman, Gerri and Frank exchange nervous glances: Where the hell is Kendall?

LOGAN

Morning, morning. Good turn-out. So, Frank? Will you whip us through?

FRANK

Um, sure. Um, I've just had word, I believe Kendall will be a few minutes late. Request for a late start?

LOGAN

No, he can catch up. Fuck that – where is he?

FRANK
(*covering*)

Stuck in traffic. That's all I know.

LOGAN

Come on, let's go.

Beat. Frank has no choice.

FRANK

So, it's twelve noon and I'd like to call this meeting of Waystar Corporation to order. Roll call. Logan Roy, present. Frank Vernon, present. Kendall Roy, absent. Roman Roy, present. Ewan Roy, absent. Ilona Hughes, absent. Datu Kassuma, present. Dewi Swann, present. Paul Chambers, present. Asha Khan, present. Lawrence Yee, present. Stewy Hosseini, present.
(*looks at Logan*)

Mr Chair, we have a quorum.

Logan grunts.

We also welcome our esteemed general counsel Gerri Kellman to the meeting.

Gerri nods.

So, everyone has received a copy of the agenda and the minutes from our last meeting . . .

He looks around – various nods.

EXT. BATTERY TUNNEL – DAY

Kendall opens the door. It's a long way down the tunnel.

437

>   DRIVER
>   What are you doing?

For Kendall, there is only forward. He gets to a bit of road or raised walkway and starts to run.

EXT. STREET NEAR BATTERY TUNNEL – DAY

Kendall emerges out of the tunnel.

There is heavy backed-up traffic. Kendall weaves, it's starting to move here and there.

INT. WAYSTAR – BOARDROOM – DAY

The board goes through the PowerPoint. The usual updates. A senior corporate figure, Noah the Corporate Secretary, takes the minutes in the corner.

>   FRANK
>   As you may remember, that project was having some technical
>   issues and some of the costs were running higher than expected.
>   I think that's all.
>   (beat)
>   Do we have approval for the minutes?

Various responses of approval.

>   (looks at Noah)
>   Okay, the minutes are approved.

A small stir outside. Roman, Gerri, and Frank strain a little in their seats, thinking 'It's Kendall, thank god.'

Ewan walks in. Logan looks at him.

>   LOGAN
>   Ewan? Can't keep you away.

>   EWAN
>   Well, thought maybe I'd show up for once? Watch the fun.

Logan looks around. Is there something strange about this? A seasoned corporate antennae twitching.

GERRI

Great to have you.

EWAN

They wouldn't let me in downstairs without a passport. Has it started?

Ewan looks around defiantly. An assistant gives him an agenda. She tries to stand over him to pour a glass of water, but he waves her away.

Logan looks at Ewan. His wheels turning.

EXT. STREET — DAY

Kendall looks at his watch. He's already eight minutes late. He calls up to Roman.

Intercut with:

INT. WAYSTAR — BOARDROOM — DAY

Roman gets up, turns away from the room.

ROMAN
(*into phone, whispered*)

Kendall? Where are you? We've already started, man, we started. What are we doing?

Kendall is running, sucking in air.

KENDALL

Tell Jess to put me through the . . . Polycom. Yes?

Roman goes to the door. To look for Jess.

FRANK

Right. Well. Moving along to um, the next item. Three-point-one—

Logan looks at all of them.

Um—

                                LOGAN
What's 'Performance Issues', Frank? This looks fucking vague,
why's it so high in the hit parade?

Gerri's phone is buzzing.

                                FRANK
Um, I'm not sure if we're hitting those? Maybe we could bump
that?

*Roman is at the door, ushering Jess in. Gerri is looking at Frank,
who's looking at Asha, who's looking at Lawrence.*

                                LOGAN
What the fuck is going on?

*Gerri makes eyes to Frank, phone to ear. Jess goes to set up the
Polycom.*

                                FRANK
I think Kendall wants to make a – comment. He has a – um
thing. He's going to speak on – and I think Ilona's phoning in
too?

The conspirators eye one another.

                                LOGAN
What is this? What the fuck is this?

                                JESS
                          (*into Polycom*)
Hi? Kendall?

                               KENDALL
                          (*on speakerphone*)
Hey everyone. I apologize. I will be there shortly. Where are we
at?

                                FRANK
We are at your item. Performance Issues.

EXT. STREET – DAY

*Kendall has stopped running. He's walking briskly. His stride
confident.*

Intercut with:

INT. WAYSTAR – BOARDROOM – DAY

> FRANK
>
> You want to wait? Where are you?

> LOGAN
>
> Fuck that. We're moving on, what is this?

> FRANK
>
> Gerri, Noah, if we wanted to halt proceedings, until— What do the rules say about voting to—?

Kendall's speech through the Polycom echoes.

> KENDALL
> *(on speakerphone)*
>
> I can do this. Dad. This is big. Look. I love my father. My father is a legend.

> LOGAN
>
> What the fuck?

> KENDALL
> *(on speakerphone)*
>
> Nothing will ever detract from what he's built and what he's done. But he is currently unfit to run this company. Not just because of his refusal to take the time to recover from serious health issues. But because every day he refuses—

The Polycom crackles.

> LOGAN
>
> Speak up. Can't hear!

> KENDALL
> *(on speakerphone; louder)*
>
> Every day he refuses to retire, he is one day closer to destroying his own legacy.

EXT. STREET – DAY

Kendall walks and talks, dodging pedestrians, moving closer to the office.

                              KENDALL

He took on levels of debt that threatened the very existence of
our firm. He's lining up dead-weight acquisitions in a sector he
has a historic regard for but which are non-growth areas. If he
pursues the full breadth of his megalomaniacal vision we will
end up with years of political conflict with the FCC, executive,
legislative and judicial branches of government. He is making
decisions for a future that he no longer understands. He's
gambling our last dollars at the track on a horse that's ready for
the glue factory and I am calling for a vote of no confidence in
him as CEO and Chairman.

INT. WAYSTAR — BOARDROOM — DAY

*Ewan scoffs. This is all ridiculous bullshit. Look at all of these
piranhas flopping. He unfolds his croissant and nibbles.*

                              LOGAN

Bullshit. No.

                              FRANK

I'm afraid since you're the subject of the vote you need to recuse
yourself, Logan.

Logan goes cold and internal. Shakes his head. Ewan whistles.

                              LOGAN

Jesus Christ, it's amateur hour at the fucking circus.

                              FRANK

You don't get to vote and you don't get to comment, is the
situation. Really you should leave the room.

Gerri manages to look shocked. Logan looks at her.

                              LOGAN

Fine. Vote!

                              FRANK

Would you mind?

                              KENDALL
                         (*on speakerphone*)
Is he there – is he still in the room?

> LOGAN

I'm sick. I can't move, fuck that. Vote! Come on.

> FRANK
> (to Noah)

Let the minutes reflect Logan Roy was asked to recuse himself.

> LOGAN
> (mumbled)

Let the minutes show Logan Roy shoved a boot up Frank's ass.

> FRANK

Well, all in favor of the vote of no confidence in Logan Roy?

> KENDALL
> (on speakerphone)

Me. My hand is raised. More in sorrow than in anger.

> LOGAN

No shit, Judas.

Frank raises his hand.

Frank. Nice to have you back.

Asha raises her hand.

Asha, yeah, oh yes? I see you.

Logan goes cold and starts reciting something under his breath.

EXT. STREET – DAY

Kendall is getting close to the building. There's silence on the line.

> KENDALL

Stewy?

INT. WAYSTAR – BOARDROOM – DAY

> STEWY

Okay, well look. As a major shareholder I think we have to take the view this is a company matter. And abstain.

That's a shock. Gerri clocks it. Roman too.

> DEWI

Against!

> PAUL

Strongly against.

Frank gets a nod from Jess who has arranged another line. Hits a button on the Polycom.

> FRANK

We have Ilona on the line?

> ILONA
> (*on speakerphone*)

Hello, Logan? Hello. Yes. After consulting with my family, I am voting in favor of the motion.

> LOGAN

Thanks for nothing. Fuck off.

Logan hits the button to hang up the phone.

> GERRI

Ewan?

Ewan looks mock-surprised to be involved.

> LOGAN

Go ahead! What we on? Four against two, go on, fuck it, join the rats. Let's finish this.

> EWAN

I vote with Logan.

Logan blinks. He looks at Ewan. Ewan stares back. Eyes move to Datu.

> DATU

I think we should take the time to consider this properly, when all parties are here.

> LOGAN

Datu, we're voting now.

> FRANK

Logan, please can you try to stay out of—?

DATU
In which case – Logan. I stick with Logan.

This is unexpected. Gerri and Frank exchange a glance.

LOGAN
Hey, Kendall – you counted, right? You alright there? Four against four? This your best shot?

KENDALL
(*off*)
Lawrence?

Roman looks at Lawrence. Lawrence looks back at him. Taking all of this in. He does not like the weakness of Kendall and Roman or Logan.

LAWRENCE
I don't have a dog in this fight. I abstain.

ROMAN
Uh-huh?

LOGAN
Young cardinals vote for old popes, ah?

Logan winks. Lawrence stiffens, as he realizes Logan has his number. Roman looks at Lawrence. Lawrence coolly returns the gaze. Lawrence has assessed the power that's bothered to show up in the room, and it's not with the Roy boys.

EXT./INT. WAYSTAR – DAY

Kendall has approached the entrance of Waystar. His sweaty hand pumps the elevator button. He's listening.

INT. WAYSTAR – BOARDROOM – DAY

FRANK
So currently, that's, um, four in favor of Logan stepping down, four to remain, two abstentions.

> KENDALL
> (*on speakerphone*)
> Gerri, you want to say anything to speak, to the senior management team's attitudes here?

Gerri doesn't like the situation.

> GERRI
> Well I'm an independent observer here. Non-voting as general counsel so I'm not sure that's appropriate?

Ouch.

> KENDALL
> (*on speakerphone*)
> Right. Thanks.

> FRANK
> Very – professional.

INT. WAYSTAR – ELEVATOR – DAY

It feels like the slowest elevator in the world.

> KENDALL
> So. Roman, where's your hand, bro?

INT. WAYSTAR – BOARDROOM – DAY

Roman's hand is conspicuously NOT up. All focus moves to him.

> KENDALL
> (*on speakerphone*)
> Roman?

INT. WAYSTAR – ELEVATOR – DAY

Kendall's phone loses reception. He pounds the door of the elevator. It opens on a floor. Wrong floor.

The doors close, Kendall continues to move up.

INT. WAYSTAR – BOARDROOM – DAY

Roman looks to the Polycom.

> ROMAN

Kendall? Ken, you there?

> LOGAN

He's off the line. C'mon, son!

> FRANK

Roman?

Logan looks at Roman: Well?

Roman starts to raise his hand. It feels very heavy.

> LOGAN

You better be smelling your fucking armpit, Romulus.

He lowers his hand.

> ROMAN

I think it's a tough one. It's tough, but maybe—

> LOGAN

Roman for me.

> FRANK

Well. I'm not sure we—

> LOGAN

Roman?

> ROMAN

Against.

> FRANK

But he started to vote? I'm not sure he can change?

Frank looks to Gerri.

> LOGAN

He *can* fucking change.

People murmur – Frank checks something with Natasha. Confusion in the room.

Whatever. Count him, out. Deadlock! Continuity prevails. I'm Chairman, casting vote, I win, it's fucking over!

Kendall arrives. He can't look Logan in the eye.

My son! You lost.

FRANK

Well I think there's some doubt . . . in terms of whether, we're
on—

LOGAN

And Kendall – Frank – Asha, Ilona. Off the board. Fired, with
immediate effect!

FRANK

Well I'm not sure you are able to do . . .?

LOGAN

Fuck you. I can do anything. By-law.
(*shouts out*)
Lucy! Jeane! Security.

FRANK

Well, I think the by-law depends on majority control and you no
longer have, since Stewy and—

LOGAN

Security!

Kendall is broken. Outside – security are summoned.

KENDALL

Dad this is an in-house— You don't have to—

LOGAN

I'm in the middle of turning the fucking tanker! Frank, you are
fired, without exit package. Asha, goodbye. Someone send a
telegram to Ilona and tell her she's no longer required and my
best to her cancer.

Kendall casts a look at Stewy. Stewy returns the look.

FRANK

I think we all need to take a beat.

LOGAN
(*interrupting*)
Meh meh meh meh meh fucking meh.

FRANK

Logan, stop, is it wise to fire the board? With the share price this
weak? Heading into a political fight?

> LOGAN

Take it like a fucking man. You're out. You're fucked. You tried to kill me but you failed and you're dead, okay? Now fuck off.

Security guys are there. Couple in suits, couple from building security.

> KENDALL

I need to get some things.

> LOGAN

Cry me a river. Go on. Out!

As security approach, Kendall, Frank and Asha start to head out.

Straight out, passes canceled, we'll send the personal belongings along. No goodbyes, thank you.

They start to walk out, stunned. The security approach Kendall.

Roman, Gerri, Stewy, Ewan, Paul, Datu and Lawrence watch them go. Logan looks at Roman.

What am I going to do with you?

> ROMAN

I don't know, Dad?

INT. WAYSTAR — DAY

Kendall is walking through the executive floor, flanked by two security guys. He walks the length of the floor, past his own office.

Security have been told to not let him go back into his office.

A buzz goes round the office as he comes through. People don't know whether to look or not to look. He can't get his face right. Doesn't know whether to say 'I'll be back' or try to smile at anyone. He can't trust that his face won't betray him.

As they reach the far end of the bullpen a security guard quickens his pace to guide him towards the elevators. That snaps something for Kendall.

> KENDALL

I know the way, okay? I know the fucking way.

INT. SHIV AND TOM'S APARTMENT – DAY

Shiv comes in with her case, chirpy.

> SHIV
>
> That was the journey from hell! I spent thirty minutes in a cab not moving.

She's taking off her shoes.

INT. SHIV AND TOM'S APARTMENT – BEDROOM – DAY

Shiv enters. Tom is still in bed. His head is pounding. Laptop closed on the bed.

> SHIV
>
> Hey!

> TOM
>
> Hey.

> SHIV
>
> What happened, are you sick?

She comes on to the bed.

> TOM
>
> I think someone poisoned me. I'm working from home.

> SHIV
>
> Did someone poison you? With booze? I got you something. I missed you.

He nods. She's glad to be home. Her phone is buzzing. She has a shirt from a nice place in a bag.

> TOM
>
> Thank you. You were away like fourteen hours?

> SHIV
>
> Yeah well, sorry for missing you.

Shiv checks her phone, takes the call. Listens.

> What – the fuck?

> TOM
>
> What? What's happened.

> SHIV
> (*into phone*)

Well more – tell me more.

> TOM

Has it happened?

> SHIV
> (*into phone*)

Call me right back.

Phone down.

The world's blown up.

She gets back on her phone making a call, walks out into the main space—

> (*to Tom*)

What do you mean? Did you know?

INT. SHIV AND TOM'S APARTMENT – DAY

Shiv on her phone walks out. Greg is on the mezzanine in boxers and a T-shirt.

> GREG

My tummy hurts.

> TOM

It's happened?

> SHIV
> (*into phone*)

Kendall, call me!

> (*to Tom*)

Did you know?

> TOM

Yes. What's happened? Has it happened?

She's calling someone else.

> GREG

I don't know if it's the noodles or the edible gold. I think too much edible gold hurt my tummy?

SHIV
(*into phone*)
Kendall did? Well who the fuck else knew about this?! *Roman knew?!*

CONNOR
(*on phone*)
I don't know why you'd expect any different.

SHIV
Not a single one of them involved me. It's complete bullshit.

CONNOR
(*on phone*)
It's like I always say, you and I are the only sane ones.

The sound of a horse neighing.

SHIV
What was that? Are you on a horse?

CONNOR
(*on phone*)
Yes I'm on a horse.

EXT. CONNOR'S NEW MEXICO RANCH – DAY

Reveal Connor is, in fact, riding his horse.

CONNOR
Yes, generally, when you're talking to me it is safest to assume I am on a horse. Shiv?

Shiv's hung up.

INT. SHIV AND TOM'S APARTMENT – DAY

Tom is on the phone getting an update.

TOM
Fuck. Okay?

Phone down, on hold.

SHIV
You knew?

TOM

I tried to call you.

SHIV

Not hard enough. Fuck. He's fired half the board.

TOM

And Kendall?

SHIV

Fired. Frank. Asha. Fired. The rebels are getting shot in the town square. I'll talk to you later, Tom.

Shiv walks out towards the door. Tom and Greg look at one another: Oh fuck.

GREG
(*whispered*)
Oh, man, they're 'shooting the rebels in the town square'?!

INT. WAYSTAR – DAY

Shiv is with Sarah, heading in.

SARAH

It would kind of put a big hole in Joyce? Her top strategist jumps ship for the front-runner?

SHIV

Thank you, Sarah. Thank you very much, that's why I'm thinking *fucking* carefully about it.

INT. WAYSTAR – LOGAN'S OFFICE – DAY

Shiv arrives to Logan in the office, Sarah waits outside.

Across the way in Kendall's office, boxes are being packed.

SHIV

You fired Kendall?

LOGAN

My children have betrayed me.

SHIV

All your children?

He's too angry to hear.

> LOGAN
>
> I've got no one to trust. Only Marcia.

> SHIV
>
> Dad? I didn't know.

Logan seems genuinely rattled and confused.

> LOGAN
>
> You work for that bitch. No one gives me an ounce of credit.
> You all stir up this poison together.

> SHIV
>
> Pop. Perspective. We all need to calm down, okay, you don't
> want a huge incident here. Kendall only acted this way because
> you took back what you promised him?

> LOGAN
>
> You push me. You all think you can push. You're midges.
> Buzzing on my eyes. I'll swat you.

*She leaves Logan alone in his office. It's not clear if Logan
understands why she is walking away.*

Shiv starts to make a call—

INT. WAYSTAR – LOGAN'S OFFICE – DAY

*Logan sits at his desk. He is on the phone. He's sitting up a bit
straighter.*

> JEANE
> (*on phone*)
> I have the White House. The president will join once you're on.
> They're very apologetic.

> LOGAN
>
> Tell them I'm on. Then put him on hold for a little while?

Logan smiles. Toys with something on his desk.

*Florence Reece's 'Which Side Are You On?', as performed by The
Almanac Singers (on Classic Labor Songs) starts to play.*

Logan takes his sweet time moving things about his desk before taking the call. As the music plays Logan's body language and comfortable smile tells us all we need to know about how the call is going.

> LOGAN

Real terrorism, eh?

He listens.

Yeah well. I took down a terrorist myself . . . my son.

Logan chuckles.

EXT. STREET — DAY

Music plays on as – Kendall walks the streets near the office. Suddenly, he is calm.

Nowhere to go, no hurry.

We follow him for a block or so as he tries to compute his feelings. Suddenly aware of the city, the details for the first time in years.

He laughs to himself. Not necessarily a good laugh.

Episode Seven
AUSTERLITZ

Written by Lucy Prebble
Directed by Miguel Arteta

Original air date 15 July 2018

Cast

LOGAN ROY	Brian Cox
KENDALL ROY	Jeremy Strong
MARCIA ROY	Hiam Abbass
SHIV ROY	Sarah Snook
ROMAN ROY	Kieran Culkin
CONNOR ROY	Alan Ruck
TOM WAMBSGANS	Matthew Macfadyen
RAVA	Natalie Gold
COLIN STILES	Scott Nicholson
STEWY HOSSEINI	Arian Moayed
GERRI KELLMAN	J. Smith-Cameron
KARL MULLER	David Rasche
KAROLINA NOVOTNEY	Dagmara Dominczyk
WILLA FERREYRA	Justine Lupe
NATE SOFRELLI	Ashley Zukerman
STREET GUY	Jason Selvig
LEON	Ryan Begay
TARA	Deborah Chavez
MARIA	Kym Gomes
ROB	Jeffrey Omura
RANDALL PIERCE	Vic Browder
ALON PARFIT	Griffin Dunne
GIL EAVIS	Eric Bogosian
JANELLE	Kimberly Bigsby
TANNER	Joey Brooks
CHANG	Tony DeMil
MAC	Manny Rubio
PHOTOGRAPHER	Toshiro Yamaguchi
HERTZ GUY	Ryan Jason Cook
PROTEST GIRL	Norma Aurel
JEANE	Peggy J. Scott

DAY ONE

EXT. WAYSTAR – DAY

Inside the car. On Logan. Thinking.

Logan's car pulls up by a side entrance. But not right by the door. Colin comes round out and opens his door, scanning the streets. Logan gets out.

He starts to make it towards the doors of the lobby as a security guy from the building comes out. A guy on the street starts filming Logan on his phone.

> STREET GUY
> Hey. Logan Roy? Can I get a photo?

Logan ignores him. Colin puts his body in the way.

> Hey I love your work, Mr Roy! Big fan.

Tiny acknowledgement from Logan?

> Love all the – misogyny and the racism.

Logan heads on in, not interested. But while Colin and Logan are distracted by the guy with the camera phone—

—his two buddies – a guy and a girl, part of a direct-action protest group – pull something from a backpack.

> PROTEST GUY
> Logan! Logan! Over here!

They rush Logan and before he can see what's happening, attack – hitting him with a water balloon full of piss.

> PROTEST GIRL
> Liar! He's a phony! Shame!

The street guy carries on filming as he shouts:

                          STREET GUY
Hey, you fucking scum. Fucking monopolist scum! I hope you
fucking die.

*Colin is on the balloon-assailant, protest girl, right away, taking her
down.*

Building security rush out as the street guy keeps filming.

    You're fucking poison, Roy.

INT. WAYSTAR – BATHROOM – DAY

*Colin leads Logan in. A gaggle of two security folk and two front-
desk folk follow, one guy on a walkie-talkie, a cop follows.*

*But once they get into the general bathroom on the ground floor,
Logan wants to be left alone with Colin as he heads towards the
sinks.*

                          LOGAN
    Leave me. No one else, thank you!

*Logan makes it to a sink. Not too fast, it doesn't matter too much
now. Runs the faucet and splashes and washes his face. He starts to
undo his shirt.*

As Colin makes a call for a fresh suit to be brought down.

INT. WAYSTAR – LOGAN'S OFFICE – DAY

On a TV, Roman is flicking.

*One news channel showing the footage of Logan getting hit. Chyron
reads: 'Protestor Targets Roy on New York Street'—*

*Roman flicks to another one reporting the same thing. Chyron reads:
'Logan Roy Attacked With Urine Balloon'—*

*Roman switches to ATN. Chyron reads: 'Why Should We Give
Terrorists Free Speech?'*

*Logan enters, shaking off Lucy and Colin. Stewy sits scrolling his
phone waiting for him, with Karl, Gerri and Roman.*

ROMAN

Are you okay, Dad?

Roman approaches but Logan shrugs him off. He doesn't like the attention and these two still aren't patched up.

LOGAN

Fine. Don't get all over me.

STEWY

These trust-fund YouTube shits, we had some (outside)—

LOGAN
(*to Stewy*)

I'm here, okay? I understand you want me to take you through my every thought?

Stewy and Logan scope each other out. Stewy needs Logan. Logan needs Stewy.

STEWY

I . . . appreciate finally getting to talk through the very major moves you're considering.

But Logan hates needing Stewy and Stewy needs to let Logan know he's not a whipping boy. Logan grunts: Karl, you explain.

KARL

It's exciting. We've become aware of some very desirable assets that are available. A block of local TV stations.

STEWY

TV? Yeah I remember that. They have it at my gym.

LOGAN
(*'funny'*)

It's so great to have the wisdom of my son's college drinking buddy in the room.

STEWY
(*'funny'*)

I love how he asks for money!

KARL

We'll want to go cash not stock. Hence—

We need you.

> STEWY
> (*silly voice, to Roman*)
> 'Aww I feel like we only talk when you need something.'

Logan isn't playing.

Fine. But, there is a pressing issue, right?

Logan thinks he knows the issue. The only dance he'll do for Stewy is this:

> LOGAN
> Local TV, it's just the beginning. A very scalable sector. Regulation's in tatters, and as people shit their pants over online, I can buy everything up and still play the little guy.

Stewy plays a little to the room.

> STEWY
> I get that. I think the bigger issue is – that everyone fucking hates you?

> LOGAN
> (*shrugs*)
> It's cloudy, it's sunny.

> STEWY
> I mean you want to push through a massive politically sensitive buy-up and I read *this* over my morning cappuccino?
> (*to Roman*)
> By the way I'd love a cappuccino.

Stewy gets a copy of New York Magazine *out of his man-bag. The cover is the Roy family under broken glass. Headline reads:*

'The Crack-Up: The Splintering of the Roys and the Fracturing of America'.

> LOGAN
> Maybe we'll buy that too.

> STEWY
> Your son's launched a lawsuit against you? You fired half the board. People say your COO's a fucking joke.

> ROMAN
> Hey!

               STEWY

People say. People say he's a coked-up dauphin who doesn't know shit from shinola and you're still not talking to each other?

Logan doesn't look at his son. It's true. Roman's hurt by his father's non-defense. They don't talk. Silence.

Now *I* could care less. I don't care which way the wind blows as long as I get blown, but even the advance whispers on local TV have people so mad they're throwing piss at you on the street?

               ROMAN
           (trying to be useful)

We don't know it was piss.

               STEWY

Great contribution, Zuck. But you're not sitting downwind.
               (beat)
You want to have a buying spree, great, we can talk. But can you figure out the visuals? This is a family business. The family's fucked. It hurts the stock. It makes the place stink up. It draws heat. Can't you fix it?

Stewy's right. They all know it. He looks at the magazine.

You know this is actually a good photo of you. You're not covered in piss?

INT. CONNOR'S RANCH – DINING ROOM – NIGHT

Connor is at his big dining table. He is eating with Leon, his land manager, and Tara, his housekeeper.

The nights are long out there. Connor eats, chews. It's good.

               CONNOR

Umm! Good. VG. VG, Tara!

The staff smile.

Food is the only thing makes me regret heading for the singularity!

               LEON

Uh-huh?

Leon and Tara smile, they hope they're not going to have to talk about the singularity again.

> CONNOR
> But nevertheless. Nevertheless, I personally can't wait to shed this human body and just – upload.

> LEON
> What will you do without a body, Con?

> CONNOR
> Freakin' relax, man! Chess and Johann Sebastian. Hello, eternity!

His phone goes. It's there on the table.

> Apologies, folks, I know I ask you not to, but this is family.
> (*takes the call*)
> Marcia?

Intercut with:

INT. LOGAN'S APARTMENT – NIGHT

Marcia is at home. Logan is around too.

> MARCIA
> Hello. Connor? I have a question for you.

Connor heads into a spot for some privacy.

INT. CONNOR'S RANCH – DINING ROOM – NIGHT

Connor reappears, excited. Still on the phone.

> CONNOR
> Yes! Yes! Of course. I'm a resource, Marcia. Use me! Fantastic. I think it's superb. Love to you. Love to Dad.
> (*phone down*)
> Okay, folks. It's happening! I am hosting a family get-together!

> TARA
> Oh. That's great. Great.

But there's a hint of reservation, she doesn't want him to get hurt again—

> CONNOR

Oh sure I know, but I'm confident, very confident they'll come this time!

He starts to make another call.

Willa. I need you to come to New Mexico for the weekend! I'm playing my joker, honey!

> WILLA
> (*on phone*)

Do you have a joker? I'm not sure it's convenient?

> CONNOR
> (*quietly*)

I'll make it up to you. Let's crunch it over email.

> WILLA
> (*on phone*)

Okay well. I guess we can chat.

> CONNOR
> (*louder*)

Oh that's great!

Tara and Leon share an awkward look.

> (*to Tara and Leon*)

Willa too! We're going to be a full house!

Tara and Leon put on big smiles for Connor.

INT. MANHATTAN – EDIT ROOM – NIGHT

Shiv is watching the political spot for Gil that they're testing.

> GIL
> (*on screen*)

The Revolutionary War, the Civil War, the Second World War, when this nation has been tested, freedom has always won out. And that's what I believe we face right now. Nothing less than a war against inequality. A war against human beings being devalued by technological change. A war we must fight to stop

467

unimaginably vast power and riches, ending up in the hands of an impossibly small number of men. I'm not afraid of this fight, I know you're not either. This fight starts here.

It ends. Nate looks at Shiv.

SHIV

All the class-war shit? Don't you find it a little jejune?

NATE

Jejune?

SHIV

It means—

NATE

I know what it means I just thought only assholes said it.

SHIV

Okay so is this you pulling my hair? Cos why are you even bringing me in? I'm not a good fit.

NATE

Shishi, I genuinely believe he's going to be President of the United States. And you know me, I barely believe in anything. Are you finished with Joyce now?

SHIV

That's as far as she'll go.

NATE

He's all over blowing the base till Tuesday. Colorado then Texas and New Mexico.

SHIV

New Mexico? And *this* wouldn't be an issue?

NATE

What?

SHIV

The – atmosphere?

NATE
(*pretend naive*)
I don't feel an atmosphere . . .?

They both sense the atmosphere.

I think as long as we have clarity.

SHIV

Right?

NATE

And to be clear. At absolutely any place at any time, with absolutely no consequence, I will fuck you and want desperately to fuck you and that is just a permanent state of affairs.

SHIV

I thought you were marrying a French doctor?

NATE

Oh, come on, you're marrying a – French doctor, everyone's marrying French doctors – I just want you to know, that is my position. So, you have all the power, and you can do what you want with it.

Shiv thinks. That's good and . . . annoying.

DAY TWO

INT. LOGAN'S APARTMENT – DINING ROOM – MORNING

Logan is in with Karolina and her assistant Rob. They're pitching to Logan, who has reservations about this. Gerri is there too.

LOGAN

When did we start having to do this shit, Gerri? If I wanted good PR I'd stand on a red carpet in a fucking see-through dress.

Gerri gives him a 'yeah well' smile. Karolina continues.

KAROLINA

The journalist is Leah Lorenzetti, you'll have seen her on things, on our things.

Totally compliant.

LOGAN

And she gets it?

KAROLINA

She absolutely gets it.

Karolina nods to Rob.

> ROB
>
> The piece will be: 'After the turmoil, the coming together'. A
> family. A dynasty. An American story. It'll be a very compelling
> package, photographs—

> LOGAN
>
> Whatever. Just as long as I don't have to read it.
> (*re print-out*)
> And this shit. Who is this guy? Alon? Is he going to bust my
> chops?

> KAROLINA
>
> Very highly regarded corporate therapist. Harvard Business
> School, former CFO at a Fortune 500. He just worked with the
> Sultan of Brunei and the Bolkiah family.

> LOGAN
>
> 'Corporate therapist'. What does he do? Ask Microsoft how it's
> feeling? Fucking ridiculous.

> KAROLINA
>
> He's more corporate than therapist.

> LOGAN
>
> How long do I have to sit there?

> KAROLINA
>
> It's very common now, a few hours.

> LOGAN
>
> Can we just *say* I did it?

Karolina looks to Gerri. She knows how to handle the old beast.

> GERRI
>
> Does it hurt that much, because, it's best not to lie, you know?
> In case?

> LOGAN
>
> In case there's a God?

> KAROLINA
>
> It's just cleaner.

LOGAN

Do they all have to be there? Does the traitor come too? Can we
Photoshop the prick in?

GERRI

Well, that's obviously your choice.

*Gerri and Karolina look at one another, uncomfortable with this area
where family meets business.*

KAROLINA

But I think the message is: A family reunited in the desert. To
reflect and regroup. Family unity is kind of what you're going
for.

LOGAN

Uh-huh.

GERRI

And frankly, if you got Kendall to drop the lawsuit, everything
becomes much cleaner for us acquisition-wise?

Logan hears this. Nods.

LOGAN

Okay, well. I'm not groveling. Get Romulus in here. And let's do
the email.

EXT. CONNOR'S RANCH – MORNING

*Connor is walking his land, enjoying imagining everyone coming.
Pre-empting his father's criticism. Maybe he's opening the doors to
the bedrooms to let some air in.*

*He checks his phone and reads an email. A disbelieving smile. He
dials Shiv, leaving a message.*

CONNOR

Shiv, it's Con, I just gotta see, did you get this email about
therapy? Cos this is like, wow. I just need to check that it's not
one of those spam things or something.

EXT. MANHATTAN STREET – DAY

Shiv is walking, Tom beside her. Shiv checks her emails.

TOM

My only thought is, I like Gil. People like Gil. He's great. I just
have this sneaking feeling if he won an election he might quite
like to line up me and everyone I know, and shoot us?

SHIV

Holy fuck. No way!

TOM

What? What is it?

Shiv doesn't reply but dials on her phone.

SHIV
(*on phone*)

Have you seen this?! I can't believe it. Dad wants to do
therapy?!

Intercut with:

EXT. MANHATTAN – KENDALL'S APARTMENT BUILDING –
DAY

Roman has answered the call. He's pressing a buzzer incessantly.

ROMAN

I thought you weren't talking to me?

SHIV

I'm not. But what the fuck?

ROMAN

Oh very much the fuck. Very much the fuck indeed. The big
man's breaking down and everyone's invited!

More buzzing.

SHIV

Not Kendall?

ROMAN

Everybody.

SHIV

Bullshit. What's he doing? Do you think he's going to kill us one
by one like in an Agatha Christie novel?

ROMAN

I've got to go. See you in Cuckooville.

Roman hangs up. He rings the bell, again, again. Eventually, Maria, a housekeeper, opens it a crack.

MARIA

Please, Mr Roy?

ROMAN

I need to talk to Kendall.

MARIA

He's not available.

ROMAN

He's not available? What's he doing? Playing with his fucking Legos? He's nothing but available.

MARIA

He – he isn't here right now.

ROMAN

Well I know he is, so – c'mon, okay?

MARIA

He's not been here for weeks. I'm sorry goodbye.

ROMAN

Will you take a message?

MARIA

I— No thank you.

ROMAN

Tell him to reply to the email. He has to come, okay. Tell him Dad wants him to—

Behind Maria, Kendall has silently approached. Roman sees him briefly through the gap in the door before it gets slammed hard in his face.

Roman recovers his pride, turns around and walks away. He gets back on his phone.

Hey. No. No I don't think he's going to play ball. No.

INT. LOGAN'S APARTMENT – DINING ROOM – DAY

Karolina takes the call. She shakes her head at Logan.

> LOGAN
>
> No?

> KAROLINA
>
> No.

> LOGAN
>
> Okay. Well. Plan B. Operation Black Sheep.

Does a little sadness creep through Logan's resignation?

DAYS LATER

INT. CONNOR'S CAR – DAY

'Sarabande' by Handel starts to play.

Leon drives a car through New Mexico.

Revealed in the back is Willa, putting on hand cream, waiting to be delivered.

INT. KENDALL'S APARTMENT – DINING NOOK – DAY

Kendall, alone, tries to read The Histories *by Herodotus. It's long. His phone rings. He dives for it.*

> KENDALL
>
> Hey, Rava?

> RAVA
>
> Hey. You okay?

> KENDALL
>
> I'm fine. What time are we doing the pick-up?

Intercut with:

INT. RAVA'S OFFICE AT MCKINSEY-STYLE CONSULTANCY –
DAY

> RAVA

Good. Just checking in.

> KENDALL

Uh-huh?
> *(he can hear something in her voice)*
What?

> RAVA

Do you ever look at Sophie's Instagram?

> KENDALL
> *(what's the right answer here?)*
Did we say yes to Instagram?

> RAVA

I was monitoring and some older kid linked to that shitty article
about you.

Hold on Kendall as he takes this in.

> KENDALL

What, I haven't been looking at anything, deliberately, Rava—

> RAVA

Okay. You should read it.

> KENDALL

What is it, what?

> RAVA

Let me – 'Kendall Roy ran the streets of New York, sweaty and
incoherent, ranting about a coup against his father, but couldn't
find his way to the boardroom to start said coup. Is he back on
drugs? We couldn't possibly say. But some people are saying
that.'

> KENDALL

Rava. That's not true.

> RAVA

Yeah. It's just that's what you used to say when it was true?

>   KENDALL
> Jesus. I'm not using, Rava, I don't touch anything, you know
> that, Jesus Christ!

>   RAVA
> I know, look, unrelated, this weekend, Iverson's got his tests, and
> if we break his routine it's gonna affect things, you know?

>   KENDALL
> Okay. 'Unrelated'.

>   RAVA
> I'm just asking. I'm happy to have them.

>   KENDALL
> No! Fuck.

>   RAVA
> Don't get angry.

>   KENDALL
> I'm not fucking angry! I bet it's Dad! He's a bully and he can't
> take someone standing up to him – I'm not on drugs, I'm not on
> drugs, I'm not taking fucking drugs.

>   RAVA
> Yeah it's the paranoid rant that is so convincing.

>   KENDALL
> Rava . . . ?

>   RAVA
> I believe you. I just don't want to break his routine. Let's
> reschedule?

*He desperately wants to kick or punch something. This shit can't
stand.*

INT. TOM AND SHIV'S TOWN CAR – DAY

Tom and Shiv are being driven to the airport.

>   TOM
> I think it's actually brave to go.

> SHIV

Thank you. I'm a hero. Can you imagine: Connor? Dad? Roman? *Feelings?* It'll be like tossing a bag of Uzis into the soft-play area.

> TOM

And, I know he spoke abominably to you. So just for context, would it be appropriate this weekend, in a bridge-building way, for me to be speaking to Logan or no?

> SHIV

Just do what you feel is right, Tom.

> TOM

Got it, sure. Because I want to have your back. But there's also my back. We're a beast with two backs.

> SHIV

I get it. You're your own guy. It's fine. I won't judge.

> TOM
> (*I think you will*)

No, of course, I know that.

Hmm. Tom wants to do what he wants but he wants her to care.

> SHIV

Ooh, and it's possible I will be breaking out to make a meeting with Gil? He might have a window.

> TOM
> (*unable to share her enthusiasm*)

Oh. Great. Great that he can get a, a bit of time away from the masses.

She gets on her phone to check for updates on that, but finds something else that concerns her.

> SHIV

Fuck? Google alert on Ken . . .

> TOM

Is he okay? He's not dead?

> SHIV

No!

> TOM
>
> No. Great. No. It's only because, he's one of those people where I would be like, no! But also, yeah?

> SHIV
>
> This is—

> TOM
>
> He hasn't fallen off the wagon has he?

> SHIV
>
> Yeah. Either that or he's been pushed under the bus.

INT. LOGAN'S MOTORCADE – DAY

Logan and Marcia sit in a large SUV as it travels to JFK. Colin and a colleague on hand for security. Karolina behind. They look comfortable and happy.

Karolina continues reading a news report—

> KAROLINA
>
> 'We just hope he is not back in a self-destructive cycle,' one friend of the family said. 'We are here for him.'

Logan nods. It's not nice but it needed to be done. Marcia smiles in agreement.

> MARCIA
>
> You shouldn't feel bad. We tried. You still have Roman.

> LOGAN
>
> Uh-huh.

> MARCIA
>
> What does Connor do out there in New Mexico?

> LOGAN
>
> I don't know. Tries to breed fuckable buffalo.

They smile.

EXT. CONNOR'S RANCH – DRIVEWAY – DAY

A sign says: 'Ranch Austerlitz'. Two black executive cars pull up. Logan gets out, followed by Marcia.

Connor and Willa greet them.

> CONNOR
>
> Dad! Marcia! Welcome to Austerlitz!

> LOGAN
>
> Thank you. Thank you. It exists!

> MARCIA
>
> Was this the name, when you bought it?

> WILLA
>
> Oh, it was racially insensitive. So, he picked the new one. It's a battle.

> LOGAN
>
> So, son, we need somewhere for them to set up? Just a few folk to help us with photos and such, chroniclers of everything.

> CONNOR
>
> Oh? Right?
>
> *(quickly readjusts)*
>
> Okay.

Oh. Connor looks on as Karolina and her assistant unload some kit from a second car.

> LOGAN
>
> *(heading in)*
>
> Good place. Plenty of room.

Connor doesn't know if he's talking to him or himself.

EXT. CONNOR'S RANCH — STABLES — DAY

Connor, Willa, Logan, Marcia are driving around in one golf cart. They drive and pull up.

> WILLA
>
> *(re Connor)*
>
> I think he should have business cards printed for the ranch.

> MARCIA
>
> Really? And what would they say?

> WILLA
>
> They'd say, 'Connor Roy. Libertarian Environmentalist Cowboy Philosopher'.

Marcia just looks at Willa.

> MARCIA
>
> They're going to be big cards.

> CONNOR
>
> Thoreau of the West.
> (*chuckles*)
> I mean the spot is not strategically the best but good place to be in an apocalypse! I'm pretty much invulnerable in terms of biohazard, famine and civil unrest. The only thing I need to ship in – is love!

He smiles at Willa. She smiles back but that's a bit much. The L-word.

> LOGAN
>
> You're doing great, son.

Logan has sprinkled his sugar, now he's done.

> CONNOR
>
> So we're doing photographs tomorrow as well now? Because this would be good? Highly photogenic.

> LOGAN
>
> Nothing fancy, words and pictures. Family shots. Whilst we're all alive. Good?

Connor has been ambushed but he's eager for it all to be nice.

> CONNOR
>
> God, now I'm thinking about it, I own a large number of beautiful spots. All around actually. There's some real humdingers.
> (*then*)
> And everyone else is okay? Shiv? She happy to pose with her bros?

A grunt. No answer. Connor motions to some buffalo.

> Do you want to take a look at the buffalo?

> LOGAN

Yes.

> (*looks over*)

Okay. I've seen the buffalo. Can we go back? I have calls.

They drive on.

EXT. CONNOR'S RANCH – DRIVEWAY – DAY

Tom and Shiv arrive. Connor and Willa go out to greet them.

> CONNOR

Well hello to the metropolitan elite! Welcome to the real America!

> TOM

Here he is, man of the people . . . who work on his ranch!

> CONNOR

Haha!

> TOM

Wow!

> CONNOR

We'll be in there tomorrow, that chapel dates all the way back to 1878.

> SHIV

The chapel, okay well at least Roman might spontaneously combust.

INT. CONNOR'S RANCH – TOM AND SHIV'S BEDROOM – EVENING

Tom unpacks and marvels, looks at a cowboy painting. While Shiv fixates on her laptop.

> TOM

Yee-haw. I have never ridden a horse. Can you believe it?

> SHIV

Yes.

INT. CONNOR'S RANCH – BEDROOM/OFFICE – EVENING

Logan walks in to a mini-office set-up where Karolina is on her laptop. He looks around with satisfaction.

> KAROLINA
> We'll introduce Alon at a little drinks party, yes?

INT. CONNOR'S RANCH – LIVING ROOM – NIGHT

A small cocktail party with an awkward atmosphere has been limping along.

Logan, Connor, Willa and Randall in one group. Shiv alone, texting. Marcia with Tom.

> CONNOR
> Randall owns the next ranch over. I said he could pop in, just wanted to say hi. He's very big in pesticide.

> LOGAN
> Uh-huh. I don't need any.

Randall laughs too hard.

> RANDALL
> You wait! You just wait.

No one knows what this means.

> CONNOR
> No. I'm always ribbing him. You know three in every hundred bunches of grapes has above the legal level of pesticide?

> RANDALL
> So you wash it!

> CONNOR
> Can't wash your colon, Mr Poison!

> RANDALL
> Why I oughtta—!

> CONNOR
> Put 'em up.

They playfully duke in front of Logan.

Marcia and Tom watch from a distance, negotiating.

> MARCIA
> Logan will talk to Shiv so long as she says sorry?

> TOM
> Well, I think Shiv's position would be that she has nothing to say sorry for?

Marcia looks at him, doubts that this is true.

> I think obviously—
>> (*best he can do*)
> She's sad about the way things happened? We could offer that?

Over with Shiv, alone. She's on her phone. She reads a text from Nate: 'I want you.'

Then another incoming: 'On the team. I think we might intersect! Make ready!'

Then Roman arrives. Connor goes to greet him either in the background or unseen. Leon is taking away his bag in the hallway behind.

What we do see is Roman enters the party, removing his coat.

> ROMAN
> Okay, the entertainment's arrived!

He sidles up to Shiv. As people say hello.

> Wow, this is like the first stage of an orgy. Like kind of exciting but also super-awkward.

Over with Tom, he moves to go join Shiv, but first makes fleeting eye contact with Logan. Tom looks away quickly, then over to Shiv.

> TOM
> Okay. I did it.

Shiv isn't following.

> I blanked your dad.

> ROMAN
> Hey, Tom.

> TOM
> (*asking permission*)

Can I—?

> SHIV

Whatever, hey, I'm not in charge of you.
> (*then, kidding*)

Go get us some drinks!

Tom nods, takes Shiv's empty glass and heads off to get them both a champagne.

Tom can't handle the aftermath of the blank and passes, looking over at Logan. This time Tom does a smile and a nod. Logan nods back.

> ROMAN

So where's the actual head-doctor guy?

> SHIV
> (*cold*)

How would I know?

He looks at her.

> ROMAN

I just hope he can cure your serious case of being a bitch.

> SHIV

Yeah fuck you.

> ROMAN

Fuck you.

That actually thaws the ice for some reason—

> SHIV

You know Dad's gonna try to 'win' at therapy.

> ROMAN

It's ironic. Cos if anyone needs therapy it's him.

> SHIV

My guy says if he'd had therapy I wouldn't need it.

> ROMAN

My guy's surprised I made it through at all.

> SHIV

I'm not sure you actually did make it through?

> ROMAN

I'm surprisingly well adjusted. You're the looney tune. You're just the best at hiding it.

Maybe. A younger-siblings thaw. From their POV we can see Tara come in and tap Connor, close to Logan, to say Alon has arrived. Connor reacts. Begins to usher Randall out. Tara goes to get his coat.

> CONNOR

Okay, Randall, I hate to kick you out, buddy, I have had word. 'Elvis' is in the building.

Connor guides Randall to Tara to show him out then comes back over to Roman.

> ROMAN

Yeah, so, I think I'm going to reveal to him you sexually abused me.

> CONNOR

Excuse me?

> ROMAN

Yeah. You just would not stop.

> CONNOR

You're one sick puppy!

> ROMAN

You're the one who tried to fuck me.

> CONNOR

Hey c'mon, stop saying that! Why would you say that? You don't think that, do you?

> ROMAN

No. But – competitive advantage. Could come in handy some day!

Tom comes over with their drinks.

> CONNOR

Roman's threatening to tell everyone I touched him as a child.

TOM

Oh? Right. Did you?

CONNOR

No! Of course not! Tom!

Logan bangs a fork against a glass.

LOGAN

Family. Now then. We are all gathered here in this beautiful home—

Connor beams.

Because there are things to address and I believe we should . . . address them. I think I mentioned all around that we will also have a small celebration of our being together with some photographs tomorrow, nothing fancy. As you age you begin to appreciate, capturing memories and pinning them . . . down. So. Allow me now to introduce Alon Parfit.

Shiv looks at Roman.

ALON

Hi to everyone. I look forward to sitting down with you all tomorrow. It takes a lot of courage and that's not lost on me. I'm very touched.

ROMAN

Me too!

CONNOR

Thanks. This family is broken. And that has consequences. A missed phone call today – a – a – bunch of kids lose their job in China. Butterfly wings. But bigger? Huge wings. Like a pterodactyl. Or the Smithsonian. So let's fix our wings!

ROMAN

This is barely comprehensible.

SHIV
(to Roman)
What photographs? Did you know this?

Shiv wants to discuss but Roman makes off. Alon is withdrawing, but Roman gets him.

ROMAN

Hi Alon, just FYI. I play it dumb but my SAT scores were off the chart. For context.

ALON

I don't need too much context. I get things pretty fast.

ROMAN

Oh okay. Well I guess that's me told . . . ooh I feel so exposed. Please don't brain-fuck me, Daddy.

Logan has had enough.

LOGAN

Right. This has been fantastic. But I'm going to bed!

ALON

I'll head on up too—

Connor walks with Alon.

CONNOR

Great you're here. Fifty years late but hey better late than never! One thing. Ask about summer vacations! I'm not saying that's where the emotional treasure chest is buried, but you know!
(*pirate voice?*)
'Get digging, my hearties!'
(*serious*)
Yeah. I've been seeing someone for decades, so you know, I'm pretty unpacked.

ALON

A lot of baggage to unpack was there?

CONNOR

Ha yeah no I'm boring really. She's bored to death just listening to me each week. Everything's terrifying isn't it. Anyway, night.

Alon touches his arm.

ALON

I think you're probably the most interesting person in that room. Night.

Connor nearly cries.

NEXT DAY

INT. HERTZ CAR RENTAL AGENCY — SANTA FE AIRPORT —
MORNING

*The following morning, Kendall picks a car from a list. The Hertz guy
waits with his license.*

> HERTZ GUY
> Can I take a credit card too?

Kendall hands it over.

> Any plans while you're here?

> KENDALL
> Maybe. Patricide. Fratricide.

> HERTZ GUY
> (*no idea*)
> Oh! Okay. Well that sounds expensive.

Kendall smiles, sort of, takes the keys. Walks away.

EXT. CONNOR'S RANCH — MORNING

*Logan looks out over Connor's land. The rural landscape feels
familiar.*

INT. CONNOR'S RANCH — TOM AND SHIV'S BEDROOM —
DAY

Shiv is on the phone. Tom is in the en suite shower.

> SHIV
> No way, now?

> NATE
> Uh-huh. No shit. I'm in a hotel in Santa Fe.

> SHIV
> I can't now, Nate. The whole reason I came out here is to do
> this, family thing. Can we schedule tomorrow?

> NATE
> He's pretty fucking busy.

> SHIV

I just can't right now.

Tom emerges from the shower, pink and shiny.

> TOM

The pressure on the faucet is moderately intense so go easy.

Shiv hangs up. Her body slumps.

> SHIV

Shit.

> TOM
> (*hand on shoulder*)

Hey! It'll be okay. You want me to come with you, into the emotional swamp? Cos soon I'm gonna be part of this whole genetic carnival. For better or worse. Haha!

EXT. CONNOR'S RANCH – POOL LANDING TO CHAPEL – DAY

People are gathered post-breakfast to head to the chapel.

> ALON

Okay, shall we?

> LOGAN

Therapy! Therapy! This way for the therapy!

Connor, Roman and Shiv fall in to make their way to the chapel. Following Alon who leads the way.

Roman hums a death march as they go.

Logan gets next to Alon.

> (*quietly*)

This is fantastic!

> ALON

Well we haven't actually—

> LOGAN

If this goes right, maybe we should get you in on a nice long-term corporate consultancy?

He smiles as they get to the chapel doors before Alon can respond or object, and calls as the kids head in—

(*cheery*)
Roll up roll up for the festival of grievances!

EXT. CONNOR'S RANCH – POOL LANDING TO CHAPEL – DAY

Willa, Tom and Marcia watch them go.

TOM
It's like waving your kids off to school.

MARCIA
They better not gang up on him. He's still frail.

Tom looks like he's not sure about that.

INT. CONNOR'S RANCH – CHAPEL – DAY

They enter and take seats.

ALON
Ahem. Okay. Welcome. I like to start off with what I think of as a little prayer?

Family – eyes to each other: Oh god, what?

'They fuck you up, your mum and dad.
They may not mean to, but they do.
They fill you with the faults they had
And add some extra, just for you.'

He smiles. An icebreaker.

I find that poem – well it can be an interesting place to start?
But I wonder if any of you feel you know how you want to start?

Everyone looks around. They're all a bit scared of Logan.

ROMAN
You're the expert, man.

ALON
Well I guess I'd say *you're* the world experts, in you?
(*smiles*)
Would anyone like to talk about what's brought us here today?

Roman looks at Connor. Connor looks at Shiv. You go. No you go.
None of them want to look at Logan.

LOGAN

C'mon is no one gonna have a pop at the champ?

Smiles.

CONNOR

Can I just say, I never touched Roman inappropriately.
(*odd*)
If he says I did, I didn't.

SHIV

(*after an uncomfy beat*)
Good to have that clear.

CONNOR

He was going to make a horrible joke? So I'm pre-empting.

Roman shrugs: Maybe. Then – silence.

ALON

Okay, look, one good place to start is—

LOGAN

I can start if you want?

Everyone looks mildly surprised.

ALON

Please?

Logan has a line prepared . . .

LOGAN

Everything I've done in my life is for my children. And I know
I've made mistakes but I have always tried to do my best by
them because they are everything to me. And I love them.

Everyone looks at each other: Fuck. That's a surprise.

ALON

Okay? Great.

LOGAN

Thank you.

                        CONNOR
    Well that's nice. That is nice.

*The kids all have a bunch of feelings about that but can't quite
muster them and nor do they want to start to quibble.*

                        ROMAN
    It is nice.

They look at Shiv.

                        SHIV
    Sure. No. Agreed.

Silence.

                        ALON
    And so? What do you feel in terms of that? Anyone?

He looks around. No one speaks.

                        ROMAN
    I hear it. I hear it.

Alon nods.

                        CONNOR
    Uh-huh. Big words. Good words.

                        SHIV
    I'm just processing. But yeah.

But no one wants to go next.

                        ALON
    You've got a lot of power in this room, Logan, do you realize
    that?

                        LOGAN
    How do you mean?

                        ROMAN
    He's got a lot of power everywhere.

Logan looks at him and Roman shrinks.

                        ALON
    Logan, how do you feel about the idea that—?

LOGAN

Look. Everything I've done is for my children. And I know I've made mistakes but . . .

SHIV

Dad, you can't just do one sentence.

LOGAN

That's what I feel, Siobhan, I can make shit up if you want?

Silence with an edge.

ALON

Shiv?

SHIV

Look where I'm at is I'm having a hard time diving in because – I guess honestly, I wonder why did he bring us here? I mean was it for this photo opportunity?

LOGAN

No. No absolutely not. I wouldn't bring you out here for a photo and an interview.

SHIV

Excuse me, there's an interview now?

LOGAN

I told you a photo and an interview.

SHIV

No you didn't. What? So this is a publicity event essentially?

LOGAN

It's optional! It won't be questions. Apparently it's 'rural wear'. I don't know.

SHIV

This is not okay. I have a publicist for this stuff. Con, did you know?

CONNOR

I think the photo's nice.

SHIV

Rome?

                         ROMAN
I don't mind.

                         ALON
Logan – do you think your children might, sometimes, be a
little, scared of you?

                         LOGAN
Ha! Fuck off. After what they've done to me? Fuck *off*!

Something snaps for Logan.

EXT. CONNOR'S RANCH – POOLHOUSE – DAY

Marcia, Willa and Tom are served coffee by Tara.

                         WILLA
Well this is nice.

                         TOM
 Shall I be mother?

He pours coffee from a French press.

   All girls together!

                         WILLA
The First Wives Club!
                    (*then, glancing at Marcia*)
The current wives club . . .

                         TOM
Do you think they're talking about us?

                         MARCIA
They will all be talking about themselves, except Logan.

A chill.

                         TOM
This is a lovely place, Willa. Are you here often?

                         WILLA
Not that often. I worry he won't let me leave! Hahah. No I'm
kidding. It's incredibly quiet. Which is great. When you lie in
bed, you know, you are seriously in the – calm?

MARCIA

And tell me do you think you'll always do what you do?

WILLA

What? The theater?

MARCIA

Yes and what you do – for money?

WILLA

Uh-huh. Well, I like my life and. I go with the flow, so. Yeah
I think I'll just – slide over more into producing or writing or
directing?

MARCIA

I knew a woman in Paris who did what you do. She was very
intelligent.

WILLA

Thank you.

MARCIA

And do you want children?

WILLA

Um, I don't know. Maybe one day?

MARCIA

Don't wait too long. That is all I will say.

TOM

That old biological clock starts a-ticking! You can always
freeze?

MARCIA

Uh-huh. That is a way of putting off life.

TOM

I'd like Shiv to freeze. Embryos not eggs. Little bit of me in the
bank! Have you thought of that?

WILLA

Um – so much advice! Maybe I'll need therapy after this!

MARCIA

My friend, in Paris who was your way, she was actually
murdered. But it was not to do with her being a prostitute, it
was to do with a restaurant that went pouf. So?

                              WILLA
    Oh? Okay!

Willa tries to smile.

INT. KENDALL'S HIRED PORSCHE – DAY

Kendall is driving through New Mexico. Fast. Peaceful.

Kendall's approaching the ranch. We see a security guard by the turn-off. Kendall begins to slow.

We're on his face. He's got a number of feelings. Excitement. He's going to tell his dad how he feels! But then there's the gateway. The actual gateway . . . Anxiety builds. Shame. His heartbeat gets louder.

As he slows, the security-guard gate makes ready to check him. Kendall thinks: is this a retreat? It just feels so complicated to go in there and get into it all? Can he do it, in public? Maybe he can do it, more empowered, later?

As the guard approaches he begins to accelerate and – he's away. It feels good. Like freedom.

INT. CONNOR'S RANCH – CHAPEL – DAY

Shiv, Connor and Roman are looking away from Logan.

                              ALON
    If they're scared of you, they're scared of you. That's the
    information you need to accept.

                              LOGAN
    Fine. I don't believe it is all.

He checks his phone. Hits something.

                              ALON
    Look can we go forward with the shared agreement to put our
    phones away while we focus on what's happening in the room.

Logan eyes Alon. The children watch, this is interesting. Who has the power in this room?

                              LOGAN
    I am trying to buy a number of television stations.

ALON

Could you do it . . . later?

Tiny smiles from the kids.

LOGAN
(*a small climbdown*)

Fine. Tell me what more you want here and I'll dance the dance.

ALON

I guess what I want you to do is tell me how are you feeling?

LOGAN

I'm feeling I need to check my emails.

SHIV

That's not a feeling, Dad.

CONNOR

Maybe don't deny Dad's feelings, Shiv.

SHIV

I turned down something huge to be here and now you're just going to tank it?

LOGAN

I'm doing therapy!

ROMAN

I don't think you are?

LOGAN

I am.

CONNOR

Well, no you're not, Dad.

Logan on phone.

The kids look at Alon: See what we have to deal with?

SHIV

Look. What I think we should actually have a conversation about is the fact that Kendall's not here. And that's because there are reports all over that Kendall's taking drugs. And I for one don't know where those have come from.

LOGAN

You don't have to worry about that.

497

SHIV

What does that mean?

LOGAN

That's not something we're dealing with today. It's beyond the remit.

SHIV

I don't think there really is a remit?

LOGAN

I had nothing to do with those stories.

The kids all look at each other, the floor. None of them believe that.

ALON

Shiv, do you believe your father?

Beat.

SHIV

Well.

ALON

Go on?

SHIV

Honestly no. I think this is all fake.

Logan stares her down.

ALON

Roman?

ROMAN

I don't know.

Alon looks at Connor.

CONNOR

I don't know. No.

ROMAN

I mean he might not have meant to but – no.

Logan boils over. He mumbles then explodes—

LOGAN

You think your generation invented talking?! There used to be nothing but analysts and hippies running screaming on LSD

about wanting to fuck their mothers. Well let me tell you I did fuck your mothers. And sometimes I'm sorry.
(*then*)
I'm sorry I'm sorry. Alright? I'm finished. I'll apologize as much as you fucking want, but I can't get into everything. That's it.

Beat.

                    ALON
Logan, if I'm ever asked if you participated fully in this family therapy I can't yet, in good conscience, say you have.

Logan composes himself.

                    LOGAN
Fine. I apologize. Maybe I'm hungry. I've got nothing to hide. Let's do it, c'mon. We can do it.

                    ALON
How about we take a break and begin again, clean slate, in the afternoon?

On the kids: Okay, let's do it.

EXT. NEW MEXICO DIVE BAR – DAY

Kendall stops and gets out of his car.

INT. NEW MEXICO DIVE BAR – DAY

Kendall enters. A few regulars, a mix of daytime drinkers. He approaches the bar, hops up. The barmaid, Janelle, is there.

                    KENDALL
Hey have you got any non-alcoholic beer?

                    JANELLE
Na-ah, sorry.

                    KENDALL
Fine, sparkling water please. Mineral water.

She gets it, looks at him. An unusual type.

                    JANELLE
Uh-huh. Tourist?

He doesn't give her anything. Hands over a credit card.

Kendall – Roy. Visiting family? Connor Roy?

Kendall's not going to deny it. Smiles.

Is he your dad?

KENDALL

No.
                    (looks at her face)
What? I probably think the same.

JANELLE

No just there's stories. He came in here one time, had a dog with
cancer he wouldn't let the vet kill. But he couldn't watch it die
either. Dragged it round the whole bar trying to get someone
to take it. Saying give her a good life. I'll pay you, I just can't
watch. Anyway, Skunkhead Tanner, he took three grand then
shot her in the parking lot.

KENDALL

Jesus.

Turns to look. Pool-playing men, Chang and Tanner.

CHANG

What? What?

JANELLE

None of your business, talking about Skunkhead.

TANNER
(off)
Don't you talk shit about me, Janelle!

Laughter, this is all good-natured.

KENDALL

Hey, also, can I get a Smirnoff, just two ice?

*She brings it. Too slowly for him. It sits there. Beautiful. He picks it
up, drinks it. That's it. That helps. This isn't real life, here. He moves
over to the guys playing.*

I heard you killed my brother's dog?

INT. CONNOR'S RANCH – TOM AND SHIV'S BEDROOM –
DAY

Shiv is getting a small bag. Tom follows her in, excited.

> TOM
>
> So?? C'mon.
>> *(as she busies herself)*
> What did everyone say!
>> *(he's 'sympathetic')*
> Nothing too horrible? Or upsetting? Or just disgusting?

> SHIV
>
> Listen, I'm going to Santa Fe to meet Gil.

> TOM
>
> Oh. So it's all, resolved?

> SHIV
>> *(kidding)*
> Yes, we solved everything. Done. Totally sane.
>> *(then)*
> I won't be more than a few hours, will you be okay?

> TOM
>
> Sure. But listen. You're okay right? Sometimes I don't know.

> SHIV
>
> Big question. Yes. Yeah.

Tom follows Shiv out and down the stairs into—

INT. CONNOR'S RANCH – KITCHEN – DAY

*Shiv enters, Tom a bit behind. Alon, Roman, Willa and Connor are
having sandwiches.*

> SHIV
>
> Can I take a car?

> CONNOR
>
> What's that?

> ROMAN
>
> What are you doing?

SHIV

The Tesla. I have a meeting in town. I'm not taking this seriously when no one else is.

CONNOR

But we're getting somewhere, Shiv, I can feel it, he's breaking down.

SHIV

You're sweet and I love you, but you're dreaming.

ROMAN

You can't go! Can she?

ALON

Shiv can make decisions as an adult. But you know, I was just saying maybe we should take a break though, get out of our heads, into the good body. Everyone, get your dad out there—

CONNOR

Dad can't swim.

SHIV

Doesn't even trust water.

Connor hands over the car keys. Shiv leaves, with a kiss for only Tom.

TOM

If it helps to make up numbers I'd be pleased to . . . get involved.

WILLA

Let's swim!

INT. CONNOR'S RANCH – BAR AREA – DAY

Connor catches up to Willa.

CONNOR

Hey, so, um, you know, about, the family photo – later.

WILLA

Uh-huh?

CONNOR

There was an idea maybe you should sit it out?

WILLA
(*she gets it*)
Yeah.

CONNOR
Cos it's just family et cetera.

WILLA
Uh-huh.

He feels terrible.

CONNOR
Sorry.

WILLA
It's okay. I'll probably end up getting murdered anyway.

CONNOR
No one's murdering you. Not statistically anyway.
(*then, he looks at her, at the view*)
Look. You know – I appreciate you.

WILLA
I appreciate you too.

CONNOR
And I think you're better than any of them.

She smiles.

I just wondered. Wouldn't you – couldn't you. I don't know how to say this except to say: love is a strange and peculiar affliction. It's like a – a cold, who knows when you're going to catch it? It's a virus. A mutating virus. Could you just stay here for a while and maybe you'll catch it?

WILLA
Con?

CONNOR
I know, but I'd still support you but you could take my money in the way that a wife does, not a – how you do now?

WILLA
Are you serious?

> CONNOR

That came out wrong. What I mean is, you'd have an allowance. And you can write and travel to New York and we can make a life in the theater. I could be your producer?

> WILLA

Gosh that's a lot.

> CONNOR

We have so many great ideas.

> WILLA

No. Sure. We do.

> CONNOR

Let's do family but different.

> WILLA

We could try.

> CONNOR

Exactly, why not! Yeah?

> WILLA

Yeah.

> CONNOR

Hey! I love you!

> WILLA

And I – I . . . love . . . you.

> CONNOR

Exactly! See? That wasn't so hard, was it?!

She smiles awkwardly at him. There's the sound of a splash from somewhere.

INT. CHANG'S HOUSE – FRONT ROOM – DAY

Kendall, Tanner, Chang and Mac (three guys from the bar) come into Chang's home.

There are a bunch of wolf posters and knick-knacks in the room.

> KENDALL

Okay. Lot of wolf stuff.

CHANG
(*earnest*)

I like wolves.

KENDALL

Okay.

TANNER

He really likes wolves.

KENDALL

Yes. Okay.

CHANG

My mom says I was a wolf child.

Tanner's lighter isn't working and he goes and finds another. He's gradually setting up to smoke meth.

TANNER

That's cos she never bothered to take care of you! That's just salesmanship of her straight-up neglect.

Chang shows off a wolf tattoo.

CHANG

Whoooo!

KENDALL

You get wolves here?

MAC

Nope.

Tanner takes out the light bulb they use to smoke meth. Mac turns on the TV at source. Tanner tokes on, then passes the bulb to Kendall.

KENDALL

I never did meth. This is like an experiment.

He takes a hit. It's really really nice. Home.

The channel that comes on automatically is ATN. Kendall is momentarily mesmerized. There's something on about extreme weather. Flooding.

My family own that.

> TANNER

That screen's only sixty-four inches. You probably have one of those – a projector, like, what are those ones, Mac?

> KENDALL

There's a thing now that Type A's actually – can't get addicted, because we are addicted.

> CHANG

You know if it wasn't for wolves we couldn't speak.

> MAC

What the fuck about that?

> CHANG

It was only from having to tell dogs what to do, that we ever actually got the need to like talk out loud, to command them—

> TANNER

This is a real person, don't start attacking his brain.

> KENDALL

I'm not a real person.

> CHANG

I saw it on *Unknown Evolution*.

> KENDALL
> (*with great clarity*)

How much more you got. We need to get more. And some weed. And some Xanax some Oxy and some cigarettes.

> TANNER

You like it?

Kendall considers.

> KENDALL

Experiment successful.

He decides to put on a show for them.

I am interested in becoming a methhead.

Laughter. And cheers.

That's cats anyway—

TANNER

What is?

KENDALL

Who only make sounds for us. They don't meow at each other.

TANNER

You want me to text our guy?

KENDALL

Sure. I got money.

TANNER

You got to work later?

Kendall shakes his head. No, no he doesn't. He's free.

EXT. CONNOR'S RANCH – SWIMMING POOL – DAY

Roman in the pool. Willa too. Alon arrives in his trunks.

ROMAN

Really dive deep. Don't be scared of what you're going to find down there!

He smiles, suddenly a little uncomfortable.

WILLA

You have to jump!

ALON

I will.

ROMAN

Jump jump jump! You pussy!

WILLA

Jump jump jump!

Rather unexpectedly, Alon takes a little run-up and then dives head-first into the pool. The shallow end.

Crack.

Alon's comes up, blood pouring from his mouth.

INT. CONNOR'S RANCH – DINING ROOM – DAY

Marcia and Logan and Tom are eating sandwiches.

TOM

I feel I should apologize. For blanking you earlier. Clear the air.

LOGAN

For what?

TOM

Ignoring you.

LOGAN
(*to Marcia*)

What's he talking about?

TOM

I'm sure it wasn't clear but I try to hold myself to a higher standard—

Karolina has appeared discreetly.

when it comes to inter-family turmoil and etiquette and—

KAROLINA

We have the journalist holding in Santa Fe, what do you want to do? Hi, Tom.

Tom's surprised to see her. Roman bursts in, soaking wet and out of breath.

ROMAN

The guy, his teeth— It's bad, I dunno, maybe, someone—

Roman rushes out. No one much reacts. Is this a joke?

LOGAN

What was that?

Eventually, Leon comes in.

LEON

There's been an accident in the pool. We might need emergency services.

They respond, get up and head out.

INT. CONNOR'S RANCH – LIVING ROOM – DAY

Tom, Connor, Marcia, Logan.

Alon enters in a towel, with another bloody towel packed into his mouth, blood seeping out. Tom is tending to him. Roman doesn't know what to do.

> WILLA
> We don't know if he got a head injury or—

Alon shakes his head.

> ALON
> (*barely audible*)
> Just my mouth.

> ROMAN
> He just dived. He hit the bottom—

> WILLA
> Did you hit your head?

Alon shakes his head. Points.

> CONNOR
> He hit the teeth.

> ROMAN
> Well the teeth are in the head, Connor, they're kind of a central feature.

> CONNOR
> It's signed, Alon, it's clearly signed, what were you thinking?!

> MARCIA
> Should I call an ambulance?

Karolina comes to find out what's happening.

> ROMAN
> I didn't think he'd jump head-first.
> (*surprised by her presence*)
> Hey Karolina.

> KAROLINA
> Hey Roman.

(*then*)

He mustn't go to sleep.

ALON
(*muffled, confused*)

I don't want to go to sleep.

Connor is on his phone immediately, pacing away. The others come in to look.

WILLA

Let's have a look. The bleeding always makes it look worse than it actually . . .

Alon takes the towel away to reveal several of his teeth are missing. A bloody grin. Their reaction shows it is very much not *alright.*

ROMAN

Jesus fucking Christ, man.

ALON
(*panicking*)

What?!

WILLA

We should get him to a hospital.

ALON
(*indistinct*)

Oh god oh no! What is it?

ROMAN

Yeah, you're okay, buddy. Fuck!

Connor returns to the group, still on the phone.

LOGAN

Send your guy. Send Colin. We should stay.

ALON
(*muffled*)

Can we go please?

CONNOR

I really feel I need to help him.
(*then, sotto voce*)
And I want to make sure he's not litigious.

Connor's off. This is an injury to Logan too. The day is disintegrating.

> LOGAN
>
> Great, fucking great. I was about to take business advice from a clown who jumps in the shallow end. And now everyone's fucking off!

> MARCIA
>
> Roman's here, Logan. Roman's still here. For photo, for everything?

> ROMAN
>
> Sure. I give good cheekbone.

Logan looks at him: Yeah, you're okay. And here.

EXT. SANTA FE HOTEL — DAY

Shiv pulls in the Tesla and valets it.

INT. SANTA FE HOTEL — CORRIDOR — DAY

Shiv with Nate, walking the corridor. Local press pass by. Shiv gets paranoid.

> NATE
>
> Don't worry, he's super-nice.

> SHIV
>
> Nate, Ronnie Reagan taught me how to gallop. I'm not going to turn green and do a shit when I meet Gil Eavis.

A journalist passes by.

> This is just a fuckload of press?

> NATE
>
> They're local, they don't know who you are.

> SHIV
>
> So naive.

> NATE
>
> Such a narcissist. Okay, so, don't fuck this up.

He lifts her hand and kisses it. Sort of pally. But definitely not. She looks at him: WTF?

EXT. CONNOR'S RANCH – DAY

Logan and Roman walk, hands behind backs, the senior statesmen, as a photographer takes shots of them.

PHOTOGRAPHER
Yeah, okay you're talking! That's nice. That's stately. That's great.

LOGAN
What?

ROMAN
We look good, Dad. We should talk.

LOGAN
Look I want you to call Japan, we, have the office. I'm tickling Sandy on local. I want you to get into the government issues of it all with the launch deal.

ROMAN
Right, sure.

Beat.

And you actually want me to do that? Or is this just words we're spewing for the camera?

LOGAN
You're COO aren't you?

ROMAN
(*pleased*)
Yeah. No sure. I got it. I'm on it. I know, I was checking.

INT. SANTA FE HOTEL – CONFERENCE ROOM – DAY

Shiv and Nate reach Gil Eavis. Tough, experienced. The full politician. When he concentrates on you everything lights up.

GIL
Siobhan Roy! The acceptable face of the Worst Family in America!

SHIV
Gil Eavis. Stalin in a sweater.

NATE

Okay, well, happy . . . meeting!

They both smile at these versions of themselves as Nate retreats. Gil looks at Shiv. Takes a beat.

GIL

So. How are you?

The light is on her and she soaks it up. She kind of wants to let him in and thinks it's good tactics.

SHIV

Really? Um. Well, my family's fucked. I'm hardly talking to my dad and my brother's suing my dad.

GIL

I'm sorry. If family isn't right, nothing feels right.

Shiv nods. He's good at making connections.

SHIV

And, how are you? Are you gonna go for it?

He considers. Can he trust her?

GIL

I'm feeling really good. I suffered some depression last year – after everything – but I'm good.

SHIV

And – what – are you thinking I can help handle the message on that?

GIL

No. That's just – the truth.

It is the truth. But it's also considered vulnerability. Both versions are true. Shiv gets it. They smile.

Look. I'm not going to make you do a dance. I'm finalizing and Nate and me want you on the team. What do you think?

SHIV

I think you're too radical.

                              GIL

You know the good politician, he figures out what people need
and sells it back to them as what they want.

She looks at him. That's interesting.

                              SHIV

So this is a job offer?

                              GIL

Well. Yes, but, there's an issue.

                              SHIV

My name?

                              GIL

One section of my base will be outraged at my even meeting
you.

                              SHIV

Well that section has nowhere else to go. So fuck 'em.

He smiles at the cynicism.

                              GIL

You know cynics are always frustrated idealists.

It's an ideological flirt. She's tempted.

If I'm going to win big, like I want to, to remake this country,
for the better—

                              SHIV

Ooo. Lah-di-dah!

                              GIL
                  (*smiling, unembarrassed of his ambition*)
I need to spike your dad's guns. The papers, the news channels.

She narrows her eyes: Oh, do you want me for that?

                              SHIV

I can't help with that.

                              GIL

No. Oh no. No! Of course. But I'm gonna go for his throat.
Legally, legislatively. Hearing, referrals. I thought I should tell
you? It'll be ugly.

She looks at him.

> SHIV

And how do you know I won't betray you?

> GIL

I guess, I – trust you.

> (*then*)

And I think – you trust me, right? That's all we can ever do.

Yes. Terrifying. She doesn't want to dive in yet.

> SHIV

I can work with Nate. I can't work for Nate. It's fine. It's just a preposition thing.

> GIL

We could figure that. The bigger question is do you want this enough to go to war with your family?

They look at one another.

> SHIV

Can I think about it?

INT. NATE'S CAR/EXT. HOTEL PARKING LOT – DAY

Shiv in the passenger seat, Nate in the driver's seat of a rental car. They are in a parking lot of the hotel.

> SHIV

He's good.

> NATE

So?

> SHIV

I don't know.

They look at one another. Shiv is feeling high and reckless.

Okay.

> NATE

Okay?

> (*then*)

Listen. It's shitty but my AirBnB has a hot tub?

He starts the engine.

                         SHIV
    Turn it off.

She leans and takes his hand and places it up her skirt and exhales, like just its pressure is relaxing.

                         NATE
    Not gonna go to the hotel?

                         SHIV
    Let's just . . . be here, a minute. So I can think.

She closes her eyes. She can think. She masturbates herself with his hand. The rest of him waits.

INT. CHANG'S HOUSE – FRONT ROOM – NIGHT

They're smoking weed – a bong is there. There's some powdered amphetamine speed on the table.

Kendall is half-focusssed on the business news, not ATN, another channel.

Waystar expansion plans. The sound is down but his date from the RECNY Ball is on a rival channel, the subtitles play out as a presenter speaks:

'Ambitious expansion plans could be on hold due to concerns about ongoing litigation regarding boardroom disruption at the global media player . . . '

The others are telling 'yo mama'-style jokes.

                         CHANG
    He so rich, he so rich that he gives Oprah a car!

                         TANNER
    He so rich, he so rich he need a golf cart to pass the salt.

                         MAC
    He so rich, he so rich his goldfish wear furs.

                         TANNER
    Okay, he so rich, he so rich that when he cums, it's like Perrier water and all the sperms have little top hats.

They love this. Even Kendall has smiles.

> You know, I don't even care. You might be rich. But we have this. And this is real. So, who's better off? You are. Fuck it. I do care.

Kendall raises his hand – it's funny. But has to make a call. As the guys focus in on a game of cards or a photo one of them has on their phone, Kendall makes the call.

KENDALL
Hey. Listen, Roman. I know why Dad hates us and we need to talk.

Intercut with:

INT. CONNOR'S RANCH – BEDROOM/OFFICE – NIGHT

Logan and Roman are in the makeshift office. Karolina too. Roman on the phone.

ROMAN
What? Where are you?

KENDALL
New Mexico.

ROMAN
What??

KENDALL
I realize now.

ROMAN
Are you high?

KENDALL
No. I'm at some guy's house and we've been taking drugs but I'm very clear.

ROMAN
Ken, will you send me a pin, just so I know you're okay?

KENDALL
I've got a lot of important information in play.

> ROMAN
>
> Just send me a fucking pin, okay? Do it now, are you doing it?

He looks at his phone to check then back up.

> I'm coming to get you, bro.

Roman hangs up.

> LOGAN
>
> You're doing the call?

> ROMAN
>
> I'm going to get Kendall. He's . . . here. And – he's not – great?

Logan gets the implication.

> LOGAN
>
> Okay. Okay. Go.

> ROMAN
>
> I'll make the call!

He's off.

INT. CHANG'S HOUSE – FRONT ROOM – NIGHT

Kendall is starting to feel a little paranoid. He has got a glass of water and it is a funny color. He doesn't want to drink it.

A knock at the door freaks the others.

> ROMAN
> (off)
>
> Hey, man? Man?

> TANNER
>
> Who the fuck is that?

> KENDALL
>
> It's okay. It's my brother.

Chang opens the door with a chain on.

> ROMAN
> (through the chained door)
> I've come to rescue you, man.

Chang checks with Kendall and lets Roman in. Kendall enjoys his brother's discomfort. Roman clocks the room, vibe and drugs.

Wow. Hi. I like what you've done with the wolves.

TANNER

I thought your brother was the rich guy with the – face?

ROMAN
(*to Kendall*)

Come on, man, let's get you out of here.

KENDALL

Hey look, I probably shouldn't even be talking to you, legally, given the ongoing situation apropos of my legal action against you as a board member for your failure to fulfill your fiduciary duty and breach of my employment contract.
(*then*)
But – I've had a major realization.

ROMAN

Is that crank?

KENDALL

We've had all kinds of fun, thanks, Mom.

ROMAN

That will make you crash like fucking – Mohamed Atta, into – Princess Di.

TANNER

Not if you stay high . . .

KENDALL

Tanner makes good points.

ROMAN

Come on, let's go.

KENDALL

How's the therapy?

ROMAN

It was all bullshit. He didn't even do it.

This pleases Kendall. Roman reaches out to take his hand. Kendall takes it up.

> KENDALL

Gentlemen, this has been divine.

> ROMAN

We should all meet up and do this again, I'll make sure he stays in touch.

They start to exit.

> TANNER
> (*after them*)

Hey, Kendall, tell Bill Gates my computer's fucked from all the fucking updates, man!

INT. CONNOR'S TESLA – NIGHT

Shiv driving. She puts on earbuds, music plays. Her face – unreadable.

EXT. ROAD/INT. CADILLAC SUV – NIGHT

Roman drives and Kendall in the passenger seat.

> ROMAN

You okay?

> KENDALL

I think so.

> ROMAN

Should I call a doctor. Or Rava? Do you want me to hit a kid so we can steal his kidneys?

Kendall just laughs. Roman starts to set up his hands-free.

Listen. I'm sorry, but I gotta do this call about the launch thing in Japan, as we go – if that's—

> KENDALL

You do your call, brother.

Kendall has his window down. The rush of air. It feels good.

INT. CONNOR'S RANCH – KITCHEN – NIGHT

Shiv enters. She creeps in. Through the dark house but there's light in the kitchen.

She comes in surprised to find . . . Logan waiting up with Connor, Marcia and Willa and Tom. Some late-night supper remains, maybe cheese and nachos.

She's not expecting this crowd. There's a tension.

SHIV

Oh . . . Hey?

TOM

Hey!

LOGAN

You're late.

SHIV

Yeah.
(*then*)
So what happened with the whole – fake therapy? Any pretend breakthroughs? Any good performances?

CONNOR

Nothing. Our therapist died.

Shiv frowns.

Metaphorically speaking. It felt like you all killed him, to me, is how it felt.

TOM

He knocked his teeth out in the pool.

LOGAN

And where have you been?

SHIV

I was meeting about a prospective job.

LOGAN

Uh-huh, that's right.

MARCIA

With your father's enemy?

Shiv looks at her, how much does she know?

SHIV

Okay, I'm going to bed.

521

LOGAN

I keep an eye on things, Shiv. I keep an eye.

SHIV

What is that supposed to mean? I had a meeting! You do what the hell *you* like on everything, forever.

A car arrives. Tom doesn't like the vibes.

TOM

Maybe we should chat this over in the morning?

He's totally ignored.

MARCIA

And he has to hear it from his so-called friends. On the telephone. Dripping poison in his ear.

TOM

It is her job?

Kendall comes in, high and unusually invulnerable.

KENDALL

Hey, hey hey! What we fighting about, muthafuckers??

Logan is immediately unsettled by his demeanor. Roman comes in after, his brother having briefly escaped his grasp.

SHIV

Jesus, Kendall.

CONNOR

Hi brother?!

Logan takes one look.

LOGAN

What's wrong with him?

KENDALL

Oh, where do we start?

LOGAN

Roman?

KENDALL

I'm off my nut, folks. Off my fucking head. Like all the papers said. Your dreams have come true, congratulations!

Uncomfortable beat as Kendall goes to get a beer and the air dies and Roman whispers—

> ROMAN

Listen, just so you know, I think the launch thing is good. I talked to the guys—

Logan waves it away.

> KENDALL

Shut up, Rome! The king is angry. The king is displeased and everyone needs to pretend he's wearing clothes.

Logan doesn't want to deal with this. He's focussed on Shiv.

> LOGAN

You'd do that to me? Eavis? The one Senate member who wants to fuck me ragged? On the same side as those animals who hit me with a face full of piss!

> KENDALL

He doesn't even fucking notice, Rome.
> *(then)*
Give him a high-five, Dad. Come on. He's waiting.

> SHIV

It's my work, if anyone, Jesus you should—

> LOGAN

That's not work. This is sabotage. Rebellion.

> SHIV

Oh, of course, it's about you? What if I actually believe in his points about the purchases, or just his whole philosophy . . .?

> LOGAN

'Philosophy'. His philosophy is to take the bread from my mouth. This is a deliberate attempt to undermine my whole business strategy.

> KENDALL

You don't have a business strategy, Dad! Your whole business model is based on seducing presidents. You're a really high-class hooker.
> *(to Willa)*
No offense.

CONNOR

Hey!

WILLA

It's fine. My aunt's an addict. But I think I'm gonna—

Willa leaves, Connor holds her hand till the very last second.

CONNOR

But you know, I have to say, I do feel a little used here today, Dad.

LOGAN

Oh you too!

CONNOR

Just where we are and what's happened, and then even tonight you just, went off and worked—

LOGAN

I took a few calls, Jesus, you can't wait?

CONNOR

Can I wait for you to finish a couple of calls? Oh I think so. I think so, Dad, I've had a bit of practice, quite a bit.

MARCIA
(re Kendall and Shiv)

Connor, your father's been busy dealing with these two – traitors.

SHIV

Disagreeing with Dad is not treason!

ROMAN

Mmmm. But, trying to make his biggest enemy president *is* kind of a fuck-you.

KENDALL

I liked those stories you planted about me, Dad. That was fucking nice.

LOGAN

You forced my hand. You're lucky that was it. It's part of the game.

KENDALL

C'mon, everybody, it's a rootin' tootin' super-fun fuckin' game for all the family!

LOGAN

Fine. I'll shut it all down, the network, cable news. No acquisitions. No company. No way to distance yourself, would you like that? You run to politics to make out you're your own man, fine, but that's not principle. You're scared to compete. You're marrying a man fathoms beneath you because you don't want to risk being betrayed. You're a coward.

Shiv, furious, walks out. Tom follows.

SHIV

You are beyond, you are . . .

LOGAN
(*after her*)
You're worse than the other two!

CONNOR

The other 'two'?

KENDALL

You know, I'm lucky. I'm a lucky person. I lucked out. I realized that. You're so fucking jealous aren't you? You're so fucking jealous of what you've given your own kids. And you can't . . . You can't work it out.

LOGAN

If I'd spoken to my uncle like that, he would—

KENDALL

What? What would evil Uncle Noah do?

LOGAN

Get him out.

KENDALL

Cos that's some big advance calling your daughter a coward till she cries.

During this, Logan struggles to get up. Roman helps him. Logan exits, knocking off a fruit bowl as he passes.

> LOGAN
>
> Fucking – nobody. You're a nobody.

Marcia follows her husband. Roman stands, tense, torn. Connor sits, somehow stronger. Kendall gets a beer from the fridge. Opens it. Makes an 'oops' face to his brothers.

INT. CONNOR'S RANCH – TOM AND SHIV'S BEDROOM – NIGHT

Tom comforts Shiv.

> SHIV
>
> I'm sorry.

> TOM
>
> Honey. You don't need to apologize. I know it's not true.

> SHIV
> *(it is)*
>
> I'm so sorry.

THE DAY AFTER

EXT. CONNOR'S RANCH – DAWN

A crack of sunrise on a New Mexico vista.

EXT. NATURE PARK, NEW MEXICO – EARLY MORNING

Kendall is up early. He's still clinging to the last of a buzz and he climbs up a hill to get the purest hit of view. You have to start at the bottom.

EXT. CONNOR'S RANCH – DAY

Connor and Willa wave Shiv and Tom off.

> CONNOR
>
> It's funny. I wanted them all here, but I feel relieved they're starting to go.

He gives her a squeeze.

> It'll be nice when it's just us.

                              WILLA
                          (*maybe . . .?*)
        Yeah.

                              CONNOR
        Home on the ranch.

*They walk towards the house. Connor looks relieved, happy, content.
Willa looks like she's dying inside.*

EXT. NATURE PARK, NEW MEXICO – DAY

*Kendall sits, looking at a spectacular view. He feels an enormous
sense of peace. Then he snorts a dirty-looking line of speed off the
back of his hand.*

EXT. CONNOR'S RANCH – SWIMMING POOL – DAY

*Logan, in trunks, makes his way cautiously into the water. Marcia
watches, huddled in a blanket.*

                             MARCIA
        That's right. There you go.

*He tries a few strokes, flails around, scrambles across the width of the
pool, half walking, half swimming.*

*He pulls himself up against the side of the pool. On his back we see –
scars. Something traumatic happened.*

Episode Eight

PRAGUE

Written by Jon Brown
Directed by S. J. Clarkson

Original air date 22 July 2018

Cast

LOGAN ROY	Brian Cox
KENDALL ROY	Jeremy Strong
MARCIA ROY	Hiam Abbass
GREG HIRSCH	Nicholas Braun
SHIV ROY	Sarah Snook
ROMAN ROY	Kieran Culkin
CONNOR ROY	Alan Ruck
TOM WAMBSGANS	Matthew Macfadyen
FRANK VERNON	Peter Friedman
COLIN STILES	Scott Nicholson
SANDY FURNESS	Larry Pine
GERRI KELLMAN	J. Smith-Cameron
STEWY HOSSEINI	Arian Moayed
NATE SOFRELLI	Ashley Zukerman
JEANE	Peggy J. Scott
GIL EAVIS	Eric Bogosian
TABITHA	Caitlin FitzGerald
SHARON PETERS	Michelle Duffy
BOB GALPIN	Joel Hatch
ILHAN	Nick Choksi
ANGELA	Lauren Patten
KARA	Jeena Yi
GINA	Mallory Ann Wu
MATT	Nick Mills
JONAS	Michael Izquierdo
AMY	Jade Kedrick
LUCY	Christine Spang

DAY ONE

INT. WAYSTAR – OUTSIDE LOGAN'S OFFICE – DAY

*Greg waits. He smiles at Jeane and Lucy. He looks in at Logan,
Roman, Gerri, Stewy with Bob Galpin and his lawyers and advisors.*

                    GREG
    Pretty great view, huh? I meant out there. Not me.

INT. WAYSTAR – LOGAN'S OFFICE – DAY

Bob and advisors with Logan, Roman, Gerri and Stewy.

                    GERRI
    . . . but look Bob, we appreciate you coming over.

Roman is texting under the table. Trying to set something up.

                    BOB
    Sure. Some people would insist on neutral territory. Turn
    everything into a mind-game.

                    LOGAN
    Uh-huh.

                    GERRI
    Where are we at, Bob?

Stewy's noisily unwrapping a mountain-energy bar.

                    STEWY
    Excuse me. I'm not here.

                    BOB
    You're at five-point-three?

Roman looks up from his phone. Bob whispers with an advisor.

                    ROMAN
    Correct.

> BOB

And I think we can live with that?

Roman perks up. Not ridiculously. He wants to nail this.

> ROMAN

Yeah?

> BOB

Yeah.

> LOGAN

Uh-huh.

Roman gives Logan a secretive thumbs-up. Logan looks away.

> BOB

It's a fair price.

> LOGAN

Oh yeah? That's nice. What a lovely guy.

> BOB

Logan. You'll have seventy local TV stations? Buy in Sandy's. You're King Kong of local.
> (*nods to Roman*)
The kid knows. The kid's smart. We good?

Bob is ready. Logan looks away. Gerri can read the room.

> GERRI

Can you give us five? We'll set you up with a room.

INT. WAYSTAR – LOGAN'S OFFICE – DAY

Outside, Gerri stands with Bob and advisors, liaising with an assistant about a meeting room.

Roman, Logan and Stewy have moved into the main office and are looking out at them.

> ROMAN

Good, right? Is it whisky time?

> LOGAN

Shut the fuck up.

ROMAN

Ugh? That's a good price?

LOGAN

So what's going on? He's selling me things I want at a fair price?
What's next?

Gerri returns as Bob and associates are led away by an assistant.

ROMAN

I think he wants out, fast.

LOGAN

So, if he does, we fuck him.

ROMAN

Dad. I think we did fuck him?

They watch as Bob consults with his lawyers, now on the move.

GERRI

It's no good if he's smiling.

ROMAN

Well, objectively, I mean, if we get what we want and he gets
what he wants—

LOGAN

You screw them out, you chisel them out, you fucking hurt
them. You make them squeal.

ROMAN

Well, sure, I like hurting other human beings as much as the
next guy but – this is, really fucking good, Dad.

LOGAN

Walk him to the elevator and tell him four-nine.

ROMAN

Oh, Dad? That's— It's insulting.

LOGAN

Alright. Gerri, you go.

She does, Logan looks at Roman.

If you can't do it fuck off! Just text on your phone, you bendy
fuck.

Roman slopes out, hurt and undermined. Stewy watches him go.

INT. WAYSTAR – OUTSIDE ROMAN'S OFFICE – DAY

Stewy catches up with Roman. Roman tries to act unbruised.

> STEWY
>
> Hey. You okay, kiddo?

> ROMAN
>
> What – that? Oh that's nothing.

> STEWY
>
> Uh-huh?

> ROMAN
>
> I got game. Sometimes you play possum. Let him punch it out till he gets tired. Then, I move in for the kill.

> STEWY
>
> Right. Nice. So – I've been wanting to ask. How's Kendall?

> ROMAN
>
> He blowing you off too? Last time I saw him he was smoking crank with some mole men. But that was, like, a month back. He's hustling.

INT. WAYSTAR – ROMAN'S OFFICE – DAY

They enter. Stewy invades the space.

> STEWY
>
> Right, VC-ing?

> ROMAN
>
> I'm maybe seeing him this weekend. If he shows.

> STEWY
>
> Yeah?

Roman's looking at his phone.

> ROMAN
>
> Fuck. Dude. I don't suppose you know a coke dealer in Prague?

> STEWY
>
> Um. Probably. Why?

Stewy dumps himself in Roman's office chair and starts fucking with the settings. Adjusting the height, back rest.

ROMAN

Tom Wom bachelor party. Ugh. Ugh. I don't have time for this shit!

STEWY

Tell you what, dude, fuck Prague. My girlfriend and her freak dogs they run – you know these parties? Rhomboid?

ROMAN

Bullshit. Rhomboid?

STEWY

Hey, I'm cool.

ROMAN

Please. Because you have a nipple ring and simply will *not* stop going on about it?

STEWY

Better than telling everyone you're 'down with Dre' because he sends you cereal bars at Christmas.

ROMAN

Fuck you, I have a reputation. I'm not taking my crew to watch, some art pricks and some tech hoes dance around in bowler hats and twizzle their mustaches out of time to the 'beatz'.
(*re chair*)
Dude. Come on. Not the lumbar setting.

STEWY

You know who else'll be there? Sandy Furness.

ROMAN

Really? Yuch. He goes to those things?

STEWY

I know, right? But he's sitting on the other half of your dad's dream deal. Packet of fifty more local stations.
(*then*)
Come to the party. Talk him into selling. Go home to Zeus like a triumphant fucking Hermes or someone. Does that make sense? I never read any of that shit.

                                    ROMAN
Sandy goes? Jesus.

                                    STEWY
Dude. Send me the names, I'll get you on the list. And bring
Kendall yeah, I need to straighten things out.

Stewy exits. Roman feels good about that.

INT. KENDALL'S CAR – DAY

*Kendall looks down intently at a new pair of Basquiat-themed
Reeboks/Timberlands in his lap as he relaces. Frank next to him,
anxious. Ken's jiggling. Up on pills. Calmed by pills.*

                                   KENDALL
Bro? How about some more bass in the back? I like to feel my
teeth dance.

Kendall pulls on the first sneaker. He feels good.

                                    FRANK
You okay, Ken?

                                   KENDALL
I'm good. And listen, try not to drag yourself in there like the
world's oldest man, yeah? And try not to breathe so loud.

A restlessness to Kendall's energy.

INT. INDUSTRIAL TECH MEETING ROOM – DAY

*Kendall and Frank in a boardroom. Ilhan finishes pouring waters as
Angela and Kara enter. Kendall's all confidence.*

                                    ILHAN
Kendall. Frank. This is Dust.

                                    FRANK
'Hey.' Great to connect. Love the name, by the way. Very funky.

                                   KENDALL
Please excuse Captain fucking Bee-Bop here.

Kendall moves past Frank to shake their hands. He's loose.

How's it going? Nice shirt. Big fan of what you do. Fucking
sweet potatoes.

ANGELA

Thank you.
(*fumbling*)
Um. Likewise?

It just sits there. Unspoken weirdness. Kendall smiles. Then.

ILHAN

Angela. Did you want to spin us through the pitch deck?

Angela pulls up a slide.

KENDALL

I don't need to hear the pitch. Because I've X-rayed your
business and I get how it works.

Kendall puts his feet up on the table. His new sneakers.

You buy bullshit from idiots and you sell it to pricks. Art-school
student makes a painting, you jack up the price, skim it, sell it
on.

Angela and Kara smile politely. That's not what this is about.

ANGELA

We're interested in increasing the reach of young artists.

KARA

. . . and the democratization of art.

KENDALL

No absolutely, I get it. You're giving a platform to marginalized
talent. I'm just telling you how this works from the outside, to
the sharks.

Ilhan steps in.

ILHAN

Maybe we should talk about funding cycles—

KENDALL
(*cutting across him*)
Look. Can I tell you something? I bought these on my way over
here because I thought you'd like them and I'm passionate about
working with you.

Kendall pushes it.

> Don't sell your soul to some monolith. We're boutique, we're
> light on our feet. Fucking rebel alliance. I'm a good guy, who
> knows the bad guys and I'll fight for you every day. I'm the
> asshole who can be your Warhol. And yeah, I just thought of
> that.

It's a convincing pitch.

> So what? Do I take off my shoes? I will. I'll throw them out the
> fucking window right now.

*Kendall pops a shoe off. Angela and Kara look at one another – he
does have a certain swagger. Maybe he's a contender?*

INT. WAYSTAR – OUTSIDE LOGAN'S OFFICE – DAY

Greg sits waiting. He's restless. Leg jigging.

GREG

What do you think? I mean I'm somewhat between the devil
and the deep blue sea here because, my boss downstairs, is like
waiting, and yet my boss up here is. Him. And I've been here
three and a half hours now. Do you have any advice?

Jeane gets a buzz.

INT. WAYSTAR – LOGAN'S OFFICE – DAY

Logan at his desk. Looking down through his glasses. Greg enters.

LOGAN

Ugh. It's the wheel.

*Greg crosses behind Logan. On his screen, Logan's trying to watch a
speech from Senator Gil Eavis. But there's a spinning buffering wheel
in the middle of the screen.*

GREG

It's buffering. You could try knocking it down to low quality?

*Logan gestures: Go on then. Greg would have to lean right over
Logan to make the adjustment.*

As Greg leans over Logan and starts fiddling with the settings, he can see the top of Logan's head quite clearly.

There will be a minor loss of crispness.
                    (*re Logan's browser*)
Wow. That's a lot of browser tabs. But, then, you're a busy guy.

                    LOGAN
I hear you boys are headed out for Tom's bachelor party?

                    GREG
Yes. That's correct. Roman's arranging. Prague has been mentioned?

The video of Gil's speech now plays on Logan's computer.

                    GIL
                    (*from speakers*)
. . . Logan Roy is a pernicious influence on our culture, he is, to be frank, a cancer to American values . . .

                    GREG
Man. That guy. What a – jackhole. Well. He just lost my vote.

                    LOGAN
Huh.

Logan hits pause. Greg feels the need to fill the silence.

                    GREG
Got a really good head of hair there. Sorry to— But it's the maternal side I think, that's carried on. So! Good news for me!

                    LOGAN
So listen. This party. Can you make sure Kendall doesn't come home in a box?

                    GREG
Okay?

                    LOGAN
I don't want him showing up dead at the bottom of some French fag's swimming pool.

                    GREG
Absolutely. None of us do, sir.

LOGAN

Keep an eye on him for me. Is that something you can do for me?

GREG

Yes, sir. In which case would now be a convenient time to talk with you about my position, because I'd like to move on from parks and into, for example, digital? I won't mention any names but there's a culture of— It can border on the personally abusive.

LOGAN

Tom? Tom can dish it out?

The first time Logan has heard something promising about Tom.

GREG

He's pretty able in that department. All I'm doing is, I'm flagging to you that I'm thirsty for the next chapter.

LOGAN

Take care of this for me, perhaps we'll talk.

GREG

Muchly appreciated.

Greg exits. We track with Greg as he walks away. Hates himself.

'Muchly'?

INT. LECTURE THEATER – DAY

Gil Eavis, midway through a speech.

GIL

. . . and it's a wave, a wave that pushes up. It starts with the voters like you. And it rises and breaks over the powerful and says, *this, here, this* is where it starts. And today we're calling time's up. Time's up on the big media owners who pervert the flow of true, pure, information. Contaminate it with their sour and bitter pollutants. Time's up for Waystar Royco, and the shadow it casts across our national conversation. Time's up for the man at the top of that pyramid – Logan Roy. The man who, it seems, will not rest until he has monopolized the provision of news in these United States.

Shiv and Nate at the back of the room. Hands dangle but don't quite touch. A magnetism between their two bodies.

> SHIV

You saw this?

Nate looks over her shoulder at her phone. Close behind her.

> NATE

ATN spot. Uh-huh. Yeah. I guess, we do? Right.

> SHIV

You're going to stand right there? In my air space?

> NATE

I am rereading for context.

> SHIV

You're cc'd.

Beneath, as Nate presses against her.

> GIL
> (off)

. . . the coverage of your local school board elections, or your city council, or the latest crime statistics, all under the control of a billionaire mogul from his penthouse in Manhattan. Logan Roy is a stain on our American values. Time is up for him and the partisan propaganda and divisive commentary his outlets pump. Sowing seeds of division and suspicion amongst the people of this nation while he feathers his nest with the super-sized profits he makes by exploiting tax loopholes his friends in government refuse to close. His tendrils continue to spread, conveniently unchallenged by those in high office. And so the question you need to ask yourself is this: do you want your local news anchor in hock to a rapacious tycoon in bed with special interests? Or do you think it's time we took a stand and protected your First Amendment rights? You see, these monopolistic practices cannot be left unchecked simply because we're too afraid of the powers that one man wields. Waystar Royco is a cancer at the heart of America and Logan Roy is out of control. And I say no. I say no more.

> SHIV

I can't believe I get paid to call my dad names. It's so cathartic.

They watch the speech for a beat.

> NATE
>
> You really think he should do ATN?

> SHIV
>
> Sure. Into the lion's den. He attacks them, righteous, Old
> Testament anti-capitalist Gil. They attack us, 'there's a red in the
> bed!' No one's mind's getting changed. We get the base fired up.
> They get the viewers. Then, once we're through the primaries,
> we pivot to center.

> NATE
>
> Gil won't pivot.

> SHIV
>
> I'll get him to pivot.

*Nate looks like, really? Gil's speech finishes to applause. Shiv takes a
call.*

> Hello?

Intercut with:

EXT. STRETCH OF WASTELAND – DAY

Tom on the phone to Shiv.

> TOM
>
> So listen, something's afoot. I've arrived at the drop-off point
> and it seems there's been a change of plan—

*Tom is with Connor, Greg, Matt and Jonas – Tom's old friends, 'The
Fly Guys' – on a stretch of wasteland. They have luggage (apart from
Roman). Greg has a rucksack.*

> I'm pretty sure I'm being pranked.

On Roman with Greg and Connor.

> GREG
>
> What's happening, Roman?

> ROMAN
>
> Just – hold your tingling wieners. All will become clear.

CONNOR

I'm not sure you understand how disruptive it is to be changing the itinerary at this late stage—

On Tom.

TOM
(*on phone*)

And I don't know what's going to happen but – you know, I have a feeling it's all liable to get a little 'disgusting' and—

SHIV

Pretty sure you're not supposed to be telling me this, Tom?

TOM

I just wanted to flag it. And calm the qualms. Because I for one—

SHIV

Tom. We're adults. It's one night. Enjoy yourself.

Tom is overcome with relief.

TOM

Shiv . . .? Honey badger? *God* I want to dock myself inside you so much right now.

SHIV

I love you too, Tom.

A town car pulls in. Kendall gets out.

ROMAN

Oh, okay. *Now* he deigns to join us. You're late.

KENDALL

Yeah well. Apologies. I've been a little busy revolutionizing tech financing.

ROMAN

. . . On coke.

They smile.

CONNOR

Okay, what is this, Roman?

ROMAN

Alright! Who wants to fuck a hobo?

Nothing.

No? Then let's roll out. Party. Down there.

Roman points in the direction of the tunnel.

GREG

Wait, what? We're going to a party in a tunnel?

TOM
(*to Matt and Jonas*)
Relax. We're not going to a party in the tunnel. It's a ruse.

Roman has a package containing five flashlights.

KENDALL

What is this? Some pop-up shit?

GREG

Am I going to need my central Europe coat?

CONNOR

Rome, what now? I'm wearing flight socks and my TSA slip-ons.
C'mon!

TOM

I get what's happening here. One minute I'm getting lured into a
tunnel, next thing I wake up in Belgium with no eyebrows.

ROMAN

You should probably dump your luggage in the car.

*Kendall, Greg and Tom start loading their bags into Kendall's car.
Roman crosses to Matt and Jonas.*

And listen, I'm really sorry, guys – but it's a pretty tight guest
list?

TOM

Oh. Roman, what? Matt and Jonas? The Fly Guys aren't . . .?
They flew in. The old team? Roman?

ROMAN

Relax, we'll figure it out. Keep your phones on, we'll first-wave
it and call you once we're inside. Take twenty for coffee.

MATT

Thanks.

JONAS

I can buy a coffee.

The guys leave their luggage in Kendall's car. Roman heads into the tunnel with Kendall, Greg and Connor. Tom is in an agony of indecision.

TOM

Gah. Oh! I can't leave Team Fly Guy. That's the Fly Guy code?
(*looks between the groups, walks*)
Keep your phones on yeah? I'll call you! Five minutes. Five.

Tom smiles awkwardly. And heads into the tunnel, leaving Matt and Jonas behind.

EXT. APPROACH TO TUNNEL/INT. TUNNEL – DAY

Roman leads Greg, Connor and Kendall into the tunnel with flashlights. Connor still has luggage. Tom runs to catch up.

TOM

Oh, man. What the fuck have you got planned for me, Roman?

Roman laughs devilishly. Tom laughs along. Then.

Seriously. What have you got planned?

ROMAN

Look. Tom, I'm sorry. Prague fell through and I was busy and I didn't have time to organize a – hot-air balloon to Monaco.

TOM
(*sounds promising*)

Okay . . . 'Hot-air balloon . . .'?

GREG

I just stepped on a snail. Oh god. I hate stepping on snails.

TOM

Roman, do you know where you're going?

ROMAN

Yeah. I came to another thing here.

547

> CONNOR

Ugh. This is a disaster on the footware front. Can I change? Guys? Stop for a shoe change?

> GREG

You kept your luggage?

> CONNOR

Be prepared. I know Roman. And I love him. But I don't trust him. He's a twenty-four-karat dingbat.

Up ahead, Kendall and Roman walking at the front of the group. Then, privately, with genuine fraternal concern.

> ROMAN

So, bro. Are you going to be okay to be around all the booze and coke? Because, I can make sure no one does it around you, man.

Kendall bristles. He doesn't need Roman looking after him.

> KENDALL

I'll be fine, man. Thank you.

Roman nods. Clocks Kendall's frostiness.

> ROMAN

I hear you're 'doing apps'.

> KENDALL

Uh-huh. I'm incubating. I've been out on the west coast sprinkling fuck-dust. Rebalancing away from crypto, into eco.

> ROMAN

Wow. It's all so futuristico.

> KENDALL

Better than being carried around in Dad's pockets like fucking Stuart Little—

> ROMAN

Hey. They're nice pockets. Spacious.

> KENDALL

How is he? Still using your fragile self-esteem as a punchbag?

                    ROMAN

He's actually got me overseeing this satellite launch out of
Tanegashima.

                    KENDALL

Wow. A spaceship?

                    ROMAN

Plus I'm heading up the local deal. Bob Galpin's selling and
I knocked it out the park. Which was nice.

                    KENDALL

Good for you, bro.

Roman enjoys the power over him.

                    ROMAN

Guess I finally broke out the cage.
                    (*then*)
'Can't keep a good dog down,' right, bro?

Roman arrived at an iron door.

    Okay! Abandon all hope, ye who enter!

Roman opens the door with slight trepidation.

INT. WAREHOUSE – CORRIDOR/RECEPTION AREA – DAY

The boys pass through a corridor. Tom and Roman at the front.

                    TOM

Is this real? Is this a real corridor? Are we at an airfield?

Connor and Greg at the back.

                    CONNOR

Yeah Willa moved out to Austerlitz. And she loves it. She loves
how quiet it is. She didn't think she would but she really does.
So. Girlfriend. I guess I for one won't be partaking in any
debauchery.

They arrive at Gina and a check-in desk with security.

                    GINA

Roman Roy and guests? Welcome to Rhomboid.

Gina produces five phone pouches.

>   ROMAN
> Okay, boys, we're pouching.

>   TOM
> Wait – how are we going to phone the Fly Guys?

>   ROMAN
> Tom, we'll figure it out.
>   (to Kendall and Greg)
> I think the big white men are going to be drinking *a lot* of diner
> coffee.

Their coats are taken. Gina sees Connor's luggage.

>   GINA
> What's in the luggage, sir?

>   CONNOR
> It's a variety of winter wear.

>   GINA
> You can leave that with us.

>   ROMAN
> Okay so this way . . .

INT. WAREHOUSE – DOWNSTAIRS SPACE – DAY

The boys follow Roman through into the main warehouse space.

>   TOM
> Wait . . . So this is it . . .? This is *actually* where I'm going for
> my bachelor party?

>   GREG
> It smells of – ammonia. And, like, the inside of handbags? If
> you're at all familiar with that smell?

>   CONNOR
> The tough thing is I've been living on central European time
> for forty-eight hours, to ease the transition. So I'll be ready for
> breakfast soon.

>   GREG
> It doesn't look like the sort of party with a lot of food?

TOM

Roman. I'm sorry – am I having my bachelor party in a very large, very cold sort of – pretend rail yard?

As they walk on – and see Stewy approaching.

STEWY

Hey, Rome. Ken?! How you going?!

Kendall wasn't expecting to see him.

KENDALL
(*what the fuck*)

Stewy?

STEWY

Bro. Long time. You look like shit. What you up to, working at Starbucks and growing the coverage?

Kendall smiles.

We good?

KENDALL

You're my third oldest friend and you fucked me like a tied goat. We're great.

Stewy smiles.

STEWY

Let me show you up.

Stewy heads towards the elevator. On Kendall with Greg.

GREG

Oh and Kendall. If you need anything this evening. Bottle of water, soft drink – I'm more than happy to be your mule on the whole soft-beverage side of things? Okay?

On Roman, as he rushes to catch up with Stewy. Privately.

ROMAN

So, dude, where's Sandy? When do we sit?

STEWY

All things in time.

They arrive at the elevator. Stewy shows them in.

INT. WAREHOUSE ELEVATOR – DAY

Kendall, Roman, Greg, Tom and Connor with Stewy.

> TOM
>
> No. I'm sure it'll be great. Thanks, Roman.

> ROMAN
>
> What did you expect? Why did you even ask me, Tom?

> TOM
>
> I thought you'd rise to the occasion.

> ROMAN
>
> Well clearly I haven't risen to the occasion.

Tom nods sullenly. Elevator arrives.

INT. WAREHOUSE – MAIN PARTY SPACE – DAY

*The boys plus Stewy step out and into the party. Stewy gets stopped
by someone he knows.*

> STEWY
>
> One second – Kendall, I'll find you.

*Roman leads them in, looking back at Stewy to make sure he'll stay
in touch.*

> ROMAN
> (*re the party*)
> Okay. This is it. Yeah? Cool right? Is it cool? Or is it like total
> fucking bullshit? Who knows?

> TOM
>
> What is this?

> ROMAN
>
> It's a physical fun palace. It's if you like it and she likes it, it's all
> good. Uh, this guy – look at the fucking bird mask like it's *Eyes
> Wide Shut.*

> GREG
>
> Wait – *Eyes Wide—* Is this – gonna be an orgy?

> ROMAN
>
> No.

GREG

It's not gonna be an orgy?

ROMAN

Greg. It's not 1997. It's not this and it's not that. Don't be so binary, Mr Betamax.

TOM

So it's – it's a bit of an orgy?

ROMAN

It's basically a collective of hot people – and Connor. At a party.
(*re a projection*)
With a monkey dressed as an astronaut. It's whatever you want it to be. It's a fucking – sandpit for emergent behaviors.

TOM
(*warming up*)
Okay! Okay. Holy shit. So can we, are we going to be able to – fuck here?

KENDALL

Not me, business is my fucking.

ROMAN

Sure. Maybe we could find you a Bloomberg terminal to stick your cock in?

CONNOR

Well, I'm out. In a relationship. Girlfriend!

TOM

Well I have to say, Roman. This is promising! This is very promising!

ROMAN

See, Tom? How about a little faith?

GREG

But there's areas though? Neutral areas? It's not— In the sense of it being compulsory.

Kendall sees Angela from Dust talking with friends nearby.

KENDALL

Angela? Dust? Yeah? Hey?

Kendall crosses to her. She's just coming up from doing a line of coke. A compromising situation.

> ANGELA
> Oh – fuck? Hey. What's happening?

> KENDALL
> We just got here. Cool. Very cool.

> ANGELA
> Totally. Same.
>> (*then; re cocaine*)
> This is actually only like the third time I ever did this, so.

Kendall smiles and nods. Neither letting her off the hook or casting judgment.

> KENDALL
> This must be synchronicity, huh? Two people meet in a warehouse and the fucking world changes?

> ANGELA
>> ('*yes but*')
> Oh. Yeah. And we really appreciated you coming to see us—

> KENDALL
> I'm super-excited.

> ANGELA
>> (*oh shit. Are we doing this right now?*)
> Oh. Totally. Me too.

> KENDALL
> Well, you have a great night, Angela.

Kendall exits. Angela watches him go.

Kendall takes a glass of champagne. Knocks it back, feeling good.

> GREG
> So maybe – one water, one wine? As a kind of informal rule for the group? Plus, they have risotto balls?! Soakers. Super-soakers.

> KENDALL
> Can I help you with something, Greg?

Greg shrinks back. Kendall goes back to the bar, leaving Greg with Tom, Connor and Roman. They look away with drinks.

> TOM

Man. It is going off tonight like Wambs, gans, thank you ma'ams! We should go talk to some girls.

> CONNOR

Little tip. Ask them where they were on 9/11. If they can't remember, they could be under twenty-one.

> TOM

Shiv gave me a hall pass. 'We're adults.' Apparently. I'm going to blow my stack, like, multiple times!

Something occurs to Greg.

> GREG

And what, Shiv? Shiv has the same arrangement. She's an adult too?

> TOM

What? No! I mean. Sure. I – I don't know. Greg, it's not a competition.

> GREG

No, it's cool. I'm sure you've got it all figured out.

Tom looks out. Suddenly less sure of his position.

Connor sees a whisky tumbler half filled with pills.

> CONNOR

What's this?

Connor puts on his reading glasses. Inspects a pill.

> ROMAN

Molly. Happy pills.

Connor nods.

Con man. C'mon. No?

> CONNOR

What? Prague time. It's two in the morning for me. I need a pick-me-up.

Roman holds Connor's hand to stop him from taking the pill.

Dude, I know my way round. 1986. Me and a Fleetwood Mac LP and a bag of weed touched the face of God!

555

> *(takes a pill)*
>
> First of the evening! First of many!

ROMAN

Connor. Do not do any more of these.

CONNOR

Got it. I am one and done.

Stewy joins Kendall at the bar.

STEWY

So. How does it feel to be out?

KENDALL

Not going to lie. Great. Seeing the kids. Growing kale.
Following my nose. Intrigued by vegan meat.

Stewy smiles.

STEWY

And about the vote and your dad, you know I had to follow the
money, right?

KENDALL

I get it. Friends are friends but money's money.

STEWY

Exactly. And, listen. Here's a question. How would you feel
about getting all the way out?

Kendall doesn't follow.

Half a bil for your share of Waystar.

KENDALL

Hello?

STEWY

I know. I'm feeling generous. I've plumped the pillows, added a
little premium.

Waiting staff pass with a tray. Stewy looks at the canapés.

Can you get me one of these but without any of this? Thank
you, I'll be right here.

KENDALL

Consisting of what?

STEWY

Straight liquid.

KENDALL

Bullshit.

STEWY

Don't worry about that. I can raise it.

KENDALL

Why would you want to be even more in? The place is a fucking antique shop.

STEWY

Ken. Just take the money and get out.

KENDALL

Well. It's not uninteresting. Because I've got a lot cooking. An artificial sun. Clean beef made in the lab.

STEWY

Great. So listen. Part two. How would you feel about talking about this with Sandy?

KENDALL

Sandy Furness? Excuse me, what the fuck?

Stewy smiles. And Stewy and Kendall head off. Roman notices them go.

INT. HOTEL ROOM – DAY

Shiv and Nate are in bed, looking at their phones. Nate's looking at a gift registry. Shiv is watching ATN's anti-Gil coverage.

NATE

These bathrobes are nice. You should ask for these.

SHIV

Uh-huh.

NATE

What's your table-linen philosophy?

SHIV

My philosophy is I literally don't give a fuck. So what's that, Nietzsche?

NATE

Silverware. These are what we have on our registry. You should go for these.

He shows her.

SHIV

You want us to have matching cutlery?

NATE

Why not? It'd be sort of horrible and cute.

SHIV

Right what and then when we get divorced and split all the stuff, we can hook up and still have the full set?

NATE

Uh-huh.

SHIV

You know this is just fun, right?

NATE

I know. This is just—

SHIV

Nothing. I mean there's no God, and there's no – anything. So there's just people, trying to be happy, in rooms. Right?

NATE

Right.

Then, casually dropped.

SHIV

And you know I'm suggesting to Gil, on ATN, he cools off on the anti-Waystar agenda.

NATE

Er. Excuse me?

SHIV

(no eye contact)

I talked to him after the thing.

NATE

Oh. Okay, well, I have spent quite some time on how it would be 'very vivid' to attack Waystar on a Waystar network.

>   SHIV
>
> It's played out. It looks like we have an agenda.

>   NATE
>
> Er, we do. Stopping overly mighty media owners setting the agenda for our democracy.

Shiv 'falls asleep' during this.

> DOJ, FCC, Batman to stop your dad eating the news.

>   SHIV
>
> Uh-huh? Even if we're going for that, isn't it in a big important speech nobody reads? Tonight he can forget the base and connect with America.

>   NATE
>
> Shiv, I appreciate you might have split loyalties on this—

>   SHIV
>
> Fuck you. I just want him to win.

>   NATE
>
> I'm just not sure he can do both at once. The base, and the rest.

>   SHIV
>
> If you can't ride two horses at once, you shouldn't be working at the circus.

INT. WAREHOUSE – BACK ROOM – NIGHT

Stewy shows Kendall through to a back room.

>   KENDALL
>
> Sandy comes to these things?

>   STEWY
>
> Oh yeah. The thing about Sandy? He *loves* sex.

Kendall shivers in disgust.

> I know. Gross. He takes the thing that he pees through and he puts it into other people. It's disgusting.

They reach Sandy.

>   SANDY
>
> Kendall. You look well.

                    KENDALL
Thank you. You look – incredibly out of place.

Sandy smiles.

    So. You wanted to talk?

                    SANDY
Has Stewy filled you in . . .?

Kendall clocks the conspiracy between the two of them.

                    KENDALL
Why do I feel like I'm about to find out you're not my real
mommy and daddy after all?

                    STEWY
Look, the truth is he wants your piece of pie, but – and I don't
want you to blow a fuse, but he's already in on Waystar.

                    KENDALL
As in?

                    STEWY
Sandy's me, I'm Sandy. We're kind of a single entity. Like a
creature from mythology. Head of a horse, dick of a swan.

                    KENDALL
Seriously? Stewy? Jesus Christ.

                    SANDY
I have a shell company attached to his private equity fund. I'm a
parasite on a parasite.

This is huge. Kendall could freak out. But—

                    KENDALL
You obviously should have disclosed this to me when I brought
you in.

Stewy makes a little noise. Maybe.

    You acted like kind of a snake?

                    STEWY
And you acted like kind of a sap, so, quits?

Kendall decides whether to blow up or not.

SANDY

You were in a tough position without having to consider whether your dad would want me . . . involved.

KENDALL

He very much would not.

Sandy smiles. Finally, Kendall smiles too. Waiter comes over and whispers something to Stewy.

STEWY

So apparently my girlfriend's having a panic attack – so I'm going to let you two catch up.

Stewy exits.

SANDY

Stewy tells me you're getting into tech.

KENDALL

I have a fund. We're small but we're engaged. Only work with good people. I'm interested in adopting an ethical posture.

SANDY

Half a billion. Smart guy could make a pretty big difference . . .

KENDALL

Just closed a deal tonight. Also there's these four Stanford grads, they have a piece of proprietary tech, it's a cluster of hydrogen lamps in a honeycomb formation and it makes a kind of artificial sun—

Roman enters. He hears the last of it and gauges the mood.

ROMAN

Wait. What's going on . . .? Dude. Are you pitching? Did you just pitch?

Instantly kills Kendall's vibe.

KENDALL

Where'd you spring from, Heidi?

ROMAN

Don't stop. I want to hear the big pitch. I might invest.

KENDALL

We were just talking.

Roman looks to Sandy.

> ROMAN
>
> To him? The enemy? Dude?
>> *(then to Sandy)*
>
> He's doing apps now. Did he say? He has this dry-cleaning one.
> It's going to revolutionize the way we get grease spots out of
> 'chinos'.

Kendall smiles along. But a sense of growing needle.

> KENDALL
>
> Rome? The adults are talking. How about you go play in the
> other room?

Roman smiles it off.

> ROMAN
>
> Sandy, could we maybe get a moment in private? Because I'd
> like to talk to you about how attached you're feeling to your
> fifty failing local TV stations?

> SANDY
>> *(polite smile)*
>
> Sure. I'm sure we can find a time . . .

> KENDALL
>
> Roman. Could you maybe back off for like twenty minutes?

> ROMAN
>
> I'm good thanks, Kendall.

> KENDALL
>
> Maybe just dial it in like *this much*. Get us a drink.

> ROMAN
>
> Haha. No.

> SANDY
>
> I would love another old fashioned.

> ROMAN
>
> Look I know you and my dad are deeply and happily in hate
> and have been for many years – but I need you to know, I'm
> my own thing. And I'm fully authorized to negotiate on Logan's
> behalf.

KENDALL
(*smirks*)

'Logan'.

ROMAN
I'm actually overseeing telecoms.

KENDALL
He's doing satellites like it's 1985. Dad's got him holding the
plastic wheel in the back and telling him he's driving.

Roman bristles.

ROMAN
You'll have to excuse my brother, he's making some adjustments
right now and he's a little 'off-center'.

KENDALL
How about you fuck off back to your little gangbang?

ROMAN
You see this? How he talks to me?

KENDALL
You're embarrassing yourself.

SANDY
Family.

ROMAN
You know he used to lock me in a cage?

KENDALL
What the fuck?

ROMAN
Back when we were younger. True story.
(*off Kendall's look*)
What? You pretending you don't remember the Dog Pound?

KENDALL
You're tripping.

ROMAN
It was a game, I had to climb into the big Alsatian cage in the
kitchen and wait for someone to come collect me.

SANDY

Oh yeah . . .? I don't know—

ROMAN

Might be three minutes, might be the whole afternoon. Four years old. Eating dog food from a cold tin bowl.

KENDALL

You need to stop talking.

ROMAN

Pissed myself in there once. He just gave me some newssheet and told me to mop it up.
(*laughs*)
I know, right? They should make a fucking movie about this shit.

SANDY

Excuse me, I'll be back.

Sandy exits.

KENDALL

What the fuck are you doing?

ROMAN

What?

KENDALL

What was that bullshit?

ROMAN

Oh, I can't— I can say what I want.

KENDALL

Yeah but you— That was – that was insane.

ROMAN

You want me to pretend none of it happened?

KENDALL

What happened?

ROMAN

So none of that happened? The Dog Pound?

KENDALL

Okay. I never made you eat dog food.

ROMAN

There was a bowl and it was filled with chow and I had to stay in there until it was finished.

KENDALL

It was a game. You enjoyed it. Ask Connor, ask Shiv.

ROMAN

I enjoyed being in a cage for three hours with a leash around my neck. Sure.

KENDALL

So now there's a leash. You're full of shit.

ROMAN

That's right, Kendall. Me. *I'm* the piece of shit. Enjoy the party, asshole.

Roman exits. We hold on Kendall.

INT. WAREHOUSE – CORRIDOR – NIGHT

Tom looks inside a side room as a couple make out. They're clothed, but the intensity suggests things are going to escalate. Tom gulps. Greg enters.

GREG

Have you seen Kendall? Because I feel like we should maybe keep an eye on him?

Tom makes a decision to make a phone call. As Tom exits, Roman is on a mission to find Connor. He crosses to him.

INT. WAREHOUSE – MAIN PARTY SPACE – NIGHT

Two men make out at the bar. Nearby, a man with his hand up a woman's top. A sense of the party kicking into a higher gear. Connor in conversation with Amy (twenties, high on MDMA).

CONNOR

—Austerlitz. It's in New Mexico. And we recycle all our rainwater.

AMY

Oh yeah? That's awesome!

Amy's half-listening to Connor and half-engaged in a conversation with her friends.

Roman enters.

>   ROMAN
> Hey Con, can I ask you something?

>   CONNOR
> Roman this is Amy and she's amazing.

Amy's talking to someone else. Connor can't stop looking at her.

> So smart. I really like her.

>   ROMAN
> Dude? That's the drugs talking.

>   CONNOR
> No, I really don't think it is. I think we have a real connection, you know?

>   ROMAN
> Trust me, it's the drugs.

>   CONNOR
> It really isn't. We're just really relaxed in each other's company. She held my hand. I think I'm in love.

>   ROMAN
> For fuck's sake, you're not in love, man.

>   CONNOR
> The only problem is I'm in love with Willa. So I can't be in love with Amy and in love with Willa. I mean, Willa's amazing and Amy's amazing maybe we can all be amazing together.

>   ROMAN
> Sure. On your Mormon sex ranch.

Connor thinks on it. It's not the most ridiculous idea.

> Look, do you remember anything about the Dog Pound from growing up?

>   CONNOR
> I remember something about a game you used to play.

ROMAN

So he did? He used to lock me in a cage?

CONNOR

Sure. The big cage. In the laundry room. At your mom's place in Cheltenham.

ROMAN

Right? What a bastard.

CONNOR

No, you liked it. You used to ask to go in the cage.

ROMAN

What?

CONNOR

Yeah, it was weird but I think you enjoyed it..

ROMAN

Okay. So I 'asked' to eat dog food?

CONNOR

It was chocolate cake. I think?

ROMAN

Bullshit.
(restating it)
Kendall locked me in a cage, I went all fucking weird, started pissing the bed and that's why Dad sent me away to St Andrew's.

CONNOR

Rome, Dad sent you away to military school because you saw *Rambo* you started marching up and down the hallway with a placard saying, 'Send me away to military school.'

ROMAN

You're full of shit.

CONNOR

Well, that's how I remember it.

Connor turns back to Amy. Interrupts her conversation.

Seriously. It's safe from biological and chemical attack and you'd all be welcome, pre- or post-apocalypse.

INT. WAREHOUSE — RECEPTION AREA — NIGHT

Guests congregate to talk on their unpouched phones. Tom approaches Gina.

> TOM
> I'd like to unsheathe please. Go bareback.

Tom smiles at a nearby woman, on a call. She looks back, disgusted. Tom is given his phone back. Dials.

INT. DINER — NIGHT

Matt and Jonas sit drinking coffee. Jonas scrolls on his phone as Matt drinks his coffee and stares into space.

A long beat.

Then – Matt's phone goes. Anticipation as Matt answers it.

> MATT
> (*into phone*)
> Hello . . .? No, I'm happy with my current provider thank you.

Matt hangs up. Jonas returns to scrolling on his phone.

INT. WAREHOUSE — RECEPTION AREA — NIGHT

On Tom, his phone now unsheathed.

> TOM
> (*into phone*)
> I'm just checking in . . .

Intercut with:

INT. ATN STUDIOS — NIGHT

Shiv is waiting.

Nate and Gil approach. Nate has Gil's ear. Shiv looks at them.

SHIV
(*into phone*)
Tom, sweetheart, listen, I'm at ATN with Gil, what is the least
number of syllables you think you can say this in?

TOM
Yeah, just so we're clear – in terms of you and me. Is this a quid
pro quo arrangement?

SHIV
What are you talking about, Tom?

TOM
(*low*)
Because if I for instance, touch a boob, do you grab a dick?

SHIV
Um. I don't know if—

TOM
Is there a rough chart of comparison? Like Celsius to
Fahrenheit? Or is it an eye for an eye, an orifice for an orifice?
I'm just trying to get a sense of the parameters?

SHIV
Tom. I can't negotiate right now. Just— We know, right? We
know.

TOM
Right. No sure, we know.

*She hangs up. Tom left feeling cut adrift. Shiv, Nate and Gil are met
by an assistant who guides them.*

SHIV
You want to run the tree on how personal stuff plays?

GIL
Issues. Issues issues issues. I can handle the soft soap, Shiv.

Nate winks at Shiv. He's had Gil's ear.

INT. WAREHOUSE – RECEPTION AREA – NIGHT

Tom, re-sheathed, waits by the elevator. Kendall comes out.

> TOM
>
> Hey, Kendall, just spoken to Shiv. Official permission for having of the fun!

> KENDALL
>
> Amazing. So happy for you.

INT. WAREHOUSE – RECEPTION AREA – NIGHT

Kendall on the phone to Frank.

> KENDALL
> (*into phone*)
>
> Frank, so listen, I've had an approach. Very interesting approach and I wanted to get your brain on it—

Intercut with:

EXT. STREET – NIGHT

Frank on the phone.

> FRANK
>
> I heard from the girls. The Dust thing. With the art?

> KENDALL
>
> I know. I saw them. It's locked down.

Kendall looks over, and catches Tom's eye. They nod.

> FRANK
>
> They wanted you to know, they loved you in the room but . . .

> KENDALL
>
> Frank. I just spoke to the girl.

> FRANK
>
> Ken. They're already setting this up elsewhere. But like I say, they loved you in the room . . .

> KENDALL
>
> What are you talking about?

> FRANK
>
> I think there's other money and they like it better.

KENDALL

Then we match it.

FRANK

I already tried. But seriously, they loved you in the room—

KENDALL

Stop telling me they loved me in the fucking room. Frank.
(*then*)
Let me talk to her, I can fix this.

Kendall hangs up and exits.

INT. WAREHOUSE – NIGHT

Kendall searching for Angela, laser-focussed.

INT. WAREHOUSE – CORRIDOR – NIGHT

Angela sees Kendall approaching.

KENDALL

Can we talk for a second?

ANGELA

Could we do this another time?

KENDALL

I just got off the phone to Frank. He told me.

ANGELA

I'm sorry. It's nothing personal—

KENDALL

Listen. And I shouldn't be telling you this, but I'm about to land a chunk of seed capital the size of fucking – Idaho so whatever it is you need I can make it happen, okay?

ANGELA

Okay.

KENDALL

Okay? We good?

ANGELA

Yeah, it's just, not about that.

> KENDALL

Then? Help me out here. Because there's something I'm not
seeing—

> ANGELA

It's the name.

> KENDALL

Which – Dust?

> ANGELA

Roy. Kendall Roy.

Kendall's confused.

It's like I was marrying Hitler and then what? I'd get to be –
Mrs Hitler?

> KENDALL

Okay. I get it. But that's not me. I'm not a Roy. Not really.

> ANGELA

I'm sorry, it's cool. We just don't want to be 'Hitler
Incorporated'. You're a—

> KENDALL

I'm solid, I'm a good guy.

> ANGELA

Well consensus is you're a coked-up prick who can't shit
straight. You think you're different, you're the same poison in
new sneakers?

Kendall's rocked. He allows the facade to drop.

> KENDALL

Angela. Okay. I'm going to be frank with you—

> ANGELA

Look. I didn't want to do this here. And I may be being
more forthright cos of the coke. I definitely seem to get more
forthright on coke I'm sorry—

*Angela goes to walk away. Kendall reaches out to stop her. Little
harder than he should.*

> KENDALL

Hey, wait—

                                ANGELA
    Hey fuck off.

Angela pushes past him and exits.

Kendall sees someone doing coke.

                                KENDALL
    Hey, man, can I get in on that?

Kendall reaches over and starts chopping out four huge lines.

INT. ATN STUDIOS – NIGHT

Gil with host Sharon Peters.

                                SHARON
    I'm joined in the studio by Senator Gil Eavis. Firstly, Senator,
    welcome. We appreciate it.

                                GIL
    Happy to be here, Sharon.

                                SHARON
    Let's jump straight in if we may? Your wife very tragically took
    her own life eighteen months ago.

Gil tries not to react. A curveball.

On Shiv and Nate watching in the wings with other staff.

                                SHIV
    The warmest of ATN welcomes.

                                NATE
    Soft-core. Horrible but easy.

With Gil.

                                GIL
    Um. I think everyone knows about that and it's something I live
    with but isn't relevant in terms of the issues I want to—

                                SHARON
    The impression you've given is that it did inform your decision
    to run?

GIL

A lot of things inform a big decision like this. What I want to talk about is—

SHARON

It hasn't been long and I guess what some people will ask is, what could possibly have caused such a tragedy and are you ready so suddenly to turn around and run for the highest office?

On Shiv and Nate.

SHIV

Doesn't he have a line for this?

NATE

It's normally – it's normally good.

GIL

What I'm focussed on what I think this country needs to do—

SHARON

But it's something you think about? Your mental and emotional state?

GIL

Yes. Sharon. I think about my feelings. Like most humans.

On Shiv and Nate.

SHIV

No. No jokes. Nate?

NATE

Yeah. I don't know.
                (*re monitor*)
Can we change channels on this?

SHARON

It must be incredibly difficult for you, especially someone who has had to deal with rumors swirling around the state of their mental health.

GIL

You know, instead of playing a pretend game of sympathy where you're trying to get your viewers to ask: 'What sort of guy has a wife who kills herself?'—

                              SHARON
        That's not what I said—

Gil tries to turn this thing around.

                               GIL
        Maybe we should talk about the guy who owns this channel,
        your boss, the owner of ATN, who's trying to buy up local news
        networks all over the country – so I'm calling for this deal to
        be blocked by the FCC, and for the DOJ to launch an in-depth
        investigation . . .

On Shiv and Nate.

                              NATE
        Is this okay?

                              SHIV
        I don't— It doesn't feel great?
                             (*then*)
        I'm going hot and cold so fast I think I might have hit the
        fucking menopause.

                             SHARON
        Would you say your emotional outbursts here could suggest
        you're not emotionally ready, temperamentally ready, to seek to
        lead the free world?

                               GIL
        If you wanna make this personal let's talk about Logan Roy.
        Your paymaster who has presumably sent you in as a hatchet
        woman?

                             SHARON
        Oh come on.

                               GIL
        Because you can tell a lot about someone from their relationship
        with their family.

On Shiv and Nate.

                              SHIV
        Oh fuck.

                              NATE
        I feel sick.

> SHIV
>
> Then you should puke. We could use the distraction.

> GIL
>
> His only daughter has come to work for me. What does that tell you about the man?

> SHARON PETERS
>
> You've got a hot temper haven't you, Gil Eavis?

Gil unmics.

> You don't want to take any more questions, is that it?

Gil shakes his head and walks off.

He passes Shiv and Nate.

> GIL
>
> They knew. They knew we were coming for them.

Gil looks to Shiv.

Gil exits. Shiv watches him go.

INT. WAREHOUSE – CORRIDOR – NIGHT

Greg catches sight of Kendall through the glass – chopping out coke. He starts banging on the window.

> GREG
>
> Okay, wait. No, Kendall . . .?

As Greg goes to cross to Kendall – Roman stops him.

> ROMAN
>
> What is it with you and him? You've been up his ass all day. Are you trying to fuck him?

> GREG
>
> No I just – I just want to make sure—

> ROMAN
>
> Make sure what?

> GREG
>
> Roman – excuse me— It's not anything.

ROMAN

Is something going on, Greg? Because I can see inside your brain. And if anything's obscured. I'll pull your fingers off.

Greg takes a breath.

GREG

If I say, you will keep it to yourself?

ROMAN

Yes.

GREG

You won't tell him will you?

ROMAN

Absolutely not.

GREG

Okay. Your dad – I think he's worried about him – he asked me to keep an eye on him?

Roman starts banging on the glass.

ROMAN
(*calling over*)

Hey, Kendall! Dad asked Greg to keep an eye on you.

INT. WAREHOUSE – MAIN PARTY SPACE – NIGHT

Kendall reacts.

KENDALL

Wait – he's been *spying* on me?

Roman crosses to Kendall. Greg has to explain.

GREG

He just – I think he was concerned.

Kendall's head's spinning.

KENDALL

Okay. Well. I'm about to do these four lines of coke and then my heart's going to explode so if you want to stop me—

Kendall gestures at the four lines of coke on the table. All eyes on Greg.

> GREG

But that's like— I don't get involved in the white drugs.

> KENDALL

Or maybe you want to explain to my dad how you let his son OD?

Kendall's not fucking around. He does a line.

> GREG

Come on . . .?

Kendall does another line.

> KENDALL

What are you gonna do, cuz?

Tom enters with drinks. Clocks the situation.

> He's counting on you, Greg. He's counting on you to look after me.

> TOM

Yeah go for it, Greg! Suck on those big white dicks, you fucking pervert!

Greg takes a step forward. Takes the rolled-up bill. Then, in very quick succession – bangs back two lines in a single, fluid inhalation.

Greg pushes back from the table, still inhaling manically. A sense of amused disbelief amongst the boys.

> Holy shit, cuz! You greedy piece of shit!

> KENDALL

And now I guess I have to go find some more.

Kendall exits. Greg stands – coke still hitting throat.

> GREG

That is – strong – drugs. I need to— Should I puke?

> TOM

Unless you can puke up your bloodstream? Oh, man, I hope you don't die! Cos if you do your heart'll be pumping so hard it'll probably bring you back to life and then you're just in a vicious circle of dying and briefly reanimating! Buckle up, fucklehead!

Tom slaps Greg hard on the back. Tom laughs. He looks over, and makes eye contact with Tabitha. And a smile. (Tom thinks, and crosses to her?)

INT. RESTAURANT – NIGHT

Logan at a table alone. Not on his phone. Tapping a finger on the table. Shiv approaches. She sees him. Tries not to feel anything.

> LOGAN
> Hello, Pinky. Glad you kept the date.

> SHIV
> Well. Family. How was the play?

> LOGAN
> You know. People pretending to be people.

Shiv sits.

> How are the wedding preparations?

> SHIV
> *(dry)*
> Very exciting.

> LOGAN
> Well I am excited. My daughter.

Logan looks at Shiv sincerely. Perhaps reaches out a hand to hers? Shiv's in no mood. Pulls away.

> SHIV
> You saw the interview?

> LOGAN
> They told me.

> SHIV
> You came after the man's wife.

> LOGAN
> They said.

> SHIV
> And you're happy with that?

LOGAN

Well tell him not to speak about my family. Not on my network
and not on any network, ever again, or I'll end him.

SHIV

So – silence the man who says you're stifling dissent?

LOGAN

I'm a bad father? How dare he? He's a bad husband. He killed
his fucking wife.

SHIV

What if your acquisitions are bad for the country?

LOGAN

Meh meh meh. Men change the world. Cowards complain. He's
using you. Can't you see it?
        (softer)
Don't let a lot of bullshit overshadow the wedding okay?

SHIV

The fucking wedding? I don't care about—

LOGAN

C'mon, stop screwing around. Let's talk. Come in. I'm tired of
this. You have potential. I always thought you were the smartest.

SHIV

So that's why you tried Kendall and Roman first? You know
what – I am the smartest. Which is why I can see through you
and this transparent little offer to buy me off.

Logan appraises her.

LOGAN

You know, I've always taken care of you, Siobhan, and maybe
I shouldn't have. Maybe I should just let them come for you.

SHIV

Like what?

LOGAN

I hear things, Siobhan.

Shiv looks to Logan: Are you threatening me?

> SHIV

Okay. You know what, Dad? If this is the way things are going—

She starts to stand.

> LOGAN

Well then I'm truly sorry.

Shiv exits, leaving Logan all alone.

INT. WAREHOUSE – MAIN PARTY SPACE – NIGHT

Couples have congregated in the cuddle puddle. Kissing and some groping. Connor at the heart of it all with Amy.

Tom's with Roman. Tom looking over at Tabitha.

> TOM

—and in terms of Shiv, where I've landed is – I think I'm going to maybe just ask for a 'handy'?

> ROMAN

Tom. Don't *pre*-rationalize. You get off and you eat the shame for dessert.

Tom smiles at Tabitha. She smiles back. Roman checks her out.

Wait. Her? This one?

> TOM

Yeah. We were talking for twenty minutes about financial derivatives and then she just asked me?

> ROMAN

My god. Holy shit. Dad would go absolutely nuts for her. You should do it.

> TOM

Yeah?

> ROMAN

Man. I'd be all over her. I'd like— I'd fucking – *urgm*. Oh yeah.

Tom feels a ripple of nervous energy.

> TOM

Okay. I need a Smint. Do you have anything?

> ROMAN

Tom. Just grab your baloney-pipe and jizz.

Tom takes a beat. He picks up two drinks and heads back to Tabitha. Roman watches them interact from across the room.

Roman watches as Tabitha leads Tom away. Roman thinks. Then follows after them.

Roman watches Tom and Tabitha through a window.

INT. WAREHOUSE – SMOKING AREA – NIGHT

Roman following Stewy through the space.

> ROMAN

So is now a good time to sit down with the old geezer?

> STEWY

Soon. Did you see the projection with all the plastic in the Pacific?

> ROMAN

So when can I talk to him? Because I would love to secure something to take home?

> STEWY
> *(hand on the shoulder)*

Romey. Be cool. Maybe eat a slider, ask if you can stick your finger in someone's ass—

Roman snaps.

> ROMAN

You know what – fuck you. I'm not your little pet that you get to kick around. You think I can't make life difficult for you? Word in the right ear, I can be your migraine, motherfucker.
> *(then)*
I came here to talk to the old man. On your word. So make it happen.

Stewy looks to Roman. Taken aback.

> STEWY

Okay, okay.

Stewy exits. Roman stands, feeling suddenly empowered.

INT. WAREHOUSE – MAIN PARTY SPACE – NIGHT

The energy and excitement of the party have gone. Connor at the bar. Sweaty. Greg drifts over to him.

GREG

I tried to hide but it finds you. Wherever you hide, the party finds you.

Connor smiles. Gina enters.

GINA

Sir, this is your final warning.

CONNOR

Absolutely. Got it. Understood.

GREG

What's happening?

Connor rolls his eyes. It's all just a misunderstanding.

GINA

Your friend keeps telling people he's in love with them. And it's making people uncomfortable.

CONNOR

My bad. Mixed messages, we just share such strong feelings on gut bacteria I think I got the wrong end of the stick.

Gina exits. Tom returns.

TOM

Oh my god, dude. That was *insane.*

GREG

Oh yeah?

CONNOR

Maybe I should go apologize . . .? Give her a hug . . .?

Connor exits. Tom continues.

TOM

Me and this girl. Went into a side room. Made out for a while, I was touching her, she goes down on me, I just splooge in her mouth. I know! Then – get this – she kisses me, and puts it back into my mouth, I swallow.

                           GREG
       Which – the splooge?

Tom's desperate to believe this is all okay.

                           TOM
       I know. So hot.

This sounds horrible to cokey Greg.

                           GREG
       You swallowed your own load?

                           TOM
       Because I've heard about it but I never knew it actually
       happened.

                           GREG
       Oh yeah? Because I haven't heard of it.

                           TOM
       Yeah. There's a word for it. I can't remember it right now.
                          (*then*)
       So fucking hot.

Tom takes a large swig of mineral water. Greg thinks on this.

                           GREG
       When are we allowed to go home?

                           TOM
       We have cars at five.
                        (*determined*)
       Greg. I am having the time of my life.

On Greg and Tom looking out. Pathetic broken men.

INT. HOTEL ROOM – NIGHT

*Knock at the door. Nate opens up to find Shiv. He has champagne
ready.*

                           NATE
       Are you ready for your bachelorette party? They were out of
       marine uniforms so I've come dressed as a political consultant.

He goes to kiss her. She stops him.

Relax. This isn't real.

> SHIV

Can I stay? But – with you – just as a human dog at the foot of the bed?

> NATE

I'll be your dog.

INT. WAREHOUSE – MAIN SPACE – NIGHT

Kendall (bit cokey) in conversation with a group of people. Connor enters.

> CONNOR

Hey, brother. I'm looking for this girl but I think she might be hiding from me.

> KENDALL

Connor. Not right now.

> CONNOR

Is there another room, you know, for humping? Because I've also lost Roman.

> KENDALL

Forget Roman.

> CONNOR

Yeah? Cos he was asking about the Dog Pound and he got kinda riled up.

> KENDALL

Uuh. He's still talking about that? Pathetic. He enjoyed it, right?

> CONNOR

Sure.

> (*then*)

I mean, so did you.

Kendall thrown.

You'd give him a real good whack on the snout. With the Sunday magazine.

> KENDALL

Well, rough house.

Connor reflects.

> CONNOR
>
> You know, Dad's theory was. You got two fighting dogs. You send the weak one away. You punish the weaker one. Then everyone knows the hierarchy and everyone's happy. So away he went.

Kendall thinks, makes a calculation. And exits.

Connor left alone. He sees a woman.

> Hey. So, can I ask? Where were you on 9/11?

INT. WAREHOUSE – SECOND-FLOOR SPACE – NIGHT

Sandy is standing. Kendall enters with renewed purpose.

> KENDALL
>
> Hey, listen, Sandy. I appreciate your offer, I'm not getting out.

> SANDY
>
> Okay. Well if you think you're going to tell your father, get back in with him, I have—

> KENDALL
> (*interrupting*)
> Keep your money, bring me in. We do this properly.

> SANDY
>
> Uh-huh?

> KENDALL
>
> Takeover. Leveraged buy-out.

Sandy looks opaque.

> SANDY
>
> A dual stock situation. That's not going to be straightforward.

> KENDALL
>
> Price in the toilet, shareholders are pissed. You and me could force him to the table.

> SANDY
>
> What about the rest of the family?

> KENDALL

Fuck the rest of the family.

> SANDY

Easy to say?

> KENDALL

No one has a clue but me. I can see it all. We take it apart. Fuck local TV, newspapers, parks. We bulldoze the whole fucking shanty town. I just keep the juiciest morsels. Turn the thing from a pod of rotting whales into one bastard great white.

> SANDY

What's your end?

> KENDALL

CEO.

> SANDY

Don't hold back.

> KENDALL

I'm the only one who knows the architecture. The – emotional and corporate architecture.

> SANDY

Well I could like it. Stewy might not like it?

> KENDALL

Fuck Stewy. He'll follow the money like a dog in a cartoon.

> SANDY

And you're sure you've got the stomach?

Kendall fixes him with a look.

> KENDALL

Yeah. I'm good.

They share a smile. Sandy nods.

DAY TWO

INT. HOTEL ROOM – EARLY MORNING

Shiv and Nate asleep on top of the sheets, both fully dressed. Wrapped up together. Intimate. Her phone goes. She grabs it.

> SHIV
> (*into phone*)

Tom . . .?

Shiv sits up.

> MARCIA
> (*from phone*)

Sorry to wake you.

Marcia's voice sends a current through Shiv. She sits up. Nate next to her, also clothed.

> SHIV

Is everything okay?

> MARCIA

He couldn't catch his breath. We've taken advice. We're sorry but we think it might not be a good idea for him to come to the wedding.

Shiv takes this in. She's hurt, but tries not to let it show.

> SHIV

Uh-huh. I think that's sensible.

Intercut with:

INT. LOGAN'S APARTMENT – LIVING ROOM – EARLY MORNING

Logan sits watching Marcia on the call.

> MARCIA

Shiv. He really is sorry.

Shiv takes this in.

> SHIV

Me too.

Marcia hangs up. She smiles at Logan. But he just gets up and walks out of the room. No sense of satisfaction in all this.

INT. HOTEL ROOM – EARLY MORNING

Shiv hangs up. Anti-Gil ATN coverage is playing on their TV.

> NATE
> Are you okay?

She's sad.

> SHIV
> I'm great. Two less wedding dinners for the caterers.

Ugh. Everything's a mess.

> I don't know Nate. I don't fucking know.

She heads into the bathroom and lets out a moan of confusion and sadness.

INT. WAREHOUSE – MAIN PARTY SPACE – EARLY MORNING

Roman, Sandy and Stewy.

> ROMAN
> —and I'd be the pointman on this, you wouldn't even have to deal direct with my dad.

Sandy nods.

> So if we can find a price—

Sandy looks positive.

> But there's potential?

Sandy's not giving anything away.

> SANDY
> It could work.

Stewy nods. Roman feels a swell of pride.

> ROMAN
> I'm excited. This is pure upside, for both of us.

Roman shakes Sandy's hand and exits. The second Roman's gone—

                              SANDY
                           (*re Roman*)
        Let's jerk him around for a bit then throw him back.
                       (*shake of the head*)
        This fucking family.

INT. WAREHOUSE — ELEVATOR — DAWN

Roman enters. Upbeat. Kendall already in there. Going down.

                              ROMAN
        Bro. How it's going?

*No reply. Roman looks up and becomes aware that Kendall's staring
at him.*

        What?

Kendall says nothing. Intense, dominating stare.

        Oh. Are you psyching me out, bro?

Roman meets Kendall's stare for a beat. Then. Roman breaks.

        Ooh. I'm terrified.

*The elevator hits the ground floor. As Kendall exits, he bangs hard
into Roman, jarring him. Roman watches Kendall go, a bit shaken.*

        Asshole.

INT. WAREHOUSE — LOADING BAY — DAWN

*Greg, Tom and Connor waiting with luggage. Nearby, other guests
stand looking at phones, checking for Ubers.*

                              GREG
        If the car doesn't come soon I'm just going to swim home.

Beat.

                             CONNOR
                           (*to Tom*)
        Greg tells me you swallowed your own load.

                              TOM
        Yeah. It was – it was pretty wild.

The light slowly dies behind Tom's eyes.

> It's cool because it's kind of like I didn't cheat? Because all the sperm stayed in my body? Like a closed-loop system.
> (*then*)
> Be really nice to see Shiv.

Connor has his phone back.

> CONNOR
> (*into phone*)
> Hey Willa, I just wanted to say – I love you. I love you so much.

Kendall enters, purposeful. Roman now lagging behind.

> KENDALL
> What's happening?

> TOM
> We have cars arriving in five.

They stand staring out for a beat.

> ROMAN
> Congratulations. I hear you swallowed your own load.

Tom just nods. Then, with tangible sadness.

> TOM
> I did.

Hold on the boys – waiting for their cars to come and collect them. It's been a long night. Kendall imperious; Roman feeling beaten down.

> CONNOR
> (*on phone*)
> It's been a really wonderful night.

INT. HOTEL ROOM – BATHROOM – DAY

Shiv checks her reflection. Tired, bit hungover. But dressed. She's on the phone.

> GIL
> (*from phone*)
> I wanted to apologize.

                         SHIV
                      (*on phone*)
   Oh. This is new.

                          GIL
   I shouldn't have brought you into it.

                         SHIV
   You know what? I don't care if you use my name—

Shiv tracks through into the bedroom, where Nate lies on the bed.

   but the truth is, you don't need to. He's scared of us.

                          GIL
   Got it.

Shiv smiles. She hangs up. Takes her bag. Turns to Nate.

Nate's phone goes. He checks it.

                         NATE
   Gil?
                       (*then*)
   Well, this is socially uncomfortable.

Nate takes the call. He motions for Shiv. 'Don't leave.'

                      (*on phone*)
   Hey . . . Yeah . . .? What just now . . .? So what did she say . . .?
   Okay, interesting . . .

*Shiv looks over at Nate on the phone: What a fucking mess. She
smiles at Nate, and exits the hotel room.*

INT. TOM AND SHIV'S APARTMENT – MORNING

Tom enters. He's jittery. A guilty conscience.

                         TOM
                    (*calling out*)
   Hey, Shiv? I'm home! And I still have both my eyebrows!

Shiv enters. Caught on the hop.

                         SHIV
   Oh. You're back already? I was just—

> TOM

God honey, I've missed you—

They embrace. Awkwardly. Each aware of how they might smell or feel. The hug breaks. They look at each other. And look away.

> SHIV

How was it?

> TOM

Which? Oh. The party? Yeah it was a – blast.

Beat.

> SHIV

So what happened?

> TOM

You know. This and that. The usual. Normal stuff.

Shiv smiles. Then. Face suddenly drops.

> SHIV

Specifically what, Tom?

Tom thought they had an understanding. Starts panicking.

> TOM

Wait. Shiv? Because I thought you said—

> SHIV

I'm shitting you, Tom.
> (*then*)
It's good to have you back.

Nice beat.

> TOM

Hey, listen I had an idea – what do you think about this? As you know since I read that thing, I'm a feminist. Well why don't I take your name instead of you taking mine? Tom and Shiv Roy? What do you think?

Shiv has something on her mind.

> SHIV

So, Tom? Listen, you know the toxic thing that you know about that I told you I didn't want to know about?

                              TOM
    Oh yeah?

                              SHIV
    I think, one way and another, I'm ready to know about it now.

Tom takes a beat. Anxiety racing. Tom slumps down into the chair.

DAY THREE

EXT. STREET – DAY

*Kendall exits his town car. Suited. Black Oxfords. All business. On
the phone.*

                            KENDALL
                          (*into phone*)
    Yeah, Frank . . .? Those girls from the art thing . . .? I want you
    to put the word around – they're junkies, they're flakes, they're
    shooting seed capital straight into their arms. Let's sink them.

INT. PRIVATE EQUITY OFFICES – OUTSIDE MEETING
ROOM – DAY

*Kendall crosses the corridor of the upscale Manhattan offices of a
private equity firm. He arrives at a meeting-room door. He doesn't
even break his stride. Opens the door to reveal – Sandy and Stewy in
conversation. They stop. All eyes on Kendall.*

                            KENDALL
    Gentlemen. Shall we?

Episode Nine

PRE-NUPTIAL

Written by Jesse Armstrong
Directed by Mark Mylod

Original air date 29 July 2018

Cast

LOGAN ROY	Brian Cox
KENDALL ROY	Jeremy Strong
MARCIA ROY	Hiam Abbass
GREG HIRSCH	Nicholas Braun
SHIV ROY	Sarah Snook
ROMAN ROY	Kieran Culkin
CONNOR ROY	Alan Ruck
TOM WAMBSGANS	Matthew Macfadyen
RAVA	Natalie Gold
FRANK VERNON	Peter Friedman
COLIN STILES	Scott Nicholson
KAROLINA NOVOTNEY	Dagmara Dominczyk
JESS JORDAN	Juliana Canfield
GERRI KELLMAN	J. Smith-Cameron
KARL MULLER	David Rasche
WILLA FERREYRA	Justine Lupe
STEWY HOSSEINI	Arian Moayed
SANDY FURNESS	Larry Pine
NATE SOFRELLI	Ashley Zukerman
GIL EAVIS	Eric Bogosian
MRS WAMBSGANS	Kristin Griffith
MR WAMBSGANS	Jack Gilpin
TABITHA	Caitlin FitzGerald
CAROLINE COLLINGWOOD	Harriet Walter
CHARLOTTE	Anna Wilson-Jones
MATT	Nick Mills
JONAS	Michael Izquierdo
BARMAID	Anna Crilly
VICAR	Richard Huw
DODDY	Tom Morley

Billy Bragg's 'Help Save the Youth of America' plays.

DAY ONE

EXT. EASTNOR CASTLE – FRONT ENTRANCE – DAY

Lots and lots of black and silver cars – Mercedes, BMWs, Bentleys – coming and going.

Some of Shiv and Tom's best friends and family are showing up – the ones who are staying at the castle.

Every couple who is arriving is being helped by a member of the staff to bring their luggage in.

Charlotte, the main wedding organizer, is also there with an iPad and a couple members of her team welcoming people.

Braziers burn by the entrance. Guests are offered a whisky as they arrive.

Tom pats a guy on the back – shakes hands but is keeping an eye out for . . .

A coach that starts to appear and make it down the drive to the main gate.

> TOM
> Okay. Here they are! Will that make it through?

> CHARLOTTE
> I don't think they will make it through, will they?

> TOM
> Well don't ask me. You're the wedding planner, Charlotte – is this part of the plan?
> *(then, approaching)*
> Hey! Hey!!

The coach pulls to a stop. It starts to reverse.

EXT. EASTNOR CASTLE – FRONT ENTRANCE – DAY

A little later. The ten or twenty folk from the bus, middle-class folk from St Paul – small-time lawyers, teachers, small-business owners, Tom's friends and family – are disembarking.

Tom is guiding them, Charlotte's team are greeting people, cases are unloaded from the other side of the bus.

> TOM
>
> Come on. Come on down!
> > *(aside to Charlotte)*
> This is not the welcome I intended.

> CHARLOTTE
>
> We'll sort it out, Tom.
> > *(calls out)*
> If you wait here we'll buggy or car you to the accommodation!

> TOM
>
> Hey hey hey!
> > *(aside, whilst smiling to Charlotte)*
> How the fuck long is that going to take?

> CHARLOTTE
>
> Not long. I can round up some buggies.

He looks at her.

> TOM
>
> I work in hospitality, Charlotte, and I can smell the bullshit. I'm going to remain calm but this is a major issue right here. Huge!
> > *(turning)*
> Dad! Hey hey hey!

An older couple are uncomfortable in their new best 'casual' clothes. And now, coming up the steps, their son is there, checking in.

> Mom? You okay?

> MRS WAMBSGANS
>
> Absolutely, Tom! Wonderful.

> TOM
>
> Good ride? You like it?

MR WAMBSGANS

Fantastic. Couple of hours at the airfield, waiting for the gang, but yes. Yes. Great to be here.

TOM

Couple of hours?

MRS WAMBSGANS

It was wonderful just sitting there. We liked watching the planes. Your father thought he might have seen the man from U2?

MR WAMBSGANS

And Arthur Laffer. You know, of the Laffer curve? Are they coming?

TOM

Uh-huh, sounds right, it's mostly rock gods and economists!

There are some other couples on the bus coming down, slightly confused, waiting in huddles as their luggage is unloaded. Other St Paul guys from high school, including Matt and Jonas. Tom waves hellos.

Hey hey it's the Fly Guys!

There's a few hellos from his old pals. His mom doesn't want to complain but his father wants to ask—

MR WAMBSGANS

Your mother is a little thirsty is the only thing?

MRS WAMBSGANS

I don't want to be a bother, Tom. It's my fault.

TOM

Oh, Mom. Say, you should say.

Tom picks up her case and walks towards the castle, past Charlotte.

(*with a smile*)

I hope you're pleased, Charlotte, my mother's dying of thirst. And I'm picking up a case. I am carrying a case on My Wedding Eve.

INT. HEATHROW HOTEL – DAY

Nate and Gil are talking. Shiv enters.

                                SHIV
Listen, I'm going to have to go. I'll see you there, you've got the
change from Sarah about the time for the embassy—
                          (*feels the chill*)
Sorry, are we okay?

                                 GIL
Yup.

Nate looks at her: No.

                                SHIV
You don't have to come down to the wedding, Gil, if you're
busy?

                                NATE
                          (*with meaning*)
We've just been doing the media monitoring?

                                 GIL
Motherfucker! I'll fucking kill him. I'll take them to pieces.

Gil starts making a call.

                                NATE
He's not sleeping. It was what's-his-name Screwdriverface. He's
got under his skin.

                                SHIV
The – the – the bit—

Nate flips the iPad: A still of a talking heads show with—

*Chyron: 'Author Asks: Could Fiery Senator Have Driven His Wife
Over The Edge?'*

                                NATE
The bit that implied he murdered his wife. Yeah, for some
reason that has 'somewhat irked him'?

Gil returns. Trying to stop obsessing.

                                SHIV
Gil, let us hit that, you need to—

                                 GIL
I know. I know, I'm focussed. I'm focussed. I'm X-raying this
briefing for salient facts.

Nate and Shiv look at each other. They can see him stewing as he tries to digest some briefing pages. He's hardly reading it, breaks off to get back to what's eating him—

I mean I don't want to get this out of proportion but – is it possible your father is the worst human being who has ever lived?

SHIV

I really don't think it's good to focus on—

GIL

Is it true he's not coming to the wedding out of – spite?

SHIV

Well – it's complicated—

GIL

I want to take him out. I want to destroy ATN.

SHIV

I'm not sure that's wise.

GIL

And if I said it was wise. Would you have a problem with that?

SHIV

In the end, I'll do whatever you want, Gil.

He looks at her. His phone goes.

GIL

My son. Probably intrigued to hear whether his father might have murdered his mother?

Gil gets up to take the call. Nate looks at Shiv.

NATE

He'll calm down.

Gil puts his hand over the phone.

GIL

If there's something – anything you can get, Shiv, I'm in a fucking knife fight holding a dildo made of American cheese.

Nate looks at Shiv.

INT. KENDALL'S CAR — DAY

Kendall is driven through rural England.

He has papers beside him that he's looking at.

EXT. PUB PARKING LOT — DAY

Not a lovely spot. A pub parking lot right by the road.

Kendall is walking in circles in the lay-by or pub parking lot. Wholly intent on his call as vehicles flash by on the A-road they've left.

Eventually, Stewy's nice black car pulls up. He gets out. Looks around at broken kids' playground stuff. Council houses.

> STEWY
> Your sister knows about Lake Como, right?

Kendall ends the call. He's jumpy. Taken some pills to keep him up, some pills to keep him calm.

She knows Venice exists and Cape Town and the Maldives? She is aware of these locations?

> KENDALL
> How we doing?

> STEWY
> But she just what – she's got a thing for fallen empires?

> KENDALL
> I got the call. You get the call?

Stewy nods into the pub. Kendall looks skeptical.

> STEWY
> We're putting together a hostile takeover of one of the largest media corporations in the world. I *think* it might be worth braving some non-vintage champagne to keep it discreet?

INT. PUB — DAY

The pub is almost empty.

> STEWY
> I got the call. Canadians are in.

(*to the barmaid*)
A bottle of champagne please.

KENDALL

So what ten days and we go in for the kill? We can't keep it on lockdown for more than about ten days, right?

BARMAID
(*shouting, off*)
John. Have we got any champagne?

She goes off to find out.

KENDALL

So like the seventeenth for the bear hug? Ten days till the end of the world. Good?

STEWY

There's just one little thing.

Kendall looks at him.

The Canadians? There's just a little static about some details.

KENDALL

Like what?

STEWY

Like – you as CEO, just, some queries. But I think it's good.

Kendall looks at him.

BARMAID

We've not got champagne. I can do a white wine spritzer?

STEWY

Relax. This doesn't work without you. It's normal co-investor shit. It's just positioning? I'll deal. Probably looking for a board seat.

KENDALL

If you tried to fuck me, I'd kill you.

STEWY

Good, and if you tried to fuck me I'd kill you too, that's why we're such good friends.

>   KENDALL
> Frank knows the Canadians, you want me to . . .?

>   STEWY
> I'll handle, okay? No leaks.

Kendall looks concerned.

> Why you so jumpy about this, Ken?

>   KENDALL
> Why am I jumpy? About screwing Rome, screwing Shiv and
> Connor? Probably – blowing what's left of my dad's fucking
> brain? About taking the company out of family control, forever?
> I don't know, Stewy, why would that make me jumpy?

INT. WAYSTAR – LOGAN'S OFFICE – DAY

*Logan is sitting at his desk. He looks out at New York City. Twitchy.
He's at his desk, he's clicking refresh on his emails. He's on the phone.
But he's not talking much. Listens.*

>   LOGAN
> Look, I don't give a fuck.

Intercut with:

EXT. EASTNOR CASTLE – DAY

Gerri is outside the castle being helped with her luggage.

>   GERRI
> But I mean, do you want me to ask?

>   LOGAN
> I'm just curious if she's going to come begging.

>   GERRI
> Okay. Because I can ask?

>   LOGAN
> I don't want to ask. If she wants to ask she can ask.

>   GERRI
> Because I can physically see her?

Shiv is getting out of a car to be met by Tom who is looking at his watch. She waves to Gerri.

LOGAN

Do *not* ask, Gerri, okay? If she comes crawling, then I'll think about coming.

(*then*)

What's going on? Have you seen Caroline? Is she still with that chinless hippy prick?

GERRI

I don't know. Everyone's just arriving. The castle is currently being invaded.

INT. SHIV AND TOM'S CAR – DAY

Tom and Shiv get into another car.

TOM

I thought we might miss the rehearsal!

SHIV

(*sweetly*)

We don't need to rehearse, we're gonna kill it.

TOM

And have you thought again about your dad and if maybe we want to reconsider and—?

SHIV

Fuck him.

TOM

Right. Right. And whether we want to go Wambsgans? Roy-Wambsgans or, as I've said, I would be willing to drop traditional and go Roy myself – in fact—

They set off. She smiles. He smiles.

SHIV

Look, I know this is kind of weird timing, but there's something I need to ask . . . to clear up.

TOM

Uh-huh?

> SHIV

I could do with knowing about the bad thing, in cruises, you know the thing that meant you couldn't sleep?

> TOM

Uh-huh?

> SHIV

No?

> TOM

I just think, maybe, Church and State, AC/DC, Ebony and Ivory, never the twain shall meet?

> SHIV

Right but you always wanted to make it public, didn't you?

> TOM

Yup. In my bones I did.

> SHIV

Exactly.

> TOM

But I did then destroy all the evidence. So?

> SHIV

I guess, if it's bad, the longer you leave it the worse it will be when it comes out?

> TOM

Uh-huh.
> (*beat*)
Unless, it, you know never comes out?

> SHIV

I bet it's not even that bad!

> TOM

It is quite bad.

> SHIV

How about you just tell me? Then I'll be in a good position to judge what you should do with the information?

> TOM

Uh-huh.

(nods, that makes sense)
I mean I guess right now, *I'm* in a good position to judge what to do with the information?

Tom is quiet, looks at the country.

This isn't very weddingy?

Shiv smiles.

Look. If I tell you everything, then you feel you have to tell Gil everything, then Gil feels he has to tell the world everything then, what people might say is, 'Let's sack the head of the division of where these terrible things happened.' And that's me.

Silence.

Honey. Really. Let's not let this spoil things?

EXT. CHURCH – DAY

Later – they've reached the church. Tom and Shiv climb out of the car. Take a breath.

> SHIV

Oh fuck, here we go.

> TOM

It's exciting!

Shiv makes a noise. Kendall is there at curbside on the phone. He ends his call.

> SHIV

Hey. Did you talk to the Wicked Witch of the North yet?

> KENDALL

I just got here, Shiv. Is this going to take long?

> SHIV

Shall we?
> *(to Tom)*
Oh fuck. Saddle up, soldier!

> TOM

Oh c'mon she can't be that bad!

Kendall and Shiv look at him. They walk towards the church.

EXT. CHURCH – DAY

Caroline is outside having a cigarette with Roman and Tabitha.

> CAROLINE
> Hello hello hello! Here they are! I knew they'd come eventually.

> SHIV
> Hi, hi, Mom.

Shiv, then Tom, kiss her. Tom and Tabitha shake hands gingerly.

> CAROLINE
> Tom. Well look at you! Very plausible.

> TOM
> Oh, well—
> *(bit odd)*
> Thank you?

> CAROLINE
> Exactly.

> KENDALL
> *(stand-offish)*
> Hi, Mom.

> CAROLINE
> Hello 'Kendall'.

She embraces him.

> KENDALL
> Bro.

> ROMAN
> Woof woof.

Roman goes to hug Kendall gingerly.

> CAROLINE
> Right, well, shall we all play happy families?

Tom, Kendall, Roman, Tabitha all start to head inside.

Caroline stops Shiv as she goes.

> Well done on Tom.

SHIV

Thank you.

CAROLINE

Tell me again why you're marrying him?

SHIV

Mom?

CAROLINE

I'm joking! I like him. And I wanted to say, I hope this can be nice. I appreciate you coming here.

SHIV

No worries, my travel agent specializes in guilt trips.

Shiv smiles – it's a joke, she can see Caroline is trying. They smile.

Just then Greg starts to make it up the path into the church, hurrying.

GREG

Hey! Apologies, did I miss anything?

CAROLINE

Caroline Collingwood. Pleased to meet you.

GREG

Likewise I'm sure – your – excellency.
           (is this a joke? he hopes so)
Greg Hirsch.

Caroline regards him.

CAROLINE

Greg – Egg?

GREG

Excuse me?

CAROLINE

Are you Greg the Egg? When you were born you looked like a little misshapen egg?

GREG

Er – I think I did – hear tell of such—

CAROLINE

Your dad tried to sleep with every man in Sausalito?

> GREG

Er? I don't (think so)—

> CAROLINE

How's your mother?

> GREG

Er, doing okay. Solvent, currently. Thank you, ma'am.

Wow. Lots of information for Greg, he heads in.

INT. CHURCH — DAY

They all head in. Greg and Caroline first. Greg sees Tabitha, approaches Tom.

> GREG

Oh my god, Tom! Did you see?

> TOM

What, Greg?

> GREG

The girl from Red Hook. From your bachelor party, who sucked your dick and made you swallow your load!

> TOM

Greg, that's not very weddingy.

Greg still needs an explanation.

She's called Tabitha and her and Roman are dating, which is cool, so please do not act like an unsophisticated rube.

> GREG

Oh, okay? Wow.

> TOM

He really liked her and it's fine – just one of those weird urban things. Like when you go to see stand-up and the comedian is your dentist? Yeah? Okay?

Elsewhere: Roman catches Shiv as she passes.

ROMAN

Er – hey, Shiv, listen, good news. I got my lump hammer out and broke some shin bones and I got the launch moved. It's on. We can throw it large at the party?

SHIV

Excuse me?

ROMAN

My satellite launch. I thought it would be cool – and Tom said—

TOM

Um, no I did not.

ROMAN

Tom?

TOM

I said we'd discuss, but Shiv's been very busy—
                    (*no criticism!*)
which is fine.

ROMAN

C'mon, don't be a fucking witch about this?

Tabitha looks at him: Not cool – he clocks.

SHIV

No. Absolutely not.

ROMAN

Fine. I'm kidding. Let's discuss.

Shiv heads in. Roman looks at Tabitha. Everyone heads down the front to talk with Charlotte who is positioning people where they'll stand during the ceremony.

INT. VICAR'S OFFICE – DAY

The vicar is with Willa and Connor. Willa is introducing herself.

WILLA

Willa. Connor's – partner.

VICAR

Fantastic and what do you do, Willa?

WILLA

I'm actually a playwright?

The vicar makes a note.

VICAR

Fantastic. America!
                    (*writes something down*)
And what do you do, Connor?

Connor hesitates, so much to explain, where does he start?

WILLA

Um – Connor doesn't really do anything, do you, Con?

Connor takes it in, smiles tightly as Charlotte comes to the door, nods to the vicar.

CHARLOTTE

I think we're all gathered now, Patrick?

INT. CHURCH – DAY

The vicar, followed by Connor and Charlotte, returns to the group.

VICAR

Okay and – just to get things straight. Am I right that the father, I understand the father is—?

CAROLINE

He couldn't be bothered.

People look at her.

I'm joking!

TOM

He's not well.

CAROLINE

That's the story, everyone remember the story!

CONNOR

So I will be performing the father role.

VICAR

Great. And Charlotte's taken you through the big picture but let's get into the details shall we?

Kendall can't bear how long it's all taking.

> KENDALL
>
> Can someone brief me?

> VICAR
>
> It won't take long?

> KENDALL
>
> I'll wing it, I swear, if I stand in the wrong place tomorrow –
> shoot me.

Kendall talks on the phone.

> Frank. I need to see you.

INT. CONNOR AND WILLA'S CAR – DAY

Connor and Willa travel in silence.

EXT. EASTNOR CASTLE – DAY

Connor and Willa arrive back at the castle. Climb out of the car.

> WILLA
>
> I didn't mean that you don't do *anything*.

> CONNOR
>
> Well that's a shame, because that's what you said?

> WILLA
>
> You know? I meant nothing like my writing? Nothing kind of—

> CONNOR
>
> Safeguarding thirty thousand acres of wilderness? That's
> 'nothing'.

> WILLA
>
> Con?

> CONNOR
>
> Being on the verge of setting up a podcast on Napoleonic
> history with a considerable level of investment interest? That's
> 'nothing'?

> WILLA
>
> Sure, no.

>   CONNOR
> 'Cracking the nut of happiness'. Like a modern-day Thoreau?
> Oh *that's* 'nothing'?

>   WILLA
> Con. You're great. You are.

>   CONNOR
> Well, here we are. 'The family pile'. The thorn in Caroline's side.
> The fish bone in her throat. When we were kids you know she
> wouldn't even let us look at it?

EXT. EASTNOR CASTLE – KENDALL'S BUNGALOW – DAY

*Kendall holds his keycard against the lock sensor on his bungalow/
cottage in the grounds. It flashes and he enters.*

INT. EASTNOR CASTLE – KENDALL'S BUNGALOW – DAY

*Jess is already there. Kendall says hi, surveys the room, puts down
his things. Cracks open the laptop. Lays out three phones, a portable
router. He takes out his wash bag. Looks at it.*

*There are a pair of Wellington boots correctly sized as gifts for each
guest and other little gifts – a welcome letter, chocolates.*

EXT. EASTNOR CASTLE – KENDALL'S WAR ROOM – DAY

After the sumptuous areas, a shabby spot. Kendall with Frank.

>   KENDALL
> Yeah, listen. You know the Canadians. Yves et cetera?

>   FRANK
> Uh-huh, what, the pension-fund guys?

>   KENDALL
> Yeah. What do they think of me, Frank?

>   FRANK
> How do you mean, what's the context?

>   KENDALL
> I can't give you context.

FRANK

Okay. Well that's very interesting context?

Frank starts to think about the three or four things this could mean . . .

KENDALL

Look. As a pal. If there was a situation where a private equity was trying to buy out a – 'major media company' – and install a new CEO, how would they view me?

FRANK

Are you serious? Fuck. So what they're co-investors?

KENDALL

You know those guys. Behind closed doors are they of the opinion I'm – the real deal, or – in training?

FRANK

And would there be room to wet the beak of an old pal, in such a situation, Ken?

KENDALL

Frank. Too soon. Get your hard-on out of my soup. I need an answer?

FRANK

Well.
('*diplomatic*')
I think they have a lot of time for you. But there may be certain questions.

Kendall hears the subtext.

KENDALL

Oh shit, really?

FRANK

Look. They think they're hotshots. They make hard jokes.

KENDALL

I need details.

FRANK

Well, sometimes when you were absent they used to refer to you as 'the calamari cock ring'. I don't know what it even—

> KENDALL

Well I think it means they think of me as a cock ring made from calamari, Frank. It's pretty self-explanatory. Jesus Christ.

> FRANK

I never laughed. I used to give them a very – cool look.

> KENDALL

Thanks a lot. Hero.

Kendall's thinking.

INT. EASTNOR CASTLE – ROMAN AND TABITHA'S ROOM – DAY

Roman unpacks. Tabitha too, then gleefully bounces on the bed. She lays back and looks at him. An offer.

> TABITHA

I guess, I would say, does it really matter? It's just a satellite launch—

> ROMAN

Well, yes. Yes it fucking does, it's kind of the whole fucking thing for me.

Tabitha gets up and picks up her bag.

Hey? Hey. Tabs? Tabitha? No don't – don't. I was sharp. Don't go.

> TABITHA

Why not? Why shouldn't I?

> ROMAN

Because. Because – you're great for me.

> TABITHA

Uh-huh. Well that's great, for you.

> ROMAN

I'm sorry, okay? It's just it's not a rocket. It's a flag.

> TABITHA

It is?

ROMAN

It's a trumpet. It's a huge fiery trumpet.

TABITHA

You're a huge fucking trumpet.

ROMAN

I was gonna meme-jack it to announce a personal rebrand. But now everything's fucked. Forever.

She watches him bang his head against something.

TABITHA

Uh-huh. And me? Am I part of the rebrand, Rome? Is that why I'm here after just four dates?

ROMAN

Yes, Tabs. You've been selected as the new face of Roman Roy. You now have to wear the approved fragrance of Roman Roy. And the new range of clothes. No, you fuckhead, you're here because I like you.

Roman comes over to her. Nuzzles the top of his head into her belly with a moan until she rubs his head.

INT. WAYSTAR – LOGAN'S OFFICE – DAY

Logan's got Karolina in. Maybe he's looking at trashy celeb magazine feature on Tom and Shiv's romance and wedding.

LOGAN

So, what are we going to say?

KAROLINA

Well I thought we were going to say illness?

LOGAN

I don't want to say illness. It plays weak. No.

KAROLINA

Okay. Well we can say – busy?

LOGAN

What sort of prick is too busy to go to his daughter's wedding?

> KAROLINA

Or we – float that Gil's campaign is kind of like a cult in some ways, 'what is this grieving senator's hold over young Shiv Roy?' kind of thing.

> LOGAN

Makes her look weak. Which makes me look weak. None of my kids have gone round the bend or topped themselves – I might have had my moments but—

> KAROLINA

No, we've always pushed that you're a good dad.

> LOGAN

Because—

> KAROLINA

Because you are a good dad.

> LOGAN

Huh.

> KAROLINA

So I mean if you don't want to say illness or work or rift I mean, do we just—

> LOGAN

Fuck it. There's no way out.

> KAROLINA

I mean if you want to go?

> LOGAN

I don't want to go. There's no other fucking way out. Karolina – tell Marcia to call Tom and tell him we're coming. Alright?

EXT. EASTNOR CASTLE – DAY

Caterers' supplies are arriving.

INT. EASTNOR CASTLE – DINING ROOM – DAY

Charlotte, the wedding organizer, is in discussion with Shiv and Tom.

CHARLOTTE

Well we can do whatever you want us to do. I'm sorry if we did the wrong thing. He just told us he was coming?

Kendall arrives.

KENDALL

Who's coming?

SHIV

Dad. And Marcia.

KENDALL

Dad's coming now? Here? Do you want him to?

Kendall doesn't want to see him.

SHIV

No, I don't want him to. He never apologized. But Marcia called Tom—

TOM

And obviously I said I'd have to ask Shiv—

Roman arrives.

SHIV

Meanwhile Marcia called Charlotte and said they were on the jet.

ROMAN

Dad's coming? Is it about the launch? Is he concerned?

KENDALL

Yeah I'm sure he's thinking about that twenty-four-seven.
(*to Shiv*)
What you going to do? You can just say no?

SHIV

I don't know? Maybe I have security – just fucking stop him?

Tom maybe makes a little noise.

TOM

No sure. Could do. I just wonder – little bit, could cause a certain atmosphere? I mean I guess he did pay, not that—

> SHIV

If he's got the balls to walk in, what do we do? Set the dogs on him? No seat, let him stand?

Tom heads off . . . As Caroline arrives.

> CAROLINE

So I hear he's coming now? That's wonderful.

> SHIV

Mom, c'mon?

> CAROLINE

It's fine. I just hope you won't forget about me once your father arrives with his Head of Middle Eastern Operations.

Shiv sees an angle of attack on her mother.

> SHIV

Marcia?

Caroline knows there's some grit there with Shiv and Marcia – an angle for her.

> CAROLINE

Yes. Marcia. Do you still find her a bit—?
> > (*knows they don't get on*)
> You know?

Shiv isn't letting her in.

> SHIV

We actually became quite close. During Dad's illness.

> CAROLINE

What a sweet little scene that must have been. Very moving, I'm sure.

Kendall spots Stewy. Gives him an eye – I need to talk.

INT. EASTNOR CASTLE – WELCOME PARTY – NIGHT

The welcome party. We take in the glittering event.

In a corner, Shiv is with the Wambsgans. Shiv is 'mm'-ing about the wine.

SHIV

Delicious!

MRS WAMBSGANS

Well I'm glad you like it.

MR WAMBSGANS

Because it cost a pretty penny.

Shiv smiles as Nate comes and whispers.

NATE

So, have you got any protein, for us to use?

SHIV

Protein. I'm not a fucking hen to lay you eggs? I'm a strategist.

NATE

I know. But, look. Gil would like a word?

Nate leads her over to Gil. Takes her arm very gently to guide her. Far across the room. Tom clocks this. It's a gesture of familiarity and intimacy and it makes him double-take.

Shiv cuts her eyes at Nate: Hey, remember where we are. He looks at her: Don't overreact. It's all over in under a second but very intimate. They don't know they've been observed.

They arrive with Gil.

GIL

Listen, I don't want to be overly dramatic, but I was assured when I accepted he wouldn't be here?

SHIV

Plans changed. I was ambushed. I'm sorry.

GIL

This is not okay from my POV, Siobhan. This compromises me.

NATE

I mean you were very eager that Gil—

SHIV

Well I didn't realize it was such a chore?

GIL

He's just weighty, Shiv. He carries his gravity. He's not a man,
he's a fucking planet.

SHIV

Look, there's no press. No pictures. We have jammers and a
fucking, hawk to take out drones. It'll be like it never happened?

GIL

I hear you might have something explosive I can use?

SHIV

Maybe. I think so. Just not yet.

NATE

Let's destroy ATN, Shiv. Wouldn't that be a nice wedding gift to
the American people?

SHIV

Yeah, sure, I'm just concerned. About collateral damage – Tom?

NATE

He'll be fine.

SHIV

Says the man who has no idea what he's even talking about.

GIL

Shiv. C'mon. I have all the arguments on monopolies in news
and the coarsening of our public sphere but I can kind of feel
myself falling asleep as I talk. Give me something salty, Shiv.
Give me a stick of fucking dynamite to shove up your dad's ass.

*Kendall walks in with Stewy and greets Nate, who is with Gil and
Shiv.*

KENDALL

Hey! How you going, man?! Too long. Still trying to teach the
world to sing in perfect fucking harmony.

They do a brief hug.

NATE

I guess. You know Gil of course?

KENDALL

Pleased to meet you, Mr Eavis.

> GIL

Likewise. How are you finding it outside the Evil Empire?

> KENDALL

Oh fine. I'm fine thank you.
> *(looks around)*
And how d'you like it here in the lion's den?

> GIL

Oh I've been to zoos before.

> KENDALL

You like drinking our champagne?

> GIL

I'm a 'champagne for all' guy, not a 'gruel for all' guy.

Roman barrels up.

> KENDALL

Hey. You know Gil Eavis, sword of the dispossessed and lover of vintage champagne?

> ROMAN

I guess technically I should take a swing at you?

> GIL

And technically I should call you libelous scum.

They smile. Roman looks Gil up and down.

> ROMAN

So, you gonna calm your shit-talk down, or do we have to ramp up?

> GIL

Well is your dad gonna stop poisoning the discourse of our great republic?

> ROMAN

You got a laptop? You seen the shit out there? We're the fucking good guys now.

> GIL

Uh-huh?

ROMAN
(*looks to Kendall*)
Join in, bro, by the way, feel free.

Kendall shrugs.

Shiv? Your guy here is shit-talking our company.

SHIV
Oh we don't talk about that, it would be a conflict of interest.

She smiles.

ROMAN
Uh-huh. Nice. Very nice.

Elsewhere—

Nate has made himself scarce. He bumps into Tom.

NATE
Hey, congratulations, man! Good to finally meet you.

Tom looks puzzled. Hand for a shake.

TOM
Right. Tom Wambsgans.

NATE
Obviously. Nate.
(*off his look*)
Nate Sofrelli?

TOM
Uh-huh? Right?

NATE
So. What can I say? The best man won!

Shiv is looking over – not crazy about this interaction.

TOM
Right. I'm sorry, as in?

NATE
You won the Shiv-off, pal, good luck!

TOM
Right and who are you again?

NATE

Nate Sofrelli? Did she never? Is this embarrassing?

TOM

Oh, right. You're a pal of Kendall's?

NATE

Yeah. And back in ancient history me and Shiv? We were—?

TOM

Right! Okay. Yes. Maybe she did?
(*it vaguely rings a bell now*)
Right. 'The best man won!'

NATE

Hahah, 'maybe!'

TOM

Aren't you married?

NATE

Getting married. She couldn't make it. Sends her love.

Elsewhere – Shiv is talking to Tabitha. Tom looks over. Not super-comfortable about the exchange.

TABITHA

Just wanted to say hi and thank you, for having me. Tabitha.

SHIV

Great to meet you, I've heard so little about you!

She's joking, but not.

TABITHA

This is amazing. And this is your mom's place—?

SHIV

Oh no. No I think – it was her uncle's, her great-uncle's, or— The story gets mangled. There was an uncle, who ended up living in Gibraltar with a monkey, and I don't know. He swindled my mom's grandpa or. I don't know. My mom— We'd always come and stay with her nearby. She lives near, to keep the wound fresh, you know?

TABITHA

Uh-huh. It's good to keep the wounds fresh right?

Shiv sees something in her – she's fun and sparky. Not a dead-eyed hanger-on.

> SHIV
>
> Right. So what do you do? Who *are you*?

> TABITHA
>
> Oh I'm nobody. Don't worry about me.

> SHIV
>
> Yeah?

> TABITHA
>
> I'm an MBA and I cashed out on my little operation and now I don't need to work but I'm a corporate coach?

> SHIV
>
> Okay well, I'm going to split because I can see my husband-to-be talking to my ex and it's making feel like I'm going to hurl, good?

Caroline comes to say hi to Tom.

> CAROLINE
>
> Just to say, it's so kind of your parents to have paid for this delicious wine, Tom.

> TOM
>
> Not at all, they wanted to make a contribution.

> CAROLINE
>
> And it's so clever the way they're letting every single person know.

> TOM
>
> Oh, good?

And she's gone. Shiv arrives—

> SHIV
>
> Okay?

> TOM
>
> I think I just got stabbed by your mom, but I'm not completely sure?

> SHIV
>
> Uh-huh. That's how it works. You'll bleed out in about an hour.

Tom looks around confused – focusses on Nate. Unnerved. He starts to guide Shiv upstairs.

INT. EASTNOR CASTLE – SHIV AND TOM'S ROOM – NIGHT

Tom shows her in.

> TOM
>
> Yeah. I just wanted to get you up here to ask – to ask. About – the table plans and – and—

> SHIV
>
> And have you thought any more about if you want to tell me about the secret thing which—?

> TOM
>
> Um, and also. Just to say, I did meet 'Nate'?

> SHIV
>
> You met Nate before I think?

> TOM
>
> Nope. No.

Tom looks at Shiv.

> SHIV
>
> No? Okay. Well, he's a good colleague and Kendall and him ran around in Shanghai. And he's a dick. I mean he's okay. But he has a certain dickish quality as well. I told you about him?

She's babbling a little, covering. Tom sits down a bit broken.

> TOM
>
> Uh-huh. Look, Shiv.

She looks at him.

> Is this real?

> SHIV
>
> What do you mean?

> TOM
>
> Am I a total jerk? Do you really want to do this? Because we don't have to?

SHIV

All the people are here, Tom.

TOM

Yeah?

SHIV
(*then*)

And plus I do, I do want to.

TOM

Is this— What level are we on? Are you fucking around on me?

SHIV

Tom?

TOM

Honestly? Gil? Gil is charismatic. And this 'Nate'? I just feel –
there are vibes?

Shiv looks at him.

SHIV

As soon as two colleagues are close, Tom? DC loves gossip.

TOM

No, sure. But sometimes there are rumors and people aren't
fucking. And – sometimes – they totally are?

She smiles.

I just – I don't know. There are a lot of layers. And we have
our plans and I love you and I think you – need me, but right
now . . . I mean, I can cope with almost anything, but I do need
to know where the – bottom of the ocean is? So will you tell me,
if I am going nuts and what's real here?

*She looks at him. She does love him. She has a moment to make a
decision.*

SHIV

Honestly? This is real.

He looks for more.

I'm not fucking around.

He holds her gaze. If she looks away, he'll know. But she doesn't. She has the nerve to hold his gaze and he decides to accept it.

                    TOM

Well, I trust you.

                    SHIV

Good. Thank you.

                    TOM

And that – puts my mind at rest.

                    SHIV

You're a good guy. When I met you I was I was a fucking mess. I need you.

                    TOM

And listen. If you want to know about the cruise-line stuff, the secret stuff. I'll tell you. Because I think we have to be able to trust, right?

                    SHIV

Tom, that would be great.

INT. EASTNOR CASTLE – BATHROOM – NIGHT

In the toilet. Kendall has done a bump of coke.

INT. EASTNOR CASTLE – WELCOME PARTY – NIGHT

Kendall heads out and bumps right into – Rava. She looks at Kendall.

                    RAVA

Hey?

Is he okay? Nope. He's uncomfy in his own skin.

                    KENDALL

Hey! Hey. When you get in? Where are the kids?

                    RAVA

Yeah good. They're jet-lagged. The happy couple okay?

                    KENDALL

Oh you know, maintaining the veneer.

RAVA

And you okay? Maintaining the veneer?

Sort of joke that would normally let her in—

KENDALL

I'm great, actually.

He's a little twitchy, looking around, wants distraction from this intimacy on offer. Feeling the coke in his throat and feeling like a fraud.

RAVA

Fine. I just wondered— You look—

KENDALL

I'm fantastic. I did like a hundred and twenty push-ups this morning, so, yeah, I think I'm, okay?

Rings pretty hollow.

RAVA

Oh, well if you did a hundred and twenty push-ups?

KENDALL

Rava, I just have a lot going on right now.

He's quite distracted by her champagne glass. She can tell suddenly that he's on drugs and she stiffens.

RAVA

Not one of your relaxing interludes?

KENDALL

Yeah I'm a big fucking stress knot, what can I tell you? Probably got a tumor eating me inside out.
(*checking her drink*)
You want another drink?

RAVA

Okay, so, I don't want to talk shop but your lawyers have gone a little quiet, is it just natural or—

KENDALL

I don't know about that.

RAVA

Well could you give them a nudge?

KENDALL

Sure.

RAVA

Great. And look, Ken. I – I know you, okay? I know you and if
you want to talk—

KENDALL

I'm good.

*End of discussion. They look around the event. A silence grows. The
perverse desire to fuck this up bubbles up in him.*

Yeah the truth is my lawyers are stonewalling because your
lawyers are trying to fuck me over. So shall we leave it to them
and then you and me can just smile, and, you know, you can
do your coy little smile and we can flirt and everything because
I love all that shit?

She looks at him.

RAVA

Have a fucking line if you want one that badly, Kendall.

KENDALL

Oh fuck you, everything isn't what you think? You know? You
can't see inside me just because I've told you the occasional
fucking thing.

But she's gone and he's left trying to feel like a big man.

*Looks around the glittering party, the beautiful evening. He sees Gerri
talking to Frank. Marches over, cokey and paranoid.*

Hey hey hey, so what the fuck's going on here? This looks
mighty fucking cozy?

GERRI

Hey, Ken, we were just – we were just saying, I came to here
when you were all kids the first time, like '83 maybe?

KENDALL

Uh-huh? Yeah? Right. Great.
    (*looks between them, realizes he's off-kilter*)
Sorry. I'm sorry. I should circulate.

They watch Kendall go and raise their eyebrows at one another. He's not in great shape.

INT. EASTNOR CASTLE – SHIV AND TOM'S ROOM – NIGHT

Shiv has a notebook.

> TOM
>
> I'm happy to tell. But do we have to do it tonight?

Shiv looks like: Nevertheless.

> It's not very weddingy? Because it's about corporate cover-up of crimes and institutionalized sexual abuse.

> SHIV
>
> Uh-huh. Same old same old.

> TOM
>
> And that's not very, 'something borrowed, something blue'?

> SHIV
>
> Still?

> TOM
>
> Okay well, there were, pay-offs, legal and semi-illegal intimidation.

> SHIV
>
> And have you personally got plausible deniability?

> TOM
>
> I think. Digital deep-clean. And I got the paper material shredded. Outside team. Inside, to sign the material out, Greg.

> SHIV
>
> Greg?

> TOM
>
> Greg. Yeah family seemed safest. But Greg's expendable.

> SHIV
>
> What – you'd – kill – Greg?

> TOM
>
> No! But we could, we can shut him up right? Family?

                              SHIV
Right.

                              TOM
And what are you going to do with it? Because if I give you the
details, it could hurt me, Shiv.

He looks at her.

                              SHIV
You're a good guy.

                              TOM
I'm not a good guy. I'm not.
                    (*beat, looks at her*)
But I do love you.

                              SHIV
And I love you.

                              TOM
And you won't let me get hurt?

*She looks at him. He looks at her. Should he trust her? She strokes his
hair or touches his face. He thinks it should feel reassuring.*

EXT. EASTNOR CASTLE – UPPER TERRACE – NIGHT

Kendall looks into the night, smoking.

                          CAROLINE
Kendall – could you spare a cheeky ciggy?

                          KENDALL
Hey, Mom.

He lights a cigarette for his mom and hands it to her.

                          CAROLINE
So. How are you?

                          KENDALL
I'm good.

                          CAROLINE
Yes?

> KENDALL

Yeah. I think. You know. Whatever it means.

> CAROLINE

I was sorry to hear how everything went with the – board thing.

> KENDALL

Roman. I never could rely on him.

> CAROLINE

No.

> KENDALL

So, how are you, Mom?

> CAROLINE

Oh you know.

> KENDALL

Not really no. No. It's quite hard, to know.

> CAROLINE

Oh well.

> KENDALL

I don't know if this is any use to you, but so you know. I used to see someone, to talk to, and I've forgiven you.

Just then there's a whirring overhead – a helicopter is coming in to land nearby.

A few curious folk come out to join Caroline and Kendall to watch it touch down in the distance.

Amongst them . . . Nate and Gil and Shiv. They look out at the helicopter arriving with a sense of foreboding.

> CAROLINE

Oh, thank you. What for?

> KENDALL

What for? For – well for – leaving us and – for – for—

> CAROLINE

For having a little bit of fun? Do you think he ever did a single thing he didn't want to do? Ever?

Kendall backs off inside. Others drift inside.

Leaving just Shiv and Nate for a moment in the half-light. He bumps up close beside her.

> SHIV
>
> Hey!

> NATE
>
> C'mon. Forbidden fruit.

> SHIV
>
> Nate.

> NATE
>
> Has the chicken laid the egg?

She considers. Looks at Nate.

> SHIV
>
> Um, nope. Not yet, no joy.

> NATE
>
> Look at you. I'm desperate to make you concentrate on nothing but me for just fifteen minutes.

> SHIV
>
> You think I used to concentrate on you?

As she goes to leave he gooses her on the butt – but she playfully blocks his hand away. Flirty.

They head in. But someone was watching from the shadows – we clock: Greg.

Greg looks like: Oh shit. I did not want to see that.

INT. EASTNOR CASTLE – WELCOME PARTY – NIGHT

A little later. We take in the scene. The champagne is flowing. We pick out our folks:

Gerri, Connor and Willa, Roman and Tabs, Kendall, Stewy.

Greg wanders in, anxiously considering what he's seen.

> CAROLINE
>
> So, Greg-Egg, how long do you give it?

> GREG

I'm sorry?

> CAROLINE

The marriage. How long do you give it?

She gives a mischievously deadpan face. Greg is worried – does everyone know?

> GREG

Oh. Is there – doubt afoot?

> CAROLINE

I mean *I* for one think they look solid as a rock!

She winks and moves on leaving Greg looking worried – shit, people are having doubts. He looks at Tom who gives him a warm thumbs-up. Maybe he should say something?

There is a sense of something happening near the entrance of the room. Logan is popping in, with Marcia, still in travel clothes, to say a few hellos. Assistants take their bags away in the background.

The world shifts as Logan arrives – everything tilts towards him, the energy in every room.

Shiv is across the room. They lock eyes. She looks away and he approaches her.

> SHIV
> (*coolly*)

Hey.

> LOGAN

Hello.

> MARCIA

Hello, Siobhan.

> LOGAN

So. I'm 'feeling much better'.

Marcia and Shiv smile at one another.

> MARCIA

He's much improved.

SHIV

Great. You weren't actually invited though? Maybe I'll see if they can make you an omelette or something? Find you a chair?

Marcia doesn't like it. Logan smiles.

MARCIA

I think usually the ones who are paying, get a chair, no?

SHIV

Oh I didn't realize *you'd* contributed, Marcia, I'm so rude. Thank you.

Logan ignores their crackle. Shiv heads off as Caroline arrives.

CAROLINE

Logan. Lovely to see you, as always. It's wonderful you made it in the end.

MARCIA

We wouldn't have missed it.

CAROLINE

Well you nearly did. But well done you! Are you feeling *much* better?

Logan grunts.

MARCIA

We were sorry not to be here to help. Has it been very busy? You look tired?

CAROLINE

Oh don't worry I haven't been making canapés. But I am seeing a new guy. Perhaps it's taking a toll?

Logan looks around.

LOGAN

So they gave this place a lick of paint?

CAROLINE

I believe it's very popular with footballers and Russians. You probably know them all, Marcia. Excuse me, I should circulate!

Stewy comes over to Logan to pay his respects.

> STEWY
>
> How's the big man? All good?

> LOGAN
>
> All very good. Everything's good acquisition-wise.

Stewy, from Logan's POV, is on the inside.

> Just need to shut down the voice of the fucking people over there.

He nods to Gil. Logan and Kendall catch one another's eye.

Logan gives him a smile.

It's quite a thing, that smile. It seems to acknowledge everything that's come before, and without denying it, says, 'Ah c'mon.' Kendall is stuck trying to decode it and also feels that old familiar tug.

After a beat, through the crowd, Logan heads for Kendall.

Kendall looks at him. Fortified by the drugs and booze in his system he can take it. Regards him with a wry smile as he approaches.

> Kendall.

> KENDALL
>
> Hey, Dad.

The room is alive to the rapprochement. Gerri looks over. Roman. Not too pleased.

> LOGAN
>
> So, what about it, son, shall we jump out of the trenches for a game of soccer? Can I bring you some corn to get you through the winter?

But Kendall can see right away Logan's oblivious about the moves that are in play.

> So, how you doing? What's the news?

Kendall is kept warm by his secret.

> KENDALL
>
> Oh, keeping busy.

> LOGAN
>
> Need a reference for your resume?

KENDALL

I'm good.

LOGAN

'Relatively punctual'. 'Prone to occasional bouts of insubordination'.

Little smiles. Logan can charm when he wants to.

KENDALL

Yeah well. You know.

LOGAN

So how long you gonna fuck about on the outside?

KENDALL

Uh-huh. You recruiting? What, a new Head of Being Continually Thwarted?

LOGAN

How would a TV network suit you? One of the big guys? When I land it? Could that work?

KENDALL

You feeling the heat on your own? Want me back? Like to put that in a press release?

LOGAN

No I'm just a lovely guy.

KENDALL

Uh-huh. Well, thanks, Dad.

Logan pats Kendall on the shoulder, heads off.

Roman starts heading over to Kendall, seeing he's free. Wanting the gossip.

ROMAN

Okay, what was all that, cocksucker?

KENDALL

Oh he was just telling me how shitty you are at doing your job.

ROMAN
(*true?*)

Fuck you.

> (*pathetically, he can't let it lie*)
> Did he mention the launch? He knows I've accelerated?

Stewy is making it over to Kendall. But he's intercepted by Caroline—

CAROLINE

Hello. Caroline Collingwood, mother of the bride. How long do you give it?

STEWY

Oh I'd say, I don't know. Forever.
> (*then*)
Or until Shiv goes away for a week. Whichever comes first.

CAROLINE

You beast!

Shiv intercepts Caroline.

SHIV

Um, Mom?

CAROLINE

Yes?

SHIV

Mom, I hear you're asking people, 'How long do you give it?'

CAROLINE

It's a cheeky icebreaker.

SHIV

Yeah. Sure. But it's kind of horrible?

CAROLINE

It's not all about you, Shiv. Other people need something to say.

SHIV

Well could you ask them about the price of fucking fish instead?

Caroline smiles. Roman arrives.

CAROLINE

I like your girlfriend, Roman.

ROMAN

Well thank you. I met her at a sex party where she was giving the groom a blowjob.

Neither Caroline nor Shiv take him seriously.

CAROLINE

Hahahhah. You should marry that one.

ROMAN

Excuse me?

CAROLINE

And, Shiv. Stop taking everything so seriously! I am trying to sparkle. When people ask me how long I give it, I say forever! And it will be forever.

SHIV

Uh-huh. Thank you.

CAROLINE

Or it'll feel like forever.

And Caroline's off with a smile.

ROMAN

She says she's being impish.

SHIV

She's being a stone-cold bitch. Listen. Last meet, tonight, if you want? In The Place?

Roman looks intrigued.

I need to catch Dad.

Elsewhere: Stewy makes it to Kendall.

STEWY

So what was the white whale saying to you?

KENDALL

Oh nothing. Think he's shoring up his position. It's not real. He's under pressure.

STEWY

You good? No wobbles? You're okay?

KENDALL

Yes I'm okay!

(*looks at Stewy, suspicious*)
I'm not going to get cold-cocked here am I, Stewy? I heard from
Frank the Canadians might not be too keen on me?

STEWY
You talked to the fucking grandfather clock? Has he signed
anything?

KENDALL
Frank? That would be rude. He – he taught me to fly in his
Cessna.

STEWY
'Your honor, in lieu of a non-disclosure agreement we have this
faded Polaroid of some conspicuous consumption.' C'mon, man!
You're not a little prince anymore, don't rely on Sir Talky of
Fuckchester? Okay?

KENDALL
He's good, Stewy.

STEWY
Look. Can we do a catch-up in the war room in five?

INT. EASTNOR CASTLE – WELCOME PARTY – NIGHT

Logan makes his way across the room.

*Unfortunately, just then, Gil rounds the corner. They can't very well
ignore one another.*

LOGAN
(*with a smile*)
Ah, Mr Fuckhead, I presume.

GIL
Logan Roy.

*The two big beasts in the room. Neither wants to speak, but
neither wants to choose the low-status option of shrinking from the
encounter . . .*

LOGAN
So. Are we allowed to talk?

644

GIL

Well I've nothing but admiration for you personally, Mr Roy.

LOGAN

Oh really?

Gil regards Logan coolly.

GIL

Well. It's the sort of thing you say, isn't it?

LOGAN

Classy. Look, what have you got against me?

GIL

You're the one making it personal. I'm just trying to do my job. Think about everyone, not just myself—

LOGAN
(*cutting in*)

The interest of each is the good of all. That, is the whole of the law.

Gil nods.

GIL

You don't need to remind me of my Adam Smith, I taught economics.

LOGAN

Uh-huh, kindergarten was it?

GIL

What about from each according to his ability to each according to his need?

Shiv makes it over to hear how it's going. Not well.

LOGAN

Sure. But what about – and this isn't me talking, but what about me, Mr Fucking Ability, busting my chops in my auto shop just so some needy fuck in the projects can jack off on my time? That's the issue, I'm afraid.

GIL

When you're a crook, you can't imagine anyone else is decent.

645

> LOGAN

I didn't make human nature. But I do know what they watch and what they read. I make my nut off of what people really want, so don't tell me about people. I'd go flat bust in a week if I didn't.

Gil's not about to be bullied. Leans in back.

> GIL

Keep singing the song, Logan.
> > (*beat – he drops the bomb*)
I'm digging. I'm joining the dots and digging you out.

Logan bustles off. Past Tom.

> TOM

Hey! Good to see you, Logan, glad you made it.

> LOGAN

Uh-huh.

> TOM

And just to say. New Mexico. Things get said. You know. And – no hard feelings.

> LOGAN

Right. Huh. Thanks.

> TOM

Well. Apology accepted!

Logan is still thinking as he starts to head upstairs. Shiv catches him up as Marcia joins him to go up.

> SHIV

Sleep well, Dad. Marcia.

> LOGAN

Thank you.

> SHIV

Could be your last good one for a decade or two?

> LOGAN

Huh?

> SHIV

The cruise situation?

Logan makes some calculations. Why is she saying this, in front of Marcia?

> LOGAN
>
> I don't know what you're talking about.

> SHIV
>
> Uh-huh. Sure. Well, you might be about to find out?
> (*smiles*)
> Unless?

Logan starts to head upstairs, severely shaken.

Marcia looks at Shiv as she goes. She knows something is going on.

> MARCIA
>
> You could afford to be a little more amenable, Siobhan. He came.

> SHIV
>
> You don't know, Marcia. Okay?

> MARCIA
>
> I know plenty.

> SHIV
>
> Maybe, maybe you do.

> MARCIA
>
> I know when I see a spoiled slut.

> SHIV
>
> Excuse me?

> MARCIA
>
> *Écoute-moi.*

> SHIV
>
> Who *are* you? Apart from a, a fucking, machine for, accumulating power and keeping yourself – safe.

> MARCIA
>
> You have no idea how vulnerable a human being can be.

> SHIV
>
> Never to do a single thing for its own sake. Have you ever had a fucking – grapefruit – without an agenda?

MARCIA

He made you a playground and you think it's the whole world. Well *va te faire foutre*! Fuck off, go on, out, see how you like it!

Marcia departs upstairs – Caroline is there.

CAROLINE

Oh you two you seem like very good—

She is about to say something tart, about how Marcia seems to be a 'very good friend'.

But it dies on her lips when she sees how fragile her daughter is right now.

It's okay. It's okay, Siobhan.

Shiv accepts a hug from her mother.

Logan looks back down. Calls down.

LOGAN

Someone will be in touch.

INT. EASTNOR CASTLE – ROMAN AND TABITHA'S ROOM – NIGHT

Tabitha is getting changed. Roman lies on the bed, finishes a call, watches her.

ROMAN
(*watches Tabitha*)
You know, you're fucking great.

TABITHA

Well thank you.

ROMAN

You're not a headfuck, or a bitch or a leech.

TABITHA

You say such pretty things.

ROMAN

Seriously. You're a unicorn. You came over here. I mean how long have we known each other? And you haven't got your meat hooks in at all, you never once asked to stay over or how it works with my dad or the trust or what my stake is, you know?

TABITHA

I'm just pathologically incurious.

ROMAN

I tell you what, Tabs, I'm like stepping up, grown-up shit.

TABITHA

One thing about grown-ups? They tend not to walk around saying 'I'm a grown-up.'

That lands. Yes. She's right as usual. He laughs.

ROMAN

What if I was prepared to marry you?

TABITHA

Hello?

ROMAN

Shiv's getting married, Kendall got married.

TABITHA

What if you came down from Olympus and proposed to a mere mortal? No. This is crazy.

ROMAN

Why?

TABITHA

Because this isn't a normal relationship.

ROMAN

Why?

TABITHA

Why? Well, one, because we never fuck.

Roman doesn't want to hear it.

ROMAN

Yeah we do.

TABITHA

Well, no we don't.

> ROMAN

Oh come on. We do! We've been busy.

> TABITHA

You – kind of – jerked off – *near* me.

> ROMAN

Well there's no need to be disgusting.

> TABITHA

Look, Rome, honestly, I've had more sexual contact with the groom than you?

> ROMAN

Tabs, please, I've asked you not to talk about—

> TABITHA

I've slept with a lot of guys, Roman. If that's a problem you better say.

> ROMAN

No. No. It's just – Tom.
> (*bleurgh*)
Look, I can't get into all this. Do you want to get married or not?

> TABITHA

Is this how you think you get someone to stay?

He looks at her.

Is it some sort of tax scam? I mean why the fuck would I marry you?

INT. EASTNOR CASTLE – SNOOKER ROOM – NIGHT

Shiv is standing in the snooker room, waiting for someone. Gerri arrives.

> SHIV

Hey hey. Gerri. Thanks for—

> GERRI

Uh-huh, what is this?

> SHIV

Just a chat?

GERRI

Right, it's your wedding, why do I feel like I'm going to get
fucked?

SHIV

Okay, look, it's late, so. Here's the situation. I know all about
the cruise-division horror show. And the cover-up. And Gil
wants to go to town on you. But maybe I can stop him. If ATN
lays off the personal stuff. Gil's wife.

GERRI

You want us to stop attacking him? 'Poor lickle fwagile
presidential candidate'?

SHIV

No. Keep attacking him through the primaries. Fire up our base.
Then back off for the general. But no more wife stuff.

GERRI

They're journalists, Shiv, not remote-control little—

SHIV

Sure they are. I just feel confident a little public comment or two
from my dad. An email. The minions realign pretty quick?

GERRI

Uh-huh. And you're – just to be clear – you're – you're—

SHIV

Yes, I'm bullying. I'm blackmailing you. I'm threatening to
destroy my father. However you want to put it.

GERRI

And you're happy with that?

SHIV

Oh come on. It is what it is.

GERRI

Uh-huh. You used to be such a nice girl.

SHIV

And Tom needs to be clean, move him on. Move him up. Maybe
abroad. Clean hands.

GERRI

You're very pushy, missy.

651

>   SHIV
> Thank you, fairy godmother.

>   GERRI
> And if I was authorized to accept can you get Mr Smith to fuck
> off back to Washington and not pull down his pants to show off
> his amazing morals?

>   SHIV
> I think I can persuade him that a dirty LBJ gets more done than
> a clean McGovern.

Gerri nods.

> Okay. Goodnight. No marriage advice from my dear old
> godmother?

>   GERRI
> Don't ask me – my husband died. Don't let him die?

INT. EASTNOR CASTLE – KENDALL'S WAR ROOM – NIGHT

Jess leads Kendall in.

>   KENDALL
> Um, Stew – what is this? I was talking?

>   STEWY
> I'm sorry, dude. Jess, would you?

>   KENDALL
> No. Stew. Seriously. My wife, my kids – I need to—

>   STEWY
> Stop. Ken – I've got Sandy on the line.

>   KENDALL
> You've what?

>   STEWY
> Sandy?

He hits speakerphone.

>   (*to phone*)
> Sandy?

Static.

> KENDALL
> (*to Stewy*)

What is it?

> STEWY
> (*nods to phone*)

He can say.

> KENDALL

You can say, Stew.

> STEWY
> (*to phone*)

Hello, Sandy?

Noise from the conference line—

> SECRETARY
> (*off*)

Can you hold for Mr Furness?

> STEWY

He was just there, where'd he go?

Kendall looks at Stewy: C'mon, man.

> KENDALL

What the fuck? You're not going to say? Is this the cold-cock?

> STEWY

I think it's best for him to say.

> KENDALL

You're such a pussy. Is this – is this Canadian shit? Because I'm the only person who can do this, Stew, you know that.

Static. Kendall looks like: Come on. Stewy avoids his eye.

> STEWY

It's about the bear-hug letter.

Kendall: And?

He can explain.

> KENDALL

What? C'mon, man!

                              STEWY
An acceleration.

                              KENDALL
Oh no, fuck off. What?

                              STEWY
This weekend.
                          (*to phone*)
Hello, Sandy?

                              KENDALL
At my sister's wedding. Are you insane? What do you want this
to be – *One Wedding and Four Fucking Funerals?*

Sandy finally connects.

                              SANDY
                      (*on speakerphone*)
Hello?

                              KENDALL
Hi. Yeah he told me already. No. Absolutely not. No way. No
fuck this.

                              SANDY
                      (*on speakerphone*)
Hey, Kendall. I'm sorry. Listen. But you told Frank.

                              KENDALL
I hinted—

                              SANDY
We've been contacted by a reporter, they know something's
cooking. We have to go now or risk a leak which kills us.

                              KENDALL
We're all together, this isn't a good time.

                              SANDY
                      (*on speakerphone*)
Well it really is a good time. Your dad's out of the loop? In the
UK. We catch him off guard.

Stewy looks at Kendall: Are you losing your nuts?

KENDALL

No. I need to prepare. Sandy? That's just human. You know,
I need to, I need prep time, for the approach?

SANDY
(*on speakerphone*)

You can't practice needing a shit.

KENDALL

But we'll be stuck here with him?

SANDY
(*on speakerphone*)

I'm afraid you're going to have to suck it up.

KENDALL

Uh-huh. Seriously?

SANDY
(*on speakerphone*)

You can't make an omelette without breaking some arms.
(*then*)

I'm sorry, okay? We'll be in touch with the letter, and let's close-
coordinate on the minute it's presented? Okay? Thanks, kid.

End of call.

KENDALL

Motherfucker.

He checks his watch.

I oughta go. I gotta go.

EXT. EASTNOR CASTLE – BOATHOUSE – NIGHT

Shiv arrives, late.

SHIV

Hey.

ROMAN *and* KENDALL

Hey!

SHIV

Where's Con?

Roman and Kendall both look at one another.

> KENDALL
>
> Con? Was he invited?

> ROMAN
>
> I thought you were going to tell him?

> SHIV
>
> Oh, man! What?

> ROMAN
>
> Do you want me to get him? I told Willa?

> KENDALL
>
> Well, I mean, What is this?

Roman pulls out a joint he has prepared. Sparks it.

> SHIV
>
> It's nothing. I just thought it would be nice. But I don't—

Roman offers her the joint.

> Um? I have things to do. You know?

> ROMAN
>
> I thought this was for old times'.

Offers Kendall.

> KENDALL
>
> Likewise. Kinda lot cooking?

> ROMAN
>
> Oh c'mon. I'm gonna be stoned out of my gourd!

> KENDALL
>
> One hit.

They pass the joint.

> SHIV
>
> To old times.

Kendall looks at his siblings.

ROMAN

So. Listen. Guys. Look. I've got something I need to tell you.
I went to Mom's. And she got me to sort through some of her
old papers. And – Shiv, you're adopted.

(*beat*)

And Kendall you're adopted. And Connor's adopted. So I think
that means everything comes to me and you can all fuck off?

He chuckles.

SHIV

Yeah. I'm sorry. I don't know why I got you down here.

ROMAN

No, it's nice. Congratulations.

SHIV

It is what it is.

KENDALL

It's nice. Tom's okay.

ROMAN

He doesn't know what he's saying he's so fucking high.

Kendall is breathing deeply.

KENDALL

Listen. Can I suggest a hug?

SHIV

Are you serious?

ROMAN

What is this?

KENDALL

Fine fuck you.

SHIV

Fuck you, come on then.

ROMAN

No way. That is so gay.

SHIV

Roman?

657

> KENDALL

Come on, you know you want to, bitch.

> ROMAN

Okay come on, bring it in.

Roman is quite eager to hug really.

> SHIV

Here we all are, happy as can be, all good friends and jolly good company.

> ROMAN

If either of you try to fuck me, I will hit you.

They break a little.

> KENDALL

You know we've been dicked over, right? By them. But it's alright. It's all alright.

> SHIV

Oh sure.

> KENDALL

There's the games and there's this – and the games don't affect this, right?

> ROMAN

That's big.

> KENDALL

What?

Kendall doesn't know what he means.

> ROMAN

Seriously. That's big of you. It must hurt, being outside, seeing me do big shit? Winning the game.

> KENDALL

Yeah, well.

> ROMAN

I hope you're okay outside, man.

Kendall is too guilty to reply, looks away.

SHIV

I like your date.

ROMAN

Yeah and she seems to loathe me, which I obviously find
incredibly appealing.

KENDALL
(*poking*)
Does she remind you a little of Mom?

SHIV

I've never done crack. But I guess Mom is like how I imagine
crack?

ROMAN

Um—

SHIV

If crack didn't get you high. You're jonesing. Then you get a hit.
And . . . *immediate* come-down.

KENDALL

'Family's a drug with no high.'

ROMAN

Side effects may include: diarrhea, nausea, shortness of breath,
anal seepage, sexual dysfunction, blindness and death.

Roman checks time. Then out of the darkness.

CONNOR

Hey?! Guys? Ken? Hello?

ROMAN

Con. Where you been, man?

CONNOR

I went to the other place – is this, was this The Place?
I thought—

ROMAN

This was the place we came. We always came here.

CONNOR

Right. I guess – I guess, maybe I just didn't come so much?

> SHIV
>
> We're turning in, bud.

They all pat Connor on the shoulder.

INT. EASTNOR CASTLE – KENDALL'S WAR ROOM – NIGHT

Kendall: not asleep. Pacing the war room. Making calls.

EXT. EASTNOR CASTLE – NIGHT

Greg has made a friend amongst the waiting staff, Doddy, a local hippy guy. He's smoking weed with him.

> GREG
>
> Tom is my friend, but is he my real friend? I mean I think I owe him this. But do I? I mean I don't want to say. But what if he finds out I knew? I mean, do I owe it to him to tell him? Or do I owe it to him to totally not tell him?

> DODDY
>
> I think tell him.

> GREG
>
> Yeah?

> DODDY
>
> Or maybe don't. I don't fucking know.

INT. EASTNOR CASTLE – ROMAN AND TABITHA'S ROOM – NIGHT

Tabitha asleep.

Roman watches her sleep.

INT. EASTNOR CASTLE – CONNOR AND WILLA'S ROOM – NIGHT

Connor is looking into the dark.

Willa is up typing.

DAY TWO

EXT. EASTNOR CASTLE – DAWN

Dawn is breaking.

INT. EASTNOR CASTLE – DAY

Morning. Shiv walks ahead. Looks back to—

Logan and Gil walking behind.

> GIL
> You know I was quite outraged when she suggested this.

> LOGAN
> I don't like being outside the US for too long.

> GIL
> It doesn't sit well.

> LOGAN
> There's a mercilessness I miss.

He looks at Gil. A challenge.

> GIL
> I don't like squalid little deals.

> LOGAN
> Fucking without a rubber. Everywhere else feels soft. Look at this fucking place.

> GIL
> Yeah well. It's all very refined.

They look at the castle.

> LOGAN
> Refined. Ha! That? All of it. Slaves, cotton and sugar. This country was nothing but an off-shore factory for turning evil into hard currency.

> GIL
> Is this where you tell me you're working for the communists?

> LOGAN

Ha! Now it fucking lies here, living off the capital, sucking in
immigrants to turn it and stop it from getting bedsores.

They walk.

> GIL

I was looking forward to taking you down. You've got a very
persuasive daughter.

*They look over to Shiv, who is walking and keeping an occasional eye
on them.*

> LOGAN

Oh, but doesn't a deal feel so much better?

> GIL

Handshake?

> LOGAN

I don't think either of us want to get dirty, do we?

EXT. EASTNOR CASTLE – DAY

*Tom is out in running gear as Greg is getting dropped back from
down a lane. He's been up all night smoking weed.*

> TOM

Hey, morning, Greg! How's the shabbiest groomsman in town!

> GREG

Urgh? Fine. Good. Good thanks, Tom.

> TOM

You okay, kiddo? Need someone to let out your dress?

> GREG

Uh-huh.

> TOM

You okay?

> GREG

Sure. Just. You know.

TOM

Good. Good man. Good to have you here, kiddo. Good to have you here, you know I rough-house you but I know it's because you can take it. You're a good kid. You're okay.

Greg feels a moment of connection.

GREG

Look, Tom, I've been up all night and I didn't know how to tell you this . . .

TOM

Is it about 'our secret thing'?

GREG

Nope. No, it's – it's, I don't know, Tom. I just— It doesn't feel right not to say, but it's a huge deal saying so— I've been wrestling and – basically, I'm pretty sure Shiv is like—

TOM

No, Greg.

GREG

I think she's having an affair.

Tom goes steely.

TOM

No. You're wrong.

GREG

Well no because—

TOM

Shut up, Greg.

GREG

Maybe I'm wrong?

TOM

Yes you are wrong, so that's all good.

GREG

Oh, well. Right?

TOM

Yes. So. Thank you for your time.

> GREG

You don't want to hear . . .?

> TOM

I don't need to hear, Greg, because it was a misunderstanding.

> GREG

I don't think it was, dude.

> TOM

Stop saying it.

> GREG

But . . .

> TOM

Shut up!

Tom goes to clamp Greg's lips shut.

> GREG

Hey. I'm just trying to—

> TOM

Fucking shut up.

> GREG

I feel sorry for you, man.

Tom can't stand being pitied and gets Greg in a headlock. Greg struggles.

> TOM

Shut up.

Tom puts his hand over Greg's mouth.

> GREG

Dude, I'm not making it up.

Tom punches him, not hard but with a quick jab to shut him up.

> TOM

Shut up, Greg. Shut up shut up shut up.

He swings him round, trying to get him quiet and releasing all his pent-up tension. He tries to put his hand over Greg's mouth.

> GREG

Why are you hitting me, Tom? I'm the only one that likes you?

Tom hurls Greg to the ground and runs off.

> TOM
>
> I'm sorry, Greg!

INT. EASTNOR CASTLE – TOM'S ROOM – DAY

Tom puts his wedding gear on.

Bravely. Manfully.

INT. EASTNOR CASTLE – SHIV'S ROOM – DAY

Hair and make-up for Shiv and her bridesmaids as she is photographed and videoed.

Caroline and Marcia and Mrs Wambsgans are there too.

INT. EASTNOR CASTLE – KENDALL'S WAR ROOM – DAY

Kendall and Stewy watch as a letter judders out from the printer that Jess has set up.

> STEWY
>
> Wanna game it?

Kendall knows it off by heart.

> KENDALL
>
> Deliver. He calls emergency board. We release the letter. The world blows up. The arbs dive in. He tells the world some fairy tales. Talks poison pills, other defenses. Board says, 'Hold on, we don't want to get sued.' Dad says, 'Fuck the shareholders.' Calls analysts, calls us, tells us to fuck off. The price rockets – because everyone knows we're going to win.

> STEWY
>
> You think there's any chance he'll just do a deal?

> KENDALL
>
> Nope. He'll never retreat. It'll be hostile hostile hostile.

INT. WEDDING CAR – DAY

'The Man That Waters the Workers' Beer' by Paddy Ryan plays.

Logan waits in the car. Shiv climbs in. They smile at one another.

They drive.

LOGAN

He's a good man, Siobhan. He is.

As they drive off through the castle gate, we stay on the car then the castle as—

Episode Ten

NOBODY IS EVER MISSING

Written by Jesse Armstrong
Directed by Mark Mylod

Original air date 5 August 2018

Cast

LOGAN ROY	Brian Cox
KENDALL ROY	Jeremy Strong
MARCIA ROY	Hiam Abbass
GREG HIRSCH	Nicholas Braun
SHIV ROY	Sarah Snook
ROMAN ROY	Kieran Culkin
CONNOR ROY	Alan Ruck
TOM WAMBSGANS	Matthew Macfadyen
RAVA	Natalie Gold
FRANK VERNON	Peter Friedman
COLIN STILES	Scott Nicholson
SOPHIE ROY	Swayam Bhatia
IVERSON ROY	Quentin Morales
JESS JORDAN	Juliana Canfield
GERRI KELLMAN	J. Smith-Cameron
WILLA FERREYRA	Justine Lupe
STEWY HOSSEINI	Arian Moayed
SANDY FURNESS	Larry Pine
NATE SOFRELLI	Ashley Zukerman
GIL EAVIS	Eric Bogosian
MRS WAMBSGANS	Kristin Griffith
MR WAMBSGANS	Jack Galpin
TABITHA	Caitlin FitzGerald
CAROLINE COLLINGWOOD	Harriet Walter
AMIR	Darius Homayoun
CHARLOTTE	Anna Wilson-Jones
MATT	Nick Mills
JONAS	Michael Izquierdo
DENIS	Tim Berrington
DODDY	Tom Morley
PHOTOGRAPHER	Cambridge Jones

'Who Do You Love?' by Bo Didley plays over—

DAY TWO

EXT. EASTNOR CASTLE – MAIN GATE – DAY

Shiv and Tom's car is returning to the castle.

Across the road outside the main castle entrance are freelance photographers looking for celebrities and shots of the media mogul and his family.

A cop with a motorcycle stationed to avoid traffic congestion waves them through.

Security guys from their own team, discreet, black suits, some in fluorescent jackets, wave them in.

There are also ten to twelve English onlookers drawn by the commotion. A younger couple with a camera phone.

EXT./INT. EASTNOR CASTLE – DAY

Confetti is thrown.

All of the close friends and family mill around, waiting their turn for the photos to be taken. (Depending on weather.) On the stone steps at the castle, or in another characterful spot.

Groups assemble. We pick out and jump cut between photos of:

The bride and groom, confetti being thrown—

Now the bride and groom and Mr Wambsgans and Mrs Wambsgans and Caroline, Logan and Marcia—

Stewy whispers to Kendall as he looks over.

STEWY

There he blows! The fucking brontosaurus. Always wants to fuck but can never get hard.

KENDALL

Yeah yeah.

Kendall looks at Stewy.

STEWY

What? Good to demonize the enemy before you have to kill him, man.

The photographer wants to assemble the next group.

PHOTOGRAPHER

And the siblings and partners?

Connor is near Shiv and Tom.

CONNOR

Just to say, I want Willa in this.

Shiv and Tom look at one another.

SHIV

Um, okay? I'm not sure . . .

TOM

I'm not sure if that's appropriate?

Connor ignores.

CONNOR

Oh no, that's fine, it is appropriate.

TOM

Is it appropriate? Or could it be problematic?

CONNOR

No it won't be problematic.

They don't want an incident, Connor seems so oblivious it's like he's just not getting it.

TOM

Um?

Tom looks to Shiv. She's going to explain, she wants to make it all clear but smiles and explains softly—

SHIV

Connor, she's been a call girl and one day that might come out and it could hurt my profile, or Tom's profile, so I don't want to be horrible but, you get it, okay?

Connor leans in—

CONNOR
(whispered, with a smile)
Okay. I get it, but, if you don't allow it I'm going to punch Tom in the face and rip my shirt open and take a fucking dump on the ground here and go apeshit because she's the woman I love. You get it?

Tom and Shiv look at one another. Connor smiles at Willa.

Roman sidles up to Tom as Shiv goes to talk to Charlotte to include Willa.

ROMAN
Um, dude, I'd like Tabs in this one, okay?

TOM
Oh really?

ROMAN
Uh-huh. Yes. I'm pretty into her. And it might be nice.

TOM
Okay. It's just—

ROMAN
It's just what, Tom?

TOM
I— We – obviously, shared a moment

Nothing from Roman.

(whispers, almost mouths)
She sucked me off, so?

Roman looks at him.

No, no. I mean. No. Fine. Sure. It's all good.

ROMAN

Thank you.

Cut to:

EXT./INT. EASTNOR CASTLE – DAY

The photo is taken.

Tom is quite aware of Tabitha.

Tom and Shiv quite aware of Willa.

After the photo's done, Kendall stalks off.

Colin comes over to Logan and Tom. Whispers.

Logan looks up. There's a drone buzzing high in the sky. Tom approaches.

SHIV

Okay?

TOM

Uh-huh. They think it's just a hobbyist but they're doing a sweep for paps.

SHIV

Good because, Gil, will be – eager, to keep things discreet.

COLIN

We'll take care of it.

LOGAN

If you find anyone? Don't be too gentle. Few bruises. Something broken, something blue, yeah?

Tom laughs. He sees Greg who looks wary of Tom.

INT. EASTNOR CASTLE – KENDALL'S WAR ROOM – DAY

Kendall arrives back. Inside Stewy is reading carefully. When he focusses, he really focusses. He has a pen in his hand, has made a couple of last-minute adjustments. Jess is on the laptop.

KENDALL

Hey!

STEWY

Hey.

KENDALL
(*re the letter*)

So? That it?

STEWY

Uh-huh. I just added we're not subject to any financing
conditions?

Stewy hands it over. Kendall reads.

KENDALL

Okay, yeah print, three of these.

*Jess starts to print but can't get things going so she starts checking his
connection and the printer.*

STEWY

And so, now, I guess – the only question is like – who actually –
you know – delivers it to him?

Kendall smiles then, realizes—

KENDALL

Are you serious?

STEWY

Well – yeah we can't just send him a fucking Domino's with this
as an extra topping. We have to be certain he's had eyes on it—

KENDALL

I know but I assumed – you?

STEWY

Oh. Right, I assumed you?

KENDALL

Fine. I just guess, if like we were planning to fuck your dad to
death, to make our fortune, I might offer – to actually do the
fucking?

STEWY

Are you scared?

KENDALL

Fuck you. No. Are you?

Stewy looks at him. Leaves it a beat.

STEWY

Yes. I am scared. Little bit. So if I'm scared and you're not scared, I guess, you should do it?

KENDALL

Seriously?

STEWY
(*looks at Kendall*)

We could ask, Jess to?

Jess tries to remain professional, but lets out a little tiny noise. She remains looking at the printer, but when we clock her look it's like: Um, really?

KENDALL

Fine. Fuck it – I can cope.
(*then to Jess*)

Okay. Are we ready or what?

Jess is looking at the printer.

JESS

Sorry, it should be printing.

KENDALL

But it's not?

JESS
(*realizing*)

Oh – shit.

KENDALL

What?

JESS

I think it's connected to a, a different printer – on their Wi-Fi network.

STEWY

Are you fucking serious?

KENDALL

Where is it, Jess?

JESS

I don't know. It doesn't say.

KENDALL

Oh Jesus! You need to find it, Jess. Now!

The door starts to open. There are papers all over the place.

Hey what the fuck!! No! Hello?! Hello?

There is Iverson.

Oh. Hey. Hey how are you going, kiddo? Sorry. Sorry, son.

IVERSON

Sorry? Mom said we could come?

KENDALL

Sorry, son. Sorry.

Iverson retreats, hurt. Kendall goes to follow. Stewy looks at him: Maybe not now? But Kendall needs to make it out—

One minute.

EXT. EASTNOR CASTLE/INT. EASTNOR CASTLE – KENDALL'S
WAR ROOM – DAY

Rava is there with Sophie comforting a sad Iverson. Kendall looks out from the doorway.

KENDALL

Hey, I'm sorry, kiddo.

Kendall's twitchy, looking back to see if Jess is there.

RAVA

They thought you could show them the place? But— Are you
okay?

KENDALL

Sure. Yes. I'm sorry, Iver.

RAVA

Okay.

(*looking at Kendall, all anxious*)
It's like five in the afternoon, Ken? You okay?

KENDALL
I'm great. I'm good. Just – some big moves.

Jess heads out – anxious.

RAVA
(*as always*)
Sure. Well, see you later.

He looks like: Yeah, you'll hear, baby.

KENDALL
Okay. Okay. Listen – I'll see you later. Okay?

Kendall watches them go.

STEWY
Okay. Jess thinks she has it. But you should go, in case.

He has a printout of the letter. He folds and puts it in the envelope.

You good? We doing this?

KENDALL
Yeah I'm doing this.
(*then*)
You'll email Gerri and the board?

STEWY
Just tell me when it's delivered.

KENDALL
You don't think I can deliver it?

STEWY
No. I know. It's just. You know, only fifteen percent of men,
when it comes to it, actually shoot an undefended enemy soldier.
There's an instinct not to kill.

KENDALL
I'm good.

*Kendall takes a breath. Then starts to walk. We stay with him down
the steps and on, round the back of the castle.*

We trace his walk from behind as he walks past: caterers wheeling in booze and ice; extra waiting staff pulling up and parking, including maybe Doddy, Greg's pal. Kendall walks round to the entrance to the castle.

We get a sense of the geography – how tucked away Kendall's entrance is.

Round the front – cars bringing guests who are staying at local hotels are arriving to bring people in for cocktail hour. He passes people. He walks briskly, can't dawdle, doesn't dare in case he stops entirely. He's preparing a face to meet the faces that he meets.

Jess appears. She has the letter printed from another printer in her hand. She gives him a look of relief.

Up the main steps into the castle and the great hall, past Charlotte's acolytes. At the entrance there are the tables where phones can be left – each in a numbered square inside a bag, watched over by a security person. Gerri is there arguing.

GERRI
Would it be possible to make an exception at all? I really need my phone?
(*looks like a problem, leans in*)
I'm the godmother and senior legal counsel, I'll be fucking keeping it, goodbye.

Kendall smiles a brittle smile, on he passes, through the great hall, prepared for cocktails and—

Into the staircase hall where Roman is with Shiv in her wedding dress, still talking to her about the launch. We catch a bit of him as Kendall passes.

SHIV
No. Phallocentric bullshit. I don't want a big fucking – dick blasting off at my wedding, okay?

ROMAN
It's not a big dick, Shiv, okay? It's not the fault of rockets or dicks, that they *happen* to be aerodynamic in shape, okay?

He's pointing to the snooker room. Roman catches Kendall's eye as Kendall keeps going – up the stairs.

Past more staff and guests descending. Past Tabitha coming down to join Roman.

Kendall heads along the corridor and on to Logan and Marcia's room. The paper feeling weird between his fingers.

The blood pumping in his ears—

He approaches. Now he could fail. Can he pull the trigger?

He hesitates, just for a beat, then knocks.

INT. EASTNOR CASTLE – LOGAN'S ROOM – DAY

Marcia opens the door.

MARCIA

Hello?

KENDALL

Hey. Is my father available?

MARCIA

What is it?

KENDALL

It's— I just need to have a word.

She looks at him.

MARCIA

Logan! It's Kendall.

LOGAN
(off; friendly)

Tell him if he wants to stop me buying papers and stations, he can fuck off, we're good to go.

Logan is messing with his bow tie in the bathroom. There is something potentially humiliating about how we find him. Shirt on but no trousers.

Come through, son!

All's good for Logan. Shiv is on board and Gil neutralized. Kendall doesn't want to do it this way. A member of staff or wedding planner arrives to check with Marcia that she's happy with a detail of the arrangements.

> KENDALL
>
> Do you want to, come out, Dad?

> LOGAN
>
> Come in. I'm not on the can.

Kendall enters.

> Nice service right? Shame it wasn't Catholic but there you go. Fucking all those kids will hurt the brand.

> KENDALL
>
> Hey. This isn't a nice thing, I'm afraid.

Logan clocks him and his manner for the first time.

> LOGAN
>
> Hello?

> KENDALL
>
> Um. Yeah. Read this.

He offers the envelope.

> LOGAN
>
> What is it?

Logan looks at the envelope. Kendall tries to retreat into the part of himself that is a businessman making an offer.

> KENDALL
>
> It's – it's – a proposal, to buy Waystar for a hundred and forty dollars a share. We're asking you to come to the table – open the books.

> LOGAN
>
> Ugh?

> KENDALL
>
> It's great value for shareholders.

> LOGAN
>
> Huh?

> KENDALL
>
> Yeah. There it is, I'm not going to get into feelings.

> LOGAN

It's— This is – a – fucking bear hug?

> KENDALL

That's right.

Kendall offers the letter. If Logan will take it, maybe he can go?

> LOGAN

Guh.

> KENDALL

Well, fine. We have the financing. Let's see what everyone thinks. Let's keep it professional. You know, it's just the situation that has arisen and you're very tough and so am I, as your son, so, I think this is just the way it has to be with us.

Logan just looks at him. Won't take the envelope.

We know several major investors are in favor. We go public with the letter tomorrow. So then we'll have to see – to see – what the arbs make of it?

Logan looks at him.

> LOGAN

Who?

> KENDALL

It's me and Stewy. And Sandy.

Logan flashes his eyes, shakes his head.

He's some of the cash so. I'm not sorry for what I'm doing which is – correct, but I am sorry for how it makes you feel.

Logan doesn't react – it's a lot of information to take on board and he's not mentally prepared his defenses. He refuses to react – it's scary to see. He is in new territory and feels any reaction may betray him. He's so emotionally overloaded he shuts down.

I'm sorry it had to be now. It was out of my hands. External factors.

Kendall puts the letter down. Maybe somewhere slightly damp and the envelope starts to absorb water. Kendall picks it up again.

Here.

LOGAN

No. Fuck off.

(scrambled)

I haven't got pants on!

Logan takes the letter and throws it in the toilet.

Do you even know what you're doing this for?

KENDALL

I— Ideas. I have – wanted to do things.

LOGAN

Uh-huh?

KENDALL

To save the business and and and do – do things that are—

· LOGAN

You can't even fucking say it.

KENDALL

I can say it.

(then)

Do, some, good, things.

LOGAN

'Do good things.'

(then)

Be a fucking nurse.

Logan laughs.

Kendall exits through the bedroom where Marcia is admiring Amir, who has recently arrived, the door still open.

MARCIA

Look at my little prince!

AMIR

Hey.

KENDALL

Hey.

Kendall walks on down the corridor as—

                          LOGAN
                     (*off; shouted*)
     Marcia!

INT. EASTNOR CASTLE – LOGAN'S ROOM – DAY

Marcia, right afterwards in the bathroom.

Logan is fishing in the toilet for the letter. Pulling it open.

                          LOGAN
     Gerri! Where's Gerri? Karl.

                          MARCIA
     Karl's in New York, Logan, what is it?
                     (*re the toilet bowl*)
     Get out of there!

                          LOGAN
     I need Gerri, I need Karl. I need—

                          MARCIA
     What is it?

                          LOGAN
     Bear hug, then they'll go— It'll— A – hostile. It makes sense. It
     fits.

                          MARCIA
     Today?

                          LOGAN
     I don't know.
               (*opening the wet and tattered paper*)
     I don't fucking know. It's not a good position I am in.

He rests on the bed or on the side of the bath. Marcia can see him
wobbling.

     If he has financing, and major shareholders? And – I'm here. By
     tomorrow? I need – I need a lot of things I don't have—

                          MARCIA
     You're alright. It's okay, Logan. Take a breath.
               (*calling him through*)
     Amir!

LOGAN

And I'm tired. I'm tired.

Marcia looks at him.

MARCIA

Logan. Amir, in here now please!

EXT. EASTNOR CASTLE – DAY

People are ferried from their hotels to the castle – different gangs of people arrive.

INT. EASTNOR CASTLE – GREAT HALL – DAY

The guests have assembled, post-wedding. In their black tie/evening wear. Cocktail time in the great hall of the castle, champagne goes around.

We might join with Amir who heads down looking for Gerri – he spots her and hones in.

Gil is near Gerri, they are being discreet but discussing how Waystar and Gil's accommodation with one another can work.

Amir whispers in Gerri's ear. Her face falls and she retreats with an apology upstairs.

Connor is crashing around. Likes the look of Gil as a target for conversation.

CONNOR

Hey. Senator Eavis, Connor Roy! Huge skeptic. Massive skeptic.

GIL

Good to know.

Gil's met entitled guys like this lots – right away he's looking around, looking for the exit.

CONNOR

Big problems with you and everything you stand for, my friend!

Connor looks pleased with his pronouncement, waits for a response. Gil looking around for someone else to talk to.

As Shiv comes over with Roman—

> SHIV
> *(to Gil)*

You okay?

> CONNOR

I look at you and I see Weimar. Hyper-inflation. I look at your face and, no offense, but I see dead babies.

> SHIV

Con?

> GIL

Very interesting. I'd have to disagree. Would you excuse me?

> CONNOR

Of course. Great to joust a little!

Shiv and Connor watch him retreat.

That's the best he can do?

> SHIV

He's going to be president, Con.

> CONNOR

Really? But I just wiped the floor with him in a debate?

Connor heads off, shaking his head.

Tom is saying hello to Mr Wambsgans and Mrs Wambsgans.

On Shiv and Roman. He's still smarting about the rocket.

> ROMAN

Is it him? You don't want a rocket launch cos of him? Would it help if it was a rocket full of – Muslim – granola?

> SHIV

Roman. It would just be fucking weird. Don't be a little kid.

She's hit him where it hurts.

> ROMAN

'Oh I'm so adult and important because I work for a man with glasses.'

Shiv sighs. Roman's frustrated his sister won't relate to him.

Is he a Jew by the way?

                    SHIV
Oh come on, man.

                    ROMAN
What? It's just a simple, friendly, slightly racist question.

She doesn't smile.

You used to be fun. When did you become one of them, Shiv?

                    SHIV
One of who?

                    ROMAN
The fucking dancey bullshit people.

                    SHIV
Yeah well sorry if I don't want to come to your freewheelin',
good-time, n-word-shouting hoedown.

                    ROMAN
The n-word, the b-word, the c-word. The world isn't a fucking
nursery school. And people don't like being taught.

                    SHIV
Wait, have you been watching our channels? I thought you
knew not to do that, with your IQ?

Roman's phone goes.

                    ROMAN
Excuse me. I actually have to go watch a satellite launch in
Japan that I'm actually in charge of? That I reorganized for you.
But you're too fucking carbon neutral to enjoy.

Roman heads off.

                    SHIV
Fine. Go on! Fuck off.

Roman starts to make a call.

INT. EASTNOR CASTLE – TOILET – DAY

*Roman slips into the toilets by the main stairs. His phone to his ear.
Another iPhone in his hand.*

                                                    687

ROMAN
(*into phone*)
Okay. Good. It's streaming. It's good. It's good. I got it. Wish everyone luck yeah? In Japanese obviously.

He watches the image on his iPhone for a beat.

Booster ignite. Plumes of smoke.

Then . . . with no noise, the rocket starts to lift then – an explosion and it falls or folds in on itself.

It blows up on the launch pad.

He's in the vestibule. A guest exits one of the two little bathrooms.

Roman watches for second. Traumatized, unable to believe.

Then after a beat or two, he just slips the phone back into his pocket.

Considers. Walks out of the toilet and returns to the party. Looks out into the crowd.

INT. EASTNOR CASTLE – KENDALL'S WAR ROOM – DAY

Stewy's waiting as Kendall returns.

STEWY
So. What happened? Tell me what the fuck happened?

KENDALL
I did it.

STEWY
You did it? Fuck. Okay. What did he do?

KENDALL
He threw it in the toilet.

STEWY
He threw it in the toilet?

KENDALL
That's a detail for our next letter to shareholders right?

STEWY
Look at you, you stone-cold killer fuck!

                    KENDALL
            (*an appeal to a friend*)
It was horrible. It was pretty fucking horrible, Stew.

                    STEWY
Yeah. I couldn't— My dad? I couldn't imagine. Hey – shall we –
Jess? Will you give us a moment?

Jess heads out. Stewy has a little baggie.

    Celebrate?

*Kendall considers. Maybe a chemical hit can make him feel not utterly
terrible?*

INT. EASTNOR CASTLE – DAY

Connor is with Willa.

                    CONNOR
So, Willa. Listen. I think I might have found a job I want to do.

                    WILLA
Okay? What is it?

                    CONNOR
President of the United States.

                    WILLA
Okay. Wow.

                    CONNOR
Yeah?
                (*looks at her*)
You don't look excited?

                    WILLA
Sure. It would be a fun project.

                    CONNOR
Is this the play?

                    WILLA
No.

                    CONNOR
Because I loved it.

                              WILLA
Sure. You just don't want to waste your money putting it on?
But running for president, that's a sound investment?

                             CONNOR
Plus I'd be planning to spend on you know, making sure your
'history' was, cleaned up?
                         (*looks at her*)
The president, Willa. That's big.

                              WILLA
Sure. But there's nothing more powerful than art?

                             CONNOR
No, sure. Apart from the power of the Executive Branch.

                              WILLA
Drama can change minds.

                             CONNOR
Sure but, I'd control the Federal Reserve?

Roman emerges. Looks around – there's Tabitha. Plus Caroline.

                            CAROLINE
Roman. Meet Denis Linton.

Roman turns off his phone.

                              ROMAN
Ugh huh?

                            CAROLINE
Denis is police and – what – commissioner? He knew your
father and me back when he did something even more boring,
right, Denis?

                              ROMAN
Uh-huh, thanks for looking after us!

They shake hands. Roman's distracted, turns off his buzzing phone.

                            TABITHA
Hey so how was it – the launch?

                              ROMAN
I'm sorry? What?

> TABITHA

How did it go?

> CAROLINE

Roman's been coordinating a satellite launch? How did it go?

Beat. Roman considers.

> ROMAN

Oh, great. It went great.

Roman's phone starts pinging as he gets inundated with texts and emails telling him his rocket's exploded. He turns his phone off.

> TABITHA

Okay, well, great! Congratulations, Rome!

Roman raises his glass and they all clink.

> ROMAN

Thank you! It's exciting!

INT. EASTNOR CASTLE – LOGAN'S ROOM – DAY

Upstairs, Logan is with Gerri. He's been kicked into action. Colin is in there. Marcia and Amir too. And another assistant/member of support staff.

He gets help putting his evening wear on.

> LOGAN

Cancel everything else. I fly out— Find out if I can leave now.

> GERRI

Now?

> LOGAN

Options. Now. In three hours, in— Are my pilots on the clock— Check who's got the hours to fly me home, or scheduled.

> MARCIA

You don't want to look panicked?

> LOGAN

Huh. Tomorrow maybe. Gerri? What's the— Where are you on that—

> GERRI
>
> Um, emergency phone board meeting for later, tonight? Or is that tomorrow?

> LOGAN
>
> Tomorrow.

> GERRI
>
> They're going to have deeper pockets, better prep.

> LOGAN
>
> Find out where that fucking shrunken Californian raisin is.

> GERRI
>
> The president? I think that's smart.

Now he's ready to go . . .

> LOGAN
>
> Come on – come on! The financials are hard. We need political support. Let's get down there. Come on, let's get going!

INT. EASTNOR CASTLE – GRAND STAIRCASE – DAY

Logan comes down the stairs, flanked by Marcia and Gerri, Amir and his assistant.

As he makes it down, there are Kendall and Stewy.

He takes a glass of champagne. Sips, defiant. A good fortifying glug.

And moves towards where they stand.

Stewy and Kendall can't quite believe it. Everything feels hyperreal. What's he going to do, what's he going to say?

He drinks. They stop their conversation.

He arrives, with Marcia and Amir and Gerri.

> LOGAN
>
> Look at you.

Kendall looks at him.

> STEWY
>
> Logan, for tonight, shall we—?

LOGAN

Oh for tonight? For tonight?

Doddy appears.

DODDY

Can I top you up?

LOGAN

Nuh.

Logan tosses his head to send him away but it could also be a nod to say yes.

Doddy begins to fill his glass.

All his simmering, controlled resentment blows up and he goes to stop him pouring with a hand that knocks the bottle which then spills on to his jacket.

What the fuck!

He flings his arm up towards Doddy, it might connect, but only very slightly.

Jerk.

DODDY

I'm sorry I didn't mean to—

LOGAN

Yeah well you did. Fucking prick. Do as you're told. Go on – get out of here.

A senior staff member comes over.

DODDY
(*explains to them*)
I thought he said yes but he said . . .

Doddy tries to return to Logan to apologize.

(*quietly*)
I'm sorry I thought you . . .

LOGAN

Stop mumbling. Don't look at me. Fuck off.

(*to the supervisor*)
Where do you get these people, they're fucking amateurs. Get out. I'm soaked through. Get him out I don't want to see him again. Ever. Okay?

As Doddy is led away, Kendall clocks him.

Nearby: Gerri is looking at her phone and crosses to Roman. He sees her coming—

ROMAN
Could you perhaps fetch me a stronger beverage?

Tabitha goes looking for a waiter. Roman knows exactly what's going to happen, but nevertheless is committed to his pretense.

Hi. Yes? Can I help?

GERRI
Um. I'm very busy on – another matter. Are you across this? I've had forty calls about the launch.

ROMAN
Well that's weird, because I haven't had any?

GERRI
Yeah. It blew up.

ROMAN
It blew up?

GERRI
Yes it exploded on the launch pad.

ROMAN
Okay. Wow. They should have told me. That's – naughty. And how bad is it? Is it bad?

GERRI
Well yeah it is bad.

ROMAN
And are— People are there people who are – from the launch site?

GERRI
I don't know. Yes. The scale means there are likely casualties. It's very unclear.

ROMAN

Does Dad know?

GERRI

No. Have you spoken to him?

ROMAN

No. Will you tell him?

GERRI

No, well it's not a good time so – I guess he's concentrating on – enjoying Shiv's wedding day.

ROMAN

Right. So, can they deal? Out there can I— I mean, this is a little detail in my world, Gerri. Not to be horrible?

GERRI

You were the lead exec, I understood.

ROMAN

I was somewhat aware of the endeavor.

GERRI

Well, yes they can deal, but we need to be prepared for any comeback. I mean I'm just thinking legally—

ROMAN

Uh-huh.

(*then decides*)

Because I did put on quite a lot of pressure to accelerate the launch even though there were concerns.

GERRI

You did?

ROMAN

Yes I did.

GERRI

Oh fuck.

ROMAN

I thought it would be nice. For it to happen on Shiv's wedding day. Like fireworks? Big fireworks.

GERRI

Well you got that right.

ROMAN

I'm just telling you because I sent quite a lot of emails and I – you know— There's no use hiding that because— I mean I'm just going to say, that's for you as general counsel to know. So you can protect me.

GERRI

Well I can try. But, fuck. You're looking at potential corporate manslaughter.

Roman looks sick.

INT. EASTNOR CASTLE – KITCHEN – EVENING

Out back: Doddy is being paid off. Colin is there with an assistant and an NDA.

COLIN

You just sign there.

INT. EASTNOR CASTLE – MARQUEE – NIGHT

Guests are seated at the many tables in the marquee.

ROMAN

Ladies and gentlemen. I give you. The bride and groom!

Shiv and Tom come on in.

Later: We pick up sections of speeches—

(NB: We won't hear all of these speeches – but cherry-pick as we move around the room on other people.)

So. Yes. It's me. I am the best man. And truly, I am the best man. No disrespect to Tom's oldest friends, I'm just superior to them. I'd like to welcome Tom to the family. I don't feel like I'm losing a sister, more that I'm gaining another, uglier, more ladylike sister. What can I tell you about Tom? Very little, nothing really sticks. He was born and grew up, in – um America. The middle. In an Applebees. I should imagine. I've never asked. His parents are here. I'd point them out but they're basically nobodies. What? Folks, I don't want to be mean – it's what a best man's speech is. They're actually incredibly lovely people. Just poor and uninteresting. I'm kidding! But I imagine what you really want to know is what went on at the bachelor party?

Roman looks at Tabitha. Who smiles at him. She doesn't give a shit. Tom clocks it. Tries not to look terrified.

Yeah nothing he was well behaved!

Tom looks relieved. Then mock indignant.

Although he did get a blow job. I'm kidding! No. I'm not. I am. Am I? No I am. I'm being horrible. It's the job.

Now Logan is giving a speech. We hear snippets of—

LOGAN
(*looking at Kendall*)
. . . I wouldn't have missed this for the world. This is a very memorable day. A day I'll never forget, as long as I live. I wanted it to be perfect. For my daughter. And it is. Nothing could ruin this. It means so much to be surrounded by everyone we love and trust and hold dear. Because nothing is more important than family.

As Logan sits down to applause, Gerri comes over.

GERRI
What about we do London, tomorrow?

LOGAN
Uh-huh.

GERRI
And I've put together the list of investor calls. Karl is making initial contact.

MARCIA
And a poison pill? Should you consider?

Okay. Marcia is part of this? Gerri looks at her.

GERRI
Yup. I'll have the options on a poison-pill defense. President in twenty-five. The EU Commissioner in the morning. Yes?

LOGAN
Yeah.

> GERRI

And have you told the others?

> LOGAN

The others?

> GERRI

The kids?

> LOGAN

No.

> (*why would I?*)

Is there an advantage?

> GERRI

Well. I don't— No also, to, to just to tell them?

That thought hadn't registered with Logan.

On Shiv's speech—

> SHIV

Okay. Who wants to hear about the bachelorette party? Well, unlucky. Because there's nothing to tell. We ate chocolates and watched romcoms while sewing. And no one will tell you different. Because we killed the strippergram. No but seriously. I want to thank my dad. We've had the occasional little difference but I'm happy to say we see eye to eye on most things. I'd also like to thank my brothers but they've basically been a pain in the ass my whole life so I'm not going to. No, I'm grateful to them being here, especially given how busy they are. Roman had to launch a rocket today.

Roman looks sheepish.

And Kendall's spinning a million plates.

Shiv looks at Kendall.

And Connor is basically an older Bruce Wayne, who knows what that enigmatic man is really up to. I wouldn't be who I am without having them as role models showing me so clearly what not to do. And I'd like to thank Tom. For being my rock. You're a good guy, Wambsgans, and I like hanging out with ya.

Frank appears behind Kendall.

FRANK

So you did it?

Gerri and Logan and Marcia looking over at Stewy and Kendall.

Shiv and Tom clocking the looking.

Tom is giving his speech—

TOM

I love my wife. I love saying she's my wife. I just love the word 'wife'.
(*some of this for Nate's benefit?*)
Wife, wife, wife, wife, wife, wife, wife. She's my wife! And she's my life. And I love her very much. And I'm going to stop talking now because I feel like I'm going to cry and it would be crazy to cry because I'm just so happy. Thank you all for being here. I love you all.

Then Caroline—

CAROLINE

My daughter didn't want me to speak. She finds me embarrassing. But I just wanted to say – I know we haven't always seen eye to eye. It's difficult when your father has stolen you away across the Atlantic! And I know I can be difficult – she can be difficult too – but I hope you also know that I think you are a brilliant, strong, extraordinary young woman, Siobhan. And I know you probably think I'm deliberately trying to make you cry or, steal the limelight. But I just wanted to tell you in front of everyone that you are special and, after my own fashion, I love you. And I wanted to say that publicly because I'm getting on, and I might not be in good enough health to say it when you remarry. That's a joke! I wanted to end on a little joke! Oh, and I love you, Tom. And you have exquisite taste!

INT. EASTNOR CASTLE – MARQUEE – NIGHT

Later: Shiv and Tom are dancing. To 'All of Me'.

Logan approaches. He cuts in, as is traditional.

Tom goes over to his mother and invites her to dance.

Tom's father approaches Marcia.

> MR WAMBSGANS

I believe it's traditional to invite you to dance?

The dance finishes.

Shiv heads off – once she is in the crowd a little, Gerri whispers to Logan.

Nate intercepts Shiv.

> NATE
> *(whispered)*

Hey excuse me. Can I get just two?

> SHIV

Thanks for the text message. What the fuck was that? 'I won't do it if you don't.' Is that a kind of anti-proposal?

> NATE

Look I just spoke to Gil and it sounds like, well, he thinks he's being very subtle and all but something has happened and I wondered what the fuck that was?

> SHIV

What's happened with what?

He looks at her.

> NATE

In terms of burying whatever it is we know about and not being scared of ATN anymore?

She plays it dead straight.

> SHIV

Oh, okay, that's an interesting change of perspective?

He looks at her.

> NATE

I brought you in, what did I do?

> SHIV

I'm going to make him win.

> NATE

He's going to win anyway.

> SHIV

I might not agree.

> NATE

Well yeah. Look, I don't want to play the bleeding heart but—
there's a reason I work with him and it's because—
  (*he's embarrassed to state his good intentions*)
inequality and—

Shiv clocks his weakness and mocks—

> SHIV
> (*mocking voice*)

'Inequality.'
  (*then*)
If you can't handle it, fuck off.

Tom clocks Shiv and Nate in heated consultation. Starts to head over.

> NATE

Who are you?

> SHIV

I'm Shiv fucking Roy. And I'm going to have two grateful
people: the president and my father.

Logan makes it to Shiv.

> LOGAN

Okay. I'm sorry, honey. I'm sorry. But you need to talk to your
brother. I think you all need to chat.

INT. EASTNOR CASTLE – MARQUEE – NIGHT

Elsewhere: Connor snakes through the party.

> CONNOR

Um. Kendall? Could I grab a word with you?

> KENDALL

Uh-huh? What is it?

> CONNOR

Oh just a thing, just a little thing. Would you mind? In private?

Gerri is over talking to Shiv, and then going to Roman.

INT. EASTNOR CASTLE – GOTHIC DRAWING ROOM – NIGHT

Kendall walks in, led by Connor.

> CONNOR
>
> I'm – sorry, bro. I didn't give you the full, full picture.

There inside are Shiv and Roman.

> KENDALL
>
> Oh. Okay. Okay.

> SHIV
>
> So what the fuck? Dad told us. How could you?

> KENDALL
>
> It, it was out of my hands, Shiv – I—

> ROMAN
>
> You're a real piece of work, you know that? You act like you're
> a fucking – guy, a decent guy, but seriously?

> KENDALL
>
> Look – we can talk. There's no need to talk to me like I'm—

> SHIV
>
> I think we get to talk to you any way we fucking like.

> KENDALL
>
> The fact is I was forced into this position against my wishes.

> ROMAN
>
> Boo-hoo. Boo-fucking-hoo.

> KENDALL
>
> You can talk to me. I'll answer any questions you have.

> ROMAN
>
> Yeah I have a question. What the fuck in the name of all the
> fuck in the universe do you think you're doing?

> KENDALL
>
> I'm trying to save the company.

> ROMAN
>
> By fucking us, forever?

KENDALL

If this works, which undoubtedly it will, you'll all be very very very rich and maybe it's for the best for this to no longer be a family operation.

ROMAN

Well no, because for one thing, our inheritance is all in stock so after this, if Dad goes loco – and pisses it all away, nothing.

CONNOR

Kendall, we're – we're— This is— Look, I can say it because I don't even care, but the fact is, right now we're somebodies, we're people, any doofus can have a few million bucks!

KENDALL

Oh come on!

SHIV

This is a unilateral decision. To fundamentally alter the nature of the family, on my wedding day. Do you have any conception of how fucking selfish you are?

ROMAN

This isn't about a dress.

SHIV

Fuck off.

CONNOR

He's right. It's about the next – one thousand years.

KENDALL

The Thousand-Year Reich? Uh-huh? That will endure for eternity? Dad is fucked? You're all – fucking – guarding a trash can full of diapers. Wake up. This is – just a little maneuver. You don't need to get sentimental.

SHIV

Look, I'm no fucking blushing bride – but the, the lack of thought, I can't believe it. To do this to Dad, today?

KENDALL

Oh, let's not pretend, Shiv? This isn't about Dad. This is because you like the power. It gets you close to the poles you like to grease. And Rome, you couldn't get a job in a fucking burger joint let alone a Fortune 500 without some nepotism and – Con, you like the glamour it gives to a fucking – freak in the desert.

CONNOR

No. I could actually do with the assistance of the family firm on my ambitions to become president.

KENDALL

Uh-huh. Uh-huh. Exactly. You're all living in a fucking dreamworld.

Logan enters.

LOGAN

Hello. How's the torture going?

KENDALL

I ought to go. This is— I shouldn't even, talk to you.

LOGAN

I don't think there's any reason not to, legal or otherwise?

KENDALL

I'm not getting into it.

LOGAN

You don't think you owe us an explanation?

KENDALL

I don't owe you anything.

LOGAN

Ha! What have you had your whole life that I didn't give you?

KENDALL

I don't—

LOGAN

I blame myself. I spoiled you and now you're fucked. I'm sorry, you're a hothouse flower and you're nothing. You're curdled cream. Maybe you can write a book or, or collect sports cars – or something but for the world, no I'm sorry, you're not made for it. You can't stand it.

Kendall considers then walks out past his father.

KENDALL

You're a fucking beast.

INT. EASTNOR CASTLE – KENDALL'S WAR ROOM – NIGHT

Kendall puts his keycard to the door, comes in. Stewy is watching the TV.

> STEWY
> Hey. Okay? I think Logan came calling to my room. I thought it was safest just to hole up here—

> KENDALL
> Right. Listen, we got – we got some more?

There can only be one thing he's talking about.

> STEWY
> Uh-huh? Shall we both, just—
> > *(lay off?)*
> You know, could be a big day tomorrow?

> KENDALL
> Sure. You got a little though? In case we want – for tomorrow?

> STEWY
> > *(yes, but)*
> Um? I'm not sure?

> KENDALL
> You wanna look?

Stewy looks at him: Have you got this under control?

> STEWY
> We're good, right?

> KENDALL
> We're good.

> STEWY
> Sandy wants a check-in at two and at four and at six GMT. Okay?

Kendall puts his phone on the side. Taps it.

> KENDALL
> Wise. Wise.
> > *(then)*
> I could just do with a straightener?

Stewy makes a decision.

> STEWY
> Okay. Well I'm all out. I think. Sorry, but we're good?

Kendall really wants a line of something but he also knows it's not cool to push it. Will make him look out of control.

> KENDALL
> Fine. Okay. Fine. Well, catch you later.

EXT. EASTNOR CASTLE – KENDALL'S ROOM – NIGHT

Kendall heads out – hungry for stimulants. Eager to get away from himself.

INT. EASTNOR CASTLE – MARQUEE – NIGHT

Connor is talking to Roman.

> CONNOR
> And wow shit, did anyone die?

> ROMAN
> We don't know. But it will be fine.
> *(watches the band)*
> And, dude, were you kidding, about the presidential thing?

> CONNOR
> No. Why?

> ROMAN
> Because I think it'd be a disaster.

> CONNOR
> Screw you. No. I think I could do it.

> ROMAN
> Right. I mean, what would you even – want to do.

> CONNOR
> Well. I would launch a campaign, against the Great Dangers.

> ROMAN
> Which are?

CONNOR

Honestly, from my readings, and sadly you cannot say this because the permitted public debate has shrunken to the size of a fucking nut. But, frankly, onanism and usury.

ROMAN

Excuse me, Harry Potter?

CONNOR

This isn't for public consumption, it's from my readings.

ROMAN

Cuck-oo.

CONNOR

And I want to not pay tax.

ROMAN

Well, tell me about it.

CONNOR

As a protest. Like Thoreau. He had it right, let me tell you. He had it all right.

Gerri is heading towards them.

GERRI

Roman, if I leave for New York after the cake is cut will you stay up tonight as linkman?

He angles her away.

ROMAN

Did you hear yet?

GERRI

About?

ROMAN

Japan? How many dead?

GERRI

Oh yeah, did you not hear? None.

ROMAN

None? None at all?

GERRI

Two guys lost thumbs and there might be an arm they won't be able to save. But they might.

ROMAN

Are you kidding? It's just an arm? A couple of fucking thumbs?

GERRI

Yeah so sad but—

ROMAN

Are you kidding? Jesus. We're not going to ruin a party over a couple of fucking thumbs!

GERRI

And the good news is, we're in a good insurance position on the satellites.

ROMAN

Okay, see? I'm making us money!

GERRI

Uh-huh. This will overall probably be revenue neutral.

Tom is approaching—

TOM

How we all going? Sorry about 'everything'.

ROMAN

Hey, Tom, guess who didn't kill anyone? But only maybe lost a coupla thumbs?

TOM

I don't—

Tom looks blank. Roman points both his thumbs at himself.

ROMAN

This guy!

TOM

Great? Well congratulations.

Tabitha joins them.

ROMAN

Tabs. It's alright, it's okay, nobody died!

                         TABITHA
Oh. Okay? That's nice.

                          ROMAN
Yeah I kinda always wondered if I was a psychopath but
apparently not. I'm actually relieved. We have to celebrate!

                         TABITHA
Okay, sure! How?

                          ROMAN
I dunno. Wanna go try to launch my rocket?
                    (*raises his eyebrows*)
Eyebrow eyebrow.

INT. EASTNOR CASTLE – MARQUEE – NIGHT

11:50 p.m. Kendall wanders the party.

*He sees person after person he doesn't want to talk to: Gerri, his
mom, Shiv, Tom, Connor, Roman, Willa, Tabitha. A buzz has gone
round, people look at him accusingly, he feels.*

He wants another bang of something to keep his head straight.

EXT. EASTNOR CASTLE GROUNDS – NIGHT

Kendall walks out of the party or get some head space.

He marches through the gardens. Greg's smoking a cigarette.

                         KENDALL
  Hey.

                          GREG
  Hey. So, I heard.

                         KENDALL
  Yeah well.

                          GREG
  Right.
                    (*then, chancing it*)
  I just wanted to say – good luck.

> KENDALL

Good luck?

> GREG

Just – you know, the place has got to change I feel.

> KENDALL

It has, right?

> GREG

It just does.

> KENDALL

Uh-huh.

> GREG

All that – the old shit, the nasty politics, the – the stuff at the cruise lines and all that?

Kendall doesn't want to hear.

You know about that?

No reaction.

Yeah, cos I helped clean it up, but you know?

> KENDALL

So listen, do you know where I can— I wouldn't mind a— Do you have some, something something?

> GREG

I wish! But you know. I kept hold of a few little bits and pieces just in case I got into trouble you know?

Kendall looks at him.

So I would think, I'd think anybody would be wise to keep me in a good role?

> KENDALL

I see you.

Greg isn't going to push it.

> GREG

Some of the guys smoke weed out the back. I think.

He starts to head off.

KENDALL

I see you, Greg. I like it, you fucking little operator.

INT. EASTNOR CASTLE – ROMAN AND TABITHA'S ROOM – NIGHT

Tabitha looks at Roman.

TABITHA

Well that was – nice.

ROMAN

Uh-huh.

TABITHA

It was, it was fine.

ROMAN

'It was fine'? She whispered, exhausted from their lovemaking. What every man longs to hear.

TABITHA

I mean, considering neither of us came, it was – it was an occasionally enjoyable way to pass twenty minutes.

She's making him laugh. It doesn't feel so heavy.

ROMAN

Two stars.

They giggle.

TABITHA

You know, you could do anything, Rome, if this goes down, with your brother.

ROMAN

Yeah?

TABITHA

Yeah. One lousy lay doesn't mean it's all over?

ROMAN

The thing is. I *could* do anything? I have the money? It's just figuring out what.

TABITHA

What did you major in at college?

> ROMAN

I went to college, but I wasn't really paying attention.

> TABITHA

Right?

> ROMAN

I just wish I knew everything, about something. One thing, to build on. Then I could just – bang – fuck them all!

> TABITHA

Rome, you don't need to take over the world tomorrow. You need to build up. And get all the way to the edge, and then when you're right there, you wait for it to happen. And when it does, it feels great.

> ROMAN

I like you and the words you say.

INT. EASTNOR CASTLE – SHIV AND TOM'S ROOM – NIGHT

Tom and Shiv get through the door.

> SHIV

So, do you wanna talk about the takeover, and how it affects—

> TOM

You look amazing.

> SHIV

Because I mean you're in on merit and if he succeeds I think it will be tough but in terms of—

> TOM

I don't care about that.

> SHIV

I mean if Gil takes off I think – well – maybe I don't even want to go back inside and our five-year plan looks a little different?

> TOM

Shush. Shiv, let's just fuck.

> SHIV

I have bad news about my hymen.

TOM

Shiv, I wanted to get married to you not for our plan or – because— Look, you're hard and you're tough but you know, but I want in, I want in on you. And I don't care. Let's go and be sheep farmers in New Zealand!

SHIV

Sheep farmers?

TOM

I mean. You can scuba?

SHIV

Yes?

TOM

Let's teach scuba! Let's just get out.

Shiv looks at Tom. There's something she's been meaning to say.

SHIV

I should say something, Tom. I should have said. But I've had a little number?

TOM

A little number?

SHIV

And I think we both agreed we were grown-ups. I mean I think we had an unspoken agreement, that we were—

TOM

Right. Did we?

SHIV

I think I always implied, you know?

TOM

Right. Okay. Do you want to say who?

SHIV

And if I've hurt you, and I've got it wrong, I'm so fucking sorry.

TOM

Was it Nate?

> SHIV

But I think, from this point on, I want everything to be really open and honest.

> TOM

Right.

> (*then*)

Can I send him home?

> SHIV

Sure.

> (*re Nate*)

Although, what if people ask why he's being sent home?

> TOM

Can I at least spit on his cheesecake?

> SHIV

Tom. I just think – I'm not sure. I'm not sure I'm a good fit for a monogamous marriage.

> TOM

Right?

> SHIV

Yeah?

> TOM

Okay.

> SHIV

Is that okay? Is that okay to say to you?

> TOM

Of course.

> (*beat*)

I mean I kind of wish I guess maybe we'd talked about it before our wedding night?

> SHIV

Yeah, maybe that would have been wise.

> TOM

Hey. Well.

SHIV

I just think, you know, I needed you, very much, I was not in good shape when we hooked up and I think the business angle, works, we know that. We have a plan on that.

TOM

Uh-huh.

SHIV

But in terms of the relationship. Is there an opportunity for something different from the – whole, box-set death-march? A different shape of relationship? Could that be exciting?

TOM

Right? Maybe. I guess.

SHIV

Right? It's exciting?

TOM

It's exciting.

SHIV

We've pulled everything else down. But love's the last one, it's the last fridge magnet left.

TOM

Right. How do you mean?

SHIV

I mean 'love' is about twenty-eight different things – it's a lumpy sack. And it needs to get emptied out because there's a lot of ugly products in that Santa sack. Fear and jealousy and control and revenge – and they get such a pretty fucking wrapping in that stocking, it looks so nice, but you open it up—

TOM

No. I'm sure. You're right. You are. Love, it's – it's bullshit.
(*then*)
But – I do love you.

She looks at him. Smiles spread.

SHIV

I love you too.

They start to kiss passionately.

EXT. EASTNOR CASTLE GROUNDS – DODDY'S CAR – NIGHT

Kendall wanders around, Doddy is smoking a joint by his car.

KENDALL

Hey?

DODDY

Hey.

KENDALL

What you got on the go there?

DODDY

Oh. Nothing?

He hides it.

KENDALL

It's cool. I can just smell it from down there. You know. It's fine. Smells like – the kind bud.

DODDY

Uh-huh.

KENDALL

Did you— Did I see you get some shit earlier? You okay?

DODDY

Oh yeah. Yeah. They paid me up.

KENDALL

For the full shift?

DODDY

Uh-huh. And a sweetener, it's actually great because now I can just go home.

KENDALL

Nice.

(*then*)

Dude, would it be weird to ask—

DODDY

Do you wanna?

He offers the joint.

KENDALL

Um. Sure. But also, I just wondered, for the party, big party and you don't have a connection for some – powder, do you?

INT. EASTNOR CASTLE – MARQUEE – NIGHT

Tom heads in. He's got a super-charge of new life.

Nate is talking to Connor and Willa.

NATE

Look, I'm not really the strategist for you. I mean, do you see yourself as a Democrat because—?

CONNOR

Don't box me in, Nate!

Tom arrives with them.

TOM

Hey, dude, can I get in?

NATE

Um, we're just talking—

TOM

Nevertheless.

Tom positions himself to cut Nate off.

NATE

Okay?

TOM

Yeah. Hey how you doing, man?

NATE

Um, good.

TOM

Yeah, so I'm really sorry, man. But there's been a bit of a mix-up with the accommodation.

NATE

Oh, right?

TOM

Yeah. I'm sorry, but there's nowhere for you to stay.

717

> NATE

Okay, well. I'm sure I'll figure something out?

> TOM

Right. But it might be smart for you to leave directly, to find something?

> NATE

Are you serious?

> TOM

I'm serious, yeah.

> NATE

I get the message, it's fine. Okay? Let's just keep things cool. I think you need to stay calm. We're grown-ups, Shiv's a grown-up.

> TOM

Uh-huh. And I think you need to go fuck yourself, and if I ever see you in the same room as Shiv again I will pay men to break your legs and if I go to jail, which I won't, so be it.

> NATE

Okay. Look, fine, I'm going to head out. I'll just finish this and—

> TOM

My mom and dad made a contribution towards the wine so I'd rather you didn't drink any more.
> (then)

Excuse me.

He stops a server.

> NATE

Are you kidding?

> TOM

Put it back, Nate. Put my wine back.

> NATE

Oh come on!

> TOM

Put it the fuck back.

Something about Tom's manner suggests Nate shouldn't protest too much.

After a beat, shaking his head, Nate tries to pour as much of the wine as he can back into the bottle as Tom watches.

Connor and Willa watch, haven't heard the exchange so it looks quite odd.

> CONNOR
>
> Waste not want not I guess?

Connor smiles at Willa. She doesn't smile back.

> Listen. I've been thinking. There could be a financial upside to Kendall's buy-up?

> WILLA
>
> Uh-huh? You gonna pursue the breathable vitamins?

> CONNOR
>
> No, funding for my campaign? And you know – side projects.

> WILLA
>
> Such as, what, you have me bumped off, to clean up your history?

> CONNOR
>
> No! You're unmurderable! No, I was thinking, if you agreed to be my putative First Lady, I'd see what theaters are available for the most exciting voice of her generation? That's you, by the way.

Connor offers his hand. Willa takes it. They shake.

INT. DODDY'S CAR – NIGHT

12:00 a.m. In the little car. Doddy does a line.

> DODDY
>
> Oh yep!

Gives Kendall the note. Kendall looks at the crystals on the phone.

> KENDALL
>
> Hold on—

(*dabs some on his tongue*)
What is this?

DODDY

Ket. Special K.

KENDALL

Oh no. No, dude. K? I can't— No I need a different high tonight. I was after some coke?

DODDY

Oh. Okay?

KENDALL

No?

DODDY

Well I know a kid. But no. This is ket.

KENDALL

Right but you can get coke?

DODDY

Yeah, I should think.

KENDALL

Then let's blow, is that cool?

DODDY

I don't know if I can drive, right away?

KENDALL

No? I can drive?

Doddy opens the door to get out and buckles, falls right over.

I'll drive. You okay?

DODDY

I'm fine.

INT./EXT. DODDY'S CAR – NIGHT

Kendall is peering through the windshield, driving not brilliantly.

KENDALL

You okay, bud, you gonna be able to find the way?

DODDY

Oh yeah. Yeah.

But Doddy has his eyes closed.

KENDALL

Let's get some air in.

Kendall lowers both their windows. They bump as Kendall changes gear.

DODDY

You alright there?

KENDALL

Yeah, just fucking – stick shift.

DODDY

You used to an automatic?

KENDALL

Uh-huh. Plus I don't drive that much.

DODDY

No? Why not?

KENDALL

Because I'm incredibly rich and I get driven everywhere.

DODDY

You're incredibly rich?

KENDALL

Yep. I'm loaded beyond your wildest imaginations. How much farther?

DODDY

Should I kidnap you?

KENDALL

Yeah, if you could fucking walk, you should kidnap me.

DODDY

I know a house?

KENDALL

Oh you know a house? It's all coming together. A place to fucking keep me?

> DODDY

Yeah, it's got a cowshed, it's only a corrugated-iron roof. So it's gonna be fucking cold like.

> KENDALL

Hey, what do you care?

> DODDY

Exactly. And so what— Are you addicted to coke? Is that why we're going?

> KENDALL

I used to be an addict. But not now.

> DODDY

Not now?

> KENDALL

The idea of addiction was a crutch I needed. I needed to feel weak. But now I'm strong. So. I'm free. Which is nice.

Kendall grinds the gears as he changes down, looks down at the shift trying to find the gear.

Near a bridge, there's an animal in the road. A fox or a dog.

Kendall's looking down momentarily, Doddy grabs the wheel, Kendall doesn't realize why, he looks up and corrects, but overcorrects and they're suddenly out of control . . .

They're off the road into the dark, river, or water illuminated in the pitch black.

Boom as they impact. Air bags deploy. All is confusion.

Then – a beat of calm. They're in the water, in the dark, lights maybe still on for a beat.

Suddenly aware of water rushing in around them from below. But it hasn't reached the open windows yet. Kendall looks over. Doddy is out of it – unconscious or dazed, lolling.

Kendall has what seems like a little while to decide on what to do.

Unclips seatbelt. Unclips Doddy's seatbelt.

The car is going down faster now. Nose-first, weighed down by the engine.

The car is kind of floating, but filling with water fast.

Kendall tries the door – no. Now the water's coming in fast and starting to rush through the windows. Then climbs up, puts his butt on the windowsill and climbs out backwards as the car starts to fill fast.

He pulls himself out as the car rocks. He's focussed on himself and his own survival. Maybe we see Doddy's body thrown around from side to side as the car wobbles and submerges, the lights shorting out.

It's dark and real. We can hardly tell what's going on.

Kendall makes it to the surface – shocked and cold.

EXT. RIVERBANK – NIGHT

Kendall swims to the side, it's not far. Scrambles up the bank, thorns, grass, under his fingernails. Brambles. Gravel under his hands.

The bank is grassy and overgrown, not muddy.

He sits for a beat and watches the water.

He comes to after the moment of massive adrenalin. They are in the middle of nowhere. Back route from the castle.

After a while, he goes back to the water's edge. Starts to walk in. He edges in but it's cold and dark and scary.

But looking at where he might dive, it starts to feel impossible. And foolish to go back in.

He retreats.

Sits. Watches. Gets up again to go into the water. But retreats.

Eventually he walks up to the road. It's dark. No houses with lights on can be seen.

EXT. COUNTRY LANE – NIGHT

Kendall feels utterly helpless. He starts to jog. Then stops, walks back to the place where the car went off the road.

Then doubles back and starts walking along the road.

It's a trudge. His clothes are wet on him.

When does Kendall think, 'I don't need to have been here'? Is it on his mind now as he looks back?

EXT. COUNTRY LANE – NIGHT

As Kendall walks away, everything is almost exactly the same: still surface on the water, nothing to show he was here. Everything's the same as it was.

He walks. On and on through the night.

Far in the distance, can he hear the sound of music from the party?

He walks on.

Then from a way away he can hear the rumble of a car.

Rescue! Or is it? He steps to the side of the road. Thinks.

There's somewhere very convenient to get out of the way, a bank or gateway. He has to do almost nothing but maybe step aside.

He sits down in a way that looks like he's having a rest, almost pretending the car's not going past.

And then the car has passed, its lights illuminating the road.

Kendall hardly had time to think. But as he watches the car recede. He thinks, 'What am I doing? What did I do?'

He stands up and, once the car is receding, steps into the road.

As he watches it go he realizes that this wasn't just grabbing some time to think.

This was the key moment.

He's made a decision.

He starts to walk back towards the party with renewed purpose.

'Okay,' he thinks, 'this is what I'm doing.'

Maybe we cut a bit faster though his travels.

EXT. HILL OVERLOOKING THE CASTLE – NIGHT

Kendall gets to a spot where he can look down on the castle illuminated at night and it seems like going cross-country would be easier than following the road?

Maybe he cuts across a signed footpath? He does know the countryside hereabout from childhood.

EXT. EASTNOR CASTLE – LAKESIDE – NIGHT

Eventually Kendall makes it to the edge of the lake which separates him from the castle.

As he starts to make it, skirting the lake, wading in the water. This is the easiest route . . .

Suddenly. A loud bang! He freaks. Ducks. What the fuck? Is he being shot at?

Suddenly the stately sounds, blasting out from speakers surrounding the castle to accompany the fireworks—

Handel's 'Sarabande' plays loud.

Then another and another and there are explosions in the sky. Fireworks.

As they blast off and the music plays he looks into the sky, crouches and thinks. What the fuck has he done?

The display seems to go on for a long time. Can he make out figures in the distance enjoying it?

The music plays. Kendall shivers.

Eventually it is over and he walks along through the shallows.

EXT. EASTNOR CASTLE APPROACH – NIGHT

Eventually.

Kendall reaches a spot where he can see the road up to the castle approach. But there are the flashlights or security lights of a security point. On a bridge, causeway or other entrance to the castle grounds.

He skirts away from the route that would take him to this security point.

EXT. WOODLAND – NIGHT

Kendall makes it through woodland.

As he makes his way he sees a pair of security guards with flashlights marching the perimeter. He crouches, waits for them to pass. Skirts round further.

EXT. EASTNOR CASTLE – NIGHT

Kendall crosses a field and a hollow and comes up past the area where he met Doddy.

He feels he's been away for a lifetime but there on the floor is the roach end of the joint Doddy smoked earlier.

Kendall looks at it on the floor as if it might be evidence of something.

There's the space where the car was.

EXT. EASTNOR CASTLE – KENDALL'S ROOM – NIGHT

1:30 a.m. Kendall makes it back. He's there. Some kind of safety.

Finally. He reaches in his jacket pocket for—

Oh fuck. It's missing. Fuck. Checks all his pockets. Where's the keycard?!

He tries the door.

This is unbelievable. He starts to walk away – get another key?

No that would be bad.

He returns, cases the windows. He hears someone passing. But when he looks, they've gone. (It was Amir, but we never see him.)

Then, surprisingly quickly, he takes his coat or jacket and places it over the pane of glass in the door, to muffle the sound, and jabs his elbow in to smash the pane.

He reaches in to open the door. But catches his wrist as he goes in – cutting it so that blood shows up. Not deep.

INT. EASTNOR CASTLE — KENDALL'S ROOM — NIGHT

Kendall goes to the bathroom. Pulls his clothes off – dumps them all in the bath and runs water on the mud and dirt.

Dabs at his wrist with a white towel.

There are business papers freshly couriered on the bed.

Does he have another wobble? Looks at the blood on the towel. The broken window. His clothes sopping wet. He picks up the phone. He dials 911. That's not the right number.

Then his phone rings.

He answers, putting it on speakerphone.

>   SANDY
>   (*on speakerphone*)
> Hey. Kendall? Sandy Furness.

>   KENDALL
> Hey.

>   SANDY
>   (*on speakerphone*)
> How you going?

>   KENDALL
> Fine. Tough.

>   SANDY
>   (*on speakerphone*)
> It will be tough. It will be.

>   KENDALL
> Uh-huh.

>   SANDY
>   (*on speakerphone*)
> But look, I wanted to say, kid, you've done the hard part. I'm just off the line with my buddies, and I think this is— I don't see how he can stop this? Your chunk? We might let Frank in, the coalition is there, kiddo. Get some sleep. It's going to be fun!

>   KENDALL
> Great.

                              SANDY
                      (*on speakerphone*)
    Great!

                              KENDALL
    Great.

                              SANDY
                      (*on speakerphone*)
    Okay. Goodnight.

                              KENDALL
    Goodnight.

INT. EASTNOR CASTLE – KENDALL'S ROOM – NIGHT

Kendall pulls the stuff from the bath. Squeezes out the water and lets it drain.

He showers. Puts on a fresh suit.

Picks up the spare keycard from the side.

Looks in the mirror.

Then, surprisingly, he trips down the steps with a certain lightness.

He heads back towards the party . . .

INT. EASTNOR CASTLE – MARQUEE – NIGHT

2:00 a.m. As he returns he's the sober guy at the party.

Everyone is a little drunk. The DJ is playing now.

He walks the perimeter of the marquee, smiling at people.

It's like a dream. No one missed him. Everything is the same. Maybe it never even happened?

There is his mom and Rory, her 'boyfriend'.

                              CAROLINE
    Hello, naughty one?

Kendall smiles. But he's anxious. What?

    Roman told me.

KENDALL

Right. Yeah, well. You know?

CAROLINE

I don't think any the worse of you.

KENDALL

No?

CAROLINE

No.

KENDALL

Well, good.

CAROLINE

You know he did always have a favorite, of you children.

KENDALL

Mom? No.

CAROLINE

You don't want to know?

KENDALL

C'mon.

CAROLINE

It was always the business. So, I suppose this is just natural.

She smiles.

Rory, what about a dance? Are you dancing, Ken?

He walks round. There are Roman and Tabitha deep in conversation. He's making sure he's seen.

KENDALL

Hey.

ROMAN

What?

Kendall is walking on, doing his rounds.

KENDALL

Hey, Con. Good fireworks?

CONNOR

You mean the ones out here or the indoor fireworks, you let off?

729

KENDALL

Yeah good one. You know. I'm sorry. I am sorry.

Kendall smiles, walks on.

Then, on Kendall as he watches. A whack against his legs. Bang. What the fuck is that?

Looks down – it is Sophie and Iverson.

Hey hey hey? What are you two doing up?

SOPHIE

We couldn't sleep.

IVERSON

We slept this afternoon.

KENDALL

Look at you two!

Rava is nearby, she can see Kendall is straight and normal.

RAVA

They wanted to dance?

KENDALL

Well, okay.

RAVA

You want to dance?

Kendall doesn't know what to say.

Iver?

Iverson starts to dance with his mom. Sophie with Kendall. They end up dancing all together holding hands in a little circle as Roman and Tabitha, Connor and Willa, Caroline and Rory, Tom and Shiv and many other guests dance around them.

'Road to Nowhere' by Talking Heads. *

---

* By the time we came to shoot this, we knew we also wanted to try Whitney Houston's 'I Wanna Dance with Somebody'. As I recall, on the night we tried the scene with both playing. 'I Wanna Dance . . .' was much more evocative.

Kendall is lost – between pretending to have a nice time with his family and just feeling the edge of almost almost actually enjoying his kids.

Then he feels something, looks down and sees faint speckles of blood just visible on the sleeve of his white shirt.

INT. EASTNOR CASTLE – KENDALL'S ROOM – MORNING

On Kendall. Asleep. His eyes flick open. A bad dream? One blink. No. It's all real. Radio on.

A verse of John Berryman's 'Dream Song 29' starts to play.*

He looks down. On the sheet a fleck of blood from his wrist abrasion.

INT. EASTNOR CASTLE – DINING ROOM – DAY

10:00 a.m. Kendall walks in. Everything is appealingly and terrifyingly normal.

He makes his way to a brunch table.

He looks around smiles. Breathes. Greg is nearby.

> KENDALL
>
> Hey. You good?

> GREG
>
> Yeah. Yeah. Pretty good.

> KENDALL
>
> Good. Okay.

> GREG
>
> There's kinda a weird vibe – with the serving folks. The hobbity people?

> KENDALL
>
> Huh?

---

* There was always some link for me between this episode and John Berryman's 'Dream Song 29' with its evocation of waking and fearing (hoping?) that some life-changingly awful act has been committed. In the end, it was far too direct to have the poem spilling from the radio, and a more mundane piece of BBC Radio 4 played much more effectively; but the episode kept a reference to the poem in its title.

GREG

A caterer, a guy – crashed or got high and nobody knows—
Some bad shit went down.

KENDALL

Really?

GREG

But the word is the family line is that we're not going to let it
spoil anything?

KENDALL

Right. Oh, good. But he died?

GREG

Yeah a kid died, maybe.

KENDALL

Wow.

Kendall is looking at some eggs.

GREG

Yeah. Bad shit. How's the scrambled egg, has it congealed?

*Then . . . Kendall sees, from far away, coming at him like a
nightmare – Colin.*

He's making a beeline for Kendall.

Kendall feels the world rushing in.

He's coming and coming. It seems to take forever.

COLIN

Kendall. Logan wants to have a word with you?

INT. EASTNOR CASTLE – LOGAN'S ROOM – DAY

10:30 a.m. Colin shows Kendall in. Logan is there. Marcia too.

LOGAN

Hey, son.

KENDALL

Hey.

LOGAN

Thanks, Colin.

Kendall watches him retreat.

Did you have an acceptable evening?

KENDALL

Uh-huh. You know?

LOGAN

I was up all night organizing my defense.

KENDALL

Right.

LOGAN

Look. So, um. I don't know if you know, but the caterer I had an issue with, he died last night?

Kendall can't get his face right sufficiently quickly. He reacts not quite right.

KENDALL

Oh, that's terrible.

LOGAN

Did you know?

KENDALL

I knew – I knew – I know, since, I just heard. But it's a shock.

If Logan had any doubts about his son being involved they're over now.

LOGAN

Right. Well. Look. Our guys, one of our guys found a keycard to your room near where this kid went into the water.

KENDALL

Oh? Maybe he – maybe – maybe he—?

LOGAN

Uh-huh. And Amir saw you last night, rather damp. The police officers are here – with Caroline.

MARCIA

We just wanted to check if you had anything stolen last night?

733

KENDALL

Um – what, as in—?

LOGAN

Did you have anything stolen last night?

KENDALL

I don't think so?

MARCIA

You might want to check again.

KENDALL

Um—

LOGAN

This kid, I think he might be a thief. Who broke into your room and swiped your card?

KENDALL

Right?

LOGAN

Let me handle this, son.

KENDALL

Right.

LOGAN

I know the guys. They know our guys. They're all good guys. We can let them know what was taken.

KENDALL

Right . . . Dad—

LOGAN

Look, this is all quite stressful. Why don't you get in my car and we'll drive you to the plane and you can just relax and maybe you should go and straighten out in the desert?

KENDALL

Um – I – I don't know?

LOGAN

Yeah. I think that would be good.

KENDALL

Um. Right. I mean, nobody did anything wrong and – you know. It sounds like. So?

Logan nods and Marcia heads out.

LOGAN

Tell Sandy you're out. Tell Stewy. The thing looks like a shit show. Go to the desert. Dry out. You've been off-balance.

KENDALL

There's nothing— I don't think. I wasn't there. So?

LOGAN

This could be the defining event of your life. It'd eat everything. A rich kid kills a boy. You'll never be anything else. Or—

Kendall looks at his dad.

Or it could be what it should be. Nothing at all. A sad little detail at a lovely wedding where father and son were reconciled?

Logan opens his arms.

You're a good kid. You could still be a good kid.

Kendall has an urge to get that embrace that is so rarely offered . . .

He looks around the room. Everything is too vivid.

'My Heart Belongs to Daddy' by Ella Fitzgerald from Live at Zardi's *plays.*

Acknowledgements

The story of the show is one of a series of very fortunate collaborations. I can't list them all, but some key thanks I owe include:

Frank Rich – my friend and fellow executive producer, frequent first reader, who originally championed my work at HBO and got me to meet Richard Plepler who was so encouraging of my working there. Meanwhile, Kevin Messick, with a keen eye for a script and a sharp edit, first commissioned me to write about US politics and opened up the path to a relationship with Adam McKay.

These relationships came together for the pilot which Adam shot, and through which he has had such a wide and long-lasting influence on the show – bringing in all the excellent pilot heads of departments – and leading us, in conjunction with the brilliant Francine Maisler, to much of the main cast. Adam has carried on being the most generous executive producer, supporting me in becoming a showrunner when I didn't even really know what one was.

The unbelievably talented and collaborative cast, including: Brian, Hiam, Jeremy, Peter, Rob, Nick, Kieran, Sarah, Matthew, Alan, Scott, Natalie, Swayam & Quentin, Juliana, JSC, David, Dag, Justine, Arian, Ash, Larry, Zack, James, Eric, Caitlin, Harriet, Danny, Jeannie, Patch, Holly, Cherry, Annabelle, Fisher, Zoë, Jihae, Dasha, Sanaa, Hope, Justin, Alexander, Pip. Neither I nor my fellow writers could or would have written what we did without knowing that they would be receptive. Their notes and thoughts and comments, not to say improvisations and freestylings, have enriched the show at every turn.

Adam McKay also brought Nicholas Britell, genius musician and composer, to the *Succession* party. Even if the show is decent, people think it is 58% better than it is because of the brilliance and depth of the work of Nick and his colleagues, Todd Kasow and John Finklea.

Simon Chin encouraged me to write something about Rupert Murdoch. Leanne Klein at Wall to Wall offered unstinting enthusiasm even when it became time to stint. Liza Marshall at Channel 4 was supportive, but we could just never make it happen. Gregory McKnight was the first person who suggested there was perhaps something in a fictional media-family show. He and my UK agent Cathy King and US TV agent Dan Erlij have supported me throughout.

Mark Mylod – the time we've spent! The care he takes! The way he marshals a set! To have seventeen things going on, to be thinking about twenty others, and then, when I appear at his shoulder with my little clutch of thoughts and adjustments, to meet each one – not without ego or a proprietorial pride, but to feel those things and ride them and still listen and adjust.

His fellow directors – Andrij Parekh, Bob Pulcini & Shari Springer Berman, Lorene Scafaria, Adam Arkin, Becky Martin, Kevin Bray, Miguel Arteta, S. J. Clarkson, Matt Shakman, Cathy Yan.

Lisa Molinaro and Holly Unterberger – constant monitor companions and friends and creative advisors. Sharp eyes, warm hearts.

Amy Lauritsen, Christo Morse, John Silvestri, Michelle Flevotomas – assistant directors who kept the train running and the mood up. And coped with changes, late and big beyond the call of duty, with barely a flinch.

Most of the writers who've worked on the show are recorded herein on episode titles: Tony Roche, Jon Brown, Lucy Prebble, Will Tracy, Georgia Pritchett, Susan Soon He Stanton, Ted Cohen, Will Arbery, Mary Laws, Anna Jordan, Jonathan Glatzer. But not all of them. My friend Simon Blackwell had just enough time to write 'alts' for the pilot before disappearing to meatier things. We also got to work in the room with Alice Birch, Miriam Battye, Francesca Gardiner, Cord Jefferson, Lucy Kirkwood, Gary Shteyngart. All brilliant. All good things sprang from the rooms where we all sat together and plotted and laughed.

Tony and Lucy, Jon and Will Tracy I've leant on most heavily to help me write – and to rewrite – when we had an episode that wasn't firing. And Tony and Lucy were most often at hand through the long months of the shoots as good companions and stout hearts. I've leant on them for creative wisdom and valued their kindness and friendship.

Beth Gorman, Ed Cripps, Jamie Carragher, Siobhan James-Elliott kept the notes in our UK rooms. Jamie for the longest stretch. He stayed up many a night transcribing and ordering and filtering, and still found time to chime in and add a thought or a historical or literary reference that left the rest of us agog at his breadth of knowledge.

Callie Hersheway Love, who I met on *Veep* and has been a constant help, guide, aide, friend and protector of my time and concentration, and has been intimately across every nook and cranny of these scripts, lately with the help of Terry McGrath. Also, Nate Elston who at first I thought I didn't need but soon discovered I was unable to function without, it's been the greatest pleasure to have his company and friendship. Ali Reilly and Danny Klain are also amongst the best of the best.

At HBO: Casey Bloys to whom I first pitched the show, Frannie Orsi, Nora Skinner and Max Hollman, Sally Harvey. HBO could not have been a happier or more supportive home, and they are brilliant and subtle executives whose guidance and support has been steadfast and sustaining.

Jane Tranter, who guided me through the US system and reassured my American partners that we were in the writers' room, not in the pub. Ilene Landress, who produced the pilot, and Jonathan Filley, the first season, and Scott Ferguson – indefatigable producer who got us on to yachts and into nations at short notice and kept the show on the road, with Gabrielle Mahon, when we could have come off the rails.

Our DPs – Pat Capone, who once made me cry with his call to arms amidst the myriad problems of shooting through Covid, Andrij, Chris, Kate. And the camera operators – who dance with the actors, Gregor and Ethan. They are the silent scene partners and need emotional intelligence that matches their iron grip and falcon's eye.

Stephen Carter, head of an art department of obsessive attention to detail matched only by his flexibility and good humour. Also my friends George DeTitta Jr., Katrina Whalen, Ben Relf, Andre Azevedo, Monica Jacobs, Alley O'Shea.

Ken Ishii, Pete and Ethan, Billy Sarokin, Andy Kris, Nicholas Renbeck – for keeping us sounding good against the odds. To catch on the fly every beat and every late-added line and improvisation clean enough to use. Extraordinary.

Merissa Marr has been my guide through the business moves from the first season and guided us towards some excellent areas and away from corporate faux pas. Brilliant on technical detail but also attuned to what we might need and what might work. Likewise Jon Klein on media. Jesse Eisinger and Matt Friedrich on legal matters. Tracey Pruzan and Derek Blasberg on society and New York. Faisal A. Quereshi on oddities, curios, cultural updates and sex parties. Eric Schultz and Ben Ginsberg on politics, and Justin Geldzahler on everything all together all at once. All invaluable.

Doug Aibel and Henry Russell Bergstein, and Avy Kaufman, who helped find and land so many remarkable acting talents.

Angel DeAngelis, Nuria Sitja, Michelle Johnson, Patricia Regan, kind, talented and warm bosses of hair and make-up.

Michelle Matland, Jon Schwartz, Midge and Danny. Costume department of dedication and flair and good humour and hard work.

Paul Eskenazi, who has helped us into and out of our many and ever-evolving list of locations.

Ken Eluto, Jane Rizzo, Bill Henry, Anne McCabe, Brian Kates, Ellen Tam and Venya Bruk – editors of subtlety and wisdom. Who made a thousand good choices before we ever started on the ones we got to worry over together. Dara Schnapper who, with Val, James and Genevieve, presided over post-production with such attention to detail and allowed me such room for manoeuvre.

To Alex Bowler at Faber & Faber who was generous enough to think it was worth starting this scriptbook ball rolling, and his colleague Steve King who has edited this volume with care and sensitivity under a ticking clock, and Jodi Gray for setting it with precision.

To the folks at HBO responsible for enabling this book to come together: Michele Caruso, Tara Bonner, Stacey Abiraj, Arielle Mauge and Andrew Kelley.

And to my support network. Sam Bain, my kind and thoughtful compadre, with or from whom I've learnt everything I know about writing film and TV.

To Pat Halpin and Phillip Rossini. For getting me in and out and putting me up.

To everyone at First Touch FC, especially Mikey, Keith, Euan, Case and John C. for keeping me roughly in shape and pretty much sane. Likewise Chelsey Kapuscinski.

To Ju, Jas, Rob, Mark, Will, Andy & Andy Yates. Rock-solid old pals.

Chris (with whom some of the thoughts about satire in the introduction to the fourth volume were discussed (i.e. he said them and I basically wrote them down)), Jo and all the family and friends who sustained my most important people while I was often absent.

And my family. I don't think I had any idea going into this how consuming it would be and how much it would take me away. The pandemic was particularly tough. I couldn't and wouldn't have done it without your love and support. M, A&A, I love you. My mum and dad and sister and her family, too. Thank you.

Jesse Armstrong